TOO MUCH, TOO SOON?

EARLY LEARNING
AND THE EROSION OF CHILDHOOD

EDITED BY RICHARD HOUSE

D1423878

Hawthorn Press

Too Much, Too Soon? © 2011 Richard House and contributors

Richard House is hereby identified as the editor of this work in accordance with section 77 of the Copyright, Designs and Patent Act, 1988. He asserts and gives notice of his moral right under this Act. The respective authors of the chapters also assent and give notice of their moral right under this act.

Published by Hawthorn Press, Hawthorn House,
1 Lansdown Lane, Stroud, Gloucestershire, GL5 1BJ, UK
Tel: (01453) 757040   Fax: (01453) 751138
E-mail: info@hawthornpress.com
Website: www.hawthornpress.com

Acknowledgements
Cover illustration © Alan Paterson
Photographs by Sylvie Hétu, Kim Simpson and Sally Goddard Blythe, by kind permission

Cover design by Bookcraft, Stroud, GL5 1AA
Typesetting by Bookcraft, Stroud, GL5 1AA
Printed by Henry Ling, The Dorset Press, Dorchester. Reprinted 2012

Printed on FSC approved paper/paper sourced from sustained managed forests and elemental chlorine free.

Every effort has been made to trace the ownership of all copyrighted material. If any omission has been made, please bring this to the publisher's attention so that proper acknowledgement may be given in future editions.

The views expressed in this book are not necessarily those of the publisher.

British Library Cataloguing in Publication Data applied for

ISBN 978-1-907359-02-6

Contents

Reviews

A timely book with a remarkable diversity of contributors. The case is made clearly for the need for change.

Kindling, April 2012

This very readable, but vastly important, book is a must for all who care about our youngest citizens.

Marie Charlton, *Early Years Educator*, December 2011

This is a timely book with a remarkable diversity of contributors. … I finished the book with my arguments against the learning and development goals of the EYFS and their statutory nature deepened and clarified. The case is clearly made here for the wrongness of the current situation and the need for change. The positive suggestions that conclude the book present a way forward that would make a significant and positive difference to early childhood education and care in this country and would be welcomed by many parents and practitioners.

Jill Tina Taplin, *New View* magazine, Autumn 2011

Many chapters in this book would serve well as the basis for professional discussion with colleagues.

Barbara Isaacs, *Montessori International*, April 2012

This book is essential reading for everyone who cares about young children and their development.

Margaret Edgington,
Newsletter for the National Campaign for Nursery Education

Every parent should read it.

Ian Atkey, *Nursery Management Today*, May 2012

Read it for a powerful look at the problems and some inspiring ideas for change.

Green Parent **magazine,** February 2012

Convincing series of chapters written by very well-informed authors questioning the government's approach to early years education. All educators – and parents – need to read this before it's too late and we lose a generation (or more) of children to the moronic system being imposed on children and their teachers. Essential reading. Should be the basis of government policy.

Susan Norman, Amazon website review

Babies are being turned into 'mini adults' with bus schedules of singing, yoga, gym, swimming and salsa classes, experts claim.

Sarah Harris, *Daily Mail*, September 2011

The 'schoolification' of early years in England has not improved most children's chances of success in the educational system, and may be doing long term damage.

Sue Palmer, Review, *Times Educational Supplement Scotland*, September 2011

The book has entirely persuaded me that we are getting it wrong. We need to let children be children and I wish the Open EYE campaign success in all its endeavours.

Rachel Hyland, *The Social Crediter*, Summer 2012

Endorsements

'The unprecedented influences of the 21st century are impacting on the young mind with unprecedented results. This timely book offers a wide-ranging collective wisdom on how to optimize the individual potential of the next generation.'

Baroness Susan Greenfield CBE FRCP (Hon), author of
ID: The Quest for Identity in the 21st Century (Sceptre, 2008)

'The concept of Intergenerational Justice lies at the heart of sustainable development. And where else should that start than in each and every child's early years? We are currently failing in that moral obligation to young people – and this powerful collection of essays reminds us of how important and how urgent it is to put that right.'

Jonathan Porritt, Founding Director, Forum for the Future

'Our early care sets the emotional thermostat for who we are by age six. These essays, taken together, present an overwhelming case for meeting the needs of children in the early years. Personally and nationally, we cannot afford to ignore their message.'

Oliver James, psychologist and writer,
author of *They F*** You Up* (Bloomsbury, 2007)

'Since 2007, Open EYE campaigners have critiqued negative aspects of the Early Years Foundation Stage and advocated a different conception of childhood than is inscribed within it. This book collates and expands those arguments, and proffers well-reasoned recommendations for policy. It is indispensable reading for all concerned with children in their early years.'

Kevin J. Brehony, Froebel Professor of Early Childhood Studies,
Froebel College, Roehampton University

'*Too Much, Too Soon?* is a timely, informative volume which should alert all of those who believe that "earlier is (always) better" that this is by no means the case when it comes to promoting early human development. "Everything in moderation", that sage Aristotelian advice, applies to the fostering of early human development, too.'

Jay Belsky, Robert M. and Natalie Reid Dorn Professor in Human and Community Development, University of California, Davis; editor (with J. Barnes and E. Melhuish) of *The National Evaluation of Sure Start: Does Area-based Early Intervention Work?* (The Policy Press, 2007)

'If print could scream, the words on these pages would be heard as a clarion call for evidence-based educational reform. In *Too Much, Too Soon?*, the authors – teachers, scientists and policy-makers – join together to demonstrate how we might achieve rich curricular aims in a more child-centered playful learning approach to early education.'

Kathy Hirsh-Pasek, Professor of Psychology, Temple University, author of *Einstein Never Used Flashcards* (Rodale) and *Mandate for Playful Learning* (Oxford)

'The "too much, too soon" mind-set has strongly influenced American education for decades. Many health and education experts now link it to increased stress and strain in children and decreased levels of creativity, curiosity, problem-solving, and social capacity. It is high time for a paradigm shift, and this book can serve as a lever to bring that about.'

Joan Almon, founding director, US Alliance for Childhood, co-author (with Edward Miller) of *Crisis in the Kindergarten: Why Children Need to Play in School* (Alliance for Childhood, 2009)

'I have watched with dismay as early years education has been caught up in the achievement-oriented values of our market culture. The diverse voices in this book challenge this agenda and affirm the overriding importance of attachment relationships, experiential learning and emotional development in early childhood.'

Sue Gerhardt, psychotherapist, author of *The Selfish Society* and *Why Love Matters*

'A challenging addition to early childhood literature; its diverse offerings conjure up the riches and complexities of young children's development, learning and well-being. The book is an essential reading, especially for those in the profession who have only worked within the parameters of the English Early Years Foundation Stage.'

Barbara Isaacs, Academic Director for the Montessori Centre International and Senior Accreditation officer, Montessori Accreditation and Evaluation Board

'Childhood should be valued as a golden phase of life which should not be hastened, accelerated, filled with adult timescales or agendas. This book holds treasures of insight, research and information which is enlightening, informative, and most important, child friendly!'

Janni Nicol, Steiner Waldorf early childhood consultant, international representative and trainer, author of *Understanding the Steiner Waldorf Approach: Early Years Education in Practice*, Routledge, 2011

'The imposition of the EYFS by the previous Government on all settings was profoundly wrong. It ignored the views of professionals and abused the rights of parents. I hope that the Coalition Government will respect the fundamental principle of choice and listen to those who truly care about the education and development of children. Read this book.'

David Hanson, CEO, Independent Association of Prep Schools

'The Early Years Foundation Stage (EYFS) curriculum is another in a long line of disturbing developments facing children in our society. I urge anyone concerned about the future of childhood to read this book and understand why the EYFS cannot be supported.'

Professor Sami Timimi, Lincoln University, author of *Pathological Child Psychiatry and the Medicalization of Childhood* (Routledge, 2002)

'The contributors to this timely book offer us thoughtful ways forward from the disastrous culture of targets, league tables and so on that has recently come to distort early years education.'

Richard Smith, Professor of Education, Durham University, co-author of *The Therapy of Education: Philosophy, Happiness and Personal Growth* (Palgrave Macmillan, 2006)

'How can parents, practitioners, academics and politicians voice their heart-felt opposition to the narrow managerialism of early years policy? This book allows an eclectic, passionate, sometimes (appropriately) strident collective of authors to speak out for children's wider, deeper interests, and to challenge and inform our understanding of what children really need.'

Rod Parker-Rees, Associate Professor, Early Childhood Studies, Plymouth University, editor of *Meeting the Child in Steiner Kindergartens* (Routledge, 2011)

'This is a book which is both passionate and carefully argued – passionate because its subject is of vital importance to our whole society, and carefully argued because its contributors know that well-intentioned policy-makers need to be convinced of the validity of the insights presented so cogently in its pages.'

Brian Thorne, Emeritus Professor of Counselling, University of East Anglia and co-founder of the Norwich Centre; author of *Carl Rogers*, 2nd edition (Sage, 2003)

'This fascinating book incites the reader to speak out, is frequently political and dares to say things which are often at complete odds with received wisdom about what's right for young children. It speaks of love, of the child's right to dream and to be unhurried. Everyone concerned with young children and society's future should read it.'

Linda Pound, early childhood consultant, author of *Influencing Early Childhood Education: Key Figures, Philosophies and Ideas* (Open University Press, 2011)

'*Too Much, Too Soon?* is a timely, erudite and fascinating book. All will celebrate the passion for the well-being of children which is inherent throughout. The contributors, each in their unique way, emphasize the necessity to pay attention to the holistic developmental needs of children and the danger of subjugating those needs to political and/ or social ideologies.'

Dr Maria Robinson, Independent Adviser in Early Development, author of *Understanding Behaviour and Development in Early Childhood* (Routledge, 2010)

Foreword

ANNETTE BROOKE, MP

As a politician I feel very honoured to be asked to write the foreword to this collection of perspectives on early child development and learning. I don't think that I can claim to be a policy 'maker', given the nature of our parliamentary system, and I certainly cannot claim to have any special expertise in early years. I completed a one-year postgraduate teaching qualification over 40 years ago, and as my subject is economics the amount of time I spent on early years must have been extremely limited. However, the course did spark off an interest in child development for me, and I am very conscious of how important this area of study should be for anybody preparing to work with children and young people. In addition, as a parent and a grandmother I have had some hands-on experience – or maybe hands *off*, in the context of this book!

As a politician I have had the opportunity to visit many early years' settings, to participate in legislation-making relating to children, to contribute to debates on a whole range of child and educational issues and to ask many questions of ministers, civil servants and education professionals. My membership of the Education Select Committee under Barry Sheerman's chairmanship also gave me direct access to the key players and issues in education more generally, including the early years.

I led for the Liberal Democrats on the 2006 Childcare Act. Looking back in Hansard, I see that I was arguing in December 2005, in the context of the Early Years Foundation Stage, that the word 'taught' should not be on the face of the bill. I suggested alternative wording, including 'experiencing' and 'learning'. I said in March 2006 at Report Stage, 'young children learn by being supported to play and by experiencing the world around them.'

'The word "taught", whatever the dictionary definition, has connotations: it implies a group of young people, children or adults receiving instruction, rather than learning by experience at the right level.' I felt that I won the argument in the parliamentary debate, but the Government would not agree to amend the Bill and hence I cannot describe myself as a policy-maker! Interestingly, Penelope Leach in Chapter 1 singles out the confusion between teaching and learning, and explains what play means.

Consultation on the detail of the Early Years Foundation Stage took place after the debate; and at this stage I attended a presentation from Margaret Edgington on the pitfalls of the proposals, and I learned a great deal – she is indeed an 'Inveterate Early Childhood Campaigner'! (see Chapter 20). When the final document on the EYFS was published, I found I agreed with the principles, but I could see the danger from so many detailed goals, targets or aspirations, and underlying them was the word 'taught'. Many of the contributors to the book discuss the implications of these.

I became acquainted with Open EYE and its members shortly after it was formed, and whilst I haven't supported all of their calls it was clear to me that there must be a transparent exemptions policy, and that the literacy goals, in particular, had to be revisited. Their campaigning led me to question more and more the rationale of the EYFS. As contributors to this book point out, the argument for a structured approach was always expressed in terms of supporting children from disadvantaged backgrounds. However, to me this just did not fit in with the need to have an approach which would be appropriate for the development of each individual child. I want all children to be able to have the best start in life, and Open EYE's campaigning was questioning whether the EYFS framework actually did that. They asked the pertinent question about what the research evidence actually showed – as discussed in Chapter 19.

Before the 2010 General Election I was calling for reform of the EYFS, and this was embedded in my Party's policy. The new Government did take this on board with the setting up of the review headed by Clare Tickell. Her conclusions are given applause by some of the contributors to this book, but still questions remain – was she given the right remit, did we need more than just reform? I do have regrets that I wasn't an 'insider' (a true policy-maker) and able to have a say on the remit, or indeed play a minor role in the review.

However, being an 'outsider' to such processes does enable one to speak out, and that is an important role to be able to play. Open EYE is about 'speaking out', and this book is about 'speaking out'. Change can indeed be brought about by the pressure of 'outsiders', especially when based on evidence and coherent arguments. A review of the Early Years Foundation Stage was a welcome response to the debate generated by Open EYE, but now the Government has published its response to the Tickell Review it is clear that there is much more still to be done to ensure that all children do get the best start in life.

Preface

STEVE BIDDULPH

Hello – my name is Steve Biddulph, and it's great to have this opportunity to write to you and most passionately support this publication of the Open EYE campaign. Some of the most outstanding and capable advocates of children's well-being in the United Kingdom today are represented in these pages. I congratulate Dr Richard House and all the authors and their supporters across the country. My own part is simply to add a word of encouragement.

I have written simple and readable books for parents that over the years have reached about 3 million families around the world. They have been especially popular in the UK, and I seem to have become to the UK's children what Princess Anne is to the UK's horses; and so I am doing my best to grasp the reins or take the bit in my teeth – which ever is the right metaphor there. As many other psychologists before me have done – such as the wonderful Penelope Leach (see her Chapter 1) or Benjamin Spock – I have moved gradually from working with families in serious trouble to looking at how our society as a whole creates that trouble. I have noticed how, in the modern and hurried world, childhood easily becomes worse if not actively protected and nurtured.

In this context, in 2008 I read the early years policy framework (the Early Years Foundation Stage) with a real sense of horror. It went against everything that I understand about early learning, and I couldn't believe it was being contemplated. It even crossed my mind that although we might have defeated totalitarianism in World War II and the Cold War, with its wish to control and regulate every aspect of life, it still arises again so easily in the bureaucratic process, if we don't see it and speak up against it.

Caring for children well involves a knowledge of how they grow and what they need. Everything that we know about early childhood indicates an awesome capacity to self-educate, to draw in what's needed and integrate it. If the adults around a child are responsive, calm and loving, and the environment is safe and stimulus-rich, then a child will grow of themselves in cognitive, language and emotional domains. Any attempt to force or structure this actually backfires. It's like ripping open a rosebud to try and get it to blossom. The results are not good. (I often suspect that if we had a government programme to teach children to speak, we would create stammerers and mutes; and if we had a programme to teach them to walk, we would create cripples.)

This isn't just opinion. There are many studies that indicate that structured approaches to early learning, such as early phonics and structured play (which is a contradiction in terms), our attempts to assess or audit a child, or caring itself – any monitoring intrusions into the normal process of care and development – all have an adverse effect. If these factors are the cornerstones that early years policy not only advocates but seeks to force on to children and teachers, then it's no wonder that the child development community in the UK has mobilized against this.

Dr David Weikart, whom some of you will remember as an original researcher of the Perry pre-school project, reported in 2006 on his final large-scale ten-nation study of what makes good pre-primary education. This huge and comprehensive study found two striking outcomes common to all ten nations studied. Weikart's results were crystal clear: children's language performance-gains *decrease* in proportion to the amount of time spent in forced group academic activities. They *increase* in proportion to the amount of time spent in free choice and expressive activities. Likewise, children's cognitive performance increases when children spend less time in regimented whole-group activities and more time in free play.

This won't surprise anyone who works in early childhood. But it must confound those who think that learning can be forced in the early years. Forced learning destroys that learning – it makes children go backwards. Given the fact of early brain wiring, and the durability of attitudes to learning found by people such as Oxford University's Professor Kathy Sylva, the harm might well be lifelong.

I encourage you in your earnest and vigorous efforts to set these bean-counters straight on the facts of how children grow. I hope this book promotes a constructive and thoughtful change of attitude from those in government, who are doubtless well-meaning, but are needing to listen closely to those who know children best. Thank you.

Acknowledgements

Putting together a book of this size and complexity requires the co-operative endeavour of a large number of dedicated and generously spirited people, and I want to express my enormous gratitude to: my dear friends and colleagues in the **Open EYE campaign team**; the many esteemed contributors to the book for the efficient and many inspiring ways in which they have contributed; to the eminent endorsers of the book for taking the trouble to read and recommend it; the **Hermes Trust** (Richard Masters) and **Ruskin Mill Educational Trust** (Aonghus Gordon) for their generous financial support; to artist **Alan Paterson** for allowing us to use his magnificent painting for the front cover; to **Sarah Brook** for being a most generous ally in the protection of childhood; and last but by no means least, to **Martin Large** and all at **Hawthorn Press** for supporting this book – and for all they have done over many years to further the cause of holistic perspectives in early childhood learning and development.

Thank you, one and all, for enabling this gift to the world of childhood to come to fruition; we are quite a team!

In the earliest years, valuable though the input of teachers may be, children are not pupils, but apprentices in the business of growing up as human beings.

PENELOPE LEACH

Introduction and Overview

Richard House, Editor

I originally intended to call this introductory chapter 'The Roots and History of the Open EYE Campaign'; yet the more I thought about it, the more I realized that what is far more important is to use this editorially privileged space to introduce the book that you are about to read. An editor needs to make a key decision as to whether a book's editorial introduction should be short and sharp, or lengthy and involved – for a strong case can always be made for either approach. In the event, I have plumped for a lengthy introductory chapter, principally because I wish to show-case the rich feast of contributions you are about to enjoy and/or be challenged by, in order to help you negotiate your way around what is, by early years standards, a long book.

I would like to begin with two revealing anecdotes, which will help set the scene for the book. First, I recently heard a story of an English early years teacher who spends 18 hours a week taken up with the assessment of her 40 4-year-olds, in order to meet the requirements of England's statutory early-years curriculum, the Early Years Foundation Stage – so spending more time with paperwork than in actually being with her children. The second anecdote concerns an 8-year-old boy who was recently heard 'boasting' somewhat about his achievements over the past year with his reading and writing. His little 4-year-old brother soon piped up, 'In the kindergarten, I've been learning to play and to not use my hands for hitting, but for work – and I'm good at it!'

The central purpose of *Too Much, Too Soon?* is to articulate what the book's contributors see as a major and growing problem in modern culture, which has been variously called 'toxic childhood', children growing up too soon, the commercialization of childhood, the 'adultification' of children, the erosion of childhood – or more simply, and quoting the title of the book itself, 'Too much, too soon'. Readers unacquainted with the early years sphere in Britain may not be aware of England's pre-school 'curriculum', which critical journalists have somewhat irreverently termed 'the nappy curriculum' – namely, the Early Years Foundation Stage (or EYFS), which became statutory in September 2008. Even before the EYFS became law, in late 2007 a group of concerned professionals from various backgrounds formed a campaigning group, the Open EYE campaign, as they shared a number of grave concerns about the EYFS curriculum (outlined in detail in Chapters 2 and 6). The EYFS and its discontents will form a recurrent theme in Part I of the book. There is plenty of information about the Open EYE campaign both on our (rather 'workmanlike') website (at http://openeyecampaign.wordpress.com), and also *en passant* throughout this book (see in particular Chapter 2).

However, the book is far more than being a critical study of the EYFS; for whilst what follows does certainly serve that purpose, more importantly it sets the EYFS within a far wider cultural context of young children's early development and learning in the modern technological world. Specifically, we are concerned with the many ways in which young children's experiences are being intruded upon by commercial and technological imperatives of the adult world which, we contend, have no place in the psyches of young children. Much of this book is taken up with making the case for such a view.

It is important to put to bed immediately a criticism sometimes heard of the kind of position argued for in this book. Thus, those holding these concerns have been summarily dismissed by some as mere 'conservatives', or uncritical 'moral panickers', or nostalgic commentators romanticizing a non-technological past, or sentimentalists yearning for some fictional golden age of childhood, or naïve technological determinists. Speaking for myself, I take great exception to being so dismissively and condescendingly labelled. What the contributors to this book *are* 'guilty' of is bringing a radical, critically reflective capacity to the breathless momentum of modern technological developments, and their impact on children's lives and consciousness. We also bring a philosophical concern with contextualizing the proper place of technology in the wider evolution of human consciousness, and a passionate wish to protect what is fundamentally human from the march of what Jean-Francois Lyotard has called 'the inhuman' in modern culture. And there is surely no more important and emotionally charged a place for the unfolding of this paradigmatic battleground than in the realm of early childhood.

Too Much, Too Soon? is being published now for a number of reasons. First, as I write the EYFS is currently being reviewed by the British Government, and this book constitutes a major intervention into those crucial debates for the future well-being of our youngest children. The Open EYE campaign has also very much 'come of age' now, with two highly successful conferences, many high-profile media reports and numerous publications having come out of its campaign team since late 2007. This book showcases in detail the viewpoints about early development and learning to which we passionately hold. But perhaps most important of all, we hope that *Too Much, Too Soon?* will provide a rallying point for a new cultural movement challenging what we call 'the erosion of childhood'; and the chapters that follow make a compelling case for the urgency of such a movement taking hold in late-modern technological culture.

A unique feature of *Too Much, Too Soon?* is that it contains substantive contributions from educators, parents, policy-makers, academics (both lecturers and researchers) and concerned citizens; and in this sense, it attempts to break down the impenetrable barriers that routinely exist between the arguably overly precious world of academia and policy-makers, on the one hand, and parents, concerned citizens and practitioners working at the coal-face, on the other. In these pages, you will see all these viewpoints eloquently and compellingly represented; and the book's key recommendations about early years research, policy-making and the EYFS, as set out in the concluding chapter by Wendy Scott and me (see pp. 323–33), articulate the parameters of an eminently achievable way forward for all open-minded readers who wish to join us in challenging head-on the 'too much, too soon' ideology that is so dominant in modern technological and political culture.

As the editor of this book, and as just intimated, what has perhaps been most gratifying is that the Open EYE campaign has spawned such a richly diverse, pluralistic collection which gives equal value to parental, practitioner, academic, policy-maker and campaigner perspectives. Such diversity is highly unusual, if not unique, in the early-childhood literature – which I see as highly unfortunate, as parents, professionals, academics, campaigners and policy-makers really do need to listen to, and learn from, one another, and to try to understand each others' multi-faceted viewpoints. Indeed, one way of thinking about what has happened with England's Early Years Foundation Stage (EYFS) is that it was government's and policy-makers' chronic and single-minded *failure to listen* that has generated a number of major difficulties with the framework to date.

A few of the contributions in the book are overtly and passionately political in their challenging of government policy, and as editor I make no apology for this. In my view, far too much public discourse around government policy-making is surrounded by bad faith – by a kind of trance-inducing false respect in which no-one (least of all specially appointed government advisors!) dare say anything overtly critical to ministers, not daring to diverge from what they know ministers are wanting to hear. In my view, such phoniness can only lead to bad policy-making; and I think there can be little doubt that this did happen in the case of the original EYFS, and the way in which it was foisted on to the early years field. The very fact that the Open EYE campaign has received such support from across the field since late 2007 indicates that the previous government made no space available for listening openly to the substantial misgivings about aspects of the framework that were undoubtedly around in the field at the time – had ministers and civil servants taken the trouble to find out, and then listen and reflect.

Indeed, I would go as far as saying that *any* consideration of the EYFS, especially academic research, which fails to factor in the political machinations of the framework cannot but gravely misrepresent it and its functioning. In Chapter 5, for example, we read parent-activist Frances Laing writing the following:

> Countless practitioners and teachers had already told me via the blog that they did not feel able to voice their misgivings about the EYFS learning and development requirements for fear of being bullied by their managers, or because they were afraid of losing their jobs. Parents were afraid of making themselves (and their children) unpopular ... Many parents are afraid that if they criti-cize the system they will face sanctions, disapproval, lose their place at nursery or school, and in the current economic climate this will not help them to maintain a job and an income.

So much for the accuracy and objectivity of those 'scientific' (*sic*) surveys that have repeatedly told us how 'universally popular' the EYFS is (cf. Chapter 19).

This book went to press a few days after the government's response to the Tickell Review was announced (on 6 July 2011), and it does appear that at least some of the concerns that Open EYE has undeviatingly pursued since late 2007 have at last been listened to and understood, and may well be acted upon. It seems equally likely, however, that at least some of our ongoing concerns will remain unaddressed after any changes to the existing EYFS are implemented. To the extent that this is so, our campaign will continue to marshal all available evidence and rational argument to challenge, in every way we can, any early years policy-making that we consider to be harmful to the well-being of young children.

The Book in Summary

Part I of the book, 'Policy-making and the Erosion of Childhood: The Case of the Early Years Foundation Stage', looks in detail at one important example of state-legislated curricula for early childhood – namely, England's controversial Early Years Foundation Stage (EYFS). Although the chapters are closely geared to the detail of the EYFS and its vicissitudes, the arguments raised have much wider applicability to any attempt by government to legislate in this complex sphere of early development and learning. First, in **Chapter 1** the doyenne of childcare wisdom over several decades, *Penelope Leach*, gives us her profoundly insightful take on the Early Years Foundation Stage. Penelope has a number of positive comments to make about the EYFS – which makes her criticisms, when they come, all the more telling. One wonders just how many of the errors made in the original EYFS might have been avoided, and huge amounts of wasted time and resources spared for a great number of people and organizations, if Penny Leach had been one of Beverley Hughes' principal advisors when the EYFS was first devised.

Over the nearly four years of Open EYE's existence, we have individually and collectively written many articles for the professional magazines, letters to the press, and participated in numerous press and media reports – for example, making the lead front-page report in *The Times* newspaper (twice), appearing on Libby Purves' BBC Radio 4 programme 'The Learning Curve' (represented by Graham Kennish) and Kim Simpson's interview on Radio 4's flagship 'Today' programme. In **Chapter 2**, Open EYE reproduces just three of our published articles, which together give a clear scene-setting perspective on just why the Open EYE campaign was founded, and set out in detail our original objections to key aspects of the Early Years Foundation Stage. Very far from being the crudely 'anti-EYFS' campaign, with which grossly inaccurate label much of the media unfairly saddled us from the outset, it will be seen that our challenges were – and continue to be – thoughtfully nuanced, sober and carefully argued.

Chapter 3, by *John Dougherty,* then sets out in painstaking detail just how much time and energy was expended (wasted?) by one school in their Odyssean efforts to negotiate principled exemption from the EYFS's early learning 'requirements' – requirements that it now seems very likely the new government will be significantly modifying when they finally revise the framework for 2012. The grotesque irony of all this will no doubt not be lost on the reader. The psychodrama, reminiscent of Kafka, that John meticulously describes – and with remarkable restraint, given its extraordinary content – shines a very revealing light on the way in which the previous Department operated at the time; and it merely adds ballast to the many challenges that Open EYE made of both the content and the procedures pursued by the Department under the previous government. For the political scientist and the policy analyst, perhaps the most interesting and important question is whether this extraordinary government behaviour was specific to the Department and the government in power at the time, or whether it says something far more general about the way institutional bureaucracies function when challenged by the citizenry speaking truth to power. Alas, such a fascinating discussion lies beyond the scope of this book; yet some of the case-study evidence presented in what follows will make fascinating data for anyone wishing to research into governmental decision-making processes, and their sometimes patent absurdity and lack of democratic (or, less charitably, their sometimes quasi-authoritarian) ethos.

In **Chapter 4,** *Pat and Arthur Adams* offer us a dramatically direct and open description of Pat's difficult experience as a childminder in the face of the EYFS, and the ways in which she saw it as impinging on, and unnecessarily interfering with, her childminding practice. Their prescient story will surely resonate with literally thousands of childminders' experiences regarding the incompatibility of a compliance-driven, hyperactive regulatory framework, on the one hand, and on the other, the kind of relaxed, unhurried, 'home-from-home' environments that many if not most childminders strive to create for the children in their charge – and where the quality of attachment relationships is seen as far more important than measuring and assessing what 'learning goals' the young children are, or are not, 'achieving'.

In **Chapter 5**, *Frances Laing* offers us a parental perspective on the EYFS, illustrating from her own personal experience how the 'too much, too soon' ethos adversely affected her daughter's early learning experience in all kinds of ways, and how she then responded by becoming a 'parent-activist' – founding her own EYFS blog-site and becoming the first parent to seek formal exemption from the EYFS Learning Requirements (or 'targets-in-all-but-name', as she calls them). Officials at all levels of government would do well to read this chastening chapter, for it shows all too clearly the way in which inflexible bureaucratic agendas and processes can all too easily create a stultifying, almost Kafka-esque milieu in which any pretence to so-called 'consumer choice' in the public services becomes little more than a sick joke.

In **Chapter 6**, members of the *Open EYE campaign group* enter into a wide-ranging dialogue about the March 2011 Tickell EYFS Review, in which due acknowledgement is given to where the review seems to be along the right lines, and with extensive discussion of those areas in which the principled concerns raised by Open EYE and by many other critics of aspects of the EYFS seem to have been missed, or remain unaddressed by Dame Clare.

First in **Part II** ('The Foundations of Child Development and Early Learning'), *Sylvie Hétu* shows in **Chapter 7** how what we are calling the 'too much, too soon' syndrome commonly starts right at the beginning of life, around birth and just afterwards, in early babyhood. As a pre-school educator-lecturer, parenting workshop facilitator and infant-massage instructor and trainer of almost three decades' standing, Sylvie brings enormous accumulated experience and wisdom to her observations of early parent–baby relating, being and learning. What is especially interesting is her association's Winnicott-like challenge to the often disempowering ideology of professional 'expertise', and the way in which such impingement into the world of parent and child can so easily disrupt, rather than help, parents in their natural intuitive parenting capacities. For parents of very young children, and for those professionals who work with parents of young children, this is indispensable reading for those who wish to deeply understand and become aware of areas where doing 'too much, too soon' may interfere with the well-being of young children and babies.

In **Chapter 8**, *Lilian G. Katz* provides a goldmine of wisdom for any and every early years practitioner, accumulated over many decades of working in the field, in which she sensitively, and with characteristic humour, outlines those curriculum practices that are unhelpful, and describes with great clarity twelve overarching *principles* of early childhood practice that should inform all practitioners. Lilian also wisely warns campaigners not to make enemies of well-meaning policy-makers, but to find ways of dialoguing with them such that we can all hear each other, and be open to being influenced and changed by each other's viewpoints (cf. Chapter 22).

In **Chapter 9**, *Sally Goddard Blythe* takes us on a journey into the neuro-physiology of child development. Sally's seminal work in this area is enormously important in providing a solid scientific basis to the more intuitive views of 'holistic' developmentalists; and all she writes here about early learning is consistent with the view that very young children need to start their life journey with healthy *physical* development, and not cognitive or intellectual development. Sally's work therefore coheres very closely with what Rudolf Steiner and other holistic theorists have written about early development and learning. Although placed in Part II, Sally's chapter could just as easily have been located in Part I of the book, as it has a lot of vital importance to say about the developmental inappropriateness of aspects of the EYFS learning requirements, based on a deep understanding of the holistic development of the young child.

In **Chapter 10**, Open EYE's *Kim Simpson* offers a deeply moving chapter on the unfolding 'self' and its relationship to self-esteem, drawing in the process on the thinking of such towering figures as Maria Montessori, Rudolf Steiner, Carl Jung and Carl Rogers. Kim seems to embrace a quite explicitly *transpersonal* cosmology, in which terms like 'soul' and 'spirit' feature strongly, and she also draws upon extensive experience and knowledge of psychotherapeutic thinking, especially psychosynthesis. Particularly notable features of Kim's chapter are her emphasis on the way in which young children are brilliant natural learners, if only adults would have the mature discernment to enable rather than over-impinge upon their experience, and would intuitively know when *not* to get in the way; and the important idea that deprivation and disadvantage can manifest in all kinds of ways in young children's lives, and not at all necessarily just in the *economic* sense. The term 'love' is very rarely used in the early childhood literature, which I think is a tragedy and a great oversight; and love seems to me to be at the heart of what Kim is writing of so eloquently in her chapter. You certainly won't find this kind of deep thinking in any audit-driven 'early learning goals' discourse; yet this kind of mature sensibility might well be infinitely more important in helping to facilitate young children's healthy and empowering development than any number of programmatic 'learning outcomes' could possibly capture.

In **Chapter 11**, Open EYE's *Wendy Ellyatt* provides us with a beautifully articulated philosophy of learning, with her wide-ranging argument convincingly showing how the taking of a managerialist 'audit culture' mentality into the education system can be catastrophic for the quality of learning, and for the *subjective experience* of learning as an empowering, personal developmental journey for the child. For Wendy, *creativity and the imagination* should be at the centre of any educational experience, being essential pre-requisites for creating rounded, balanced citizens; yet genuine creativity is so easily damaged by a regime of targets, outcome-obsessiveness and programmatic competencies. Wendy Ellyatt argues that the position of Britain's children at the bottom of international league tables on well-being, together with our deteriorating comparative *academic* performance, is due, at least in part, to the alien curricular regimes that now increasingly dominate education systems in the Anglo-Saxon West; and she is surely right in arguing that government needs to be commissioning independent research that searchingly examines the longer-term impact upon children's consciousness and being of the current educational regimes to which they are relentlessly subject (cf. Chapter 19).

In **Chapter 12**, another Open EYE stalwart, *Lynne Oldfield*, introduces us to the Steiner Waldorf approach to creating a developmentally fitting 'foundation' for early learning, grounded in the holistic pedagogical thinking of the great seer Rudolf Steiner. The carefully unhurried Waldorf approach contains so many of the principles and practices that recur throughout this book, that one is left in awe at Steiner's remarkable holistic thinking, which he annunciated in such detail a century ago. In this chapter we find eloquently described the principles of free play, rhythm, repetition, physical development and the 'movement-based curriculum', a culture of 'oracy' and care of the senses, all couched within a language-rich, *genuinely* 'developmentally appropriate' milieu which minimizes pro-active adult impingement into the child's world, and makes a very strong case against over-intellectual early learning, and the long-term harm it can do to the child. As Lynne so evocatively puts it – and many psychoanalytic theorists would strongly concur – 'The Rights of the Child should include the right to be a dreamer'. Young children in a Waldorf setting, then, learn emotional self-regulation in a quite unselfconscious way, which approach coheres closely with Guy Claxton's work on the key importance of *un*conscious learning (cf. Chapter 21).

In **Chapter 13**, the celebrated American child psychologist *David Elkind*, who 30 years ago wrote his classic book *The Hurried Child*, lays out the reasons why play is so important in children's lives. In his chapter, David sets out clearly and compellingly the harm that is done to children in a play-impoverished environment, and he also begins to explore just what we can do to set right this chronic and worsening imbalance in children's lives. Surely every contributor to this book would agree with David Elkind's statement that 'Play … is instinctive and part of the maturational process. We cannot prevent children from self-initiated play; they will engage in it whenever they can. The problem is that we have curtailed the time and opportunities for such play.'

Then, in **Chapter 14**, *Tricia David* continues with the theme of play, with a sophisticated analysis that both acknowledges the central importance of play, and yet by no means adopts the kind of uncritical attitude to play of which some 'holistic' commentators are arguably culpable. Tricia also focuses on the neglected theme of the *politics* of play, looking at what she terms the 'highjacking' of play (e.g. by policy-makers), and the ways in which this can and does occur. Tricia usefully reminds us, then (contrary, perhaps, to many other of this book's contributors), that play is not necessarily a universal, culturally transcending phenomenon, and there are, perhaps, risks in uncritically eulogizing about play without any reference to its cultural and discursive specificities. Such a quasi 'postmodern' argument clashes head-on with the kind of view annunciated by the likes of Carl Jung and Rudolf Steiner, who argued that there *do* exist 'universal' human archetypal experiences, and that there therefore exists a complex dynamic tension between the universal, on the one hand, and the particular and the unique, on the other.

The final chapter in Part II, *Hillevi Lenz Taguchi's* **Chapter 15**, offers a challenging critical perspective on Reggio Emilia, developing what she terms a 'relational materialist analysis'. Hillevi illustrates just how easy it is for us to be caught up in constraining 'modernist' thinking, just when we are convinced that we've transcended it! A chapter informed by post-structuralist, post-Cartesian and post-humanist thinking (as developed by thinkers like Foucault, Derrida, and Deleuze and Guattari) is very important in a collection such as this, as it is from this body of ideas that perhaps the most incisive challenges to 'modernist' approaches to development, learning and education will emerge in the future. Hillevi leaves us with much food for thought, for example, when she writes that Reggio Emilia *'still doesn't manage to transgress the dominant binary divides that haunt modern liberal humanist education; that is, human/non-human; discourse/matter; culture/nature; mind/body'*; and when she challenges just where *learning itself* is located: 'A relational materialist approach to learning is critical of the idea of learning in terms of inner mental activities inside a separated human being ... Thinking and learning take place *in-between* heterogeneous actors, rather than being something localized inside a human superior mind separated and located above the material world and other organisms.' Her vision of 'an ethics of immanence and potentiality', which 'is about opening yourself up to the endless possibilities of what children do, are capable of, and can become', is certainly one which the contributors to this book would subscribe to.

Part III, 'Advocacy, Research and Policy-making for Children's Early Years' Learning', is launched in **Chapter 16** by another of Open EYE's founder-members, writer and campaigner *Sue Palmer*. Sue draws upon her extensive background in the teaching of phonics, spelling and grammar and her work for the government's National Literacy Strategy, to show how a mechanistic, programmatic approach to literacy learning not only does not work, but probably leads to a decline in 'standards' – and a possibly life-long impact on young children's self-esteem and love of learning. In the process, Sue also draws upon her first-hand experience of the highly successful Finnish education system to show how a language-rich, music- and story-oriented approach in an unhurried kindergarten environment provides a highly effective, 'bottom-up' foundation for later learning that the 'top-down' literacy strategy has been unable to achieve. Sue Palmer ends with a passionate call for the government's revision of the Early Years Foundation Stage to do much more than mere 'tinkering'; for as she writes, 'we need root and branch reform. I now believe the only way to change the culture is to raise the school starting age to six (or preferably seven), and institute a separate Foundation Phase with a totally different ethos, similar to those Finnish kindergartens.' Whatever the Realpolitik of such a proposal might be, Sue Palmer certainly makes a compelling and persuasive pedagogical case for such a change.

In **Chapter 17**, *Sebastian P. Suggate* presents the results of his doctoral journey into the highly complex field of empirical research into literacy. He shows all too clearly how the field is fraught with methodological specification difficulties – and perhaps most important, how empirical results can be turned on their head, depending on the controls involved and the time-scales over which effects are measured. In his own doctoral research, Sebastian made the extremely important discovery that, all things being equal, children who are introduced to quasi-formal literacy learning at a relatively early age show no significant enhanced reading abilities by the age of 10 or 11, compared with a control group of children in the Steiner system who were not introduced to formal literacy learning until the age of 6 or 7. He then outlines six aspects of reading that he believes account for why earlier readers lose their advantage in the longer run. These findings add considerable empirical ballast to the intuitive and practice-based views of many of the other contributors to this book regarding early literacy learning (goals); and in any rational world, these findings would lead educational policy-makers to think long and hard before supporting any policies that impose quasi-formal literacy learning on to young children under the age of 6. For Sebastian, '*ableness is not readiness*'; and 'Being able to learn to read is not the same as readiness – if we view readiness in terms of what is the long-term benefit from learning to read early'.

In **Chapter 18**, Open EYE's *Richard House* continues the critical research theme with a chapter that casts severe doubt on the veracity of allegedly respectable educational research in/on the early years. In a close analysis of EYFS-relevant research commissioned by the Department for Education, he shows how such research findings are easily politicized and misleadingly manipulated for political purposes. The difficulties are compounded when one factors in the major methodological problems with 'positivistic' research, which includes the self-fulfilling way in which the unarticulated metaphysical assumptions that are made about 'reality' at the outset of any research project can so easily determine, or at least constrain, any conclusions that can be reached; and the way in which unquantifiable 'intangibles' can be more important than what is measurable and quantifiable (cf. Chapter 21). Associated problems with the Millennium Cohort Study and the Effective Provision of Pre-School Education (EPPE) research project are highlighted, and it is argued that longitudinal research into the long-term societal impact of educational policies can yield disturbing findings. Adopting a more 'postmodern' approach to research which takes explicit account of issues of power might be one effective way of responding to these methodological difficulties.

Chapter 19, by *Aric Sigman*, presents a very different research-based chapter, being a *tour de force* of the extensive scientific research evidence on the effects of televisual and ICT technologies on young children. In a long and relentlessly engaging review of the evidence, Aric draws upon his extensive knowledge of this specialist scientific literature to paint a disturbing picture of the mounting evidence of harm that these technologies perpetrate in a plethora of ways on young children – including amounts of screen time, language acquisition, the highly questionable value of so-called 'educational computers', brain function and computer use, effects on reading, effects on learning, brain development, and social disengagement. A key argument is that it is *the medium itself* that should concern us, and not merely the content of young children's experiences with these technologies.

With evidence showing overwhelmingly that 'Exposure to screen technology during key stages of child development may have counterproductive effects on cognitive processes and learning', and that 'Even moderate levels of screen viewing are increasingly associated with a wide range of health risks', Aric Sigman proposes what he calls an 'Educational Buffer Zone' be introduced, through which the early years of education would be 'cordoned off' from these technologies, thus 'providing a buffer zone where a child's cognitive and social skills can develop without the distortion that may occur through premature use of ICT'. It is indeed difficult to imagine that anyone reading, and really taking in, the avalanche of negative evidence on early ICT could conceivably still think it appropriate to statutorily impose these technologies on to young children – which, despite repeated challenges from both Aric and Open EYE, is still the case with England's Early Years Foundation Stage curriculum. At the very least, there is an increasingly overwhelming case for education authorities explicitly to reconsider the role of screen technologies in nurseries and schools.

In **Chapter 20** the tireless early childhood campaigner and founder-member of Open EYE, *Margaret Edgington*, is interviewed by the book's editor, Richard House. In a reflectively wide-ranging and refreshingly frank chapter, Margaret covers a wide canvas of themes, including her early training experience; the auspicious tradition of Britain's specialist nursery schools and the dangers posed to them by the Single Funding Formula; the short-termism of policy-making and the possibility of early years being taken out of the hands of 'party politics'; the appropriate balance between statutory intervention and professional autonomy in the early childhood sphere; the limitations of current early years training, and the tension between academic and experiential learning in teacher training; the history of the Open EYE early childhood campaign, and the lessons that can be drawn from its many successes; and a detailed consideration of her hopes and fears for the future of the early years in Britain. Fittingly, Richard concludes the chapter by writing, 'Were I the Early Years minister, you would most definitely be my chief advisor; and if the current minister, Sarah Teather, or her successor(s) or advisors, happen to read this, there is still time! ... '

In **Part IV**, 'Ways Ahead to Achievable Futures', Open EYE's *Grethe Hooper Hansen* lifts the discussion in **Chapter 21** to a quite new level, offering us a perspective on the 'paradigm shift' which the so-called 'new science' is increasingly embracing, and which is fundamentally challenging so many of the taken-for-granted assumptions of the conventional 'modernist' learning paradigm which, for the most part, we uncritically take for granted. 'New paradigm', 'new science' thinking, supported by many prominent academic and professional authorities, is open to embracing new ways of thinking about 'reality', and is often informed by an explicitly *spiritual* cosmology (broadly defined).

In her chapter, Grethe refers to how – in line with both psychoanalytic and Steinerean (Rudolf Steiner's) thinking – we are only conscious of a very small proportion (perhaps 5 per cent) of our mental processes; and if this is indeed the case, it surely has revolutionary consequences for how we work with young children in their early formative years – for at present, the implicit assumption is that 'the 5 per cent' with which practitioners work constitutes the whole. Grethe goes on to show how the much-neglected research of Bulgarian scientist Georgi Lozanov throws considerable light on how human beings learn. For Lozanov, the richest and most effective learning is acquired *indirectly* (through unconscious parallel processing, as in the example of children learning to read); and Lozanov 'provides a myriad ingenious ways of distracting the conscious mind from the target material' (with the latter kind of approach being the *polar opposite* of the conventional educational approach to teaching and learning). Thus, when the conscious mind takes over, unconscious quantum learning grinds to a halt (an insight that Rudolf Steiner clearly had himself in relation to young children's consciousness); and 'This is the most common mistake that teachers make, since it is very difficult to adjust pedagogical practice to absolute faith in the enormous capability of the unconscious'. Carl Rogers' important thinking around the notion of 'freedom to learn' is also surely relevant here; and there is also a rich potential for cross-fertilization between these 'new paradigm' perspectives and the kinds of deconstructive, post-structuralist thinking exemplified in Hillevi Lenz Taguchi's Chapter 15.

In **Chapter 22**, and in what we believe to be a unique 'first' in the early years literature, the ex chair of the Education Select Committee, *Barry Sheerman*, has laid out in detail an insightful policy-making perspective, from the vantage-point of his key position over many years as chairman of the parliamentary Select Committee. Barry shows the extent to which early childhood has become a key aspect of policy-making over the past decade or so, and describes the role his committee had in this process. At a number of points, he touches on the 'too much, too soon' theme – writing, for example, of how his committee became 'convinced … that formal learning should not be thrust upon children too early'; that 'we worried that some schools would transform the reception class into the first part of Key Stage 1'; and that 'the Select Committee in March 2009 … did recommend that the [EYFS] Early Learning Goals should apply to slightly older children, so that they are genuinely something that children at the end of the fifth year would be able to achieve rather than having unrealistic expectations for younger children'.

Barry Sheerman also interestingly concedes that 'Ministers might have been persuaded that a prescriptive early year's curriculum that even the less well-trained could deliver, alongside more inspection and assessment, could be the quickest and cheapest way of transforming the system' – a concern to which Open EYE has consistently referred since 2007. His hope that 'the Education Committee will play a part in the restoration of balance between trusting parents, families and professionals instead of allowing too much interference from central government – a softer and more flexible policy stance' is certainly one which the contributors to this book will share.

Not wishing to spare Barry's blushes, Open EYE had a wonderful experience of meeting with him at Westminster, and of really being listened to thoughtfully and open-mindedly; and as pointed out in Chapter 20, it seems ironic that the very qualities that we believe a really effective education Secretary of State should possess seem to occur in abundance in those very parliamentarians who are not in government itself, like Barry and Annette Brooke. Perhaps there are lessons for government here regarding the kinds of qualities that currently seem to dominate the choosing of 'Cabinet material'.

Finally, in their concluding chapter *Wendy Scott and Richard House* draw together the central themes of the book and propose several eminently achievable *recommendations for early years policy-making*. They suggest that the necessarily oppositional stance taken by the Open EYE campaign needs to evolve into constructive engagement with policy-makers and more mainstream educationalists. The recommendations constitute a first but substantial step in this direction. Significantly, only one of the co-authors (Richard) is a member of Open EYE, so this collaborative chapter illustrates how it is possible for activist campaigners and respected authorities in the field to work constructively together to produce a set of proposals which, if implemented, would be of inestimable benefit to young children's healthy development and well-being.

This 'recommendations' section, closely informed by theory, research and practitioner experience, is the one that politicians, journalists and perhaps academics may wish to go to first, as it provides pointers to the practical policy changes behind which all these interests can unite in the cause of arresting premature pressures on young children – a concern which lies at the very heart of this book. Indeed, this concluding chapter locates the concerns explored in the book within the wider cultural context of *the erosion of childhood*, heralding what Wendy Ellyatt has termed 'moving *from awareness to action*', through the anticipated development of a new grass-roots cultural movement centred on the overarching theme of the erosion of childhood, which is now of such concern to so many people (see www.savechildhood.net).

Picking up, finally, on the theme of Grethe Hooper Hansen's provocative chapter, one of the defining features of 'the modern mind' is the arrogance that the conscious, control-fixated ego demonstrates in assuming, first, that human learning is overwhelmingly conscious, and so it is at the conscious level that we need to focus in order to construct effective pedagogical practices. But if this is just plain wrong – which Steiner, Montessori, Lozanov, Guy Claxton and a host of psychoanalytic thinkers believe it to be – then *we will almost certainly have to quite fundamentally re-think our whole approach to working with young children*. There are many clues in this book to the way in which this 'paradigm shift' might appropriately begin to take form; and at the very least, we can begin by teasing out, and making explicit, just what the metaphysical assumptions are about learning, the 'mind' and intersubjective experience that frameworks like the Early Years Foundation Stage might be making – and I venture that in the process, we might well be very surprised, and healthily and appropriately disturbed, by what we discover.

But now over to you, the reader, to take this important thinking forward.

Policy-making and the Erosion of Childhood

The Case of the Early Years Foundation Stage

In Part I the contributors give their concerted attention to England's statutory early childhood curriculum, the Early Years Foundation Stage – focusing on both those aspects of the curriculum's content that are concerning, and also on the ways in which its practical enactment by government seems to have been deliberately geared towards stifling or neutralizing any meaningful dissent from the framework. A notable feature of Part I is the inclusion of chapters by a professional childminder (and her partner) and two parents, who have all found the courage and perseverance to take on the full panoply of government power in their principled and compellingly argued challenges to the framework.

We are particularly delighted that the world-renowned and respected childcare expert of many decades, Penelope Leach, leads off the book with a chapter that is replete with her characteristic sound sense and perennial wisdom about young children. Part I also contains detailed commentaries from the Open EYE campaign on both the EYFS itself and also on the Tickell review of the framework. The detailed arguments developed in this latter chapter are highly relevant not only to anyone interested in England's EYFS and its vicissitudes, but also to anyone concerned with the legitimate role of central government in intervening in early childhood experience, and the many dangers that such intrusions necessarily entail.

CHAPTER I

The EYFS and the Real Foundations of Children's Early Years[*]

PENELOPE LEACH

The first decade of this new millennium has been an exciting period for people involved with the early years. In fact it is easy to forget that 10–15 years ago, the idea of government saying anything about the care and education of the 0–5s, let alone anything we *liked*, was pretty much unheard of. Now, the early years, and the importance of early intervention when problems arise during them, is a focus of attention from cabinet level downwards. Overall this is a welcome change, and it's important not to lose sight of that amidst the many cogent criticisms that have been made of its details – many of which are discussed in this book.

The previous government's document *Every Child Matters*[1] was an initiative that was launched in 2003, at least partly in response to the death of wVictoria Climbié. It is a vital policy document that was the first of three government papers leading up to the Children Act 2004. Its aims, now widely known, are to ensure that every child, no matter what their background or circumstances, is supported to: be healthy; stay safe; enjoy and achieve; make a positive contribution; and achieve economic well-being.

---

[*] This chapter is an updated and extended version of an invited keynote address given at the first Open EYE conference, 'Early Learning and Its Discontents', Resources Centre, London, 16 February 2008.

A further sweeping vision, with far-reaching commitments to change, was set out in the *Ten Year Childcare Strategy*.[2] The vision was of social services, children's centres and extended schools in every local community working together across professional boundaries to provide integrated childcare and early years education, and ensuring that all children received services and support tailored to their needs. The recently elected Coalition government has so far published several reports and Green papers on children's issues, including two on parenting: *The Foundation Years* by Frank Field and *Early Intervention: The Next Steps* by Graham Allen.[3]

This continuing governmental focus on early years care and education is welcome, but of course, it is principally motivated by economics. Governments are concerned to reduce the numbers of children in poverty and disadvantage, and believe that the way to do that is to get parents into paid work and therefore children into non-parental childcare. This is the most reliable and sustainable route out of poverty. Plans and policy initiatives such as these are inclusive of all children, and are intended especially to benefit those from disadvantaged families, such as lone mothers. They can, however, be over-inclusive in that they tend to treat all children under school age as an integrated group, with no special proposals or arrangements for infants and toddlers – except in terms of their eventual 'school readiness'. This is unfortunate. It cannot be assumed that the types and patterns of care that produce the best outcomes for pre-school and older children are also the best for the under-twos. Infants and toddlers have different needs and developmental patterns, and these are the real foundations for children's early years.

However, encouraged by these kinds of government policies, other-than-mother care in the first two years of life is becoming increasingly common in the United Kingdom – as in most of the Western world. Although much of the care of infants while their mothers work or study is undertaken informally, often by fathers and grandparents, the use of formal, purchased childcare for this age group is increasing, especially the use of group care. Other (and perhaps more desirable) options – such as paid leave for the first year – are available only to those who have been in work, and who can afford the drop in income that comes from forgoing a wage for maternity benefits. That is by no means everyone. But given that there *is* a trend towards more and earlier non-familial care, the underlying intention of the Early Years Foundation Stage (EYFS)

– to establish detailed standards of care that must be upheld in every setting, and which parents can count on their child receiving wherever they seek childcare – is welcome. But if the intention was good, some of the implications are not. As Dame Clare Tickell put it in the introduction to her independent review,[4] ' … although there is strong support for the EYFS, it is not perfect and there are clear areas where it can be improved'.

Too Much, Too Soon

Alongside the rapid increase of non-familial care in infancy, and influenced by a decade of much-quoted work on early brain development,[5] and by evidence from the government-funded Effective Provision of Pre-School Education (EPPE) study of the benefits of pre-school education to school readiness and performance,[6] there has been a growing tendency for politicians, policy-makers, professionals and the media to focus on *cognitive* (rather than any other aspect of) *development* and on early years *education*. It is worth noting that the only universally free childcare that we have in England is free part-time pre-school education places for all three- and four-year-olds (and now a lot of disadvantaged two-year-olds as well). It is also notable that while we are constantly reminded that care and education are inseparable because babies learn from birth, nobody reminds us that they are inseparable because all children need caring for all the time.

Disproportionate interest in cognitive development has peaked in the EYFS where Literacy and Numeracy (and problem-solving and reasoning) were stated to be equally as important as physical development and social-emotional development. This extraordinary statement, which was confirmed verbally by the then Minister Beverley Hughes herself but has been revised by Tickell in her EYFS review, may or may not be true for some three- or four-year-olds, but it is clearly not the case for 0–3-year-olds. And even for those 'older' children (all of four …), some of the Learning Goals – such as those for literacy – sadly set up many children, especially boys and, of course, summer-born children, to fail before they even start school. We anxiously await the Coalition government's response to these concerns in its legislative reply to Dame Tickell's review of the EYFS, which is discussed at length elsewhere in this book (see Chapter 6).

Aspects of the EYFS which would be unfortunate and unhelpful if it were 'Guidance' only (as were earlier stages, such as *Every*

Child Matters) are a truly grim reality for many practitioners and academics, because the EYFS is statutory. With every care-provider legally obliged to provide the EYFS and assess and record (and share with other carers) each child's progress through it, the implications, not only for parental and professional choice in child-rearing but also for training and staffing, have been immense. The irony is that a well-meant attempt to legislate the foundations of the early years has unwittingly risked undermining them in some very specific ways.

Emphasizing 'Cognitive Development' and 'Education'

The emphasis on cognitive rather than other aspects of development, and the reiterated use of that word 'education', constitute a wide-ranging area of risk. Applied not only to children coming up to the age of compulsory schooling but also to babies and toddlers, these phrases clearly suggest that school success matters more than any other outcome, and that 'school readiness' should be constantly in view, even when caring for babies. This has a markedly disempowering effect on parents. A mother who took part in a study of childcare I was carrying out[7] told me, when her baby was eight months old:

> I know it's time she started in the nursery. We've been having such a great time in the park and at the pool and with other parents from my antenatal class that I've been putting it off. But babies these days don't just stay home with mummy and play, do they? It's time she was mixing with other children and doing all those proper activities …

Parents aren't the only ones who are feeling undermined. Some childcare workers such as childminders, and even some grandparents, are intimidated (e.g. see Chapter 4). Registered childminders are permitted to join networks that would allow them to become early education providers for three- and four-year-olds, but many are not keen to do so because, as one put it, 'I'm not a teacher and I don't want to be a teacher. I don't do education I only do play.' It is no coincidence that the numbers of registered childminders have declined precipitately since the introduction of the EYFS in September 2008 (see Chapter 4). This was entirely predictable by anyone with an understanding of early childcare and child development. We need to help parents – and others – understand that far from being second best but good-enough-for-now teachers, they are something different, and something more.

By the time children are ready for Key Stage 1, teachers in school settings have unique roles to play in their learning, like *teaching them* skills that do not come out of free play – such as phonics – and helping to motivate them to keep going with the inevitably boring, repetitive practice that some kinds of necessary learning – such as times tables or irregular spellings – require. But in the earliest years, valuable though the input of teachers may be, children are not pupils, but apprentices in the business of growing up as human beings. And it is that apprenticeship (rather than a legally binding Early Years Foundation Stage and Profile) upon which their formal education will be built. Babies, toddlers and pre-school children will learn something (good, neutral or bad) from any experience that is shared with other people, adults and/or children, especially when they are sharing with 'personal people': parents or other loved adults.

Attachment: The Platform for Living (and Playing)

A new baby is not a fully formed individual. His brain, as much as his body, must grow and develop, and learn how to coordinate its parts and function to his command in whatever environment he is born into; and it is not a teacher he needs for that, but a parent-partner. It was Donald Winnicott who famously remarked that 'There's no such thing as a baby'; and it is a message that we need to put out to all parents. Mother (or, sometimes, father or carer) and baby form a 'dyadic system' in which both are active partners. It is the interaction between them that organizes the baby's experiences today in the light of what he made of yesterday, and in doing so actually builds the physical connections and layers within his brain and nervous system that shape the person he will be tomorrow. Research confirming the importance to babies' future development of them being securely attached to at least one person – and preferably at least one spare for insurance purposes – is widely known.[8] But what isn't yet widely understood (and certainly isn't acknowledged in the EYFS) is that that attachment relationship is not just important to babies' emotional development, but to every aspect of their brain development.[9]

Helping Children to Become Learners

Babies and toddlers don't need adults to *teach* them, but they do need them to help them learn, by providing a securely affectionate environment in which their play is facilitated and admired from the very beginning: hugs and talk and song and laughter and books. And 'scaffolding', erected by people who are sensitive to be able to see what the child himself is currently trying to do, to help him surmount each new self-imposed challenge.

The more we can show parents how vital the environment and relationship they provide for their babies are, and how clever and how keen those babies are, the readier parents will be to treat them as intelligent beings – and that's one of the most desirable self-fulfilling prophecies I know.

The EYFS practice guidance for the first 18 months supports much of this – it certainly says nothing to the contrary. But it ignores the vital fact that children get most out of those social exchanges and playtimes when they are with the people they are most attached to – usually parents. Tickell emphasizes this in an important paragraph in her review (viz. 3.4) headed 'The foundations of healthy development', which opens with the statement that 'The contribution of parents and carers to their child's early development cannot be overstated ... strong bonds ... are critical'.

There's a great deal of research that shows that even when children spend most of their waking hours in non-parental care, the Home Learning Environment – the activities and outings, conversations and songs they get at home – has much more effect on every aspect of their development, than anything that goes on in childcare. In fact, I would say (though I wouldn't make it a legal requirement that everyone should agree with me!) that the best way to help babies discover their new world, toddler explorers to grow into pre-school experimental 'scientists', and preschool children become curious, confident, able learners is to give them the warm, responsive care that makes for secure attachments. If we lead parents and other loving carers to feel inadequate compared to professionals, fewer children will get as much of that as they might have done otherwise, and we shall all have lost something important.

Confusion around Teaching, Learning and Play

The second area of risk I want to single out is a certain confusion between teaching and learning – and the consequent confusion about play. Substituting the word 'learning' for the word 'education' helps somewhat, because it makes it easier for people to realize that we are talking about something that comes more from within the child than from outside him, especially where under-threes are concerned. 'She learns', rather than 'I teach her'.

The EYFS uses that word 'learning' a lot but, sadly, it ruins the effect by tacking on the word 'goals'. A child cannot produce adult goals from within herself: goals have to come from outside. So even if the EYFS doesn't tell a parent to *teach* her child, it tells her that she has to accept pre-set goals for his learning: make sure he learns what he should in order to meet those goals by the end of the year in which he turns five.

It is important that people see early learning as coming from inside children because that's what makes clear its interconnectedness with play, and therefore the inappropriateness of many 'learning goals'. And play, *real* play (see Chapters 13 and 14), is the other foundation of the early years that I believe the Early Years Foundation Stage may be undermining, despite the insistence in the documentation that it is 'play-based'.

We could talk all day about what 'play' is – and is not – but in this context what really matters is that play is spontaneous, and child directed and controlled (see Chapter 13). Children play because that's what children do. They start playing a particular game or with a particular object or piece of the environment because they think it will be interesting and fun; they go on because it is interesting and fun. And they stop when it's not interesting or fun any more.

By definition, then, while play can be facilitated, even suggested by an adult, it cannot be 'managed' or directed, and it cannot have an actual 'purpose' (a 'learning goal', like understanding number, for instance). An activity or 'game' – such as a sport or a jigsaw puzzle – that *is* managed by an adult, and for an adult purpose, may be fun for a child so she willingly does it and learns something from doing it; but it isn't *play*.

If 'managed play' can be fun and educational, what's so important about 'real play'? Real play is integral to the development of all children everywhere. It is children's means of finding out about their particular world and how it works; of discovering and developing their own abilities and acquiring adult skills, and all at their own pace.

Worldwide, most children's play goes on without any adult management or even input, and without purpose-made toys too.

However, spontaneous play with loaned pieces of the adult world – from wooden spoons at 6 months to the family garden hose at 4 years – and with the kinds of toy that allow creativity and experiment, is *especially* important to children in urban Western environments where they are kept so separate from everyday and real-world adult concerns.

A two-year-old in rural Africa sees maize planted and watered, and has a go himself in his play. He sees it growing, helps to pick it (playing at being a grown-up); sees it shucked and ground and made into the porridge which everyone eats, including him; he knows that it is milking the cows and goats that provides milk for everyone to drink; and he can soon see, then understand, even share, adult worries about sick animals, unseasonal weather and flattened crops or drought. It's very different for urban children, especially those in Western urban environments who are cut off from most of the natural world by a layer of concrete, and from most meaningful adult concerns by the mysteries of work that is called 'going to the office', involves sitting at a computer all day and produces something incomprehensible called 'money'. Toddlers cannot understand, let alone share, worries about 'the mortgage' or 'the market'. But if they're allowed to play freely, they can find out how – and even why – adults do some of the mysterious things they do, and try some out too.

For small children there is no distinction between playing and learning; between activities that are 'just for fun' and those that are 'educational'. And it is important that there *shouldn't* be a distinction, at least until children are in full-time school and discovering the difference between *lessons* and play. Toys, including 'educational toys', and other playthings *are* fun, of course – if they weren't, children wouldn't play with them. But things that aren't toys are fun, too, and things that aren't particularly *fun* can be interesting …

Looking round a well-equipped nursery, I am often struck by how little of its bright content is recognizably anything to do with the natural world *or* the adult world. How many two-year-olds recognize those dear little baking sets as miniatures of what goes on in the kitchen at home? *Does* anyone at home roll out dough with a rolling pin? And if they do, is that rolling pin likely to be six inches long, and purple? Few homes have as many toys as a nursery, but provided the adults will share their 'toys', there is just as much, and perhaps more, potential for play and learning in many homes as there is in the nursery.

It is really important that parents and caregivers should be confident that facilitating children's learning is something they themselves can do – indeed, can't avoid doing as the children play – not 'teachers' secrets' or a 'government programme'.

Almost every contact between an infant and an adult can be another interesting and useful learning experience *if the adult will make it so*. My grand-daughter did not learn to wave bye-bye just because her parents and grandparents demonstrated and encouraged (dare I say, 'taught' her?), but because the school-crossing patrol lady waved to her every morning when she and her daddy took the bigger ones to school. She came to recognize a social gesture, and then she came to realize that what you do with social gestures is reciprocate. More seriously, I have the honour to work with a General Practitioner who won't touch a paediatric patient who can speak until or unless she has helped that child to learn what the relevant body-part and instrument is called: 'Naming is important', she says. 'Knowing what something's called gives them at least a *bit* of control, and then I can ask permission before I do anything – like "May I feel your tummy" or "Can I look in your ear with my auriscope?"'

Adults are crucial to children's learning – *all* adults, everywhere – but not *only* adults. Children matter, too; and despite the assumption that the EYFS mostly goes on in group settings, it does not adequately acknowledge the importance of peers to even the youngest children. Now that so many children are without closely spaced brothers and sisters or groups of cousins, and are kept, for their own safety, from playing out in the street with groups of neighbouring children, companionship has to be arranged, and it needs to start long before pre-school playgroup age. In what Jerome Bruner, perhaps the most respected of all child developmentalists, calls the 'quiet revolution' of infant development research, it has become clear that the 'social context' in which a child lives and learns is crucial. It is not just because children are social beings (a meaningless truism!) but because, as Bruner puts it ' … through social life with peers the child acquires a framework for interpreting experience and learns how to negotiate meaning … Making sense is a social process.'[10] That inter-meshing of emotional, social and cognitive development is the real 'foundation stage' of infancy.

Of course, some babies get all the play and stimulation they can use from people available to them at home – parents, older siblings, other relatives. There is the uncle who takes rough-and-tumble play to the very line between enjoyment and fear; the toddler who delights in making the baby laugh (or cry!); the grandmother who loves to show picture books and talk about them, and the grandfather who willingly goes on and *on* building up blocks to be knocked down, or pushing toys away for the baby to reel back in.

However, some babies and young children are under-stimulated, even if they are lovingly cared for.[11] Some research singles out one-child families in small urban homes, and babies cared for by relatives doing a somewhat-reluctant favour to young lone mothers. And to the amazement of mothers attending baby groups for the first time, a lot more get less stimulation than they can *use*. The EYFS documents are right to emphasize stimulation, but there can be too much as well as too little (see Chapter 7).

Over-controlling Play

My third risk area is the extent to which parents and carers control, and feel they should control, play. There is a fine and very wiggly line between freedom to play and being neglected. It is as important not to *bombard* babies' and toddlers' brains with stimuli as not to force-feed their bodies – a crucial point that is frequently made in this book (e.g. Chapters 7 and 12). Until babies can sit up alone, move around on the floor and reach out for things, they cannot play much on their own any more than they can feed themselves, so there has to be adult input. But *how much* input is a minute-by-minute judge-ment call. Even in toddlerhood, when children can indeed instigate a lot of their own play, it can be difficult to balance child freedom and adult control. Let's face it, toddlers left to get up on their own on Sunday mornings, while hard-pressed parents have a lie-in, seldom make it an opportunity to build new worlds with Lego. They mostly climb into the parents' bed or watch cartoons on television. The flow of a child's creativity is easily stopped by adult 'management' (or interference), but it usually takes at least a little bit of adult help and guidance to get going. The fine line on which I am focused right now, though, is not the one between freedom and neglect, but the one between freedom and control – or between autonomy and interference.

Meaning nothing but well, a father fixes the suction pad of a big rattle to his six-month-old daughter's high-chair tray. She reaches, touches, tugs at it – and explodes in frustration. He tries to demonstrate how to make it rattle by just bashing it. No good. He tries soothing and scolding, but neither soothes her. She wants that rattle *off* so she can hold and shake and mouth it. Infants don't just want to be entertained, they want to do things, to manage. To discover, again and again 'I do this, and *that* happens'.

Risk Aversion

The final risk I want to consider in this chapter is our risk-aversion; not really addressed in the EYFS but subtly encouraged by its emphasis on keeping children safe and in group care. If adult over-management is limiting, even spoiling the self-generated, free and exploratory play that is so vital to children's growth and development, some of that is due to our over-concern for children's physical safety. How can an adult be *over*-protective of a baby or toddler? Isn't physical safety the number one criterion of good care, whether at home or elsewhere? And isn't keeping her child or her charge safe every caregiver's main responsibility? Well, yes, of course – but only within reason. Just as feeding a child well does not mean giving her more and more food, so keeping a child safe does not mean putting more and more limits on her activities.

Child safety is a very emotive topic. There is much that can be said about the importance of allowing children to play freely even though that involves risks; and about how important it is to let them actually *take risks* as they play, because they have to learn to understand which situations *are* risky, and manage themselves in them. I had personal experience of this dilemma because a horribly steep gravel path led up to my two-year-old grand-daughter's house. How I dreaded her hurtling down it to greet me and falling and grazing herself as she'd done before. But her mother and I, at the top and bottom of the slope, had to let her run because that was the only way she could learn either to stay on her feet or to go more slowly.

Yet however much we all agree that some freedom to take risks really matters to children's learning, it takes only one single nationally publicized tragedy to change people's minds. A three-year-old, exploring freely around his grandparents' garden, drowned in a small garden pond while no less than six loving family members went to the toilet, to fetch the coffee, to clear the table ... – each assuming that another was watching the child. A four-year-old, allowed to set her own physical limits, fell off the top of a slide and broke her pelvis. And of course a few years ago, another vanished from a holiday apartment, and has never been seen since. When we hear about, let alone suffer, events like those, the rage of 'What if ... ', and the despair of 'If only ... ', wipe out everything but the need to keep children safe. Put the babies in play-pens with some nice rounded toys. Put the toddlers in playgroups or nurseries which are *built* to be safe, or take them to soft rooms to use up their energy. When the older children (four and over!) are not at school, keep them indoors with television and computer games – whatever it takes to keep them safe.

But too much caution can put real limitations on children's play, and therefore on their development. What's more, there is a vicious circle operating here: the more cautious we feel, the more hazards we think of, and the more protective we become. Many will remember the idiocies publicized by the Children's Play Council some years ago: children banned from making daisy chains in case of 'infection' from the ground; a school long-jump competition held on grass and guesswork instead of sand, because sand might be 'dirty' and have 'germs'. And yo-yos and conkers banned from school playgrounds for fear of injuries. Those quasi-comic restrictions are not a thing of the past. In many primary schools right now, the running games – versions of 'tag' or 'it' – that have always been the mainstay of playground fun are banned for fear of collisions; and handstands, cartwheels, somersaults and leapfrog are forbidden in case of falls.

The trouble is – as some Health and Safety regulations make clear – that as soon as you try to foresee every hazard, then *everything* becomes dangerous. The just-walking baby could trip over the toe of her own new shoe and hit her head on the edge of the terrace; the toddler could catch his fingers in that drawer; drop that cup and cut himself on its broken edge; fall over the back of the sofa he's riding like a donkey, instead of on to its soft seat; strangle himself with the scarf he's dressed himself up in. And the older children could not only bang their heads together in the playground, but if allowed out into the street or to neighbour's gardens, could fall off their bikes or submit to the lures of strangers. Curiously, the most statistically probable accident – getting hit by a vehicle – is seldom mentioned.

But this is child-proofing gone mad. There is much to be said for proofing children's surroundings from causing damage – by gating stairs from babies, for example, or controlling speed limits for cars using residential streets – but this is proofing children from their surroundings: from anything not designed for them and passed by Health and Safety. Of course that adds to the sense that they will be better off in children's centres or nurseries. But the more we isolate them into 'safe' children's settings where non-family adults are paid to take responsibility for them, the more restrictive we have to be.

A lot of keeping babies, toddlers and small children as safe as they can reasonably be depends upon tactful, tuned-in supervision by an adult who knows exactly what the child's capabilities are, and can therefore see whether his new ambition (to get to the *top* of the climbing frame instead of the platform) is something he can manage alone; something he can be helped to manage with a bit of personal scaffolding, or perhaps something he should be distracted from. The lower the ratio not only of adults to children but of adults who know the children in that intimate way, the more difficult that kind of supervision is. When there are not enough such adults to the number of children (and in nurseries and preschools, that is almost always), it is sometimes tempting for the carers or the managers, who will be held responsible if anything goes wrong, to substitute environmental manipulation for supervision. If there is nothing to climb on, there's nothing for anybody to fall off. I know a nursery that has removed its toddler-size climbing frame after a child was pushed and fell. He was unhurt, but his mother was furious. Now the children are deprived not only of the learning and self-management (and fun!) involved in climbing, but also of the learning and self-management that eventually *prevent* pushes and falls.

I also know more than one childminder who has a garden but will not allow any water play, even a water-table or a washing-up bowl, let alone a paddling pool, on the grounds that if there is water out there, she has to be there too – and take the children in with her to answer the door or go to the toilet. One of the childminders is registered in a network as an early-education provider. Even if there is no water in the garden, she really does prefer the children to be indoors where she can see them all and, even better, seated around the table drawing, doing puzzles or building with Lego. After all, that's educational.

It isn't only low ratios of adults to children they know well that lead some caregivers to be over-protective. Many worry about what parents will say – and often with good cause. It is hateful for a parent to come and collect a small child, and find that she has a bump on her head or a bite on her arm. And it is almost inevitable that she will feel that if *she'd* been there, it wouldn't have happened. But the truth is that caregivers ought not to be expected to take more care, or be more cautious than 'reasonable parents'.

Managers and Litigation

Unfortunately caregivers, teachers and their managers are often controlled by local authorities with a (sadly realistic) fear of being sued by the parents of any child who gets hurt. Why are children's playgrounds so unimaginatively equipped? Because anything outside the recognized 'safe stuff' lays councils open to law suits and charges, every time a child falls off something and perhaps fractures a wrist. Why are parks cleared of the fallen trees and piles of autumn leaves that children would so love to scramble over and jump in? Because if a child were to hurt herself and a parent chose to blame the Parks Department, the result could be a court case that would be both embarrassing and financially crippling. Last week I saw a letter to a nursery manager:

> It has come to our attention that washing up liquid has been added to the water table to provide bubbles. Please note that this is not play material but cleaning equipment. Its use is not covered by the Nursery's insurance and is inappropriate.

Childhood without bubbles? Whatever next?

Notes

1 *Every Child Matters*, presented to Parliament by the Chief Secretary to the Treasury, September 2003.

2 'Choice for Parents, the Best Start for Children: A Ten Year Strategy for Childcare', HM Treasury, Department for Education and Skills and Department for Work and Pensions, December 2004; downloadable at: http://webarchive.nationalarchives.gov.uk/+/http://www.hm-treasury.gov.uk/d/cfp_leaflet_020205.pdf (retrieved 24 June 2011).

3 Frank Field, *The Foundation Years: Preventing Poor Children Becoming Poor Adults*, HM Government, Cabinet Office, London, December 2010; downloadable at: http://webarchive.nationalarchives.gov.uk/20110120090128/http://povertyreview.independent.gov.uk/media/20254/poverty-report.pdf (retrieved 24 June 2011); Graham Allen, *Early Intervention: The Next Steps*, Cabinet Office, London, January 2011; downloadable at: http://www.dwp.gov.uk/docs/early-intervention-next-steps.pdf (retrieved 24 June 2011).

4 Dame Clare Tickell, *The Early Years: Foundations for Life, Health and Learning*: An Independent Report on the EYFS to HM Government, April 2011.

5 Allan N. Schore, 'Early brain development', *Infant Mental Health Journal*, 22 (1–2), 2001, pp. 201–69.

6 Department for Education, Effective Provision of Pre-school Education (EPPE) project, 1997–2003.

7   P. Leach, J. Barnes, L.-E. Malmberg, K. Sylva and A. Stein, 'The quality of different types of childcare at 10 and 18 months: a comparison between types and factors related to quality', *Early Child Development and Care*, 178 (2), 2008, pp. 177–209; and J. Barnes, P. Leach, K. Sylva, A. Stein and L.-E. Malmberg, 'Infant care in England: mothers' aspirations, experiences, satisfaction and caregiver relationships', *Early Child Development and Care*, 176 (5), 2006, pp. 553–73.

8   H. Steele, 'State of the art: attachment theory', *The Psychologist*, 15 (10), 2002, pp. 518–23; S. Gerhardt, *Why Love Matters: How Affection Shapes a Baby's Brain*, New York: Brunner Routledge, 2004.

9   R.M.P. Fearon, M.J. Bakermans-Kranenburg, M.H. Van Izendoorn, A. Lapsley and G.I. Roiseman, 'The significance of insecure attachment and disorganization in the development of children's externalizing behavior: a meta-analytic study', *Child Development*, 81, 2010, pp. 435–56.

10   Jerome Bruner, *The Culture of Education*, Cambridge, Mass.: Harvard University Press, 1996.

11   P. Leach, *Childcare Today: What We Know and What We Need to Know*, Cambridge: Polity Press, 2010.

CHAPTER 2

Challenging Government Policy-making for the Early Years: Early Open EYE Contributions

MARGARET EDGINGTON, RICHARD HOUSE, LYNNE OLDFIELD AND SUE PALMER

In this chapter, we reproduce just three of Open EYE's published articles, which together set the scene for just why the Open EYE campaign was founded, and setting out in detail our original objections to key aspects of the Early Years Foundation Stage.

1 Challenging Government Policy-Making for the Early Years: The 'Open EYE' Campaign[1]

MARGARET EDGINGTON, RICHARD HOUSE, LYNNE OLDFIELD AND SUE PALMER

In late 2007 a diverse group of early years authorities, including ourselves, launched the 'Open EYE' campaign (www.savechildhood.org), raising serious questions about what was then the impending compulsory Early Years Foundation Stage (EYFS) framework, and initiating in turn a wide-ranging debate about the legitimate role of government intervention in early childhood. With a major national conference, a strongly supported Downing Street petition, and the assiduous lobbying of Parliament, the aim of the campaign has been to persuade the government to reconsider this flawed legislation.

Some aspects of the EYFS are certainly laudable. We are not against government intervention in the early-years sphere per se, and we appreciate the resources that recent governments have devoted to the field. However, several aspects of the EYFS legislation are strongly contra-indicated by existing research – most notably, the highly problematic EYFS literacy goals. Foundation Stage Profile data indicate that most children are unable to achieve these goals by the end of reception year. Children taught to read and write at 6–7 years old commonly achieve literacy competency quickly and easily, and with far greater enjoyment.

In a revealing letter written to 'Open EYE' in late 2007, the then early years minister Beverley Hughes asserted that the six areas of development in the EYFS framework 'are equally important' – thereby assuming that literacy, problem-solving, reasoning and numeracy are of equal importance for this age-group as are (for example) physical, social and emotional development. Yet crucially, there exists no research evidence whatsoever to indicate that these six developmental competencies are 'equally important' for this age group. Indeed, to the contrary, evidence strongly suggests that for children under 6, certain kinds of development are far more important (e.g. physical and social development) than are others (e.g. cognitive development).[2] The compulsory EYFS framework is therefore based upon a quite erroneous view of child development, with little if any convincing research evidence to support it.

From the original 'Desirable Outcomes' in the late 1990s, through the Curriculum Guidance for the Foundation Stage of 2000, and now to the EYFS, the demands have become increasingly prescriptive and more demanding for both practitioners and children; and as from September 2008, the Statutory Guidance stated that all providers, 'regardless of type, size or funding', 'must by law deliver' the learning and development requirements. This quite unprecedented compulsion is particularly distressing for settings such as the Steiner Kindergartens, which have developed a highly effective 'holistic' early-learning approach over many decades, right across the globe.

There are also wider concerns. The compulsion enshrined in the legislation at what is a pre-compulsory schooling age not only contradicts principles of educational diversity, but raises profound issues of civil liberties and the parental right to choose the kind of early-learning experience parents wish for their children. There are also grave concerns about a flawed consultation process, and the cascading of the 'audit culture' right into the earliest of years, where its values, practices and accompanying mentality are singularly inappropriate.

A very important public/private-sphere boundary may have been crossed in this legislation, and starting in late 2007, the Open EYE campaign actively brought these grave issues to the attention of Parliament, in the hope that a much-needed re-assessment of the legislation might, with MPs' support, be granted by the then government. For the state to define what is 'normal' child development, and then to enshrine this in law, is a dangerous and quite unprecedented development in modern political life.

2   Westminster Magazine 2008 'Advertorial'[3]

The Children, Schools and Families Parliamentary Committee (Chair, Barry Sheerman MP; see Chapter 22) recently held a special meeting on the Early Years Foundation Stage (EYFS). Coming on the heels of 70 MPs having signed Early Day Motion 1031 raising Open EYE's concerns, and over 7,000 citizens having signed our Downing Street petition (including such notables as Steve Biddulph, Penelope Leach, Camila Batmanghelidjh, Margaret Forster, Philip Pullman, Bel Mooney, Dorothy Rowe, and Professors Tim Brighouse and Janet Moyles), a welcome 'window of opportunity' now exists for a comprehensive, dispassionate investigation into EYFS.

Some of Minister Beverley Hughes's own early-years special advisors have recently expressed reservations about EYFS in various letters to the press; and on 22 May 2008, *The Times* reported[4] that in a document 'shelved' by the Department, Ms Hughes's advisors recently strongly advised the revision of EYFS's more developmentally inappropriate literacy Learning Requirements. In the light of such widespread concern, it is surely better that any agreed shortcomings in the framework be rectified now, rather than waiting for a two-year review, by which time substantial damage might have already been done to our youngest, most vulnerable children.

Every Committee witness expressed shortcomings about the age-inappropriateness of some EYFS Learning Requirements, with added concerns also expressed about the likely impact of a legally enforced, assessment-driven approach upon practitioners. A compulsory framework can never, it was argued, substitute for a properly-trained and -remunerated workforce.

Open EYE has never been 'against' regulation, nor against EYFS in its entirety. Rather, we have highlighted certain aspects of EYFS which many believe are highly problematic. We argue for qualified 'support-with-reservations' for a framework which has some substantial flaws, as opposed to the uncritical, non-discerning support for EYFS that routinely emanates from both the Department and from narrow vested interests in the field.

Steiner settings have been granted special dispensations enabling them to escape the pressures emanating from the Local Authority outcomes duties. However, this doesn't go nearly far enough. Numerous mainstream and independent practitioners deeply unhappy with the EYFS Learning Requirements have contacted Open EYE, and it could raise serious schisms right across the sector if Steiner settings alone are given these special dispensations. The only tenable solution is for whole settings to be allowed to apply for principled exemption from the controversial Learning and Developments Requirements – not least on grounds of equity and fairness alone.

This is surely a time to lay aside vested and ego-driven interests, and to place trust in an all-party committee of MPs of experience and integrity, who can thoroughly investigate EYFS, and propose sensible and workable changes if they deem any to be necessary. We hope that the Department will find the magnanimity to listen carefully and open-mindedly to whatever findings might result from a Committee inquiry, and to reform the existing framework in time for September, if such action is clearly recommended.

3   The Early Years Foundation Stage and Open EYE – Two Years on[5]

MARGARET EDGINGTON, RICHARD HOUSE
AND LYNNE OLDFIELD

It is now almost two years since we first announced the launch of the Open EYE campaign for open early years learning in *The Times* and the *Times Educational Supplement*, and set out in detail our concerns about key aspects of the Early Years Foundation Stage (EYFS) framework.

We wish to introduce some tempered realism to recent uncritical statements by prominent authorities in the field about the alleged successes of the EYFS since its inception in September 2008. We believe that such viewpoints do not at all represent accurately the full reality of EYFS on the ground, eighteen months after implementation.

Open EYE wishes to acknowledge the many positive and helpful aspects of the EYFS, e.g. the admirable principles and the necessary Welfare Requirements. Certainly the EYFS has reminded all practitioners working with young children that outdoor play is an entitlement, and that children can and should initiate their own learning within an enabling emotional and physical environment. We are certainly not calling for a wholesale 'dismantling' of the EYFS, and **we have never done so**. However, we continue to express serious concerns, now shared by many across the sector, as to the inappropriateness of the statutory learning and development goals, and the uses to which they are being put.

The Statutory Learning and Development Requirements

In December 2007 we pointed out the conflict between the EYFS principle of the Unique Child and the legislated requirement for 'the early learning goals – the knowledge, skills and understanding which young children should have acquired by the end of the academic year in which they reach the age of five' (EYFS Statutory Framework, p. 11). We also highlighted the danger of a young and under-trained workforce focusing on 'delivering' outcomes and gaining a distorted view of child development through uncritical use of the age-related learning and development 'grids'. More recently, we have strongly criticized the 'audit culture' mentality which has entered the early years sphere via the Local Authority Outcomes Duty.

Many of the 'teaching to test', assessment-driven characteristics of the primary school are now invading our nurseries and other early-years settings. Ed Balls, (the then) Minister for Children, School and Families, wants (and believes it to be appropriate that) our children 'hit the ground running'. The language of industry is rapidly colonizing the art of education – with the talk of 'targets', 'outcomes', 'delivery', 'rolling out', 'drilling down' etc. increasingly dominating the sector. This kind of discourse limits the ways in which we can all think about our delicate, subtle work with young children.

Children's author John Dougherty (see his Chapter 3) recently described his story-telling session in a local school, with teaching assistants who began by sitting by the children with clipboards to assess the session against the EYFS profile targets. They realized quickly that they were missing the children's joyful responses, and put their clipboards down. But had they continued in this vein, how could they have been a role model for attentiveness and listening? What message would they have been sending out to the children? What would have happened to their quality of awareness when 'boxed in' with prescribed assessment targets? Open EYE asks, has the DCSF commissioned any independent qualitative research into such negative unintended side-effects of the EYFS framework? – sadly, we believe not.

The 'overwhelmingly positive' responses to the EYFS recently claimed in October 2009 by Sue Ellis, National Director for the EYFS, therefore needed to be viewed with considerable caution. Undoubtedly practitioners, like Open EYE members, have welcomed the principles of the EYFS; but they also have to live daily with the contradictions and tensions within EYFS and its implementation. Statistics drawn from small-scale surveys do not by any means reveal the whole reality of children's experiences, or those of the teachers 'delivering' the inescapable compulsory targets. Any claimed 'commitment' to the EYFS needs to be viewed against the reality of the 'compulsion' to 'deliver' (and the consequences for your setting if you don't!), and the propensity of early years practitioners to comply with, and make the best of, *whatever* the government might dictate to them.

How many young early years workers in their early to mid-20s will have the confidence and are articulate enough to stand up against government impositions that, in their heart of hearts, they know to be unnecessary and harmful? This is especially true when training increasingly offers little if any space for critical thinking about the EYFS framework. Following a decade of unprecedented change and a barrage of new initiatives, it is not surprising that many practitioners feel helpless and have lost confidence.

We continue to maintain that the Learning and Development Requirements are unnecessary and over-prescriptive.

The Centralization of Education

Open EYE member Wendy Ellyatt has recently outlined the threat to educational creativity and innovation from 'rigid government-imposed frameworks', producing a conformist culture in early years education.[6] Ellyatt compellingly argued that this is particularly inappropriate due to the fluid, constantly changing nature of early childhood development.

The announcement in 2009 that Steiner schools had obtained exemptions from certain of the Learning and Development Requirements obscured the fact that they were still required by legislation to assess children against targets that bear little relation to their own values and curriculum. The EYFS profile remains compulsory even for these settings.

Childminder Pat Adams (see her Chapter 4) was refused EYFS exemption despite full and enthusiastic support from the parents of the children she cares for. In addition, the EYFS exemption process itself is so daunting that even on the most generous of readings, it cannot in any way be taken as a genuine demonstration of respect for healthy diversity or parental choice in matters of early years education. With a heavily legislated state-imposed curriculum for pre-school children now in place, where can parents go if they sincerely believe that the literacy, numeracy and ICT goals of the EYFS are inappropriate?

Although the limited exemptions secured by Steiner settings did give welcome publicity to the right to apply for exemption on the grounds of educational differences, there is little understanding that a second ground for exemption exists. This is from the Human Rights Act of 1998, Chapter 42, Article 12, which gives 'parents the right to choose their children's education in conformity with their religious beliefs or philosophical convictions'. When the Liberal Democrat MP and Shadow Minister, Annette Brooke (see her Foreword to this book), asked DCSF Minister Dawn Primarolo to define this possibility, she replied, 'The term "religious and philosophical convictions" is a concept that is understood in case law, such as that on the European Convention of Human Rights. It refers to a cogent and serious belief-set or *conviction worthy of respect in a democratic society*' (our italics).

The exemption route remains very much an 'obstacle course' which is exceedingly difficult and onerous to negotiate. Yet even if the process were to be reformed and simplified, this would still not rescue children in maintained settings from the unsatisfactory aspects of the EYFS, particularly if the school entry age is lowered to four. The profile remains statutory for everyone – even if successfully exempted from the learning and development goals, or unfunded.

We still maintain that this legislation is a breach of the basic human right to educate children according to personal convictions, and that it represents an unjustifiable legal intrusion into the non-compulsory pre-school domain.

In autumn 2009, John Tranmer, chairman of the Independent Association of Preparatory Schools (IAPS),[7] spoke out against the 'loss of freedom' for private, voluntary and independent (PVI) providers to choose their own curriculum for the under fives. This is made all the more puzzling by the fact that – as yet! – there are no mandatory curricula for older children in independent school settings. He added, 'It is fundamentally wrong that the government, or more accurately a collection of pseudo-educationalists and bureaucrats, dictate to us', and he vowed to campaign to reverse the imposition of the EYFS, and to encourage members to apply for exemption. Such centralization of education, particularly in the early years, is deeply disturbing.

The Starting of Formal Learning

There was also a major conflict between the recommendations of the Rose and the Alexander (Cambridge) primary reviews – the former being government sponsored, the latter being independent. Sir Jim Rose recommended a new school starting age of four, whilst the Cambridge review recommended that the EYFS be extended to the sixth birthday. The cavalier dismissal (not to mention the gross misreading) of Professor Robin Alexander's Cambridge Review by the government (and by the opposition) strongly suggests that pre-decided politicized agendas were taking precedence over rational argument and evidence, and we also find this deeply disquieting – not least because the delicate early years sphere is surely the very last place where ideologically driven agendas should prevail.

Open EYE has consistently advocated that a genuinely play-based EYFS should be extended at least to the end of year 1.

Conclusion

Despite some 8,000 signatures on Open EYE's Downing Street website petition that was open in 2007–8 (and with many more signatures on paper), and recommendations from the government's own early years advisers that certain of the EYFS learning and development goals are inadvisable, there was no effective response from the previous government. We believe there to be a grave danger of what is, in some key respects, inappropriate legislation being uncritically accepted by a compliant workforce, as the framework rapidly becomes unquestioningly institutionalized. Although we certainly have no wish to see the EYFS dismantled in its entirety, we therefore agree with the recent call by Purnima Tanuku, Chief Executive of the National Day Nurseries Association, for a 'reviewed and [much] improved' version.

Open EYE will continue to call on the government to downgrade the legal status of the EYFS learning and development requirements to professional guidelines only. We also advocate a truly independent, root-and-branch review of the EYFS, which will enable teachers to make the necessary distinction between those aspects of the EYFS which are progressive and helpful, and those which are not.

Above all, for the sake of all children in their earliest and most vulnerable years, we need to find the courage and the wisdom to get this right.

Notes

1　An earlier version of this article first appeared in *The House Magazine: The Parliamentary Weekly*, No. 1244, Vol. 33, 14 January 2008, page 27.

2　See the Parliamentary Office of Science and Technology, 'Early Years Learning', Report 140, June 2000.

3　This advertorial originally appeared in *The House Magazine*, 2008.

4　Alexandra Frean, 'Pre-school literacy targets "are too ambitious and should be dropped"', *The Times*, 22 May 2010.

5　The first version of this article appeared in *Every Child Journal*, 5 (1), 2010, pp. 14–17.

6　Wendy Ellyatt, 'Learning & Development: Innovation – Free ways', *Nursery World*, 3 September 2009; accessible at: http://www.nurseryworld.co.uk/news/login/930827/Learning---Development-Innovation---Free-ways/

7　*Daily Mail*, 26 September 2009.

CHAPTER 3

Against the Government's Grain: The Experience of Forging a Path to EYFS Exemption

JOHN DOUGHERTY

Choice in education has become something of a government mantra over the last couple of decades. Successive education ministers have pushed the idea of 'parent power', assuring us that the ability to choose our children's school amounts virtually to a human right. It is odd, then, that whilst trumpeting our entitlement to choose between different schools, our political leaders have simultaneously been doing their utmost to turn those schools into carbon copies of one another. Diktat follows diktat, and edict follows edict, commanding that teachers teach this or that aspect of a subject in such-and-such a way to children who fall into age-range X or Y. As former children's laureate Michael Rosen has argued,[1] the laying down of the curriculum in British state schools is at present 'an utterly totalitarian process'; and the teaching of that curriculum is 'to a very large extent … controlled by the same system'. While this system, this totalitarian process, remains in place, the idea of choice in British state education can be no more than a myth.

There are, of course, still individual differences between schools; but all British state schools are directed according to a centrally imposed philosophy of education which takes no account of other views, and the option of choosing to have your child educated according to a different philosophy is available only to those who can afford either to pay or to home educate.

I was a member of the first cohort of primary school teachers to be trained in all areas of the National Curriculum, and I taught in that system for eleven years. As time went on I was forced more and more to work against my own philosophy in order to satisfy the dictates of central government and its agencies, and much of what I saw, and was obliged to implement, worried me. I was particularly concerned at the inroads that the 'academics is all' philosophy appeared to be making into the early years. And I decided I wanted something different for my own children. When my summer-born son, aged four, was in his Reception year and – pushed on by a philosophy that believes even young children must be constantly stretched and challenged – turning from a confident and proud early reader into a reluctant and grudging scholar, I discovered an independent school near us which practised a different philosophy. One of the hallmarks of this philosophy was a belief that the early years – up till around six or seven years of age – should be a time for imaginative play, for socialization and stories, and for practical tasks to develop little fingers and little minds. If I sent my son there, no-one would make him sit pointless SATs; no-one would send him home with a book that would make him feel uncomfortable when he couldn't read it; no-one would force him to do tasks for which he was not yet developmentally ready. I was convinced, and so, after a couple of visits and a lot of conversation, was my wife.

My son thrived at kindergarten, and before very long his little sister joined him there. Having failed as a teacher to make the slightest dent in a system that I believed to be increasingly bad for especially the youngest children, I felt happy that I had at least rescued my own children from it.

Until, that is, the day when our daughter's kindergarten teacher told us that the government was to impose upon all pre-school settings the duty to teach reading and writing using a phonics-based approach. To be honest, at this point I assumed there must be some mistake. Perhaps my daughter's teacher had been misinformed, or had at least failed to make a distinction between state and independent schools. After all, schools outside the state system were not required to deliver the National Curriculum, in whole or in part, to pupils who legally had to be in school; surely it would be absurd to insist that they delivered a mandatory pre-school curriculum to children who did not? Sadly, as I was about to discover, absurdity was no barrier to the whims of government.

A meeting was called at school to discuss the new Early Years Foundation Stage, and a group of parents, myself included, volunteered to co-ordinate our response. As luck would have it, one of the group was a lawyer well used to deciphering Acts of Parliament and Statutory Instruments,[2] and her reading of the situation was not encouraging. The government had indeed decided to impose a framework on all early years settings. This framework would have two distinct groups of requirements – one to do with welfare, and the other regarding learning and development – and any setting in which young children were cared for, with the sole exception of the child's own home, would be legally obliged to have regard to both sets of requirements. This meant that every nursery, every pre-school setting, every playgroup and every childminder was to be required by law to guide the children in their care towards the achievement of 69 goals, some of which were clearly neither achievable by our kindergarten's teaching methods, nor desirable according to its philosophy.

We met with our MP. He was initially surprised by our objections, but once we had explained them, he seemed to understand completely and was in sympathy with our position. He explained that the EYFS had started out as an attempt – partly in response to the tragic case of Victoria Climbié – to improve welfare safeguards for young children, by ensuring that every agency and organization with partial responsibility for a child communicated about that child's safety. The situation in which we now found ourselves was, he assured us, a result of 'cock-up' rather than 'conspiracy'. This was doubtless true, but of little comfort as we entered upon what would turn out to be more than two years of hard campaigning.

Next on our list was a meeting with what I shall call the Representative Body, or RB for short. This was an organization with which our school was affiliated, and which had undertaken to speak on behalf of a number of schools whose methods were based on the same philosophy as ours. The RB had been involved in the consultation with the Department for Children, Schools and Families (DCSF) prior to the implementation of the EYFS, and was keen to put our minds at rest: the Minister had assured its members that no compromise to our philosophy would be necessary. Our schools might have to apply for exemptions from some of the EYFS requirements, but we would be able to carry on absolutely as normal.

This highlights one of the shortcomings of the sort of consultation process employed: small organizations like the RB simply do not have the legal or political resources to keep up with either the machinations or, in our MP's words, the cock-ups of government. Our lawyer parent pointed out that, first, the verbal assurances the RB had received were worth nothing if the law stated otherwise; secondly, that the law as written did indeed state otherwise; and thirdly, that whilst the Act contained the power for ministers to make Regulations for settings to apply for exemptions, it appeared that this power was not, after all, to be exercised. In the absence of Regulations detailing the arrangements for exemptions, the law would apply to all pre-school settings outside the home, without exception.[3]

This put the RB in a very difficult situation. Not only had it been reassuring all the schools in the network that there was no cause for alarm and that they could carry on as normal once the EYFS was in force, but it had entered into protracted discussions with the DCSF regarding a number of other issues, some of them involving much-needed funding for schools with which it was involved. To now challenge with any vehemence plans which had advanced so far could have fatally compromised these other negotiations.

It's easy to see how behind-the-scenes politics – very much part of the process of government decision-making – can generate such difficulties. As a consequence, it can often be very difficult for citizens to openly 'speak truth to power'; in the worst cases, everyone ends up saying to politicians only what they know the latter wish to hear. Even in more moderate examples, it can be possible for those in power to believe that they are 'consulting' with someone who is entirely happy with the proposals under discussion, when in fact the other party's position reflects a considerable compromise on their part. In any case, the RB was not in a position to openly back us to the hilt, although it would – armed with the information our group had provided – continue to negotiate directly with the Department.

And so began a new phase for us: a phase involving long meetings, endless redraftings, and the consumption of rather a lot of biscuits. We would meet at one another's houses, discuss our options, go away and draft letters and documents, email these to the rest of the group for comments, finally agree on the wording, send them off, and wait for what, before long, we knew would be a thoroughly unsatisfactory response from the minister's office.

We wrote a letter pointing out that a number of the EYFS goals would necessitate our children's teachers employing methods which directly conflicted with the kindergarten's philosophy, and invited the minister to visit the school and talk with us about it. The DCSF replied that the EYFS was a flexible framework which was capable of encompassing many different philosophies, ours included, and that it was perfectly possible to follow it without compromising our principles in the least.

We sent a collection of self-drafted documents explaining in what ways specific EYFS goals conflicted with our philosophy, but also pointing out how the philosophy which underpinned the EYFS was clearly not compatible with the philosophy that underpinned our kindergarten, beginning as it did with a different view of both child development, and the purpose and nature of early years education. The DCSF replied that the EYFS was a flexible framework which was capable of encompassing many different philosophies, ours included, and that it was perfectly possible to follow it without compromising our principles in the least.

We asked the DCSF to explain exactly how a framework which insisted children should, by the 30th of June in the school year in which they turned five, be able to 'Use their phonic knowledge to write simple regular words and make phonetically plausible attempts at more complex words' and 'Write their own names and other things such as labels and captions, and begin to form simple sentences, sometimes using punctuation' was compatible with a philosophy which stated that pre-school education should not involve any teaching of reading or writing. The DCSF replied that the EYFS was a flexible framework which was capable of encompassing many different philosophies, ours included, and that it was perfectly possible to follow it without compromising our principles in the least.

Given the obvious conflicts between the EYFS and our kindergarten's philosophy, and given the department's assurances that we would not have to compromise our philosophy in any way, we asked that an exemption process (such as had been mentioned in the consultation, and for which the RB had strongly indicated a need) be put in place.

The DCSF replied that an exemption process was not necessary, as the EYFS was a flexible framework which was capable of encompassing many different philosophies, ours included, and that it was perfectly possible to follow it without compromising our principles in the least. It added that although an exemption process had at one

stage been considered, some of the very small number of respon-
dees to the consultation had said very clearly that there was no need
for one because they liked the proposed framework so much. It did
not seem to occur to the DCSF that this was rather like justifying a
refusal to offer a vegetarian option on the grounds that the carnivores
say they don't need one.[4]

We had also managed to scrape together enough money to instruct
a campaigning solicitor to professionally review the legal position.
She suggested that we might have a case for Judicial Review, and sent
a letter on behalf of the parents' group as a metaphorical warning
shot across the bows. The letter reiterated some of our concerns;
cited our rights under Article 2, Protocol 1 of the Human Rights Act
to have our philosophical convictions[5] respected with regards to our
children's education; and requested a copy of the draft Exemption
Order and any ministerial guidance regarding its application. It also
raised concerns regarding the consultation process, in particular the
fact that parents – major stakeholders, one might assume – had not
been invited to contribute, and requested copies of the responses to
the consultation. Naturally, the reply wasn't terribly helpful, but at
least the point had been made that we were willing to use lawyers to
make our case for us if necessary.

In the mean time, our local MP had been continuing to meet with
the Minister for Children in order to communicate our concerns. He
was clear that there was indeed a problem, but confident that it could
be resolved; and soon he was able to table a Parliamentary Question,
which received a Parliamentary Answer to the effect that none of the
schools in our network would have to compromise their philosophy
in order to comply with the legislation, and that no school would be
penalized for following such a philosophy. In the mean time, the RB
had received a letter from the minister's office containing much the
same assurance.

A few informal chats with some very high-powered solicitors reas-
sured us that this created what is in law called a 'legitimate expectation' that the law would now be interpreted in the light of the
minister's assurances – in other words, we appeared to have reached
a point where our kindergarten was safe. There was still a question
mark over whether our teachers would have to complete the official
assessment forms – to which we also had a number of philosophical
objections – but we believed we could deal with that question when
it arose.

In the mean time, the Independent Schools Council had begun to make waves, apparently having belatedly realised the incongruity of the situation: institutions which were free to ignore government learning targets once their pupils were of compulsory school age would have targets from the same source imposed by force of law on their pre-schoolers. It was at this point that the government announced a review of certain of the EYFS goals, in particular two that we had consistently raised as problematic, and – even better – announced that the Statutory Instrument containing the exemptions procedure would include a process by which settings could seek exemptions. It seemed that our campaigning, in conjunction with other representations, had at last done the trick. We thanked the solicitor who had helped us, and went off to celebrate.

We had celebrated too soon, however. The exemptions procedure turned out to be extremely unwieldy – in all probability, deliberately so. Settings wishing to obtain an exemption from any of the EYFS learning and development goals would have to first approach the Local Authority for their written opinion on the necessity for the exemption(s) in question. They needed to inform all parents of the decision to seek exemption and include the results of the consultation with the application. Without the consent of at least 50 per cent of the parents, the application would not be considered. Oh, and of course there was a form to fill in, to include the applicant's objections to each goal for which modification was to be sought, along with the reasons for those objections and the proposed modifications. Once all that was done, the application was to be sent to the Qualifications and Curriculum Authority (QCA), who would consider it and then consult with the provider and/or an assistant to the Secretary of State, before a decision was made.

As if that wasn't enough, any exemption granted would last for only two years before the process would have to begin all over again. Furthermore, no class* exemptions would be available, which meant that even the smallest and most poorly resourced kindergarten in our network would have to apply individually, regardless of how many others were applying on identical grounds.

In the mean time, we heard that OFSTED, the schools inspectorate, was taking no account of the ministerial assurances, and had received no guidance to the contrary. It felt very much as if we were back to square one. It was decided that we – the parents' campaign

---

*   Class in the sense of 'category'.

group – should begin work on the exemption process. It was at this point that we were contacted by a past pupil of our school, another lawyer who wanted to help. The involvement of this individual led to our school instructing another firm of solicitors who in turn instructed Counsel to provide an advice in conference.

The conference was held, and was attended by representatives of the Open EYE campaign and the RB in addition to our own group (as well as some parents who agreed they would potentially be the named Applicants if the case proceeded). Consequently – although considerable concern was expressed by one RB representative as to the effect our chosen course might have on negotiations she had been conducting with the DCSF on an entirely separate issue – a letter before action was sent to the Minister for Children. The gist was that:

- the EYFS represented the first time that government had sought to direct independent schools in what or how they must teach;
- according to the new legislation, a child whose parents were at liberty to keep him or her at home all day climbing trees and playing imaginatively, would now if sent to a pre-school setting have to submit to government prescription;
- the philosophy of the claimants' child's kindergarten was well-established and supported by other evidence;
- the philosophy of the kindergarten was incompatible with that driving the EYFS, despite the department's mantra of its being a 'flexible framework';
- the exemption regulations as framed were geared towards 'failing providers' and were unsuitable for kindergartens such as the claimants' child's;
- the government's refusal to make proper provision for such kindergartens meant that they were at risk of being failed by OFSTED;
- such refusal was inconsistent with the government's commitment to diversity in education; and
- the regulations were therefore in breach of human rights legislation, in failing to respect the philosophical convictions of parents with regards to their children's education, and in discriminating against the group of parents to which the claimant belonged.

It went on to request that the government acknowledged the conflict between the two systems and confirmed its intention to provide a suitable exemption. The government's reply was as unhelpful as expected. The lawyers had had to issue the letter before action within three months of the enactment of the primary legislation, and had only just done so, yet the response suggested that this letter was 'premature', on the grounds that neither claimants nor claimants' child's kindergarten had applied for an exemption. Put baldly, the response was that we couldn't claim the exemption process was unsuitable until we'd actually gone through it and proved it so. It did at least accept that there might be a conflict between the kindergarten's philosophy and some aspects of the EYFS, which was progress of a sort.

Our solicitor responded by saying that the claimants would try the exemptions process out, and that he trusted that if having tried this and found it wanting, they decided to issue proceedings after all, the government would not then claim it was too late to do so. And so we waded into the exemptions process. Night after night, meeting after meeting, email after email, discussion after discussion, as we tried to work out exactly what wording to use in our discussion of each goal or target which we had decided to address.

Of course, the problem was that the application process did not allow for the possibility of anyone's wanting to argue that the entire philosophy underpinning the EYFS – a philosophy that sees education as travel in a straight line through a series of goals; a philosophy that sees normal child development in the early years as something which has to be managed by adults with an agenda; a philosophy that believes in setting targets and then measuring the child against them – was the problem. The only problems we were allowed were specifics: we do not agree with this or that goal, for this or that reason.

While we were working out the details of the application, we were also consulting with the other parents. Unsurprisingly, they were unanimous in their support – after all, they had all chosen the kindergarten because of its philosophy. School representatives were also consulting with staff from the Local Authority, who were a little less supportive: whilst they approved of the kindergarten and its philosophy, and agreed that some EYFS goals ran counter to our educational principles, they had their own interpretations of some of the goals, which differed from ours. Moreover, they could not agree that the entire philosophy of the EYFS learning and development requirements was in conflict with ours; if that was the case, they wanted to know, why were we not applying for exemption from the whole framework? We had to point out to them that this was not an option.

Filling out the application form, it must be said, was not fun. It was not – nor, I think, was it meant to be – a means of communicating, designed to build understanding. It felt more like a game, where someone else knew the rules and we had to guess at them. We spent a lot of time debating whether this sentence or that would more nearly tick the invisible boxes we were sure the DCSF had set out like tiny traps. As it turned out, we scored quite highly: the majority of requested exemptions and modifications relating to literacy and ICT were granted, although not those relating to maths.

It seemed to us that there was a real inconsistency here: our staff were no longer expected to teach children about letters, but were expected to teach them to recognize numbers, even though the kindergarten's philosophy explicitly states that the teaching of any abstract symbol should be left until the start of school proper.

Be that as it may, it was a victory – and was reported as such by those news outlets, local and national, that took up the story. We had faced down the government juggernaut; forced the DCSF to move from a position of arguing that the EYFS was a flexible framework into which our philosophy and approach could fit, to one of admitting that there were indeed conflicts between their approach and ours.

But it was a hard-won battle, and it did not feel over. Now we had to revisit the process, and begin a second application in order to once more argue our case for the exemptions and modifications we had been denied.

While we were working on the re-application, the school was inspected. OFSTED gave it a glowing report, and reserved some special words of praise for the kindergarten – words which might not have been so flattering had the inspectors been compelled to judge it against the whole EYFS learning and development framework.

On we worked. In the mean time, a meeting was arranged with the QCDA (formerly the QCA), the agency responsible for handling exemptions, at which we hoped to discuss our reapplication.

And then, everything changed. The Conservative–Liberal Democrat coalition government took office and – to headlines such as 'Learning goals for toddlers may go as "nappy curriculum" is abandoned'[6] – announced a comprehensive review of the EYFS under Dame Clare Tickell (see Chapter 6), whilst the new Education

Secretary, Michael Gove, announced the axing of the QCDA. It was decided that – for the moment, at least, and having had a successful OFSTED inspection – we could survive with the exemption we had. There was every possibility that by the time we had finished the lengthy reapplication process, we would find that we instead needed an exemption from something completely different. Better to keep our heads down, and wait.

Such, then, was the looking-glass world we had entered. It was a world in which reason did not seem to apply; in which powerful people in far-away places made decisions which affected our children and responded with unthinking mantras to our objections. But most of all, I believe, it was a world inhabited by politicians who honestly believed they were doing good, and who did not realize that the philosophy of education to which they held was a philosophy at all. As far as they were concerned, their view of education was the truth; it was How Things Are; it was what everybody knew to be so. When they were challenged, they did not or could not see that the challenge was not just about this or that sentence, but about their whole way of thinking. In their minds, we thought the same as they did and were merely quibbling about the details. And so our objections simply did not make sense to them, because although we were using the same words, we were speaking a different language.

Still, we had won for our children a victory of sorts. We had forced, or helped to force, a change in government policy. And, I think, without us, and without all those other little groups out there who protested, and wrote letters, and campaigned, and applied for exemptions, it is just possible that the 69 goals of the EYFS might have been here to stay.

Author's Postscript

Just as we were about to go to press, I was told that the Department for Education has written to the school to say that its exemption has expired, and that a fresh application must be made – starting from the beginning of the process – unless the kindergarten is now willing to be judged against delivery of all 69 goals. This is in spite of the fact that the Tickell Review has already recommended these be reduced to only 17 and has recommended immediate class exemptions for kindergartens such as ours.

Notes

1   http://www.michaelrosen.co.uk/liberation.html

2   A Statutory Instrument is a document drafted by a Minister and/or his/her advisors, which does not form part of the relevant Act of Parliament but which has legal force by virtue of that Act. The document containing the EYFS requirements is such a Statutory Instrument (also sometimes known as 'Secondary Legislation' or 'Regulations').

3   The government had by this point announced that individual parents would be allowed to apply for exemptions if they could demonstrate that the EYFS learning and development requirements conflicted with their philosophical beliefs. However, settings would not be eligible for exemption. At this point, the guidance for such exemptions had not been published. The Act passed by Parliament gave the power to Ministers to make regulations for whole-setting exemptions, but by the time the government came to draft the exemption regulations, the relevant Ministers had decided that they would not exercise this power. Apparently they are allowed to do this.

4   Author's note: I didn't keep detailed notes during this period, and so the exchange of correspondence may not have been exactly as described. Any sense of frustration that the reader infers from this exchange is, however, entirely accurate.

5   Relevant convictions included the belief that premature forcing of a pre-school child's intellectual processes could be detrimental to the child.

6   Greg Hurst and Joanna Sugden, 'Learning goals for toddlers may go as "nappy curriculum" is abandoned', *The Times*, 6 July 2010.

CHAPTER 4

The Impact of the EYFS on Childminders

ARTHUR AND PAT ADAMS

Pat's Story

I suppose I should have expected what was to eventually come when, one Saturday morning in 2001, we were woken by the thud of a large and heavy envelope suddenly hitting the hall floor. It was the Guidance to National Standards for Childminding, and was the first official document I received from OFSTED. Amongst other things, the booklet told me: 'Children need regular drinks', and that I should 'change nappies or garments when soiled or wet', and so on. In contrast to the documentation I had received previously from Social Services, the booklet seemed to assume that the childminder had little or no knowledge about children, and needed to be told everything.

I have been a childminder now for more than 23 years, and I first started when my daughter was 2 years old. I started out of necessity because I wanted to spend as much time with my daughter as possible before she started school, but I also needed to earn a wage. Because I was at home each day, friends started asking me to look after their children from time to time. When this started to become a regular occurrence, I decided to do it correctly, and so registered with Social Services as a childminder.

I don't know whether I was just lucky, but the first few children I cared for, and also their families, were very easy to get along with, and made the job relatively easy. It hasn't always been like that, but, on the whole, I've had more positive than negative experiences, so that when my daughter started school, I decided to continue child-minding. I now find myself with 23 years' experience, and more than 50 children that I have cared for, some of whom I am still actively in contact with. I don't wish to blow my own trumpet, but I must be doing something right because I have never had to advertise my services. All of the parents who have approached me did so thanks to other parents recommending me and, quite often, I have had to turn people down because I don't have the places for any more children.

As time progressed, OFSTED became more dominant, and more of its paperwork began to arrive. On top of that, SureStart also started sending out their own booklets and paperwork, telling me how to care for children and offering courses, most of which were free, on all aspects of childcare. In early 2003 came *Birth to Three*, another large package that looked like it had cost quite a lot to produce. Then, in 2007, I found out about the Early Years Foundation Stage (EYFS). Although the EYFS is supposed to be building on existing frameworks, its tone sounded very different. The EYFS documentation contains many instances of the words 'should' and 'must', and the whole thing is now statutory so that failure to follow it is, technically, breaking the law.

In October 2007 I attended an introductory one-day session that was presented by my local SureStart office, to learn more about the EYFS and what was expected of me. I didn't like what I heard because, despite all the spin, it seemed to be turning children into commodities, with me being expected to keep steering them towards the next learning and development goal. I prefer to let children progress at their own pace as naturally as possible, and as long as I make available a wide range of toys and games suitable for their abilities and offer them help and guidance as appropriate, the children will continue to learn and develop happily. I tried to explain my concerns, but the SureStart people were not really interested because they were not prepared for people speaking against the EYFS. In the end, I had a long chat with a senior SureStart person, who told me 'It is only you who feels like this. It is only your opinion', implying that everybody else was quite happy with the EYFS. I knew this was wrong, because, even at that meeting, five out of the seven people on the table I sat at had already expressed concerns about what they were being told.

Over the next few days, my husband, Arthur (with whom I have co-written this chapter), and I started to use the internet to try to find out as much as possible about the EYFS and the arguments for and against it. One of the first items we came across was a Teacher's TV programme about the Swedish approach to nursery education, and I knew then that I wasn't just being awkward, and that my gut feelings about the EYFS were correct. Further investigation led us to the petition on the Number 10 Downing Street website, and from there to the Open EYE group themselves.

As the start date for the EYFS drew closer, SureStart began offering courses on how to implement the EYFS that were specifically aimed at childminders, and were taught by a member of the National Childminding Association. I booked myself on to a course that was to take place over three Saturday mornings in May, and was surprised to find that only about two-thirds of the 25 places had been filled. The letters from SureStart had kept emphasizing that places were limited and that demand was high, yet this was clearly not the case. Another surprise was that, of the childminders who did attend, many of them expressed concerns about what they were being asked to do in order to satisfy not only the terms of the EYFS, but also the requirements of the OFSTED inspector who would be inspecting us on how well we could show, by paperwork, that we were adhering to the EYFS.

When I attended the next session of the course, there were even less attendees than at the first session, and this was also true of the third session. Of the childminders who did attend all three sessions, a small number told me that they were seriously thinking of giving up childminding, and that the EYFS was a major factor in their decision. Since then, I have spoken to two of those childminders and they have, indeed, now given up childminding.

Throughout the run-up to September 2008 and the impending implementation of the EYFS, I kept the parents of the children I care for fully informed and up to date with what was happening, passing on web links to newspaper articles about the EYFS, enabling them to make up their own minds and come to their own conclusions. In the event, all of the parents agreed with me, and even wrote to Ed Balls, the then Education Minister, with their concerns. Neither set of parents received a reply from Mr Balls directly, although they did receive replies from civil servants elsewhere in the country. The letters were very similar and, as expected, were unsympathetic, although they did say that EYFS providers would be able to apply for exemption from the learning and development goals of the EYFS, once regulations had been laid before Parliament. I may be wrong, but it looked to me very much like exemption was something of an afterthought because the regulations were made on 2 July 2008, passed on 9 July, shortly before the summer recess, and became law on 4 August, less than a month before the EYFS was due to come into force.

Eventually 1 September arrived and the EYFS did become law. There was a lot of coverage on television and in the newspapers, but for me there was very little difference, because I carried on child-minding in exactly the same way as I had been doing in previous years. Of the childminders I spoke to at the local playgroup, all bar one were of the same opinion as myself, considering the EYFS to be unworkable and having no place in a home environment. Parents who listened in on and joined in with the conversations also said that they wouldn't expect childminders to have to go to the lengths required by this legislation.

I was (and still am) worried about what OFSTED would have to say about me at their next visit, and I expect the inspector to downgrade me to 'unsatisfactory'. The only way I could think of for avoiding this was to apply for exemption from the EYFS, and so, with the backing of the parents, my husband and also the Open EYE group, that was what I decided to do. It was difficult, first of all, to discover exactly what I would have to do because at that time there was no mention of exemption on the websites of the Department for Children, Schools and Families (DCSF), OFSTED or SureStart. We eventually found something on the website of the Qualifications and Curriculum Authority (QCA) because it is the QCA who would eventually scrutinize my application, and either allow or deny my exemption.

To say the exemption process is convoluted is an understatement. First of all, I would have to contact my local authority and arrange to discuss my proposals with them. Then I had to arrange a ballot of the parents whose children I was looking after. I then needed to achieve a 75 per cent majority in favour, or I would not be allowed to submit my application, which was the final step.

Arranging a meeting with the local authority proved to be more difficult than we had expected. After a month, I had not received a reply from the Childcare Strategy Manager, and so I had to write to the Strategic Director of Childcare Services asking her to pass my request to the appropriate department. Two weeks later, I received a reply from the person I originally wrote to, who, in our area, is part of SureStart, offering me a meeting at the SureStart office in town at 10.30 a.m. This was totally unsuitable because, at that time, I was caring for three children, the oldest of whom had just started at playgroup and we would need to leave the house at 11.30 a.m. to get her there. After a number of telephone calls, we finally managed to arrange an appointment for 6.45 p.m. at a local community centre. I had offered to allow the meeting to take place at our house, but this had been declined. As there were going to be three SureStart people at the meeting, Arthur came with me for moral support.

The meeting began with SureStart asking me to explain my situation and the reasons behind my application, even though I had outlined all of this in my letter to them. They seemed to be surprised that anyone would question the EYFS, and we spent some time going around in circles. Their only suggestion was to offer support to help me incorporate the EYFS framework into my childminding provision. As this was not what I wanted, I turned this offer down.

Although we then had to devise a ballot paper and provide an accompanying letter explaining my reasoning, the ballot of the parents (all four of them) went much more smoothly. All of the ballot papers were returned, there were no spoilt papers and all four parents voted for exemption, so I achieved 100 per cent majority, and was then able to proceed to the next stage.

The application form required separate reasoning for each of the 69 learning and development goals that I wanted exemption from (cf. Chapter 3), plus background information about myself and my childminding philosophy. I found this to be very difficult because, whilst I am not necessarily against all of the goals, it is the goals as a whole, and that I would be expected to steer children to achieve as many of those goals as possible by the time they reach their 5th birthday, that I objected to. I decided, therefore, that I would have to apply for exemption from all 69 of the goals.

The QCA would only accept applications electronically, which, in a way, was a good thing because, by now, the form was 32 pages long, together with a two-page document of background information about me and my philosophy on childcare. However, it took a large number of attempts to successfully submit the form, thanks to the incompatibility of our word processing software and that used by the QCA computer systems. In the end, Arthur found a way of converting the form to a PDF document, which the QCA were then able to accept.

The QCA website said that a decision would take up to 12 weeks, which it eventually did. Needless to say, my application was refused. The reasoning given was that I

> have not been able to demonstrate that you are unable to secure that your early years provision meets the early learning goals because it is governed by established principles relating to the learning and development of young children which cannot be reconciled with the early learning goals. Your application does not contain sufficient evidence to demonstrate that this circumstance applies and is therefore refused.

I don't know quite what sort of evidence they were expecting from me, but it is very difficult for a childminder to produce any documentary evidence to back up their philosophies. Steiner or Montessori schools, for example, would have a prospectus that outlines their philosophy, but I don't know of any childminder that has anything like that. In other words, it is almost impossible for a childminder to gain exemption from the EYFS.

I was very unhappy with the decision, but there was very little I could do about it, as there is no right of appeal. I could, though, submit a second application, although the QCA said that 'if the application and evidence provided does not differ from their earlier application it is unlikely to result in a different decision'. This made it very difficult for me, because my first application had already taken a great amount of time to prepare, and a second application, with all of the associated stages that go with it, would have been even harder to prepare.

I was required to inform the parents in writing of the QCA's decision, and they all told me they were still happy with the way I was caring for their children. They also said that I should carry on in exactly the same way and that they would continue to support me.

I showed the QCA reply to a number of people who were interested in what I had been doing. One person, who worked in the legal profession, offered to help me draft a letter asking the QCA to clarify a number of points that would explain the reasoning behind their decision. Altogether, this letter asked for no less than 22 things to be clarified. The reply from the QCA (who by now were the QCDA), on the other hand, answered some of those points, but by no means all 22 of them.

Since then, there has been very little change. I continue to care for the children in as spontaneous and stimulating a way as possible. One change is that the EYFS Review, led by Dame Clare Tickell, has now published its findings, and although I welcome a lot of its recommendations, there are still some areas I am not entirely happy about. For example, the recommendation that 'all early years practitioners to have at least a Level 3 qualification' does not seem to give any credit to people who already have a large number of years experience of childcare.

At the time of writing, I have yet to have my first post-EYFS OFSTED inspection. As the recommendations made by the Tickell Review will not come into force until September 2012, any inspection must be made under existing EYFS requirements. As you can no doubt imagine, I await this with trepidation.

Arthur's Story

I know that Pat is a good childminder. I know this because I can see how the children she cares for develop and grow; I know this because our house, shed and garden are full of toys and games to suit a wide variety of ages; I know this because I have occasionally had to help by carrying children who don't want to go home to their parent's car; I know this because I quite often come home to find Pat flopped on the sofa, exhausted after a working day that can often last for more than ten continuous hours. I also know that OFSTED don't see it in quite the same way.

At her last inspection, Pat was downgraded from 'good' to 'satisfactory'. However, all of the 'problems' found by the inspector related to paperwork. For example, the inspector found that Pat didn't have written permission to put sun cream on to the children, even though there was implied permission from the parents because they include sun cream in the child's bag. This isn't good enough for OFSTED, though, who expect to see something in a way that they can clearly understand. The result of this is that Pat's registration would be marked as 'satisfactory' for three years unless she asked for a second inspection, something she wasn't prepared to do. There doesn't even seem to be a system whereby the inspector can give the childminder a certain amount of time in which to comply.

I have always helped Pat with her childminding, by doing her accounts and tax returns, by helping her with things like forms and so on, and also the policies that she is now required to have. So when Pat started getting concerned about the EYFS, I decided to try to find out as much as possible, to see if we could understand it more, and somehow come to terms with it. Unfortunately, I didn't like what I found.

Government leaflets and websites were presenting the EYFS as something that would benefit all children, and something that would be detrimental if children weren't exposed to it. After all, when there is that much money being spent on something, it has to look good. Scratch the surface, though, and it is a different story.

To me, the EYFS seemed to have been devised to move reception class away from school and into nurseries, playgroups and also, therefore, to childminders, so that children could then begin formal learning almost as soon as they start school. This was confirmed some months later when I heard Ed Balls, the then Education Secretary, on Radio 4 saying that 'the world has changed', and that 'children starting school need to hit the ground running'. Despite there being a lot of evidence that shows that children benefit from a later start to formal learning (much of it referred to in this book), the government had decided to ignore this and to press ahead with a policy that was quite the opposite. This also seemed to explain why the EYFS is statutory for all settings when the National Curriculum isn't. Because most of the workforce who are expected to implement the EYFS work for small private companies or are self employed, then it is the only way that the government can ensure their policies are implemented. To me, that is an abuse of government power.

One night in the early spring of 2008, as I was trawling the internet, I found something that surprised me. Following a search engine link, I opened a document on the OFSTED website that showed the number of nurseries, playgroups and childminders for a particular quarter. Delving further, I found a page that listed all of the documents that OFSTED had published on this topic stretching back to March 2003. What OFSTED hadn't done, though, was to link those documents together in any way so that trends could be seen, or, if they had, that information had not been published. It was then a relatively simple matter for me to key each quarter's numbers into a spreadsheet, and to then graph those numbers.

The graphs appeared to show a clear link between the EYFS and the number of registered childminders. From March 2003 until December 2006, with the odd quarter in which numbers fell slightly, there had been a sustained increase in childminder numbers. However, in the first quarter of 2007, the quarter in which the EYFS was announced, the number of childminders fell by 1,575. Subsequent quarters also showed large falls until, by March 2008, there had been a total fall of nearly 7,000 childminders. I wrote up a small document about my findings and included the facts, figures and graphs, with the intention of forwarding the document to anyone whom I thought may be able to highlight this consequence of the EYFS.

I decided to monitor each quarter's figures as they were released, and then update my document with those figures. Even now I continue to do this, even though by now (as I write) the EYFS has been in place for nearly three years. Altogether, there were 14 consecutive quarters in which childminder numbers fell, with the largest fall (1,671) occurring in the quarter immediately after the EYFS became law. In just 3½ years there had been a total fall of 14,296 childminders, an overall reduction of very nearly 21 per cent of the workforce, and an average of more than 1,000 childminders a quarter. With less childminders, the number of places offered by childminders also fell until eventually there were 45,544 less places than there were in 2006. It wasn't until December 2010, the first quarter after the Tickell Review started taking evidence, that childminder numbers began to rise again, with a very slight increase of 172 childminders (0.3 per cent). The next quarter showed a slightly larger rise of 346 childminders and I would suggest, although I have no way of proving this, that it is the Tickell Review and the likelihood that the EYFS will eventually be relaxed that have finally begun to stem the flow, and reverse the situation.

Some people have suggested that the fall in childminder numbers was a good thing because the introduction of the EYFS had caused bad childminders to leave, leaving only the best childminders to continue. I don't subscribe to this view and, in any case, there is no way of proving it, simply because no-one has ever attempted to find out. If OFSTED, the DCSF or even the National Childminders Association had asked those childminders why they were giving up, we would have been in a much better position to comment. We may even have known which section of childminders had been affected the most. Unfortunately, we don't.

One of the groups of people I emailed my document to after I had first written it was the Open EYE group. The response was almost immediate (even though I had emailed the document late on a Sunday evening), asking for permission to forward the document to other interested parties. Within days, Pat found herself talking to a number of journalists who were interested in the story, and wanted comments from a childminder who wasn't following the government line. The following week, Pat was interviewed by a reporter for Radio 4's 'Woman's Hour' and was the springboard for a discussion about the EYFS itself. Later in the summer, she was interviewed by BBC News for a report that was shown the week before the EYFS became law.

This may seem a little naïve, but the level of interest in these findings was high, and the way that Pat was thrust into the limelight was totally unexpected. Her five minutes of fame are over now, of course, but I like to think we played some small part in making the government think a little about what they were doing. Unfortunately, it took a change in government for the Tickell Review to be announced, although any of the accepted recommendations will not be implemented until September 2012. I realize that the government doesn't want to be seen to be playing 'fast and loose' with our children's future, but it would be nice if they would announce a slight relaxation in the enforcement of the EYFS in the interim period.

CHAPTER 5

A Parent's Challenge to New Labour's Early Years Foundation Stage

FRANCES LAING

'You are writing what many parents are thinking. We're just too afraid to say it.'

ONE PARENT'S RESPONSE TO THE BLOG 'A PARENT'S GUIDE TO THE EARLY YEARS FOUNDATION STAGE', 2010

Introduction

When my own child was born, I did not know my daughter and I would be confronted with something called 'The Early Years Foundation Stage' (EYFS). I hadn't considered how the English early years system was different to that of other countries – despite the fact that I had lived in Germany for ten years previously. As a trained teacher in Adult Education, I still find it interesting and disturbing that so many of us make so few connections between what happens to children in the early years and what kind of adults they grow into.

The birth of a child unleashes a flurry of activity. I've heard it likened to an emotional bomb going off in someone's life. 'Bomb', 'blessing' or both – the average new parent is on a very steep learning curve. Preoccupied with managing important everyday parenting tasks – establishing breast-feeding, putting food on the table, holding down a job (if you have one) – how many of us have the head space to grasp how the early years education system is run in its entirety?

Disturbingly, I have learned that the **majority** *of parents in England have no knowledge at all of the ways in which early years target-setting has been criticized by experts and academics in the international research community, and why.* In this respect parents are in an extraordinarily vulnerable position. Those with children under five and their families appear to be at the mercy of any ill-informed and ill-advised early years policy that governments choose to throw at them.

But parents remain the *primary educators of children.* If we include both waking and sleeping hours in our calculation, between the ages of birth and five a child can spend as little as *10 per cent of their lives* at kindergarten, nursery or school. Despite playing such an important role in children's lives, parents are marginalized by the system – they are *disenfranchized* and *disempowered* in all sorts of ways.

Parents are also faced with a kind of insidious censorship. The information that comes their way – be it early years newsletters and magazines produced by local authorities, schools or nurseries in England – is *often* patronizing, overly complicated, full of jargon and uncritical of governmental policy and approach.

A parent at the school or nursery gate also experiences a certain kind of power relationship. When a child is born, most people recognize that it is the mother, primary carer or father who knows the baby (and its needs) best. Enter the Early Years Foundation Stage (and its learning and development requirements), and parents or carers are often no longer properly acknowledged as the parent-professionals they are. Suddenly it's the nursery and school staff who know best, and too often the predominant mode of thinking is: 'If only parents would understand what we are trying to do – it's complicated for them – we have to explain it ... '.

Just because parents are short on time and resources does not mean that our brains are completely fried. A great many of us understand how government policy affects our everyday lives and the lives of our children – why we need a humane food, environment, fiscal, welfare and benefits policy, *and* experienced and independent journalists who will ask searching questions about education.

I launched the blog, 'A Parent's Guide to the Early Years Foundation Stage'[1] in August 2009 to ask (and answer) some of these questions. Amongst other issues, the weekly blog posts documented the process of our application for what they call a parental exemption to the 69 EYFS Learning and Development Requirements for our child. We believe we are the only parents in a state-funded school to have applied for (and been refused) such an exemption in the whole of England (other exemptions have been granted, but these were for whole settings, and that's a different – but equally tortuous – application process; see Chapters 3 and 4). Our apparent uniqueness has attracted considerable attention from academics and the media.

This chapter was completed in September 2010. At that time my daughter had turned five, and was moving on from her reception class and out of the English EYFS curriculum. The EYFS Government Review was completed in 2011 and I have updated the chapter, and given a brief opinion on the proposed changes.

With regard to the parental exemptions process, I believe nothing has changed. A slimming down of the Learning and Development Requirements and the EYFS profiling has been proposed, with the number of targets-in-all-but-name being proposed to be vastly reduced. Yet ignoring the advice of the best people in Early Years, the present government may introduce a developmental check for two-year-olds – intended to measure how well these young children form relationships and interact with others. One step forward and two steps back? ...

What *has* changed is our collective consciousness of what is happening. There is a growing awareness that government consultations are being misused as political weapons – wielded in an attempt to crush open, public, democratic discussion, and to stifle dissent. Many of us now understand the mechanics of this process. Crudely put – it goes something like this:

Step 1   Government consultation is announced.
Step 2   Consultation responses are formulated and submitted.
Step 3   The deadline passes: government spin machine 'leaks' selective responses to major newspapers and the trade press.
Step 4   Government declares the whole thing a success and does what it wants anyway.

The Early Years Foundation Stage and the Tickell Review were marketed as furthering the cause of social inclusion. Where is joined-up thinking on policy here? My child's father, Richard Atkinson, grew up under Thatcher's regime and has worked in welfare and disability rights for 30 years. He writes:

The coalition government's actions give the lie to their bland, caring statements – in 1962 Nye Bevan, founding father of the National Health Service, looked back on the then new Welfare State and proclaimed it to be 'in place of fear' – fear of sickness and ill health, old age and unemployment – 60 years later, the government intends to reinstate that fear (with far-reaching cuts in benefits for disabled children, their parents and carers).

I say: let us stop pretending that such cuts do not hit the under-fives hardest. They are the ones who suffer most when mothers, fathers and carers struggle to put food on the table, or can no longer do paid work when the local nursery closes – or no longer have access to free books because of local library closures.

There is much I still need to write and say about the events of *this* year (2011) – about the latest international petition to Stop School League Tables for Five Year Olds and the parliamentary Early Day Motion which ensued – and about the international petition to stop phonics testing for young children and the Early Day Motion which accompanied it.

But this chapter has an important topical and historical focus. My writing here concerns *experiential* learning – it relates to experience: a crucial experience for parents and children: the years from birth to five which, in our case, included our child's first year at school.

I hope the painstaking documentation of this experience exposes how politicians and civil servants saw to it that a misguided and cruel policy has been imposed on the youngest and most vulnerable of our children. Whilst some of these people are now touring the globe enjoying the fattest of pensions, we are left to clear up the damage they have done. The futures of our children are still being endangered by political expediency. We should never forget.

Judging by the huge international response to the Stop School League Tables for Five Year Olds petition, I am supported by thousands of individuals across the globe when I say: 'We are resolved to prevent such a thing ever happening again'. There are other parents setting out on the journey we undertook. There are teachers and heads of schools, students in universities, schools and colleges who want to know about this challenge. I hope this chapter, this book and my blog prove helpful for them.

A Parent's Challenge to New Labour's Early Years Foundation Stage: Blog Chronology and Background to the Challenge

Our daughter was born in August 2005. From the age of two – she had been attending a very experienced childminder – she was in a family atmosphere with pets, good food and excellent care. The EYFS – the curriculum for children from birth to five – did not become statutory until September 2008. The year before (as part of a pilot programme) we had witnessed our childminder experience the increasingly bureaucratic and intrusive EYFS monitoring process (cf. Chapter 4), and had written our first exemption request letter – but the framework wasn't statutory then, and so the paperwork was minimal.

Shortly after the EYFS was introduced, our childminder stopped taking children under five altogether. In September 2008 our child changed settings to attend the nursery attached to our chosen primary school. By August 2009 she had experienced a year of part-time nursery care.

August 2009 – My daughter's report at the age of three and the Data Protection Act

At the end of this nursery year in August 2009 I was given a brown envelope. I felt as if I was the only parent on the planet to be shocked that the system gives parents a 'report' when their child was still aged just three. The descriptions in it bore little resemblance to the (still) three-year-old child I knew and loved. I wondered why.

I raised these issues with the setting, and I was told: 'We can only write what we can see'. Much later it became clear to me that the EYFS system itself is pushing people who work in nurseries towards a kind of tunnel vision. There is a danger that some are increasingly seeing *only* the things that the system is looking for: the 69 Learning and Development Requirements; the targets-in-all-but-name. (Looking back at the events of the past year, I lose count of the number of times this point has been reinforced by academics, researchers, psychoanalysts, and print and broadcast journalists, and continues to be made by the fellow contributors to this book.)

Around the time I received my child's report I attended a National Union of Journalists training workshop with the journalist Heather Brooke. Heather is a US citizen by birth, and became famous for the

MPs' expenses story. In the United States it was possible to walk into a government office, request information and examine it, very easily. In the UK it took her many years to access the information that she wanted. I came away from the training with a copy of her book, *Your Right to Know*.

I decided to use the draft letter in the book to obtain my daughter's records from her nursery, and received them within the required ten days. How many parents know that you have the right to look at your own child's records in nursery or school just by writing a simple letter?

The records consisted of a large sheet with the EYFS Learning and Development Requirements, together with a sizeable number of dated post-it notes. The notes contained comments and observations about my daughter's behaviour at nursery. At that point I was aware of some of the criticisms of the EYFS Learning and Development Requirements – but I wanted to see for myself how they were being used with my own child. I knew that unless I queried what I believed to be inaccurate assumptions, the comments that had been made about her (at the tender age of three) would flow into her first year of school unchallenged. They might well also influence her entire school journey and later life.

I took photographs of the Post-it notes and the comments, removing my child's name, and published these on the blog. I had thought long and hard about the information I was prepared to share with the world about my child, and still do. It was clearly in the public interest to publish. The target-setting affected every child in England.

I believe the need to fulfil certain compulsory 'targets' led to the staff of the nursery *short-circuiting* information about my child and *drawing false conclusions* about what she could and couldn't do and *why*. And there was more …

The EYFS system has been much-praised for its welfare provision. My experience has led me to believe the short-circuiting I am talking about can actually *jeopardize* children's welfare instead of safeguarding it. Take a child who comes into nursery one day and is unusually quiet, for example: instead of talking to the parent about this unusual behaviour, a staff member who does not know the child so well, or who is not taking child psychology into account – or who is poorly trained, or under pressure from the targets – can be tempted to defer to a label. For example, the child simply 'has difficulties interacting with adults'. Meanwhile there could be any number of reasons to explain the child's change in behaviour.

I had talked to Open EYE (the national Campaign for an Open Early Years Education) and fellow parents online. My gut instinct was that I needed to do everything I could to protect my child from the pressures of the targets (the Learning and Development Requirements) contained within this programme. So I began to find out how to apply for an exemption for our child.

From the outset, this was difficult. I realized that we were the only parents in a state-funded school to apply. (I believe I'm the first person to ask why this was the case. Could it possibly have something to do with the difficulties of the process, I wonder?; cf. Chapters 3 and 4) The guidance notes we received from the local authority included a huge flow chart and 30 pages of notes, which I photographed and published on the blog. I studied Parliamentary records and found that parents could apply for an exemption if they had a 'cogent set of beliefs'. However, an exemption could only be granted following a meeting with the local authority and the school. It was up to the school to decide whether they would grant our daughter an exemption. Even then, the decision would then have to be ratified by Parliament itself.

So we had the meeting with the school and the local authority. We are not blessed with the most progressive local authority in the country. The local authority representative turned up late. I made the most of the visual aids available (the headmistress's computer), and showed the headmistress and the nursery manager the film produced by Fergus Anderson for Open EYE called 'Too Much Too Soon'.[2]

Looking back, that meeting showed me something fundamental about what practitioners are struggling with. I can't watch that film without a tear coming to my eyes. At the parental exemption meeting, both the former headmistress of the school and the nursery manager watched it, but didn't (or couldn't) comment. Later I understood – they were simply towing the government line.

At the meeting we were requested to list our objections to all 69 Learning and Development Requirements. As far as I was concerned this was another attempt to confuse us. Our objections to each one of them were the same: they shouldn't exist as compulsory targets. The local authority representative disputed our use of the word 'targets' and 'testing' in the meeting. She said there was no 'testing' in the early years. We now know from our own experience that she was wrong. We were applying for the exemption on 'moral, religious, philosophical, educational and political grounds'. The education system had no right to impose this system on defenceless children.

We felt so strongly about these issues that we had applied for an exemption in the summer holiday before our daughter started school. We constantly feared that the school would turn around and tell us to take our child elsewhere.

September 2009 – First day at school. Rejection of Early Years Foundation Stage exemption request

In August 2009 my daughter was due to move on from the nursery attached to the school and start her very first year at a state-funded Church of England Primary school in the North West of England. She was still only three at that point, as her birthday lies at the end of August.

The exemption refusal letter (see my blog entry for August) suggested to us that we access information regarding a different school for our child. It did not acknowledge that effectively we had nowhere else to go. We could not move house; there were no schools in the district that had exemptions to the EYFS system, and the EYFS itself was ubiquitous and compulsory in every school anyway. Home education was not an option for us.

As I recall, in the first four weeks our daughter attended school for just two hours each day – first mornings and then afternoons. This system has been changed now. Two hours a day wasn't enough time for me to travel home, so I spent my time in an internet cafe – writing my reaction to the exemption refusal and speaking to editors to get my statement on the refusal published.

I'd also had a sweatshirt printed with a slogan on it which showed our opposition to the targets. On the very first day at school a nearby nursery manager came up to me and said how glad he was that I was wearing it. He didn't agree with the EYFS and the targets. Apart from anything else, he said it was a very expensive system to set up and the money could be better spent elsewhere (helping children with special needs, for example).

October 2009 – 'We don't do things like that here'. Was it possible to mitigate the harmful effects of the target-setting?

There were happy moments in that first year at school – but always in the background, as parents, we had something unpleasant to deal with, with regard to the targets (the targets-in-all-but-name).

We understand very well that teachers and parents are constrained by the system in which they are operating. Some people believe that nursery and reception teachers can mitigate the negative effects of government policy through their skills as teachers and practitioners. I believe they shouldn't have to spend precious time and energy on this – and parents shouldn't have to, either.

Our daughter was, I believe, the youngest in her class at school. Although her nursery teacher was kind, helpful and understanding, we objected to the fact that our daughter was constantly being measured with exactly the same yard-sticks as children a year (or more) older than she was. We objected to a one-size-fits-all approach to policy-making. I learned (and worried) about the research that shows summer-born children are more prone to mental illness than others (because of the pressures they are under). All children develop differently, and it is simply not appropriate to use the same system of measurements for everyone.

I watched and listened to my daughter, especially during her first term at school. Within a few weeks of attending reception class, she started to say repeatedly: 'I can't write yet, mummy', with a worried look on her face. Both my partner and I had to work very hard with her to make sure she knew that everyone learns differently, and at different times, and to explain that the other children in the class were quite a lot older than she was.

November 2009 – 'Do you know what your child needs to do to improve?' Launch of Parliamentary Petition

On an international and national level, our democratic deficit continues to shock me. We have it on a local level, too, in our institutions. In November 2009 we didn't even have a Parent Teacher Association at our school.

It was around that time I realized that parents had nowhere to go with their criticisms of the EYFS framework as it was laid down in law, and only a change in the law would change the system. We investigated the possibility of a judicial review – but we inquired at a solicitor about the cost of doing that, and were quoted a price of tens of thousands. It was out of the question for us. So, with the support of other internationally known early years education specialists I launched my first Parliamentary Petition for reform. It was a modest demand – the petition called for the Learning and

Development Requirements to be 'downgraded' to 'recommendations only'.

I regularly published the 'homework' that our child received on the 'Parent's Guide' blog, with personal details removed. There was constant pressure from the local authority to push reception-age children towards the targets. One day we received a local authority questionnaire which contained the question: 'Do you know what your child needs to do to improve?'. Our answer to this question was: 'She doesn't need to *improve*. She is *four* years old – and she is fine as she is.'

January 2009 – Homework at the age of four?

I agonized for some time about what to do with the homework sheets that were coming our way in the school bag, and with the reading record book. We had always spent time reading aloud as a family – usually at least an hour or two a day. We didn't have a television, and as a whole with extended family we spent a lot of time talking. Our house is full of books. We are quite a high-tech family – but we limit screen time.

After several months of 'homework', we made the decision that our child was better off interacting with other family members rather than sitting down with a worksheet. We were aware that our child was still just four years old. Legally speaking, she was of non-compulsory school age anyway. She didn't even have to go to school in the first place, so we figured she didn't have to do the homework. Or the reading practice. So we stopped doing them. After a while the school stopped putting worksheets in our school bag.

March 2009 – Blog media coverage

In March I was approached again by journalists who wanted to interview me about the parental exemption. Some assumed there were no other parents with similar views, and that opposition to the learning and development targets was confined to what they saw as 'minority groups' such as the Steiner schools. I believe these commentators were missing the larger issues – the factors which prevent parents speaking their mind and speaking out.

A letter of mine was published in *Nursery World* magazine as 'Letter of the week'. The new director of Curriculum Development,

David McVean, had written in and indicated he was keen to hear from those affected by the EYFS legislation and the exemptions process. David wrote: 'I am keen to learn from the experience of those at the sharp end.' I replied:

Okay, David. To my knowledge, we are the only parents in a state-funded school to have applied for (and been refused) what they call a 'parental exemption' to the Early Years Foundation Stage Learning and Development Requirements.

We applied last August, with the 'cogent set of beliefs' demanded by the Government. (I am a Quaker and my partner is an atheist.) I also documented our application and the entire process on a popular grassroots blog at www.parentsguidetoeyfs. wordpress.com.

Disappointing, David, that you feel comforted by the 'tight' timeframe and the fact that 'an applicant is only exempt once a decision is made by the Secretary of State'. Our feelings as parents and as a family, put bluntly, are as follows.

The parental exemptions process is a farce and an infringement of the human rights of any child.

Any parent who looks up to, trusts or relies solely upon the advice (and spin) of the Government or Secretary of State to 'educate' their child is, in our opinion, in a very sorry state indeed.

For reasons of political expediency, the Government is unable to admit that the EYFS learning and development requirements are, educationally speaking, a huge mistake. Soon after the election they will be changed, but too late for many of our children. Our child started school at just over four years. In the first week she was sent home with homework in her school bag. We have enjoyed reading together from an early age, but wholly reject the developmentally unsound EYFS targets the Government has tried to impose on us. So, for the past six months, homework has stayed in the school bag. Since she is of non-compulsory school age, we see no reason why she should do it.

The school, thankfully, has at last realized that as a family we are not gullible enough to swallow government propaganda about EYFS profiling. Last week our daughter won a prize at school for best portrayal of a character from a storybook. Aged just four, she chose Pippi Longstocking.

David, to use a well-worn but still effective phrase, 'we weren't born yesterday'! Stop your 'spin'. Like Pippi, the many movements to abolish the EYFS compulsory learning and development requirements and the profiling are now strong enough to lift a horse with one hand.

By way of a prize for penning this letter I received three books from the editors of *Nursery World* – one of them the wonderful 'A Child's Work' by Vivien Gussin Paley – a validation of my feelings as a parent that children's play is a means of understanding the world, and is constantly being undermined by a target-orientated culture. The book points to a fundamental misdirection in today's educational programmes and strategies.

April 2009 – Party manifestos and another democrat deficit

The parliamentary e-petition I had launched earlier in the year was shut down unexpectedly for six weeks during the election. The government had promised that petition deadlines would be extended to compensate for this, but in the end this didn't happen. Yet another democratic deficit. I had planned to obtain many more signatures at the forthcoming Open EYE conference in June. The Liberal Democrat manifesto had promised to make the EYFS 'less bureaucratic'.

After the election I heard from other journalists – the confusion unleashed by the formation of the coalition government meant that spokespeople on early years policy were impossible to get hold of.

May 2009 – 4th May – Are EYFS scores being used to predict SATS scores … ?

I had spent time on early years websites and caught a glimpse of what early years practitioners were saying about the EYFS. Some teachers and nursery workers described a tendency to 'mark children down' in nursery so that a noticeable improvement could be shown in the first year at school. I wondered whether this was what had happened to my child.

Other practitioners on the websites I visited described how EYFS Profile Scoring (which takes place in the year in which a child turns five) was being used in schools to predict how the children would perform later in life and in the much-criticized SATS tests in which children are obliged to take part towards the end of their time in primary school. I started describing the EYFS Learning and Development Requirements as the 'SATS for Under Fives'. Countless practitioners and teachers had already told me via the blog that they did not feel able to voice their misgivings about the EYFS Learning and Development Requirements for fear of being bullied by their managers, or because they were afraid of losing their jobs. Parents were afraid of making themselves (and their children) unpopular.

June 2009 – Bullying and the under-fives. Open Eye conference

In June 2009 I attended the Open EYE conference in London. Many of the conference delegates knew about and had read my blog. Back at school I was busy sitting down with the acting headmaster of our school, discussing improvements in our anti-bullying policy. Our child was not yet five and had been bullied for eight months. The school considered adopting my suggestion to extend their anti-bullying policy to cover the foundation stage unit.

July 2009 – EYFS profile and first school year report

We received the long-awaited EYFS profile for our child. At the school gate a fellow parent commented: 'We don't know what the average is' – an insightful comment. As far as we were concerned, there was no 'average', as each child develops differently.

We were glad to see our child's affection for her very kind and skilled nursery teacher. The EYFS scoring, however, was meaningless, as we simply didn't agree with the targets or the tools which were being used. We didn't want or need another report for our child. She was still only four years old, and too young.

August/September 2009 – EYFS review. A consultation or a cover for the cuts?

One of the criticisms levelled at people who question the EYFS Learning and Development Requirements (and target-setting for under-fives) is that they are ignoring the ways in which requirements (and the system) are supposed to benefit *disadvantaged* families. The argument goes like this: middle-class and so-called 'advantaged' families have the means to take their children out frequently, to provide them with stimulating activities, to read to them, to buy books and so on: *disadvantaged children*, however, are supposed to have more limited access to these things and therefore are in greater need of the so-called structures provided by the EYFS, the Learning and Development Requirements and the English childcare system.

This argument ignores several key issues. First, that there is no evidence internationally or nationally to support the notion that the early years Learning and Development Requirements help children from so-called 'disadvantaged' families. Secondly, families on lower income levels, according to the government's own reports and studies, are less likely to access childcare in the first place.

In 2009 the Westminster government announced what they called an Early Years Foundation Stage review and e-consultation – one of its declared intentions was to 'address the situation of disadvantaged children and their families'. Disadvantaged parents and families will have difficulty taking part in this consultation at all. Some of the barriers to participation include the following:

- The fact that the consultation is eleven pages long, and requires a considerable level of IT skills and access to a computer to complete.
- The consultation is inaccessible to parents who do not have English as a mother tongue. (There are a number of these in our reception class.)
- The consultation was launched in the summer holidays when many parents struggle for childcare and cannot afford to take the time out to complete it.
- The underlying assumption that parents are not *professionals*. Respondents were asked to give responses either as parents or professionals. If you classify yourself as a parent you are not required to answer any of the questions about the Learning and Development Requirements or the educational content of the EYFS. You can tick the box 'other' but are requested to justify your stance. This approach excludes some parents altogether. One home-educating mother told me she didn't take part because there was no category for her to contribute her views. Home-educating parents sometimes use childminders or part-time nursery settings. It is also quite common for parents of school-age children to change to home education, or for home-educated children to return to school.

In the pre-amble to the government EYFS review the government pays lip-service to the Freedom of Information Act. It reserves the right to publish certain responses to the review and not others. I predict that the so-called consultation will be used to justify more cuts.

Shortly after the launch of the EYFS review (as a journalist and editor of the blog 'A Parent's Guide to the Early Years Foundation Stage'), I requested an interview with the leader of the review, Dame Clare Tickell. I was refused. Another example of the sort of censorship we all struggle with.

Conclusion: On Parents, Children, Governments and Moral Blackmail

Returning to the anecdote I used to begin this chapter: 'You are writing what many parents are thinking. We're just too afraid to say it.'

I'm aware that *anecdotes* sometimes don't stand up too well to *academic* scrutiny. Nevertheless as a result of writing about the Early Years Foundation Stage, I have learned that:

- Many parents are afraid that if they criticize the system they will face sanctions, disapproval, lose their place at nursery or school, and in the current economic climate this will not help them to maintain a job and an income.
- Many parents are afraid that if they criticize the system they will be seen as trouble makers. They fear their child will be victimized or bullied.
- Many parents are afraid of breaking away from the parent cliques at school or nursery.
- No parents wish to be seen to 'hold their children back', to 'restrict their education', or to 'deny them opportunities' – therefore many hold back from criticizing the Early Years Foundation Stage. Some parents are afraid that *their* child will 'fail' at school.

What are the consequences of such fears for the future of our society? Schools and nurseries are, after all, legally obliged to seek out and support parental input – don't fears like these prevent parents from engaging fully with early years settings?

As a result of the recent work I have done, I have come to the conclusion that the previous government's Early Years Foundation

Stage policy was sold to the general public in England on the basis of moral blackmail, and the exploitation of parents' deepest fears. Many parents appear to have swallowed government propaganda wholesale – propped up by the seemingly endless shock-horror tabloid headlines about how disgraceful and shaming it is when a child *(still?)* cannot read at five.

At five, my child enjoys listening to stories and is very enthusiastic about speaking, communicating, drawing, writing and – yes – (mostly) going to nursery and school. She is healthy, happy, sociable and enjoys learning. She will read when she is ready. I see one of my jobs as a parent is to ensure that she has the confidence to ask questions and tell me when the time is right for her to move on to the next stage of learning. And *life*. To do that I need to listen to her as best I can. *I am absolutely convinced that if we had pushed her too hard to read and write – as the flawed English EYFS system wanted us to do – she would not be the confident child she is today.*

I look back at her first year at school and realise that we both learned many things about education and the friends we have. Perhaps we didn't learn the things we were supposed to learn, but I hope our insights stand us in good stead for the challenges to come. We've said goodbye to the EYFS – only to find in her second week of Year One that the pressure of 'too much, too soon' is starting again. Daughter tells me her school work is 'too tricky'. I ask her which bits are too tricky – she hangs her head and says sadly: 'All of it'. But she says she feels safe, has friends, her teacher is kind – and she likes the library and school dinners ...

The dialogue with our schools, our elected representatives and researchers continues. I would like to express my thanks to all those who care about young children – and the fellow contributors to this book: many of the writers here have sustained and supported my parenting practice and the challenge we have been able to make to the Early Years Foundation Stage.

I was once told I could not be both a mother *and* a journalist. A mother loves her child – and love clouds judgement? I prefer to hold on to the hope that *love* can *inform* judgement.

Notes

1   See: http://parentsguidetoeyfs.wordpress.com/
2   See: http://openeyecampaign.wordpress.com/video/

CHAPTER 6

The Tickell Review of the Early Years Foundation Stage: An 'Open EYE' Dialogue

THE OPEN EYE CAMPAIGN[1]

This email dialogue was created over a period of three days by a small group of active Open EYE members. Open EYE has brought together a unique and multi-disciplinary group of early years experts who value and celebrate their pedagogical diversity. The range of views and comments expressed in this chapter are not therefore necessarily shared by all the contributors.

1st posting: The Tickell Review was always very likely to be a mixed bag, or a curate's egg, from our campaign's viewpoint. Just to be clear for readers, since the Open EYE campaign was founded in November 2007, it has stood for the following changes to the EYFS framework (cf. Chapter 2):

1 **TOO EARLY LITERACY** – the compulsory EYFS literacy goals were seen as being developmentally inappropriate (which leads into a wider critique of the notion of formalized 'Learning Goals');

2 **A PLAY-BASED EXPERIENCE?** – we questioned whether 'structured' play linked to learning outcomes can ever be meaningfully authentic play;

3 **AN 'AUDIT CULTURE' IN THE EARLY YEARS?** – we argued that early-childhood experience is the very last place where 'audit culture' values and practices should hold sway;

4   **THE EFFECTS OF THE EYFS ON EARLY YEARS PRAC-TITIONERS** – we questioned the utilitarian approach dominating the EYFS guidance throughout, which verges on a kind of 'developmental-obsessiveness', and the enormous bureaucratic demands of the framework;

5   **STATE-DEFINED 'NORMALITY' IN CHILD DEVELOPMENT** – we questioned the government's definition of what is 'normal' child development being compulsorily enshrined by legal statute; and

6   **HUMAN/PARENTAL RIGHTS** – we believed the EYFS legislation to be directly compromising of parents' rights to choose the pre-school, pre-compulsory school-age environments that they wish for their children.

It seems to me that perhaps the key issue for us to consider in this discussion forum is to what extent Dame Clare's Review has responded to our concerns as outlined above, and to what extent it fails to address key issues of early years philosophy, that it arguably tinkers with at the margins, but fails to address head on. Shall we start, first, with the positives, as far as we see any in the Review – who'd like to start? …

2nd Posting: Given that Dame Clare Tickell was not asked to say whether there should be a statutory framework and, as with all government-initiated reviews, she had a very specific brief, I think she has made some positive suggestions for improving the existing EYFS framework. I welcome the move to a framework which is simpler, less bureaucratic and more easily understood (including by parents). I am also very pleased that Dame Clare has recommended that the new document should be evaluated for plain English, and hope this will bring an end to the misrepresentation of the EYFS requirements. I agree that local authority personnel and OFSTED have sometimes asked for paperwork which is not asked for by the EYFS framework. I particularly support the retention of the themes and principles related to the unique child, positive relationships and enabling environments. I believe these have been helpful in reminding practitioners of the values which should underpin work with young children and have been used effectively by many leaders and training providers to educate less experienced practitioners.

I also welcome the retention of the statutory welfare requirements, which are necessary to safeguard children, and the general approach to early learning which the EYFS promotes; however, I do think there are many contradictions, which, hopefully, the plain English review will sort out. I am delighted that Steiner schools and independent schools will be able to apply as a group for exemption from the learning and development requirements, but believe that all outstanding and good settings should also be able to apply for exemption.

3rd Posting: Glancing through, I can't find a clear statement of what it sets out to do – probably because the real purpose is to flatten all opposition once and for all. Is it a review at all? For me, a review begins with an overview of the situation that you're reviewing. But the introduction just says that it summarizes information and highlights successes. No mention of failures, of opposition to it, other points of view, the thousands who resigned as childminders (see Chapter 4) and so on. In other words, from the very beginning, it treats EYFS as a *fait accompli*, the right and only way to go, and now an integral part of education. Rather than challenging its existence, we have the power only to cross the T's and dot the I's. It's not actually a review, but a propaganda document cherry picking areas of discussion so as to strengthen its preconceived notions. I don't think there's really any point in engaging with it – it is set up so that you can't deviate from its thinking and agendas.

4th Posting: I agree with some of the previous posting – i.e. that it wasn't really a proper review and was really just about tweaking. This is all the Labour Party promised, though, when they introduced the EYFS in 2008. There is much in the EYFS that is useful and positive, and that's why a majority of practitioners like it so much. But the Open EYE campaign's main campaigning point, which is the total inappropriateness of the Learning and Development Requirements and their negative impact on thinking and practice, still stands.

5th Posting: Curate's egg indeed! ... I do have some sympathy with all that's been said so far. The problem with being asked to share any 'positives' from the Tickell Review is that one can easily end up supporting proposals that are (slightly, but only slightly) less bad than what they would be replacing – so the comments I make below should be seen very much in that light. That is, this (the current

EYFS) isn't at all where I'd wish to be starting from, but if, for a moment, we do assume it to be a given and a *fait accompli*, then perhaps at least we should be grateful for the following:

1 It is good that Tickell strongly privileges 'communication and language' over early literacy in early learning;

2 It is at least a move in the right direction that the 'learning goals' are proposed to be reduced from 69 to 17 (but again, no doubt we will come later to the question of whether, *in principle*, early 'learning goals' are at all appropriate for young children);

3 It is heartening that Steiner and independent settings would have an easier route to exemptions under Tickell's proposals compared with the near-impossible-to-negotiate labyrinthine procedure (see Chapters 3–5) set up (!) by the previous government (though there is only the need for any 'exemptions' at all because of the existence of a *statutory* framework – which again, I'm sure we'll come to later in this chapter);

4 It is surely positive that there is some attempt to simplify current assessment procedures (though again, we will likely return to the *principle* of assessment later). Thus, it is heartening that Tickell is recommending that the controversial EYFS Profile be 'radically simplified'; but there seems to have been no consideration of its existence *in principle*;

5 For me, one of the most important positives of Tickell is her emphasis on *physical development*, as one of the three 'prime' areas of focus (the others being Personal, Social and Emotional Development; and Communication and Language). If we *have* to have this kind of programmatic framework (which again is open to contestation), this one is perhaps as good as any;

6 It is good that there is direct attention given to the notion of *dispositions to learning* (e.g. through Personal, Social and Emotional Development) – Lilian Katz writes about this notion very eloquently in her Chapter 8 (and I am assuming that Tickell is doing something more than just paying lip-service to what she no doubt knows to be an important early years pedagogical principle); and finally,

7 It is surely good (but also pretty unexceptional 'mom 'n apple pie' stuff, too) that OFSTED and the local authorities should not 'create unnecessary burdens by asking for things that are not specified in the EYFS'.

So we have identified some positives, albeit with quite substantial caveats: does anyone else have anything else to say about 'positives' in the Tickell Review, before we expose it to a more 'critical gaze'?

6th Posting: I think any reluctance we might have to engage in this forum discussion is due to the very nature of the report, which writer Iain McGilchrist (author of the iconic book *The Master and His Emissary: The Divided Brain and the Making of the Western World*)[2] might describe as the (pathological) compartmentalization of the left brain. Good early years teachers keep themselves global and integrated, which makes it very difficult to plough through reports like this, and to pick out the vital points. Integrated thinking is absolutely vital when working with small children: that sense of knowing what every action will entail for each one of them. Government personnel are so focused down that they see a straight line where teachers feel a cloudburst.

It is this lust for compartmental thinking that is ripping apart the early years, and all education, but it is much more apparent in the early years sector. As Professor Guy Claxton and others (including psychoanalytic thinkers) have shown,[3] learning is fundamentally *unconscious*, not conscious, and therefore follows a parallel, not serial process. This is the key issue behind play: the government's concept of 'planned, purposeful play' is a contradiction in terms, only they're unable to understand this essential insight. As soon as play becomes planned, purposeful and adult-led, it ceases to be a self-initiated, unconscious and therefore a global, integrated, parallel process. *Integration* is the fundamental issue in education, which Finland and the other Scandinavian countries clearly understand, and the UK doesn't. This is also the paradigm-shift problem (see Chapter 21), and unfortunately most of the top people in the land are firmly entrenched in the world-view of rational positivism (cf. Chapter 19), which is not *wrong* but only a partial view that, in its limitation, distorts everything. I know we all know this; I'm just trying to put it into words that might be useful and able to be thought about.

The 'ambition to become fully graduate led' is another example, because in most universities, students are taught to stay in the head, so the more qualifications they have, the worse they get (see Chapter 20). In reality, those whose heart centres are closed (which, tragically, is most graduates, by the time university has chewed them up) shouldn't be allowed anywhere near small children.

So the entire report is flawed by compartmentalized thinking (which is why it's difficult to criticize: one just gets drawn into its agenda) – something that governments excel in. As long as the EYFS exists, it involves government control in the background, which will inevitably corrupt everything by its inappropriate way of thinking. Education should be led by educators, health by doctors, etc., because only the people deeply involved in these respective fields have the mind-set to define the pitch and deeply understand the issues.

7th Posting: This form of dialogue is very useful for clarifying where we stand, and I am interested to see how it develops. My own concerns are less about Tickell, and more about the whole way that we are approaching human learning and development. I therefore struggle to dissect such a review as Dame Clare has actually done a very good job at doing what she was asked to do ... I also think that one of the most powerful dangers of the current system is that people are constantly being made to focus down and comment on specific details rather than being encouraged to consider their decisions within the context of the greater whole. It is a well-known research trick that by using closed rather than open questions and systems, you can then proclaim statistically accurate support for any policies that you want to push through.

I think my problem with the way that early years policy-making has been approached over the past few years is the rarely challenged assumption that the most important thing is that children need to be made 'ready' for later schooling rather than for happy fulfilled lives. This has resulted in increasingly complex observation systems to support and measure what policy-makers think they should be able to do, and has taken teachers' attention away from the real needs of the child. It is also based upon the conformity of each child's attainments to pre-defined and externally defined norms. The EYFS provides a prime example of the old mechanistic way of doing things – the whole is dissected into every component part, and a system put in place that ensures standardized inspections and the maximization of required results. Such consistency and continuity are qualities that are great for the factory floor, but is this kind of detached management approach really suitable for nurturing young hearts and souls? And who is evaluating whether what we are measuring is either right or appropriate for the children's subsequent well-being, happiness and fulfilment?

In my mind Dame Clare Tickell has done an admirable job at assessing the current EYFS (in other words, doing exactly what she was asked to do), but there has been no exploration of alternative value systems or approaches of looking at early years practice, and we are instead being invited to rubber-stamp yet another newly revised 'manual for practitioners'. Where is the research looking at how current approaches are impacting on intrinsic motivation, spontaneous exploration, creativity and long-term well-being? Who is looking at the impact of the EYFS on teacher–child relationships when the teacher's attention has been so significantly moved from the child to the outcome? And what precautions are we taking to ensure that the maintenance of the system itself isn't becoming more important than the welfare of the children within it?

8th Posting: I so agree with this last posting. I also think that Dame Clare Tickell has done a good job with the brief she was given. She has taken on board many of the issues raised with her. But as the previous poster wrote, there has never been a discussion about whether a goal-driven approach *is* appropriate for young children, and that was never part of her brief. In trying to listen to a huge range of people, whilst at the same time addressing the government's 'readiness for school' agenda, Dame Clare has actually played into the hands of those headteachers, local authority personnel and OFSTED inspectors who are driven by data, forecasting and target-setting. It is so easy and depressing to see how the proposed three-point scales for each 'learning goal' will be used to the detriment of children and practitioners. The Open EYE campaign has consistently argued against the compulsory Learning and Development Requirements for such young children, some of whom do not legally have to attend any form of provision. Simply reducing the number of goals is not nearly sufficient, and there is still likely to be too much emphasis on measuring children against a narrow set of targets. The suggestion that some five-year-olds should be judged as 'emerging' or, in other words, below the 'expected level' on the proposed three-point scale is particularly deplorable, and is rooted in a fundamental misunderstanding of the great diversity of young children's development. It will inevitably increase early labelling, with the consequent impact on children's confidence and self-esteem.

I will always argue that early childhood is the very last place that there should be any nationally prescribed expectations, and I find it very sad that so many practitioners have accepted these without question. Along with my like-minded colleagues, I will continue to campaign for there to be no compulsory requirements for children aged from birth to 5.

9th Posting: From the previous postings it appears that we share a loss of confidence that early years' advisers and government early years' teams have a broad-enough understanding of early childhood, despite the welcome suggestions for simplification and change. The proposed reduction of the existing EYFS's 69 early learning goals by 52 to 17 merely confirms that there were some very serious misjudgements made at the outset, as we have always argued. We cannot ignore the potential damage to the self-esteem of young children and their intrinsic motivation towards learning that such misjudgements would have had, and are still having. The only sure way to avoid premature and developmentally inappropriate targets in the future is to remove any statutory requirements for learning and development from the EYFS altogether, lest it is again inappropriate, as well as extending it to the end of year 1.

Although also appreciating much of what Dame Clare has indicated so far in the EYFS Review, I don't agree that she has done all that she has been asked to, as the review fails to address some very serious concerns. In a workforce of nearly 100,000 strong, the 3,000 respondents to the EYFS consultation represent less than 5 per cent of the total, which leaves one questioning the oft-repeated claim that it is 'universally acclaimed' (cf. Chapter 2).

It seems imperative that the Department for Education considers, at the very least, the possibility that the crisis in education that we hear so much about could have more to do with top-down approaches and the introduction of developmentally inappropriate targets at too young an age, than it does a failure of the education system *per se*. This is fully understood by education systems which are thriving and not in crisis internationally, which introduce full-time education after the sixth birthday. However, this is the one principle that policy-makers seem quite unwilling to countenance, especially in England. Children generally will not enjoy their education if they have experienced negative feedback before the foundation of their personalities has had time to become established, and their sense of their own potential affirmed. It must be premature and inadvisable to assume that, just because there has been a review, everything in the garden will turn out to be rosy. A loss of confidence in early years' policy-makers is a loss of confidence per se, and scrapping mandatory requirements is a fail-safe way of protecting early childhood from unforeseen negative consequences.

10th Posting: I am in strong agreement with the various critical viewpoints expressed in recent postings, and especially with the 'paradigmatic' perspective expressed several postings ago. As Professor Liz Wood pointed out some years ago, educational policy-making is indeed part of a 'paradigm war',[4] which is also playing out in society more generally, between the forces of 'modernity' on the one hand, and critical postmodern, sometimes spiritually informed thinking, on the other. The latter approach rejects as false many of the assumptions and practices accompanying the technocratic, modernist worldview and its associated mind-set; and thankfully, there is at least some early years literature that takes such critiques very seriously (e.g. see the work of Gaile Cannella, Glenda MacNaughton, Peter Moss, Peter Fitzsimons etc.). But the problem with such a hyper-critical perspective is that it can be something of a conversation-stopper! – that is, we end up rejecting out of hand policy-making initiatives like the EYFS, and the possibility of a constructive conversation with policy-makers who are wedded to this world-view then becomes close to zero. In this current forum, I think we need to pay at least some attention to the content of the EYFS and to the Tickell recommendations, in the hope that some of our critical perspectives might be able to be heard and at least thought about (sadly, based on our past experience, just the latter would perhaps constitute major progress in advancing our paradigmatic position!).

I do have a range of specific criticisms of the recommendations, however – starting with the complete lack of any consideration of the appropriateness of ICT and computers in early childhood settings and experience. Dr Aric Sigman, amongst others, quoting copious health-related research findings, has written very incisively about this critical issue (see Chapter 18); and I find it extraordinary that Clare Tickell has completely ignored what, for some, is an issue of *child-sanctioned child abuse* (i.e. the state-enforced use of computers in the lives of very young children) – and this is especially the case, given that we know that Dame Clare received some very strong and detailed critical representations about this issue in the consultation submissions. One can only assume that this is known by Dame Clare to be 'beyond discussion', and is now uncritically institutionalized in the early years. If this is so, it brings home with terrifying prescience just how powerful is the ideology of technocratic modernity that underpins such pernicious and age-inappropriate developments. I and my colleagues will continue to campaign against this madness with renewed intensity until some sanity begins to prevail in this sphere. When we read in the summary of her Recommendations that 'I do not recommend banning mobile phones in early years settings' (p. 59), the prevailing hegemonic view is perhaps abundantly clear.

Trying not to repeat issues mentioned earlier by my Open EYE colleagues, other concerns I wish to mention here include the compliance-inculcating, de-professionalizing impact of the EYFS remaining a mandatory, state-imposed framework on pre-compulsory age children (this being an issue that could still well be challenged in a Judicial Review); the notable failure to distinguish clearly between support for the *general principle* of some kind of early childhood framework, and support for the *particularities* of the EYFS per se; the failure to release childminders from the impinging intrusions of the EYFS (cf. Chapter 4); the failure to problematize the very notion of early learning 'goals' and the accompanying audit and surveillance culture; the failure to engage in a wide-ranging discussion of the radically contested terrain of 'developmentally appropriate learning' for young children; the failure to problematize 'assessment-mindedness', and just whose anxieties and well-being are *really* being addressed by such an assessment- and observation-obsessed early childhood milieu; the continuing dominance of a 'ready for school' ideology pervading the thinking of the report, as opposed to seeing early childhood as an autonomous period in its own right (the DfE Tickell press release of 30 March 2011 referred to making the EYFS 'more focused on making sure children start school ready to learn');[5] the failure to engage with repeated critiques that have been made of the philosophically incoherent notion of 'structured' or 'guided' play; the report's superficial and uncritical engagement with cherry-picked positivistic research (cf. Chapter 18) that cannot but confirm and reinforce the unarticulated assumptions about learning and development that underpin and drive the EYFS; and finally, the uncritical acceptance of the discourse of 'a good level of development' accompanying the EYFS Profile.

I also wish to take the discussion towards wider issues and, thereby, to a different level. As suggested earlier, if we accept the discourse of the EYFS and the Review's approach to investigating its procedural minutiae, the danger is that we miss the opportunity to open up wider questions and perspectives which, if not considered, leave the policy-making discussion at best narrowly and inadequately conceived, and at worst, simply irrelevant to the issues which it is professing to address. Just two thoughts will suffice here.

First, from a psychoanalytic standpoint, there has been no attempt to seek to understand the deep *psychodynamics* that almost certainly underpin and drive early years policy-making. I recently realized, for example, that the EYFS framework may well be serving a crucial unconscious function in the early childhood sphere, such that people commonly simply ignore the noxious *content* of the compulsory framework because the unconscious function that it is serving (through its very existence) as a *reliever of anxiety* by far outweighs any issues to do with the procedural content of the framework.

Thus, from a *psychodynamic* standpoint the EYFS can be seen as serving as a kind of 'container' (to use the psychoanalytic jargon) for all of the inevitable anxieties that early years practitioners experience (consciously and unconsciously) in their work; and the EYFS has therefore perhaps taken on a psychodynamic significance for practitioners in 'holding' them and containing their many anxieties. A grotesque irony is that the sheer volume of bureaucratic demands within the EYFS merely adds to such anxieties – so that we end up with the absurdly self-fulfilling situation whereby massive *additional* anxieties are generated by the EYFS framework itself, and *the framework itself* is then unconsciously used by practitioners as a 'psychological object' for containing those very same anxieties! In short, then, *the very existence* of something called 'EYFS' is perhaps far more important than is its *actual content*. If this way of understanding is anything like right, it suggests that critics of early years policy-making may need to start thinking far more subtly and creatively in terms of how we address what we see as the major shortcomings of the framework.

Second, there is the issue of the distribution of income and wealth, and relative poverty in Britain. According to government statistics, income inequality in the UK is now greater than it has ever been, with the gap between the poorest and richest actually accelerating.[6] The celebrated book by Richard Wilkinson and Kate Pickett, *The Spirit Level: Why Equality is Better for Everyone*[7] (Penguin, 2009) shows how the degree of inequality in income/wealth within a given society, and the associated levels of relative deprivation, constitute *the* crucial variable in accounting for levels of subjective well-being in advanced Western societies. Wilkinson and Pickett discuss the impact of rates of income inequality on family life, and the way in which *educational outcomes are far less unequal in societies in which the income distribution is far more equal* (like Sweden and Finland) than they are in the UK (which has one of the most unequal income distributions in the 'developed' world). Thus, the general quality of social relationships is lower in more unequal societies; and inequality has a major impact on the quality of family life and relationships, with social inequalities in early childhood development being long entrenched before the start of formal state education.

In light of this, perhaps the core reason why governments have been so hyperactively intruding into early years experience is because *those very same politicians have no political will to address the main cause of unequal early life chances* – i.e. the grossly unequal distribution of income and wealth in Britain. So they are left with the only other option available: i.e. symptom-tinkering policy intrusions into the personal sphere in increasingly desperate attempts to socially engineer more equal early life chances via the policy-making process (whilst leaving the income distribution untouched – and, indeed, *worsening*).

In this sense, recent Conservative and Labour governments (or 'Blatcherism') both stand equally condemned, because it is their hand-wringingly supine homage to the sanctity of 'the free market' system, and to the excesses of the holders of economic positional power, which are directly responsible for the predicament in which so many socially deprived young children and families find themselves. On this view, then, perhaps it is these latter individuals, and the politicians who do little or nothing to address the causes of early childhood deprivation, towards whom we should be directing our campaigning zeal, and not so much those policy-makers (like Dame Clare Tickell) who are simply tinkering with the *symptoms* of a system which is, in reality, impossible to reform successfully without addressing the fundamental causes of early deprivation.

That's rather a long posting! – would anyone like to make any further points before we bring this stimulating forum to a close?

11th Posting: I totally recognize and empathize with the comments above re the unequal distribution of income and wealth in Britain, and how this inequality has an impact on early years' policy-making, with government laudably attempting to create better outcomes for what are referred to as 'disadvantaged' or 'deprived' children. However, I think that concentrating on economic disadvantage, as if it were the only sort of deprivation, is misleading, and it is just this focus which has been the main political justification for the mandatory framework in the first place. There is a more fundamental disadvantage affecting children across the economic and social divide, and that is the disadvantage of low self-esteem. Children who feel good about themselves and their potential can, and often do, overcome the negative effects of economic disadvantage. Economic disadvantage does not in itself give rise to failure, and in many cases can be the means to strive for success.

The reason that policy-makers see disadvantaged children as being limited is because they are viewed materialistically rather than spiritually. Children, who have had their self-image impaired through a lack of emotional warmth, and harsh, unenlightened and/ or inadequate parenting, are much more likely to grow up with a sense of poor self-esteem. Such deprivation is not the sole property of children who are disadvantaged economically, and such a view can be very emotive and also misleading, giving rise to all manner of justifications for earlier and earlier learning goals and social engineering. However, those children who arrive in nursery school with their self-image already impaired will approach early learning goals with little confidence in their ability to succeed.

Many of our concerns about the framework reflect the fact that premature targets and goals have far more potential to further handicap children who already have a sense of lack of worth, rather than these same targets and goals raising their outcomes. Low self-esteem is actually a psychic wound, which can best be healed by children being put back in touch with their own innate goodness, the seat of a positive sense of self. This, I believe, should be the central role of pre-school nursery education as a real 'preparation for life', instead of the new government's seriously flawed mantra that the early years should be 'a preparation for school'.

If we view all children as full of potential, we would be less concerned with their economic or social status and instead have the highest expectations for their future, providing healthy soil for their potential, and offering that extra encouragement and respect so essential for positive attitudes and dispositions towards learning, especially for the psychologically and spiritually deprived children.

12th Posting: I agree with the previous posting, and would add that there is an increasing body of research to show that young children in the UK are being subjected to unnatural cultural pressures that are eroding not only their natural learning dispositions but also their sense of personal meaning and contribution. This has profound implications for a world where personal belief, empowerment and creativity are now recognized as essential criteria for personal success.

Why do we have children who can read, but have lost the desire to do so? Why do we have such high levels of child depression and psychological dysfunction? Why do we have the worse binge drinking in Europe? And most importantly, why are so few people looking to the education system for the answer to these questions? No matter how much we are asked to accept the purity of its intention the 'schoolification' process now starts with the statutory nature of the EYFS, and if we get this wrong we set up yet another generation of children who will come to see learning as a burden rather than a joy.

To sum up the main thrust of our forum discussion, what stands out are our shared concerns about the overly and unjustifiable intrusion by governments into the non-compulsory early years arena, by setting goals and targets for development and learning. The discussion does acknowledge some aspects of the EYFS thought to be positive, such as attempts at refinement and simplification. We have always taken a supportive position for those aspects which are undoubtedly of benefit to children and, whenever possible, will continue to do so.

Many of the points we have highlighted have not been addressed in the Review, and would seem to offer Dame Clare Tickell some real insights from an experienced diverse group of people who have childhood at the heart of their concerns. However, no approach has been made from the Early Years' department to engage with our group in order to be open-minded enough to debate the issues. These issues include the apprehensions about any real benefits from early learning, and the view that much within the EYFS is inappropriate at such a young age and is, therefore, 'too much too soon'. It is also noticeable that there seems to be a systematic ignoring of the inappropriateness of ICT and computers in early childhood settings, despite universal research which is putting the subject into real question.

The crisis in education generally is also addressed, which is likely to have come about through the failure to address some of the concerns we and others have frequently voiced. The Review has concluded that young children will still be measured against targets, even though many are not in early years settings, and we find some of the new measurement labels such as 'emerging' to be deplorable.

We hope to move Dame Clare and her team away from assumptions regarding 'disadvantage', as only relating to social and economic matters.

Notes

1 This dialogue was created by active members of the Open EYE campaign. Names have not been ascribed to particular contributions, as it is the substance of the discussion that matters rather than the specific views of the participating personalities. The following Open EYE members participated in the discussion, which has been edited by the book's editor, Richard House, and with the content being agreed and 'signed off' by all participants as an accurate-enough representation of our deliberations: Margaret Edgington, Wendy Ellyatt, Grethe Hooper Hansen, Richard House and Kim Simpson. See also the epilogue to this chapter.

2 Iain McGilchrist, *The Master and His Emissary: The Divided Brain and the Making of the Western World*, New Haven, Conn: Yale University Press, 2009.

3 For example, see Guy Claxton, *Hare Brain, Tortoise Mind: Why Intelligence Increases when You Think Less*, London: Fourth Estate, 1997.

4 Elizabeth Wood, 'A new paradigm war? The impact of national curriculum policies on early childhood teachers' thinking and classroom practice', *Teaching and Teacher Education*, 20, 2004, pp. 361–74.

5 Department for Education, 'Early Years Foundation Stage to be radically slimmed down', press release, 30 March 2011, updated 16 June 2011; accessible at: http://www.education.gov.uk/childrenandyoungpeople/earlylearningand-childcare/a0076193/early-years-foundation-stage-to-be-radically-slimmed-down (retrieved 25 Jun 2011)

6 *Evening Standard*, 13 May 2011.

7 Richard Wilkinson and Kate Pickett, *The Spirit Level: Why Equality is Better for Everyone*, Harmondsworth: Penguin, 2009.

The Foundations of Child Development and Early Learning

Perspectives, Principles and Practices

Part II contains a diverse range of perspectives on early development and learning which, when taken together, set out in great detail the kind of foundation that young children need in order to facilitate effective and successful formal and cognitive learning (including literacy learning) in the longer run. Professor Lilian Katz presents the compelling arguments around 'dispositions to learn' for which she has a world-wide reputation, and there are also chapters on infant massage, play, the central importance of physical development and movement, and the approaches of Steiner Waldorf, Montessori and Reggio Emilia to laying true and appropriate foundations for children's learning.

Amongst a highly distinguished roll-call of contributors in Part II, we are especially delighted to include a chapter on the importance of play by Professor David Elkind, who has (in North America) been championing an unhurried beginning to life for young children for well over three decades. For any student or policy-maker wishing to draw up an alternative 'foundation stage' grounded in perennial wisdom and the latest progressive thinking and research on early development, the chapters in Part II will be indispensable reading.

CHAPTER 7

The Myth of Early Stimulation for Babies

SYLVIE HÉTU

What I have found is that a baby – though she doesn't know words yet, or information, or the rules of life – is the most reliable judge of feelings. All a baby has with which to take in the world are her five senses. Hold her, sing to her, show her the night sky or the quivering leaf, or a bug. Those are the ways – the only ways – she learns about the world – whether it is a safe and loving place, or a harsh one.

JOYCE MAYNARD, FROM THE NOVEL *LABOR DAY*

Having worked for 30 years as an educator and then as an infant massage instructor, working mainly with families with babies, I have had the extraordinary opportunity to see before my eyes literally thousands of babies, which has given me direct and extensive experiential knowledge about them. I am also involved with a programme bringing nurturing touch daily to schools and family life, and this adds to ongoing opportunities to dialogue with both teachers and parents. Because I have worked in 18 countries around the world and in collaboration with colleagues from 50 countries, I have a certain 'accumulation' of data, leading me to have strong feelings and views about something that is happening with babies and children. Finally, Education is what I studied at university, and I have never stopped studying it, keeping myself as updated as possible about leading progressive thinkers interested in the phenomenon of education.

I have accepted the offer to contribute to a book like this one simply because of the book's title, which for me captures a dramatic cultural occurrence which society commonly fails to see, or to acknowledge. I think we are caught in a desire to evolve and grow that is flirting with a post-Darwinist philosophy: I will win, I will be the one, I will rise above the others – not to mention fighting to be the winner, no matter what happens to the other, weaker ones. And with this phenomenon starting as early as in the lives of babies, manifesting in all kinds of ways, then we may be heading for more and more problems. I believe that several of our approaches with babies have an effect on the nervous system, to which we are not paying enough attention.

With this humble contribution, I will try to highlight some aspects of what is happening around babies, and I invite the reader to be aware of and reflect upon these issues, and to contribute suggestions for improvement. It is useful to witness certain books on the market with titles like *Why Love Matters*, and *The Science of Parenting* (Gerhardt, 2004; Sunderland, 2008). These books have the most up-to-date scientific knowledge, and their authors conclude that love is what matters … and that science is there to support that statement.

What neuro-science and biochemistry are revealing could provide an excellent basis on which parents and educators can draw for making educational choices. For educational choices we have to make, facing the fact that more and more children are diagnosed as 'hyper-' this or that, as falling on the autistic spectrum, asthmatic, over-agitated, having headaches, pains in their body, etc. Furthermore, how is it that we have created a world in which medication is needed for children in order for them to be able to cope or thrive? And do we wish to support such a development? What *do* we support?

Perhaps we do not know any more, and this is where sound reflection, combined with the study of physiology, can be a bridge for helping us to understand part of our mystery as human beings.

Birth

The thread that is often present right from the moment a baby is conceived, if not before, could well be termed 'The best … '. Parents will seek the best doctor, the best hospital, the best midwife, the best this and that. But what do we mean by 'best'? What is giving birth, and what do babies need?

Although there still exist on earth women who believe that nature knows best, there is an ever-growing movement of women believing that giving birth vaginally is a Stone Age practice, and who think: why would we even want to do that, when we can choose when to give birth with no harm, and be in control? (so they say). Well, this is where the story of this chapter really begins, because there are studies now showing that babies who are born even just a bit earlier – and that is what elective caesareans always are, with the baby being extracted from the mother earlier than the due date – have a greater likelihood of becoming 'hyperactive' in later childhood, when they reach school age.

We take great risks when we play with nature in this way. Women's bodies know how to give birth, and most of the time the baby knows when to get out – and, furthermore, knows its way out! I cannot imagine the shock the baby must experience, being cocooned in the womb, and then suddenly being pulled out without warning!

This is just the tip of the iceberg. Now that we know how wise babies are, and with birth being more and more medicalized, we will gain in using science not only to make sure that babies are safe at birth, but to make sure that medicine gives the birth experience and babies

back to their parents. We do understand, of course, that before medicine was what it is now, some babies did die. Parents who have been helped by science to keep their baby alive are surely very grateful, and with valid reason. I am not condemning science per se here but, rather, trying to discern where it might have gone beyond its legitimate role. I believe that medicine has invaded birth to too great an extent, with women and babies having given up their inner wisdom to science. And my wish is that science will help us indeed to discover that the more we leave a baby 'alone' with his parents at birth, the better.

Specialists increasingly stipulate that our first experiences are those that register the deepest, and last the longest. Biologically, this can be seen with how myelin, the coating we have on our nerves, forms within the whole of our nervous system (cf. Chapter 9); and emotionally this concords with approaches where, in psychology, each human being can have personal understanding of some aspects of their personality by recalling experiences they had as babies and children, and thus discover deeper understanding in some aspects of their adult behaviours.

My question will be, then: why do we separate babies from their mothers at birth, in order to conduct all sorts of tests? Why do we 'evaluate' those babies right from the start? This is where, for me, the *too much too soon* syndrome begins. In several hospitals, the baby is taken, washed, is given some kind of vaccine with some kind of vitamins, weighed, and then given to the mother. And we wonder whether this influences the baby? Up to the 1980s, the general view was that babies did not feel. We now know, however, that babies are extremely sensitive beings, so why don't we give them the opportunity to arrive in the world gently? Scientific people could do research into what kind of neuro-pathways are created when a baby is taken away, washed, weighed, etc. before being handed to the parents.

When I meet parents in classes where they share about their babies' birth, I cannot start to explain the pain that lives in so many mothers. Some are literally enraged about what happened, others are totally distressed. Others seem to be in cloud-cuckoo land when they share about how the birth went well, but that they could not feel anything towards the baby once the doctors finally gave them back their washed baby. Then they also share about their babies either always crying, or not wanting to be separated from them, and so on. Winnicott was the first specialist stating that mother and baby are one; at birth they are one entity, one 'being'. If this oneness is rent asunder, problems happen for both parties. Parents often share their birth stories, and when things go 'naturally' we have, simply, a more relaxed baby and mother. In addition, when mothers just follow their instincts, and stay with the baby, everyone feels better, and the problems almost magically disappear.

Today, certainly in the West, women are immersed in a general societal protocol that they cannot give birth without the medical system. That would be for me the first step: Give back to mothers the wisdom of their capacities to give birth, and secondly, conduct research on the influence of the type of birth the baby experiences on neurological patterns, and later personality traits. Not that I wish to suggest deterministically that birth would become the 'cause' of who we are; I am more belonging to the philosophy that we should get out of the way, in order for who we are to emerge with as little interference as possible. The works of Michel Odent and Frederic Leboyer, those doctors who understood and wrote a lot about the fact that we need to welcome babies with care into the world to prevent later problems, surely need to be removed from our shelves, dusted off, and given to parents and medical students. The way in which we welcome babies into the world has a major influence on later behaviour.

The Early Weeks

As we move on, hours, days, weeks after the birth, our little cherubim become the objects of all possible futures that need to be 'educated' as early as possible. This starts with controlled schedules, controlled feeding, controlled crying and controlled sleeping. Week after week I meet overwhelmed parents, bending under so much pressure to get it 'right'.

Now we do know, with the help of neuroscience, that babies cannot be controlled, and that they cannot control us. Bye-bye to the 'spoiling myth'. But this myth still lives so strongly, only in a modified way. It is not any more a matter of fear of spoiling the baby; it is the matter of making sure that the baby is 'the best'. These expectations about our babies create so much pressure on parents, albeit often unconscious. Another phenomenon we observe, too, is that parents are determined to continue to live their life as they did before the baby was there. Therefore, we educate our babies … to not be babies! And we do it far too soon. And there is a price to pay for all the involved parties.

Now no matter if one takes it from the neurophysiological or the philosophical angle, we have here an important issue. Biochemistry and neuroscience have shown us that babies tend to adapt in order to protect their nervous system. So although parents think that they are 'educating' their babies to stop crying, for example, in reality they are forcing the baby to become quiet in a way that has a deep impact. Indeed, the baby's nervous system needs to protect itself, as excessive crying damages it. The baby therefore does stop crying, but as a matter of self-protection. And the happy parent will be convinced that the baby has been 'educated' not to cry. The long-term consequences are terrible, because the departure point, a need to be answered, is not addressed or resolved. Babies cry in order to communicate their physical and emotional needs. And if those needs are not met, there are high chances that the baby will experience that 'the world is not a place to be trusted'.

Excessive crying brings the nervous system into such an alert mode, involving the reptilian brain, with excessive demand on the sympathetic part of the autonomous nervous system, and a chain reaction of biochemicals that are to be used in case of danger. This is the famous 'flight or fight' mode, necessary in urgent situations. No human being can survive for long in that state without damaging parts of his bodily system.

On the other hand, you have babies who are quite persistent, and will not give their parents a break, continuing to demand their due,

no matter what the due is. Then, those parents who have tried all of the 'controlling methods' will likely be in absolute despair. Some of them get depressed, some get exhausted, and some get utterly discouraged: disillusion is now the common mode, and on top of everything else, these parents then start to have a really poor image of themselves. They think they have a 'bad' baby, or/and that they are a really bad parent.

It is crucial to understand that trying to *educate* our babies is not only 'way too soon', but has devastating consequences. What babies need, as stipulated by several authors, is *love, attention, human contact and their needs answered*. Furthermore, there is a 'sacred place' between parents and babies that should be honoured and left untouched.

Government Policies for Babies

Things get complicated when the government starts to impose its views about 'best practices for babies' via the health system and state-employed health professionals. Do not get me wrong; I have nothing against the fact that we, as a society, have a collective desire to ensure our offsprings' well-being. What horrifies me is that ideologies become so-called 'truth' – and then policies. Government policies for babies then become collective beliefs that are often far away from either what parents feel is right for their babies and, worse, sometimes harmful for them.

I will take a simple example. In most countries now, parents are told that they have to put their babies to sleep on their back in order to prevent cot death. This is a policy you need to follow as a parent, otherwise you are told that you are putting your baby in danger. In a nutshell we have here a series of challenges. First, there is a lot of controversy about the view that putting a baby on her back for sleeping will reduce risk of cot death. A policy of this kind also contributes to generating a collective fear: that of the death of our baby. No one can prevent death. Even the best parents who 'put their babies on their back to sleep' can lose a baby, because death is surely often a mystery greater than the modern mind can begin to understand.

Parents are therefore again caught between fear, their own intuition and their own observation of their baby's needs – and what the government has told them they ought to do. Over the years I have observed parents being deeply distressed, simply because their baby would not sleep on their back, but will sleep if placed on their tummy, or on their side, or tucked alongside the parent, either in a bay carrier or in bed. The collective neurosis created by this policy is impossible to describe. Few parents are sufficiently self-confident to by-pass these policies. Other parents, I know for a fact, will lie to the health professionals about what they do with baby, in order to avoid the discomfort and conflict of feeling 'caught out'. Now this is extraordinary, isn't it?

We have become obsessed with protection because some babies are, indeed, at risk. What we need to look at is how governments, and social and health services, can *really* contribute to the well-being of babies. It is not by telling parents what to do that we will help babies; rather it is simply by ensuring that parents are considered the most important persons in the world for building a healthy society. Government policies and resources could be better used by providing high incomes to parents, ensuring adequate food and housing for them and their babies, community centres where parents 'just' meet (not to be told what mouth hygiene is). Parents need to be allowed to 'parent together', beyond the gaze of empirical researchers.

I am taken aback by how seriously government and health professionals take themselves in being the ones deciding what the first best food is for babies, and at what time – as if humanity hadn't been able to work these things out in the past! This topic generated one of the funniest open discussions in one of my infant massage parents' classes, where in the discussion, parents decided to discuss first food. There were eight parents in the class, from various backgrounds and various cultures. None of them had the same 'first food for their baby'. It was a very animated discussion, the kind that you really remember, and I did not give any personal opinion. I was simply facilitating the discussion, and was quite enjoying myself! Parents too were enjoying themselves, between banana, grapes, rice, oatmeal, sweet potatoes, cooked pears, coconut purée – there you have it. If anyone can prove to me that anything on that list is not a good first food, then so be it. With my benevolent smiles the parents realized that they were all good parents, and that they had one point in common: they would give their baby one food at a time, just to make sure that the baby reacts well to it.

The latter would, in my opinion, be a good policy. But even that ... When I was a baby, my mother had health government papers about what she had to do with me. She recently found those papers and gave them to me. That was, to the day I am writing these lines, 56 years ago. Wow! ... I was to be given meat at *one week* old; and formula milk was better, as it had all the correct measured quantities of this and that. Oh well. What will the government say in 50 years from now, I wonder? I sincerely hope it will not be 'too much too soon'.

Health: Vaccination and Antibiotics, a False Security

In one article that I read some years ago, it said: 'Vaccination is the modern baptism'. I am aware that this subject can surely become a polemic, or at least a very hot potato. Nevertheless, I have to include it here, as these substances are something given to babies, often very early on – strange substances that still have controversial and contradictory opinions being expressed about them, that invade our babies very, very early on.

What concerns me is that when I was a young parent myself, three decades ago now, there still existed doctors (who are probably all dead now) who witnessed the birth of massive vaccinations for babies and children, and who chose deliberately *not* to artificially immunize their babies and children. They all claimed that there were no real foundations to this practice, and far too much that was unknown and uncertain around vaccinations.

They used to sign papers for parents who chose not to vaccinate. Now, this practice has disappeared, and the new generation of parents and medical professionals have, for the most part, stopped even questioning these practices. Vaccination has become the norm, accepted as a matter of fact. The very few parents choosing not to immunize find very little support, not to mention that they lie about their child not being immunized, as a result of the horrified reaction they receive from health professionals and other parents.

In several countries, immunization is obligatory. Parents have therefore lost total control over health, and philosophical and social choices around their children, starting in babyhood. It also seems that the medical system has contradicted its very own motto of scientific evidence and 'evidence-based practice', not being able to really measure the effect of collective immunization, or of collective non-immunization.

We might well be invading our babies far too soon; consider, for example, the higher and higher incidence of babies being ill, despite having been immunized, and having all sorts of health problems at an earlier and earlier age. This is the first generation of babies almost exclusively born of immunized parents, so we are talking about the second generation of almost entirely immunized people. Despite all this, and nutritional education, we seem collectively to have lost control over several diseases, including diseases involving the immune system. So what is going on?

I am willing to meet any politician or heath professional reading this chapter, and would be tempted to say that I am an 'irresponsible person' who contributes to putting society at risk by even questioning the value of immunization. I will meet the politicians in 30 years from now when I will be an old lady, and we will then discuss all of this – when humanity will start to lose its war against mutant bacteria and viruses, and researchers will discover that the people surviving tend to be those who never had vaccination or antibiotics (or very little). I think it is time that we all request, or demand, unbiased studies about the value of immunization, and that we put hygiene, good water and nutrition in the picture as well. There might well be a far less invasive way of protecting our babies' immune systems.

The case of antibiotics now at least has the attention of biologists, who are starting to admit that we have weakened babies' immune system by given them antibiotics as soon as they have an infection. Now, doctors are being educated to reduce the amount of antibiotics they give to babies. The repeated administration of antibiotics (often wanted by parents as well) can surely be linked to another manifestation of the 'too much too soon' phenomenon. It might be that we need to learn to stay calm if our babies tasted the cat litter, drank water from the flowerpot, or ate some sand on the beach.

The Early Months

Babies now have 'schedules' that are as important as those of adults. When I teach infant massage classes – and I am myself in a paradox in doing so – it is quite common that babies have a class every day. Baby music, baby yoga, baby gym, baby singing, baby salsa, baby language, baby Einstein, baby sings and baby swim classes are all very common nowadays. With infant massage, we simply promote nurturing touch, inviting parents to read their babies cues, and reducing external stimulation such as light and noises. We are, in fact, quite opposite to all other classes – and yes, we are still a class.

I have seen nurses teaching music and movement to babies, and without warning putting on quite loud/strong music, and leaving very little time for parents to even figure out what was happening, let alone their babies – swinging babies from one side to another to the sound of music coming from a poor-quality sound system. I was observing the babies, and most of them had the kinds of eyes that say, 'What in the world is happening to me?' Is *this* what we call 'early stimulation'? If it is, then I believe we all need to take an urgent second look at all this.

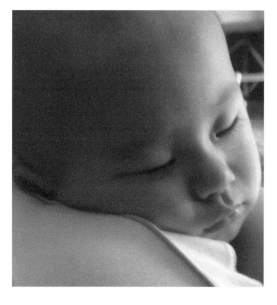

Babies respond well to human voices, human faces and human touch, and they will naturally open themselves to the world. Some time ago, I did a three-day workshop on the use of the voice, and the lecturer said that it is quite dramatic what is happening on the planet at the moment; for all cultures in the world have lullabies – but this is the first generation of parents who do not routinely and intuitively sing to their babies. Singing used to be as natural as talking, and now it has become something that nobody wants to do because it is not 'cool' to do so, because we were told we don't have a good voice, or simply because we have always listened to music and songs, instead of producing them ourselves.

Babies need the calm presence of their parents, the day-to-day house sounds, and human beings around them. That *is* the 'stimulation' they need. They also need to be protected from too much stimulation (cf. Sardello and Sanders, 1999). Most specialists will agree that babies in the modern world are either too stimulated, or not stimulated enough. In the 'not-enough' category, we often deal with families that do not have sufficient financial and emotional support to care for their baby. We go back to the same principles: support the parents so that they can support their babies.

Day Care

Other people are caring for babies at younger and younger ages. Babies are then forced to attach to persons who do not have a deep life-interest in them, with 'loving' the babies in their care being a task of their job. Lest I be misunderstood, I do know very loving persons who work with babies, and I have even been one of them myself many years ago. When the babies were two years old, they were changed to another department, arriving with a whole new team of staff. When I think about it now, it really upsets me. Babies and young children need consistency and stable figures (Elfer, 2007; Elfer and Dearnley, 2007). I believe that people can have difficulties in long-term relationships because of the several attachment adjustments they had to make when they were babies, and much clinical evidence from psychoanalysis and psychotherapy supports this view. Certainly, many specialists agree that what happens to babies and young children can have an influence on their whole life.

My own parents, who became grandparents when my children were born, also loved my children. They did not love them like I did, but they surely did not like them like the carer would 'love' the babies under their care. Though it is unfashionable and 'politically incorrect' to say so, I believe that there is a vital link with one's family that is beyond our normal comprehension. Naturally, children have 'attachment figures', and this work was clearly developed by John Bowlby and all his followers (e.g. Bowlby, 1997). Bowlby himself had a traumatic experience when his nanny, to whom he seemed to have bonded more deeply than to his own parents, simply left.

It seems, then, that the 'love' (which seems to matter highly even within a neuroscientific perspective) can never be the same for babies raised in day care compared with those who are with the parents or parental figure that remains. Having lived through the (probably necessary) age of feminism and women's liberation, it is now important to find a proper balance between women's needs and *babies'* needs (cf. Biddulph, 2006). Placing babies in day care has now become 'fashionable', and it is quite common that even women who choose to stay at home with their babies are accused of cutting off their baby from formative social experiences. I personally know some parents who have experienced this. What we have done is create *artificial* sociability to replace naturalistic familial environments, as we put babies of the same age into the same homogeneous, controlled group.

A man who has been a teacher for a number of years in primary schools, and has therefore seen several generations of children, recently told me that he has noticed that the children are now unable to look up to the healthy authority of adults (cf. Sigman, 2009). They do not see the adult; they only see their friends and their peers, and have no idea about how to relate with one another, possessing little or no morality, and therefore bullying, intimidating, ignoring, or even attacking, barely being able to realise they are doing so. This is a psychologically and culturally complex issue (Lasch's notion of a 'culture of narcissism' is also perhaps relevant here), but the teacher told me that he thinks it is because children are placed at a younger and younger age with a group of the same age, with adults who are with them purely doing their job, and not for a deep personal love for the child as a person.

It is therefore hardly surprising that healthy attachment and respect will not develop in the same way in such children. The baby is at higher risk of disengaging, and may well find some kind of compensation with his forced equal siblings. In a cartoon, I saw a 'chain' production of babies where it was the government that was 'taking' them before they were born – just as if they were in the army, all in line. We need unbiased and interest-free long-term research into the effect of separating babies from their parents before the age of three; I am convinced that it would produce very interesting results.

The other point that needs to be considered around day care is the economics of the phenomenon. I believe that economics are prevailing over common sense in terms of what is really needed for babies. In day care, babies are often ill, and I am wondering whether it is really because of the bacteria, or whether their immune system has become weaker because they do not experience deep, consistent love. 'Too much too soon' can be an experience of others, and their runny noses having to share everything at too young an age. Discouragement may actually lead to a weaker immune system. There might also be an unconscious process occurring here, for if as a baby I become ill, my parents have to stay home with me.

I find it shocking that the national curriculum for schools has now reached down to babies – with day-care professionals needing to monitor babies for what they are supposed to be able to do. I was pleased to dialogue with several day-care people recently who said they would just not do it. For me, this is a welcome sign that common sense has not been totally extinguished.

The 'levelling' that is the norm in day care is also concerning, for where do we leave a place for uniqueness? – for the fact that some babies will be slow in this and faster in that, like any human being. Furthermore, if your baby is not doing this at this age, then you as a parent are referred to specialists, who will then evaluate *you* as a parent; and your baby will go through all sorts of tests which are invasive and impinging anyway, bringing in their wake yet more anxiety to the parents, with this then felt by the baby too.

Is there any need to ask ourselves whether our baby is developing so-called 'normally'? Institutionalizing our babies puts all of us in a mould that children will later on try to break.

My own daughter walked at 22 months. She was, in that realm, 'slow'. Now, many years later, she has been a gymnastic teacher for seven years, has studied dance at college, and is now studying kinesiology at university to help dancers and sports people. I am glad she was not in day care with people worrying that she did not fall within 'the norm'.

The last argument that some people bring in favour of day care for babies is that some parents *do not know how to care for their babies,* and that it will be much better for their baby to be in day care with competent carers. This argument will be addressed in the next section.

Lost Insightfulness

Once a mum arrived in one of my infant-massage classes with a pile of books, and she was in tears. She wanted me to tell her what book she should follow, as all the books were contradicting one another. As an infant-massage instructor, I am not allowed to give advice; I am only allowed to guide parents to find what is best for them and their baby by asking questions and reflecting. I simply asked her, what is your favourite book? – and she immediately pulled it out from the pile! So I said: 'Well, it seems that this is the book that's most helpful for you and your baby', and then she said, ' … but my mother-in-law, and the doctor, and the midwife … '.

Modern parents are often lost under the weight of too much information. There is so much information circulating around babies now, and it is available after just two clicks of a mouse. The available information *is* often contradictory. In a way, I do not see that as a problem – on the contrary, opposing ideas often bring birth to new ideas, and more clarity.

It is very important to remember that parents do have insight about their own babies. They do have a 'little voice' that tells them what is best for their babies. All specialists working around parents should only aim to help parents to access that inner wisdom, which cannot be found in any books, or in any leaflets. It takes a lot of courage to let go of anything we personally think is 'true', and just create a cocoon around parents so that they find what is best for their baby, which is often very simple. We can contribute towards 'de-cluttering' all the information that is given to parents, to replace it by an ambiance where insightfulness will be able to bloom.

Protecting Babies, Revised Stimulation

Nowadays, babies experience several stimuli, at a younger and younger age. They are placed in car seats, in baby bouncers, in front of computer screens, in front of TV; they travel in cars, in buses, in trains, in planes, on the underground; they walk on the street in strollers facing outside instead of facing the person who pushes the pushchair; they hear telephones and the radio; they have monitors watching for them; and they 'swim' in electromagnetic fields of wireless internet.

I propose that we develop a culture of protection for babies. If we want the next generation to start to free itself of all sorts of syndromes, I propose a simple approach to baby raising, filled with love and parent-to-parent support, so they enjoy observing their babies unfolding naturally, as they surely will. Let us leave behind races for crawlers, and replace it by crawlers crawling freely in a safe environment, while their mum chats away happily. Let us force ourselves to really study the dangers of putting our children in the presence of electromagnetic fields, and instead of having to monitor them, just have them near us.

Let us replace the over-escalating need to have so-called 'educational toys' that babies find boring anyway after a couple of tries, and keep it simple with natural toys. Let us move out of the ever-escalating presence of plastic everywhere (baby having a plastic bottle, plastic teeth ring, plastic spoon, plastic plate, plastic high chair, plastic fence, plastic bib, plastic fruits and vegetables, plastic car set and plastic clothes).

Babies' senses, reflexes and nervous system need to be protected (Sardello and Sanders, 1999) so that they can unfold safely. Protected and consciously chosen voice, smell, balance, hearing, sight, touching and being with someone they love is what they need. This is what 'education' is for them. And yes, babies are at the centre of our universe, when they arrive. This is just the way it is.

Last Insight

Babies are kings, not the children

The authority needed around a baby should be ruled by love and abandonment of self for 'being with'. A 'matter of fact' presence, as Winnicott might have called it. A 'going-on-being' presence that is hard to describe, being beyond self-interest, although imbued with a deep responsibility that is difficult to capture in words. We can well witness that attitude when we contemplate Mother and Child Raphael paintings, or any and all artistic attempts to illustrate what circulates between mother and babies. This will happen if the mother is given loving support herself. That happens naturally for some couples, or with extended family and friends. Our post-industrialized society has meant that genuine community groupings now exist less and less, and mothers suffer from isolation at a level never to date experienced in human history. Before, and of course still in some communities around the world, the 'baby and mother' were taken in charge by society as a whole. Naturally, mothers had other mothers, their own mother or their sisters or their cousin around them, so it was not a big deal to have a baby; it was part of the course of life. Now mothers have to go to specialists, or to classes, in order to find the sharing and support necessary for their capacities to be with.

The infant-massage classes run by the International Association of Infant Massage (IAIM, nd), to which I have belonged for 28 years, have put, along with the well-being and respect of the baby, parents *supporting one another* at the core of their values. What fascinates me the most, having read literally thousands of parents' evaluations over the course of my activities with this programme, is that most of the time, parents will write under 'What did you like best about the course?' – 'Meeting other parents'.

In a way, they also feel empowered if they learn strategies to help with their baby's colic, constipation and sleep problems, but even researchers around this programme say that it is *the whole* that works, not its pieces; and that often, the togetherness experienced by parents is what enables them to feel that they are not alone in their new adventure, and other parents wonder the same things; and parents with older babies can be the best advisers in the world. Parents simply need the presence of others to be able to care for their babies, and the financial security to do that.

I invite all governmental leaders to seriously consider helping parents to be with their babies, at the very least for one year, and even better, for three years, with the possibility of up to six years. In the longer run, such a change alone would surely save society a King's ransom of otherwise needlessly wasted remedial resources.

If there *is* to be organized advice or special classes, perhaps it should be to protect babies, giving their being and their senses the opportunity to develop, and to unfold in due time. Nothing else is needed.

References

Biddulph, S. (2006) *Raising Babies: Should Under-3's Go to Nursery?*, Harper Thorsons.

Bowlby, J. (1997) *Attachment: Volume One of the Attachment and Loss Trilogy: Attachment Vol 1*, London: Pimlico.

Elfer, P. (2007) 'Babies and young children in nurseries: using psychoanalytic ideas to explore tasks and interactions', *Children and Society*, 21, pp. 111–22.

Elfer, P. and Dearnley, K. (2007) 'Nurseries and emotional well-being: evaluating an emotionally containing model of professional development', *Early Years*, 27 (3), pp. 267–79.

Gerhardt, S. (2004) *Why Love Matters: How Affection Shapes a Baby's Brain*, London: Routledge.

International Association of Infant Massage (nd) Website: www.iaim.net

Lasch, C. (1979) *The Culture of Narcissism: American Life in an Age of Diminishing Expectations*, New York: Norton.

Sardello, R. and Sanders, C. (1999) 'Care of the senses: a neglected dimension of education', Chapter 12 in J. Kane (ed.), *Education, Information, and Imagination: Essays on Learning and Thinking*, Prentice-Hall/Merril: Columbus, Ohio, pp. 223–47.

Sigman, A. (2009) *The Spoilt Generation: Why Restoring Authority Will Make Our Children and Society Happier*, London: Paitkus.

Sunderland, M. (2008) *The Science of Parenting*, London: Dorling Kindersley.

CHAPTER 8

Current Perspectives on the Early Childhood Curriculum[1]

LILIAN G. KATZ

With the early childhood curriculum so much in the news in Britain today, not least through the recent Dame Clare Tickell Review of the Early Years Foundation Stage (EYFS), this chapter shares my current perspectives on the early years curriculum. However, I should mention that the ideas and concepts that I shall present here are based largely upon my own experience and study, and are grounded largely in North American practices and research. I will leave it to the reader to decide which of the ideas presented here are appropriate to the traditions and constraints operating in the contexts in which early childhood work takes place in Britain.

I have also now lectured in more than 50 countries, and I am always impressed by the similarities of the problems we early years educators face – for example, low status, poor pay and limited understanding among those who set policy and who are in charge, and so forth. The policy and governmental strategies introduced in England, in particular since the EYFS was introduced in 2008, certainly seem to have engendered strong and intense divisions amongst the various groups involved.

Some readers may be familiar with my work, and will know that I like to talk in terms of what are called *principles*. You could say that I make them up – not out of the blue, of course, but based on extensive and constant study, and a long, rich background of experience – my own, and the experiences of early childhood teachers who have shared their experiences and insights with me over many, many years of my career.

Before I get into the principles, I think it helps to keep in mind that anyone who has to design a curriculum – at any level and any subjects – must address four questions:

Question 1: *What* should be learned? Here we think through the aims, goals and objectives of our work.

Question 2: *When* should it be learned? As we struggle to answer this question, we must take into account what we know (and don't know) about the nature of development.

Question 3: *How* is it best learned, taking into account our answers to the first two questions. These answers are usually captured by the term 'pedagogy'.

Question 4: *How* can we tell how well we have answered the first three questions?

Answering this fourth question involves evaluation and assessment, examining outcomes, or performance standards – as our regulatory agencies call them. But I prefer to call them *effects*. A very big question for us is: *when* do we get the really important effects? We must certainly be concerned about the possible differences between short- and long-term effects. This is a very serious issue in our field, to which I will return later.

Alas, I cannot do complete justice to all of these important questions in such a short space – it is really a whole term's work. Also, I should warn the reader that in what follows, I may say something unkind about your favourite practices or activities! If I *do* say something unkind in this regard, please don't take it personally: take it professionally – that is, consider what I have suggested, and if it doesn't make sense to you, dismiss it. It is important to remember that we don't all have to agree with each other – on everything. If we were all alike, we'd only need one of us! And, of course, *I* might be wrong! (but I doubt it!).

The ideas presented in what follows are arranged into four parts, as follows:

Part I – What do we mean by 'a developmental approach' to early childhood education?

Part II – What should be learned?
Part III – How is it best learned?
Part IV – Some concluding comments.

I. What Does It Mean to Take a Developmental Approach to the Early Childhood Curriculum?

In terms of principles of practice, I will highlight two broad principles.

Principle 1: A developmental approach means that what we teach and how we teach changes with the ages of the learners, and the experience that comes with age.

Development is a particular kind of change. It is about change that is due to a combination of biology, maturation and experience (environment). Development has many dimensions, just two of the important ones being:

a   *The normative dimension* – i.e. typical by age; and
b   *The dynamic dimension* – the recursive cycle, how behaviour patterns tend to 'feed on themselves' – both positive and negative ones. Children caught in a negative cycle need the help of an adult to break the cycle.

A developmental approach to early years education takes into account *both* dimensions: the normative (what most children can do) and the dynamic (what young children should be able to do – based on what we know about long-term development). It seems to me that many of us, both in Britain and in our field in the USA, are suffering from the 'Push Down' phenomenon – that is, doing earlier and earlier to children what we should probably do later.

I also want to note that recent research on early neurological development (Blair, 2002) suggests that young children benefit greatly from *continuous, contingent interactions*. The best example of such continuous contingent interactions are *conversations*; they are sequences of behaviours involving two (or perhaps three or four) individuals in which participants respond in contingent fashion to the other in a sequence of such behaviours. But there must be something to talk about that is of interest, of concern, and that matters to the participants.

PRINCIPLE 2: Just because children *can* do something – i.e. normative – does not mean that they *should* do it.

What children *should* learn and *should* do must be decided on the basis of what best serves their development in the long term (dynamic) – to the extent that we know it! And there is still a great deal that we don't know about long-term effects.

II. What Should Children Be Learning?

Given what we do know, this is a surprisingly difficult question. I suggest that we can think about it in terms of four types of learning goals.

(a) Knowledge/understanding – I put this first on the list, not because it is more important than the other three, but because in most societies, educational institutions are charged with the responsibility for helping the young to acquire what it considers to be worthwhile knowledge.

There is of course a big question concerning what constitutes knowledge in the early years. I have attached the term 'understanding' here for what are probably obvious reasons. However, my intention is to emphasize helping children to understand more and more deeply and accurately the knowledge they are acquiring. I suggest that if children are coerced into behaving as though they understand something, but they really don't, then we undermine their confidence in their own intellectual powers, their own questions, ideas and thoughts, and they soon give up (Dweck, 1991).

(b) Skills – Skills are different from knowledge. They are usually thought of as small units of action that can be observed, or fairly easily inferred, from observation of behaviour. There are very many of them, depending on how specific we want to be. There are, for example, verbal skills, many social skills, physical (e.g. fine and gross motor skills, etc.).

Skills or skilfulness tend to require practice, and for young children should be acquired in the context of a sense of purposefulness.

(c) Dispositions – These are difficult to define. I usually think of them as habits of mind with intentions, and motives (not attitudes). It may help to think of the distinction between having:

- reading skills vs the disposition to be a reader; and
- listening skills vs the disposition to be a listener.

There are many examples. The main point here is that it is not much use to have the skills if the process of acquiring them is so painful that the learner never wants to use them. Clearly, we want children to acquire, for example, the skills involved in reading *and*, alongside this, the disposition to be readers – a life-long disposition to be readers. Dispositions cannot be learned from instruction – but they *can* be damaged by it! In addition, many important dispositions are most likely in-born; perhaps we could think of them as pre-dispositions. And perhaps they are stronger in some children than in others.

It seems reasonable to assume that the most important ones are in-born, e.g. dispositions to learn, to make sense of experience, the disposition to become related to others, the disposition to co-operate, protect and defend oneself – and perhaps many others, not all equally desirable.

I suggest that unless a child lives in a chaotic environment (which by definition does not make sense) – all children have the disposition to make the best sense they can of their experience. I suggest, also, that in addition to those that are in-born, many dispositions are learned from being around people who have them, and who are observed enacting them – see, for example, Graver Whitehurst's research on young children who observe adults reading and come to think of it as 'something people do' (Whitehurst, 1996; Storch and Whitechurch, 2001). So I suggest that we should ask ourselves: Can the dispositions we want to encourage and support in the children we teach be seen by them in us? And dispositions must be *behaved* in order to be strengthened.

(d) Feelings – Of course, many capacities for feeling are inborn. But many important feelings are learned from experience and simply cannot be learned from instruction, exhortation or indoctrination – although I do believe that adults do have a role in helping children to learn appropriate feelings (e.g. if a child is very upset about not getting a turn with a toy or activity, the teacher can say matter-of-factly something like, 'I know you're disappointed … but there's always tomorrow, and it might work out better tomorrow' – thus learning early on how to cope with set-backs and disappointments, from occasional – not frequent – incidents.

I usually hear a lot of talk about feelings of *self-esteem* and their importance – especially in the United States. I think that 'self-esteem' is a much misunderstood concept, and I suggest that it is better to focus on feelings of confidence, competence and so on. It should also be born in mind that self-esteem or self-confidence cannot be gained from flattery, from certificates with pictures of smiling bears saying 'You're special!'.

Self-esteem is often confused with narcissism; pre-occupation about how one looks to others, what others will think of us, a pattern of feelings that lead to emptiness, boredom and so on. Self-esteem is also strengthened with experience of overcoming difficulties, coping with low-moments, observing and noting one's own progress.

PRINCIPLE 3: If we want children to have self-esteem, we must esteem them.

This means we must give them opportunities to make decisions, choices, be consulted – and genuine choices, not phoney ones.

In sum, then, all four categories must be addressed and assessed explicitly, not by default.

In passing, it should be noted that there is interesting evidence that gang leaders have high self-esteem, and provoke incidents in which they can demonstrate to those around them how powerful they are (Baumeister et al., 1996). We must also periodically assess the progress of children in all four categories of learning goals, and not with tests! – but by developing portfolios of their work, of observations we have made of their behaviour, documenting their work, and so on.

PRINCIPLE 4: The younger the children, the more important it is to strengthen their dispositions to look more closely at events and phenomena in their own environment that are worth learning more about.

It is important to strengthen children's in-born disposition to make sense of *their own experience*. I recall visiting a Head Start programme some years ago during the last week of March in a large city in Wisconsin. All the four-year-olds were sitting around tables, and their task of the morning was to paste cotton balls on a page with a printed picture of a smiling lamb. Being a resident of Illinois, I was surprised to see the focus on a lamb, as the state of Wisconsin is known to us as 'the dairy state' – indeed, it says so on their automobile licence plates. But I thought that perhaps there was some nearby sheep farming, and that since it was the end of March and the beginning of spring, there might be some recent births of lambs nearby. So I asked one of the boys, 'Have you been to see some lambs?', to which he answered, 'No'. I then asked, 'So why are you doing this?', and he hesitated at first, and then responded with a slightly questioning tone, 'Because lambs like to march'. Somehow he was trying to make sense of the preceding calendar ritual and the irrelevant task at hand. It also reminds us of how developmentally inappropriate it is for preschoolers to spend time daily on the calendar ritual.

A developmentally appropriate curriculum is one that helps children to make better, fuller and deeper sense of their own experience. As children get older, we must help them make better sense of others' experiences and environments, those far away in both time and place.

PRINCIPLE 5: Unless children have early and frequent experience of what it feels like to understand something in depth, they cannot acquire the disposition to seek in-depth knowledge and understanding – to engage in life-long learning.

This is a very important disposition to nurture in a democratic society.

Another important factor about dispositions is that once they are lost or damaged, it may be that they cannot be 'put back in' later, e.g. the disposition to go on learning, finding things out, looking things up, and so on – this is all so important for citizens who have a right to vote in a democratic society.

PRINCIPLE 6: We must keep in mind the distinctions between the academic and the intellectual goals of education at every level.

In the USA many policy-makers, bureaucrats, government officials and many parents (parents are just like people) think that during the pre-school period, there are only two alternative curriculum approaches: 'Skill and drill, academic instruction' versus 'Play and paste'. Those are by no means the only two alternatives, however; and I suggest that we have a major responsibility to help our leaders, decision-makers and parents to understand the distinction between *academic* goals and *intellectual* goals. As children grow older, we must consider both.

It may help to clarify some distinctions between the two.

Academic Goals are activities which entail small, specific bits of information, knowledge and skills. Usually they are items that can be correct or incorrect. They are usually taught out of context, and the elements are learned by rote and are regurgitated, memorized and practised in work-sheets and exercises. They also have no internal logic: they are systems of symbols that developed over a long period of human history and activity, and must be learned, e.g. the alphabet and punctuation.

Intellectual Goals address the dispositions to make sense, analyse, synthesize, theorize and speculate about cause-and-effect relationships, make predictions, hypothesize, speculate, ponder, conjecture, and therefore they should be involved in in-depth investigations – that we refer to as 'projects' or 'project work'. Indeed, I used to see wonderful project work all over the UK in the 1960s and 1970s – where did it go, and why?

It should also be kept in mind that enjoyment is not the goal of education – it is the goal of entertainment. The goal of education is to engage the mind fully – including its moral and aesthetic sensibilities; and when we do that well, learners find it enjoyable and satisfying. I would emphasize satisfying – but that is a *by-product* of good teaching, and not the *goal* of teaching/education.

In my view, children in early childhood programmes are routinely engaged in far too much mindless and banal activity – colouring, and cutting and pasting the same silly pictures. These are often items made by the teachers; colouring pre-printed pictures of smiling animals. In the United States, too much time is spent on the holidays; two weeks of making Valentine cards, and so on.

PRINCIPLE 7: Introduction to formal academic instruction too early, and too intensely, may result in children learning the academic details, but at the expense of the dispositions to use them.

I refer to this as the *damaged disposition hypothesis*. As I have already suggested, it is not much use to acquire skills if the processes of acquiring and learning them is either so painful or boring that the dispositions to use them can be damaged, instead of strengthened. We are also informed by the research of Rebecca Marcon (2002), who followed up very low-income children who had been in two different kinds of preschool programmes – one very academic, and the other based on the High/Scope curriculum. When she followed these children through into their elementary school years, the children in the academic programme did not have any advantage, and in fact its damaging effects seemed to be greater for boys.

So why more damaging for boys? While this is difficult to interpret, I suggest that boys do not so easily accept being placed in the passive role that is implied in the academic curriculum approach, whereas girls seem to accept passivity more easily.

PRINCIPLE 8: Children come to school with different frequencies of exposure to academic types of activities, e.g. counting, reading signs, listening to stories, being read to, learning songs, holding pencils, trying to write their names, etc.

As a consequence, they vary in school readiness-related skills, but I suggest that it is a good idea to assume that they all come to school with powerful intellectual dispositions – e.g. to make sense of experience (unless they are growing in a chaotic environment).

It requires substantial intellectual skills to cope with stressful environments; just because children are poor doesn't mean that they don't struggle to make sense of their environments and the actions of the people around them, just as children from affluent families do. These intellectual dispositions must be supported, appreciated, strengthened and used: in other words, it is important not to confuse socio-economic status with intellectual powers, even if it may be related to academic or school readiness.

PRINCIPLE 9: The younger the children, the larger the role of adults in helping them to achieve social competence.

This is a big topic – a whole book could easily be devoted to it. Evidence piles up just about daily that unless a child achieves at least a minimal level of social competence by about age six, he or she is at risk for the rest of his/her life. The risks include school failure, dropping out, employment difficulties, marital adjustment difficulties and parenting problems. Many young children get into the negative recursive cycle – e.g. a child with a poor social approach and communication skills may be avoided or ignored by peers, and will therefore lack opportunities to polish whatever skills she or he might have, and to acquire and build new ones – and is therefore more avoided and ignored, in a negative recursive cycle.

Such a cycle can only be broken with the help of an adult, and it must be done, and is relatively easy to do early in life, and very hard to do once into the primary school years. There is some research to indicate that children who are consistently rejected by their peers eventually find each other and gain – finally – a sense of belonging to a peer group based on their shared bitterness, animosity, if not hatred, for the out-group (Baumeister et al., 1996).

It is important to emphasize that social competence is not learned through instruction. Young children must have the opportunity for small group work, with individuals making their own contributions to the total achievement. They must have the opportunity to take responsibility, to argue, resolve differences, co-operate, listen to each other, help each other, and so on.

III: How Is All This Best Learned?

Given this view of what should be learned, and when it should be learned, then how is all this best learned?

PRINCIPLE 10: The younger the children, the more they learn through *interactive* experiences, active vs passive, interactive vs receptive experiences, or from the transmission of information.

In other words, the younger the children, the more is learned through direct experience vs indirect experience. That doesn't mean that children don't learn through passive, receptive experiences – e.g. stories, movies, TV – some things we might not want them to learn. But the disposition to go on learning – the goal of all education, life-long learning – the later ability to learn stuff that is not yet known, requires early interactive experience, discussion and arguing skills. And I think we have some data to show that these kinds of dispositions and skills are better learned in mixed-age groups (Katz et al., 1990).

PRINCIPLE 11: Young children must have opportunities to work on a topic over an extended period of time.

The children's work and play should be satisfying. I think we underestimate children's capacities to gain satisfaction from hard work, from effort at something that is important to them.

Principle 12: Children should be working part of the time at investigating phenomena and events around them that are worthy of their attention and understanding.

I believe that one of the responsibilities of adults is to educate children's attention. This means that children should be involved in in-depth investigations of worthwhile topics. Remember that teaching is not only covering the subject, it is also *un*covering the subject; so that children deepen their knowledge and understanding of what goes on behind the scenes, how things are made, where they come from, how they grow, the sequence in which things occur, the tools people around them use, the materials involved, and the long processes involved in providing and producing so many of the things important for our safety and survival and a good quality of life. What is crucial is what the people around young children do, and know, in relation to their well-being and safety. This is one reason why the project approach can be so effective.

IV: Conclusion

I have tried to share my own views of what education is about. To me it is about developing certain dispositions in the young. These dispositions should include being reflective, inquisitive, inventive, resourceful, full of wonder (wonder-full?), wonderment and puzzlement. These dispositions should include the habits of searching for evidence; they should also include the dispositions to be tender, courageous, caring, compassionate and should certainly include some humour as well! But I refer you to the definition of education provided by the British philosopher of education, R.S. Peters (1963):

> To be educated is not to have arrived at a destination; it is to travel with a different view. What is required is not feverish preparation for something that lies ahead, but to work with a precision, passion and taste at worthwhile things that lie at hand.

I really believe that each of us must come to care about everyone else's children. We must come to see that the well-being of our own individual children is intimately linked to the well-being of all other people's children. After all, when one of our own children needs life-saving surgery, someone else's child will perform it; when one of our own children is threatened or harmed by violence on the streets, someone else's child will commit it. The good life for our own children can only be secured if it is also secured for all other people's children. But to worry about all other people's children is not just a strategic or practical matter; it is a moral and ethical one: to strive to secure the well-being of all other people's children *is also right*.

As we address those who make the national policy decisions, we should approach them with the assumption that they have good intentions – even if that assumption is difficult at times! Do your utmost to resist the temptation to become opponents; and remember that adversaries and enemies tend to become alike in many fundamental ways.

Come together with your colleagues – those you disagree with, as well as those you agree with, and work out a position statement about what you know and what you believe. Make a well-reasoned statement, and then propose modifications in the law that will address our best current understandings of how children best grow, develop, and learn – with the sincere intention of helping the decision-makers to achieve their well-meaning intentions.

And – remember, finally, that whoever might be the leader of your country in 30–40 years from now might well be in someone's early years setting or programme today; and I hope she is having a good experience!

Note

1   This chapter is substantially based on the keynote address given by Professor Katz to the first Open EYE Conference, London, 16 February 2008.

References

Baumeister, R.F., Smart, L. and Boden, J.M. (1996) 'Relation of threatened egotism to violence and aggression: the dark side of high self-esteem', *Psychological Review*, 103 (1): 5–33.

Blair, C. (2002) 'School readiness: integrating cognition and emotion in a neurobiological conceptualization of children's functioning at school entry', *American Psychologist*, 57 (2): 111–27.

Dweck, C. (1991) 'Self-theories and goals: their role in motivation, personality, and development', in R.A. Dienstbier (ed.), *Perspectives on Motivation. Nebraska Symposium on Motivation, 1990*, Lincoln, NE: University of Nebraska Press, pp. 199–236.

Katz, L.G., Evangelou, D. and Hartman, J.A. (1990) *The Case for Mixed-age Grouping in Early Childhood Education*, Washington, D.C.: National Association for the Education of Young Children.

Marcon, R. (2002) 'Moving up the grades: relationship between preschool model and later school success', *Early Childhood Research and Practice*, 4 (1): downloadable at: http://ecrp.uiuc.edu/v4n1/marcon.html (retrieved 25 May 2011).

Peters, R.S. (1963) 'Education as initiation', Inaugural Lecture in the University of London; reprinted in his *Authority, Responsibility and Education*, London: Allen & Unwin; rev edn, 1973; also in R. Curren (ed.), *Philosophy of Education: An Anthology*, Chichester: Wiley-Blackwell, 2006, pp. 55–67.

Storch, S.A. and Whitechurch, G.J. (2001) 'The role of family and home in the literacy development of children from low-income backgrounds', *New Directions for Child and Adolescent Development*, 92 (Summer): 53–72.

Whitehurst, G.J. (1996) 'A structural equation model of the role of home literacy environment in the development of emergent literacy skills in children from low-income backgrounds', paper presented at the Annual Convention of the American Educational Research Association, New York, NY.

CHAPTER 9

Physical Foundations for Learning

SALLY GODDARD BLYTHE

Learning is not all in the mind but is also a physical activity.[1] One of the first tasks a young child needs to master is physical control of his body in space, with movement experience acting as both the challenge and the teacher. Throughout life, movement acts as the primary medium through which information derived from the senses is integrated, and knowledge of the world is expressed. Even thought and perception are an internalized simulation of action.[2] A child's motor abilities are therefore essential tools for learning, and motor skills at different stages of development provide a reflection of maturity in the functioning of the central nervous system – the relationship between the brain and body – which provides the foundation for learning.

A child's brain is not the same as an adult brain. Different regions of the cerebral cortex, the largest structure of the forebrain which contains the higher brain centres controlling intellectual, sensory and motor functions, mature at different rates. The first area to mature is the motor area, followed by the sensory area, with association areas being the last to mature, continuing growth into the twenties or thirties.[3] The higher problems of thinking, planning and problem solving performed by the frontal lobes take years to develop.[4]

At birth, connections to the superficial layer of the cortex are only tenuously formed. The neonate is equipped with a series of survival responses to various environmental stimuli which enable him to breathe, to 'root' or search for the breast if the side of his face is touched, to suckle and to grasp if something is placed in the palm of his hand, or pressure is applied to the soles of his feet. He also has a series of reflexes which evoke responses to change in position. These innate reflex responses are mediated at the lowest level of the brain – the brainstem – but as connections to higher centres in the brain strengthen during the first weeks, months and years of life, the functional direction and organized control of movement proceed from the lowest (brainstem) to the highest level of the central nervous system (cortex). 'The process of corticalization is characterised by the emergence of behaviours organised at sequentially higher levels in the central nervous system with lower levels being recruited into the service of higher functions as maturation takes place.'[5]

Children's motor development is dependent primarily on overall physical maturation, especially skeletal and neuro-muscular development combined with physical interaction with the environment. Children need opportunity for exercise and practice, not only to develop strength but also control and dexterity. Infants have a natural repertoire of rhythmic motor activities which involve kicking, waving, punching, stretching, rocking and twisting, and these rhythmic activities or primary motor vocabulary provide an important transition from uncoordinated activity to coordinated motor behaviour,[6] but they occur in the context of *opportunity*. Opportunity requires the space and time to experience physical activity in all sorts of different ways, from the gross motor movements involved in rolling, walking, running and jumping to the fine motor skills needed for feeding and writing. Development of the pincer grip needed to hold and use a writing implement comfortably provides one example of how these dual processes of maturation and experience interact in the early years to develop the more complex motor skills needed to support academic learning.

If an object is placed in the palm of a new-born baby's hand, the neonate will grasp the object by curling its fingers successively around the stimulus, beginning with the middle finger, followed by the ring and little fingers, index finger and thumb,[7] with the thumb usually nestling underneath the index finger (see Figure 1). In the first few days after birth, this Palmar Reflex is strong enough to support the baby's weight if suspended.

The Palmar Reflex remains present in healthy infants up to the fifth month of life, but should be inhibited by higher centres in the brain by the age of one year. The process of inhibition is a gradual one. By the fifth month, the infant starts to be able to let go of an object, although initially this may occur as much by accident as by design.

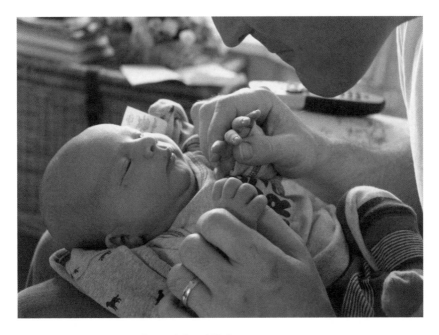

Figure 1   Palmar Grasp Reflex in 4-day-old baby

This is the stage when the infant will start to drop its toys or food, and then whimper in frustration when it cannot retrieve the object itself. Parents quickly tire of the game, but the infant is learning to do something very important: he is learning how to 'let go'. This is a precursor to being able to bring the thumb and forefinger together without the whole hand opening or closing. Modification of the Palmar Reflex also occurs as a result of other motor experiences. If, for example, infants are given plenty of 'tummy time' when awake, the action of using the hands to support the weight of the body also helps to moderate sensitivity to touch in the palmar region of the hand and inhibit the grasp response (see Figures 2 and 3).

When a child starts to apply fine motor skills to tasks like holding a pencil to write, he starts by repeating earlier patterns. He will, for example, use a cross-palmar grasp with the whole hand clutching the chalk or pencil, and usually with the arm turned inwards. As the arm is not well supported on the writing surface, the child uses gross rather than fine motor actions to draw or write. A little later, a similar grasp is used, but the child notices that he can control the pencil better if he extends his index finger. Eventually he will learn to use a tripod pincer grip, with the third finger supporting the pencil, the forearm

Figures 2 and 3
Upper body weight, supported using the arms and hands, helps to inhibit the Palmar
Reflex and develop head, neck and upper body strength

supported on the surface and the arm turned outwards, enabling
him to use fine motor actions. This later dexterity is dependent on
successful completion of earlier stages. If a young child is forced to
write before he has the motor skills in place to support writing, there
is a risk he will remain 'stuck' at an immature stage of motor competence. Figure 4 shows the writing grip of an older child who still has
a Palmar Grasp Reflex.

Figure 4
Palmar Grasp Reflex evident in the writing
grip of a school-aged child

Why Does Physical Development Matter?

Children in England and Northern Ireland already start compulsory education earlier than in any other country in Europe, with the
exception of the Netherlands and Malta, and earlier than children in
either the United States or Australia.

Table 1 Age of Compulsory Education in other European Countries

Age	Country
4 years	Northern Ireland
5 years	England, Malta, Netherlands, Scotland, Wales
6 years	Austria, Belgium, Cyprus, Czech Republic, France, Germany, Greece, Hungary, Iceland, (Republic of) Ireland, Italy, Liechtenstein, Luxembourg, Norway, Portugal, Romania, Slovakia, Slovenia, Spain, Turkey

In Scotland, compulsory education starts at age five, although many children start at four because schools have a single intake at the beginning of the school year. Local authorities set a cut-off date (normally 1 March) defining the cohort of children eligible to start school at the beginning of the following school year (normally in August). This means that Scottish children do not usually start school below the age of four years and six months.

In England and Wales, compulsory school starting age is set at five, although the majority of children actually start school at four. The cut-off date is the same as the beginning of the school year, with the result that children born in August can start school in the September, just after their fourth birthday. These children are in every sense biologically and developmentally 9–12 months younger than their peers who were born earlier in the academic year, and are in many cases placed at an academic disadvantage if forced into reading and writing before they are developmentally ready to do so. Children who have developmental delays in kindergarten, and which are not corrected, can go on to develop distorted learning,[8] 'Incorrect perceptions, poor learning skills, and inability to conceptualise have a cumulative effect and result in increasingly uneven development.'[9]

There are considerable individual differences in the age at which children are 'ready to read', with some children being ready as early as 4–4½ years of age, while others are not ready until 6+ years. One school of thought used to believe that reading readiness coincided with signs of biological development such as the onset of shedding of the first milk teeth, which usually begins between 6 and 6½ years of age, in line with the time when children in many other European countries begin compulsory education.

The Early Years Foundation Stage (EYFS) framework, which became law in England in the autumn of 2008, set out up to 500 developmental milestones between birth and primary school, and required the under-fives to reach targets on 69 writing, problem-solving and numeracy skills.[10]

While many of the aims of the document were praiseworthy, a number of the *specific* learning goals and targets in relation to reading, writing and numeracy skills failed to take developmental stages, neurological maturation and individual developmental differences, including gender differences, into account.

Boys and girls develop different skills at different times in development, with girls tending to be ahead of boys in the development of the fine motor and language skills needed for reading and writing in the early years, while boys show increased maturity in spatial skills from an earlier age.

> The most profound difference between girls and boys is not in any brain structure *per se*, but rather in the *sequence* of development of the various brain regions. The different regions of the brain develop in a different sequence in girls compared with boys – this is the key insight from the past five years of neuroscience research in brain development. In 2007, the world's largest study of brain development in children published their most comprehensive study to date, demonstrating that there is no overlap in the trajectories of brain development in girls and boys.[11, 12]

In other words, the brains of boys and girls are different at various stages in development.

Children who are forced into reading and writing at the expense of developing the supporting physical skills before they are ready risk experiencing specific learning difficulties and under-achievement later on (cf. Chapter 17). As one former head teacher of a primary school in the Midlands said, 'Alas, for some children this "one size fits all", or "practice more of the same" approach simply doesn't work'.[13]

While all children should be provided with the *opportunity* to develop literacy and numeracy skills in the early years, the setting of specific literacy and numeracy *targets* in the early years runs a risk of labelling children as under-achievers before they begin formal education, also potentially depriving them of the necessary sensory-motor and play experiences which are needed to develop the physical skills, which support all higher aspects of learning.

Examples of some of the above-mentioned targets set out in the original EYFS document included:

- Write their own names and other things such as labels and captions, and begin to form simple sentences, sometimes using punctuation.
- Use a pencil and hold it effectively to form recognizable letters, most of which are correctly formed.
- Re-tell narratives in the correct *sequence*, drawing on language patterns of stories.
- Reads a range of familiar and common words and simple sentences independently.
- Shows an understanding of how information can be found in non-fiction texts to answer questions about where, who, why and how.
- Reads books of own choice with some fluency and accuracy.
- Recognizes, counts, orders, writes and uses numbers up to 20.

Emphasis on literacy and numeracy outcomes (targets) failed to take into account that in early development there are crucial 'windows of opportunity' for developing certain skills at different times. In the first three and a half years of life, pathways involved in control of posture, balance and eye movements develop at a faster rate than they will at any other time for the remainder of life. These pathways are entrained as a result of physical interaction with the environment – through crawling, rolling, falling over, climbing up and down stairs, jumping, playing 'peek-a-boo' with Mum and rough and tumble play with Dad. These physical activities help to develop proprioceptive awareness. Proprioception is the feedback the brain receives from the muscles, tendons and joints, which helps to draw an internal 'map' of the physical body in the brain, enabling a child to know where his body is in space, even when the eyes are closed.

The cerebral cortex – the seat of cognitive learning and reasoning – also develops at a prodigious rate in the early years, but different regions develop at different times in development. The right hemisphere is slightly ahead of the left up until approximately 7 years of age, and has more downward connections linking it to the areas involved in basic physical functions, such as control of movement, sensory processing, emotion and emotional memory. The right side of the brain processes information holistically, seeing the whole picture but not the details contained within. It has limited verbal language abilities, but understands the non-verbal aspects of language, and it has other specialized abilities. Thus, it is primarily visual in the way that it processes information; it is the expert in solving visuo-spatial problems such as puzzles and mazes, and it is good at drawing. The right brain has a natural ability to copy musical melodies and rhythm, meaning that it is particularly receptive to learning through song, rhythm, rhyme and dance. It is the side of the brain that entertains fantasy and believes that anything is possible. The years of optimum right-hemisphere development between 4 and 7 are the years when learning is naturally linked to sensory-motor activity.

Sequences of information like the alphabet or, later on, multiplication tables can be memorized easily if they are learned through movement or put into rhyme, rhythm or song. These are the years when children need to be engaged in play, in exploring the physical environment, building sand-castles and dens, playing games, learning traditional dances, rhymes and stories, learning patterns through movement which imprint the information into the brain to form the basis for the pattern recognition (visual perception) of letter and number symbols, directional awareness (b or d, 2 or 5), as well as strengthening the body through gross motor activities. The right side of the brain sees whole words as pictures, but it cannot take the words apart to build words from individual letters. This is a left-brain skill which is also linked to auditory discrimination and auditory processing.[14]

The left hemisphere also develops rapidly through the early years, and has its own specialist functions. As it increases in maturity, the left brain is logical and analytical. If it cannot solve a problem as a whole, it will attempt to break the problem down into smaller components and examine them piece by piece. It has specialist centres for speech and understanding verbal language, for phonetic decoding, timing and aspects of numeracy, but it cannot solve mathematical problems without the support of the right hemisphere. The executive functions of both sides of the brain are built upon the firm foundations of sensory motor integration, which are primed in the first 3½ years of life, developed between 4 and 7 years of age through physical interaction and play, and which go through an important stage of neurological reorganization between 6½ and 7½ years of age – when pathways linking the two hemispheres, the balance mechanism and a part of the brain involved in the regulation of fine motor control and certain sequential tasks (the cerebellum) complete a stage of myelination (the neurological equivalent to insulating an electrical circuit). This is the same age when children *begin* compulsory education in many other countries.

Centres in the right and left sides of the brain process written material in different ways. While the right brain allows children to recognize whole words visually (like pictures) by shape, usually recognizing the first and last letter and guessing at the letters in between, reading centres in the left brain and connections to the right brain do not develop until 6½–8 years of age in girls, and 7–9 years in boys. 'It is the reading centre in the left brain that allows children to match sounds to letters and enables them to sound out words phonetically',[15] so that they can learn how to spell. The building blocks for phonetic decoding are assembled in the early years through learning to listen to, and to use, music, stories, rhyme, tongue twisters, conversation and 'sounding out'. Spoken language has its origins in music, which contains all the elements of speech – pitch, tone, rhythm, timing, cadence and phrasing. The phonetic aspects of written language have developed from an oral tradition and the medium of speech. Learning to read begins with visual and auditory pattern recognition; writing begins with drawing.

In What Way Does Physical Development Influence Educational Performance?

Maturation of pathways involved in control of the body, particularly those relating to balance, posture and proprioception, provide the basis for subsequent control of coordination, oculo-motor functioning (eye movements) and visual-perception. The ocular-motor skills of convergence and tracking are essential for a child to visually follow a line of print without letters and words separating on the page or the eyes jumping further along the line, to the line above or the line below. While visual acuity (eyesight) can be corrected with glasses, oculo-motor dysfunction is often linked to immature postural control, and responds to physical exercises aimed at improving functioning within the central nervous system.[16] Oculo-motor dysfunction can also affect visual perception (how the brain interprets visual information), with the result that the image the brain sees is a distorted version of the original. Children whose physical skills are under-developed in the pre-school years need *more* time and opportunity to develop their physical skills through free and structured play *before* reaching a stage of 'readiness' for sedentary and fine motor tasks such as reading, writing and numeracy.

Reading, writing, listening, the ability to sit still and focus attention on one task without being distracted, are all linked to maturity in the functioning of the central nervous system (CNS). Not only is the CNS developed through physical play, but CNS maturity is *reflected* in specific physical skills such as postural control, balance, coordination and control of eye movements. Control of eye movements is essential for reading, writing, copying, aligning columns correctly in maths, catching a ball and the ability to ignore irrelevant visual stimuli within a given visual field in order to focus attention on one task.

Thirty years ago, all children were assessed by a school doctor prior to starting school at rising 5 years of age, using a range of simple tests such as standing on one leg, stacking a pile of blocks, and hopping across the room. As the drive towards 'evidence-based' medicine gathered momentum, it became necessary to justify routine testing with access to effective remedial intervention. At the time, it was not known what to do with children who failed these tests, but whose problems were not severe enough to fit into any diagnostic category or to qualify for physiotherapy, occupational therapy or referral to other medical agencies, and routine testing of all children was phased out. As a result, many children with immature physical skills or a slower rate of neurological maturation in the early years simply slip through the net, and are at greater risk of becoming part of a hidden percentage of educational under-achievers.

A series of studies carried out in the United Kingdom between 2000 and 2005 examined aspects of physical development in 672 children in primary schools in Northern Ireland. They revealed that 48 per cent of 5–6-year-olds and 35 per cent of 8–9-year-olds in mainstream schools still had traces of infant (primitive) reflexes which should not be active beyond the first year of life. The presence of primitive reflexes at key stages in development provides indicators of immaturity in the functioning of the CNS, with particular effect on postural control, balance, motor skills and dependent functions. Some 15 per cent (49) of the 5–6-year-old group had a reading age below their chronological age. Of these, 28 also had elevated levels of retained reflexes. When reflex scores were compared to educational achievement, elevated levels of retained reflexes were correlated with poor educational achievement at baseline.

The same projects also introduced a development movement programme into the school day (i.e. the INPP Developmental Movement Programme for use in schools with special needs children) for children in the 8–9-year-old group. Children who undertook the developmental movement programme showed a statistically significant greater decrease in retained reflexes than children who did not undertake the exercises, and also highly significant improvement in balance and coordination, together with a small but statistically significant increase in a measure of cognitive development over children who did not undertake the exercises. No difference was found in reading, handwriting or spelling in children who were already achieving at or near their chronological age; but for children with high levels of retained reflexes *and* a reading age below their chronological age, those who undertook the exercise programme made greater progress. The researchers concluded that retained infant reflexes were correlated with poorer cognitive development, poor balance and teacher assessment of poor concentration/coordination in the 5–6-year-old group. Neurological scores and teacher assessment at baseline predicted poorer reading and literacy scores at the end of the study. In other words, there was a link between children's neuro-motor maturity and educational outcomes.

Other researchers have documented a correlation between retained infant primitive reflexes, poorer reading performance[17] and Attention Deficit Hyperactivity Disorder (ADHD).[18, 19] The Northern Ireland study was followed by an independent project undertaken with 64 children in schools located in areas of social deprivation in Northumberland. This project set out to investigate whether:

1 Retention of three primitive reflexes was present in children in mainstream primary schools in the United Kingdom;
2 There was a link between immature motor skills and lower performance in reading, writing, spelling, maths and drawing;
3 Retained primitive reflexes responded to a developmental movement programme (the INPP programme for schools)

Teachers found that 88.5 per cent of children in the 7–8-year-old group and 40 per cent of children in the 4–6-year-old group had signs of residual primitive reflexes. Higher scores on tests for retained primitive reflexes correlated with lower performance on the draw a person

(DAP) test. The DAP test provides one measure of non-verbal cognitive performance. Non-verbal cognitive performance, often treated as the poor relation when assessing children's educational performance, contributes up to 90 per cent to effective communication, and is fundamental to children's spatial, social and communication abilities, including the ability to 'read' and respond appropriately to the body language of others. Five pupils who had been referred to the Behaviour Support Service during the research period responded well to the developmental exercise programme, and all case referrals to the Behavioural Support Service were closed within one term of starting the INPP programme without any specific behavioural intervention having been carried out. Although the numbers involved are too small to infer a direct causal link, the findings suggest a possible relationship between non-verbal skills and behaviour. Teachers also reported that the experience of teaching the developmental exercises permeated into good behavioural strategies, including the continuation of a calm and positive atmosphere in the classroom after the exercise sessions.[20]

These findings are not confined to the United Kingdom. Similar projects have been undertaken in Germany, Mexico[21] and Hungary. In Hungary, reporting on the use of a daily developmental movement programme in a school in Budapest between November 2009 and February 2011, the teacher wrote:

> It was an amazing experience for us to see that even those children who were apparently coping with school very well showed a (partly) very immature nervous system. We had no idea that they had traces of primitive reflexes, and were very surprised by the high scores that were found of those reflexes during the testing procedures.
>
> As their form teacher, I saw those children every day, for long hours. I started to observe the signs of their compensatory mechanisms. I found that they were very smart and adept at compensating for their physical shortcomings.
>
> The signs were, among others: almost a spastic way of holding their pencil; the position of their legs and feet under the chair/table; supporting their head with their arm, elbow; mouth and tongue movements during writing; turning their booklet, sheets, difficulties with conducting their written tasks, etc.
>
> Being an elementary school teacher, I used to think before that those signs were signs of tiredness or lack of energy, primarily

resulting from insufficient focus and concentration. All these were problems which in my eyes they could easily overcome if they only wanted to.

But what I had learned about the reflexes made me wiser now. I altered my point of view and we started with the daily exercises. We called it our 'slow gym', introducing and anchoring a new way of thinking and feeling for the children about themselves. They had to learn how to slow down.

This brought fantastic and new things in their lives, and also in ours. For example: they had to realise very soon that if they paid more attention to the others than to themselves, they could not concentrate on their own movements and had less success realising them. Their physical balance was improving week by week. During the process I could observe several children 'falling apart' for a certain period of time, or just the opposite: improved concentration during the realisation of their tasks.

Also the signs of mixed laterality started to disappear, and the quiet atmosphere in the class, each time after finishing the exercises, was remarkable.

After ending the Program I recently re-tested the children. I could not believe my eyes: these were definitely not the same children standing in front of me as the ones 15–16 months ago. They didn't stumble, didn't falter across their own feet, were not suffering from dizziness any more, their laterality had been established, and whilst waiting, they were lined up quietly in a row. I was amazed and extremely happy.

They can read much-much more fluently, their handwriting shows a dramatic improvement, they 'got wings' in mathematics, their attention and concentration span is excellent, and they are happy about their own achievements, which is motivating them to want to tackle more and more difficult challenges.

When I visit them, their faces are radiating from happiness and they are proud to show their school results to me.[22]

Whereas in the United Kingdom increased emphasis has been placed on the teaching and assessment of literacy and numeracy skills in the early years, other countries are not so anxious to force their children into reading and writing. Finland, for example, gives priority to parental involvement in the early years, offering flexibility in childcare options, physical interaction, outdoor play and learning through (guided) experience until the age of starting formal school. Children in Finland do not start compulsory education until seven years of age.

The principle aims of the curriculum, as described in a leaflet produced by the Ministry of Social Affairs and Health in Helsinki, are as follows:

> To promote the child's overall well-being so as to ensure the best possible conditions for growth, learning and development. Hence the child is able to enjoy the company of others, experiencing joy and freedom of action in an unhurried, safe atmosphere. The child is an active learner whose learning is guided by curiosity, the will to explore and joy of realisation. The core of learning is in the interaction between children, adults and the environment. To this end, the environment should be versatile. Nature and the immediate neighbourhood are important elements of the environment, and the environment enables the use of all senses and the whole body for play, movement, expression, experimentation and insights.
>
> Playing, movement, exploration and self-expression through different forms of art are ways of acting and thinking peculiar to children. Parents have the primary right to and responsibility for their child's education. They also know their child best. Therefore, the educators have a key role in sharing the day-to-day education and care of the young child with the parents.[23]

A typical day for the pre-school child takes physical and developmental needs into account. Some children may arrive as early as 7 a.m., but the formal day begins at 8 a.m.:

8–8.30	Breakfast time
8.30	Morning meeting of children. As a group, children talk about what has happened in the calendar and what they are going to do today; read a story or sing together.
9–10	Work activities
10–11	Outdoor play
11	Circle time – reading a book or singing together
11.30–12	Lunch. Some children may go home after lunch
12–12.30	General story time
1–2	Rest or sleep time. A special rest area is provided
2	Snack
2.30–3.30	Indoor play to finish things off as concentration tends to drop off at this time of day.
3.30–5	Outdoor play (unless the weather is very bad)

Children are equipped with suitable clothing for outdoor play in all weathers, and plenty of outdoor space and toys are provided. The only time children will not go out to play is if the temperature falls below −15 degrees centigrade! There is also a rest area provided where children can snuggle down on a small bed with a blanket for the set 'rest period' in the early afternoon.[24] Early years education concentrates on getting the whole child ready for formal learning by developing physical (including visual) skills through outdoor play and indoor games and activities, and developing the auditory system through singing, speaking and listening to stories. It also recognizes that children under the age of 5 need rest periods.

Dame Clare Tickell's review of the EYFS, published in March 2011, has recommended that the 69 targets set out in the original document be reduced to 17, giving particular focus on three key areas:

1 Communication and language;
2 Emotional development;
3 Physical development.

Whilst none of these areas are mutually exclusive and should be developed alongside each other, research suggests that it is a child's physical development which acts as the linchpin that holds all areas together. In the early years, training all aspects of physical development *is* the primary curriculum which provides children with the tools they need for education so that good teaching can be effective.

Notes

1 E. Silvester, 'Inspiring Partnerships. Case studies by schools for schools', DVD produced by the Youth Sport Trust, 2006; see www.youthsporttrust. org

2 A. Berthoz, *The Brain's Sense of Movement,* Cambridge, Mass.: Harvard University Press, 2000.

3 O. Spreen, D. Tupper, A. Risser, H. Tuokko and D. Edgell, *Human Development Neuropsychology,* New York: Oxford University Press, 1984.

4 F.P. Rice, *Human Development: A Lifespan Approach,* Englewood Cliffs, NJ: Prentice-Hall, 1995.

5 S.A. Goddard Blythe, *Attention, Balance and Coordination: The A,B,C of Learning Success,* Chichester: Wiley-Blackwell, 2009.

6 E. Thelan, 'Rhythmical behavior in infancy: an ethological perspective', *Developmental Psychology,* 17, 1981: 237, 257.

7   H.F.R. Prechtl, 'Über die Koppelung von Saugen und Greifreflex beim Säugling', *Naturwissenschaften*, 12, 1953: 347.

8   M. Mutti, M.A. Harold, M.D. Sterling, N. Martin and N.V. Spalding, 'Quick neurological screening test II (QNST-II)', Los Angeles: Western Psychological Services.

9   M. Critchley, *The Dyslexic Child*, London: William Heineman Medical Books, 1970.

10   Statutory framework for the Early Years Foundation Stage (EYFS), London: Department of Education and Skills, 2008.

11   www.singlesexschools.org/research-brains.htm

12   R.K. Lenroot, N. Gogtay, D.K. Greenstein, E. Molloy Wells, G.L. Wallace, L.S. Clasen, J.D. Blumenthal, J. Lerch, A.P. Zijdenbos, A.C. Evans, P.M. Thompson and J.N. Giedd, 'Sexual dimorphism of brain developmental trajectories during childhood and adolescence', *Neuroimage*, 36 (4) (July), 2007: 1065–73; downloadable at: http://www.ncbi.nlm.nih.gov/pmc/articles/PMC2040300/ (retrieved 25 June 2011).

13   P. Griffin, Personal communication, 2008.

14   S.A. Goddard Blythe, *The Well Balanced Child*, Stroud: Hawthorn Press, 2004.

15   S. Johnson, 'Teaching our children to read, write and spell', *Lilipoh*, 49/12, 2007.

16   W. Bein-Wierzbinski, 'Persistent primitive reflexes in elementary school children: effect on oculomotor and visual perception', paper presented at the 13th European Conference of Neuro-Developmental Delay in Children with Specific Learning Difficulties, Chester, UK, 2001.

17   M. McPhillips and J.A. Jordan-Black, 'Primary reflex persistence in children with reading difficulties (dyslexia): a cross-sectional study', *Neuropsychologia*, 45, 2007: 748–54.

18   N. O'Dell and P. Cooke, *Stopping Hyperactivity – A New Solution,* Garden City Park, NY: Avery Publishing Group, 1996.

19   M. Taylor, S. Hougton and E. Chapman, 'Primitive reflexes and Attention Deficit Disorder: Developmental origins of classroom dysfunction', *International Journal of Special Education*, 19 (1), 2004.

20   S.A. Goddard Blythe, 'Neuro-motor maturity as an indicator of developmental readiness for education', paper presented at the Institute for Neuro-Physiological Psychology Conference, Miami, 11–12 April 2010; due to be published in Proceedings of the PWN Conference on Movement, Sight and Hearing – The Basis for Learning, Warsaw University of Applied Education, 17 September 2011.

21   G. Garcia, 'Results from the first evaluation of the INPP Programme for schools at the Liceo de Monterrey, Mexico', presented at the Institute for Neuro-Physiological Psychology Conference, Miami, 11–12 April 2010.

22   E. Kotormánné Erdei, Report from form teacher at Bakáts Tér Primary and Music School, Budapest, personal communication, 2011.

23   'Early childhood education and care in Finland'. Brochures of the Ministry of Social Affairs and Health 2004: 14, Helsinki.

24   S.A. Goddard Blythe, *The Genius of Natural Childhood*, Stroud: Hawthorn Press, 2011.

CHAPTER 10

The Unfolding Self –
The Essence of Personality

KIM SIMPSON

Freedom and Independence

> Supposing I said there was a planet without schools or teachers,
> where study was unknown, and yet the inhabitants – doing
> nothing but living and walking about – came to know all things,
> to carry in their minds the whole of learning; would you not think
> I was romancing? Well just this, which seems so fanciful as to be
> nothing but the invention of a fertile imagination, is a reality. The
> young child learns everything without knowing he is learning
> it, and in doing so passes little by little from the unconscious to
> the conscious, treading always in the paths of joy and love. How
> wonderful it would be if we could retain the prodigious capacity
> we had as children, of romping happily, jumping and playing,
> while learning at the same time the whole of a new language in all
> its intricacy?
>
> DR MARIA MONTESSORI, *THE ABSORBENT MIND*

How wonderful it would also be if we all shared Maria Montessori's
insight in realizing that in the early years, learning is not a problem.
Just imagine how liberating this would be for parents, for teachers
and especially for the child. As Montessori says, 'the young child
learns everything without knowing he is learning it':

> It is as if nature had safeguarded children from the influence
> of adult reasoning, so as to give priority to the inner teacher

who animates each of them. They have the chance to build up a complete psychic structure, before the intelligence of grownups can reach their spirit and produce changes in it. (ibid.)

Although Montessori was not the only early years' pioneer to hold such views, these quotations give a clear demonstration of the thrust of this chapter. It is so vital that children in the early years are protected from approaches which attempt to form their psyches in line with adult-centric goals and expectations. This protection will ensure that self-development is given a priority in the first few years of a child's life. If the potential in early childhood for self-education were truly recognized, then providing psychological and spiritual nutrients, both at home and in early educational environments, would be at a premium. The role of adults is essential in establishing healthy boundaries to maximize potential but, in their urgent quest for self-discovery, children recognize only too well the difference between support and control, and whilst they welcome the first, they are intrinsically programmed to resist the second.

I am not going to apologize for the idealism behind such a view as, with the Children's Society report in 2009 (Layard and Dunn, 2009) revealing that our children are some of the unhappiest in Europe, a bit of idealism is just what is needed if there is to be a change in the dynamics.

Over 35 years ago, I used the words 'The Freedom to be myself' in my promotional literature, as a succinct means of drawing parents' attention to the main focus in my nurseries. I knew even then that each unique child needed an enriching environment where, being free, they were able to follow their own inner teacher. I recognized that 'inner teacher' as the dynamic energy of will, which guided each child from within to develop a right relationship with themselves before they could develop a right relationship with others and with their world. I became determined that narrow and prescriptive approaches to what children should do, and when, how and what they should learn, would not take them away from their unique being, their intrinsic self. I also knew how important it was not to hold children back, but to provide an environment with a rich tapestry of learning potential.

The vast majority of parents recognize such an approach, as they passionately want their young children to enjoy their childhood, but they also, quite rightly, want them to learn. Prospective parents visiting my nursery express their relief when they are told that self-confidence, well-being and a joy in learning are our priorities for their children. Coupled with their relief, they also say that they are being led to believe that they should be teaching their children early if they want them to succeed. Parents welcome the message that children will succeed if they feel good about themselves, and with self-esteem as the true foundation on which everything else must be built.

It is very easy to come to a consensus that it is very difficult to stop children from learning. Who was it in the first two years of life that taught them to sit up, stand, crawl, walk and talk? It was the miracle of natural development, which literally unfolds unconsciously in every healthy child in every corner of the world. This unfolding has its own timescale and its own pattern, and we interfere with it at our peril, with the inherent dangers of diverting this natural 'flow'. Loving support and guidance are natural to parenting and this, of course, should be available when the need presents itself.

This free unfolding epitomizes the joy of childhood. Each child is unique and it is only by being free to follow their own internal developmental agendas, endowed by nature, that each child can develop and build their own unique individuality … – their emerging sense of self, more free from unnecessary early conditioning and adult expectations and fears.

In his book *The Philosophy of Freedom*, Rudolf Steiner wrote, 'I call a thing "free" which exists and acts from the pure necessity of its nature, and I call that "unfree" of which the being and action are precisely determined by something else'.

One of my happiest early memories was playing with my siblings in the hop fields of Herefordshire. We dug in the wonderful reddish earth, making our own sweet shop. Copious amounts of damp earth were dug up and moulded into bars of chocolate, with equal squares divided appropriately, whilst old rusty containers were pressed with soil to make different shapes, turned out and decorated with crushed red brick and white chalk dust to make intricate and unique patterns on top. The grown-ups were busy picking hops, with occasional help from us, but we played contentedly, extending, experimenting and creating what to us were pure culinary delights; not for consumption, of course, though I might have had a little taste! We were free and independent but, most of all, happy. I was almost five years old at the time, and life seemed perfect! There were no adults to judge or interfere with questions like 'How many bars had I made?', 'How many squares of chocolate were there?', 'Were the rusty containers round or square?' and would I remember to wash my hands? And heaven forbid what would have happened if they had appeared with 'clip boards!'. Come to think of it, I cannot ever remember being told to wash my hands during my childhood, but I learned from those around me! In early childhood, this is how freedom looks, and this state is so aptly expressed in the words of Friedrich Froebel: 'Play is the highest expression of human development in childhood for it alone is the free expression of what is in a child's soul.' The world is badly in need of children showing us what is in their souls; a revelation from the inside-out, for which a minimum of interference is essential.

The Centre of the Personality

Invariably in counselling and psychotherapy, a point is reached where certain old patterns need to change and new more healthy ones established to address whatever issues have brought the adult into therapy in the first place. Clients invariably discover that for any changes to take place, there needs to be a recognition of a loss of contact with their centre; the stable point in any personality. Throughout life, many of us will identify with this situation and find ourselves out on a limb and unable to retrace our steps to the core of our own being; this is part of the human dilemma. Losing ourselves amongst the myriad of roles we play, and the myriad of expectations we have had thrust upon us, is par for the course. However, so identi- fied can we become with those varying aspects of our personality that it can become difficult to come home to 'self' with the purpose of re-emerging more whole. However, the difference between the adult and the child is that the adult can engage consciously with person- ality reconstruction, whilst the child is at the mercy of both positive and negative forces, with little chance of any self-conscious rescue.

This is the dilemma facing the young child if it is diverted away from its natural unfolding, by a lack of understanding of the importance of self-construction. Those unnecessary confusions and complexities in the adult psyche have come about through the universal failure of educators and parents to realize sufficiently that, in the first few years of life, it is essential that each individual develops a healthy personality with confidence in their own innate goodness. This is the essential quality of the soul present, though unrealized at birth, which reflects the light of the child's essence rather than developing characteristics. This is the 'golden thread' which we need to honour and support in everything that we do with and for our children. They cannot honour this themselves and are dependent on those around them for a constant reflection back of their innate purity and goodness. Unfortunately, young children are still at the mercy of the behaviours of the role-models in their lives, which makes the responsibility of those role-models even more imperative if negative patterns are not to be imitated and made as if their own.

Regrettably, children continue to be moulded from pre-conceptions about what they must learn and how they should turn out. The United Nations Convention on the rights of the child clearly states in Article 29: 'The education of the child shall be directed to: a) the development of the child's personality', amongst other things. We ignore the development of the essential personality at our peril, and we need to halt the current belief that we can quicken the release of human potentialities through the child, before the child is ready and able to release these for himself. In the words of author Steve Biddulph (from his Preface to this book), 'It's like ripping open a rosebud to try and get it to blossom'. The rosebud has everything it needs already within in order to unfold its beauty.

The child's personality unfolds gently and slowly, emerging like the butterfly out of the chrysalis during the early years of life; but it needs to retain its unique being, and this is the 'golden thread'. However, when the butterfly first emerges it is colourless, chaotic and unattractive, but if we wait a while as it gets its act together it reveals itself to us in all its glory. There was no one there to tell it when to emerge, or what to do to enable the transformation to take place. It was guided from within! Also, there was no one there to divert its energy of will into becoming something other than itself.

> A teacher or a culture doesn't create a human being. It doesn't implant within him the ability to love, or to be curious, or to philosophise, or to symbolise, or to be creative. Rather, it permits or fosters or encourages or helps what exists in embryo to become real and actual.
>
> (Abraham Maslow, *Toward a Psychology of Being*)

What exists in embryo in the child's personality is akin to the rosebud, which gently unfolds after it has received the right nutrients from a healthy environment. The soul of the child is the deepest place wherein resides transcendent potentialities which can never be taught, such as love, compassion, simplicity, wisdom and humility. 'Be who God meant you to be and you will set the world on fire' (St Catherine of Sienna). Setting the world on fire doesn't happen by magic, and it needs the best foundation; one where mind, body and spirit have been allowed to integrate, infused by the light of the soul, before, in Wordsworth's words, 'Shades of the prison-house begin to close upon the growing child'.

At the present time, however, we have become so focused in our education of pre-school children on what they can learn and how earlier and earlier they can be cajoled to do so, that we fail to realize the importance of this essential foundation. This has led, and is still leading, to mechanistic thinking, ensuring that we constantly put the cart before the horse and then lead our young charges to the water, ignoring the reluctance and significance of their not wanting to drink. Assumptions are then made that this reluctance must be the result of some sort of dysfunction for which 'early intervention' (a new political mantra) is considered to be the only recourse. This is gross ignorance because these same children, given more time, less targets and less legal compulsion, would quite happily drink the water when they are developmentally ready.

The education page in any daily newspaper will highlight over and over again the crisis in state education in our country. Billions of pounds are invested each year with the most laudable of aims, and yet nearly 50 per cent of children leave without any decent GCSE qualifications. So the latest suggestion for improving this situation is that children need more discipline. Whether they do or whether they don't, this is just one more guesstimate which will inevitably lead to yet more interventions and more changes with the well-meaning purpose of ensuring more children succeed. And still policy-makers fail to look at the beginning.

My perturbation is that we have all become so concerned about early education, that children in the UK (and particularly England) are getting insufficient time to embrace their childhood independently and freely. Seeing the non-compulsory early years as a 'preparation for school' (another political mantra) is a clear example of how our priorities have become muddled and distorted. If the early years were focused primarily on a preparation for life, then children would already be prepared for school; but once the word 'school' enters the rhetoric, everything seems to go pear-shaped! Schooling, in the UK, usually means formal education and developing the powers of the intellect, such as the 3Rs. Dr Rudolf Steiner was adamant about the damage which could be done to the young child by stimulating the conscious intellect prematurely, and this is exactly where the root of the problem lies. That doesn't mean that children should be held back intellectually, but there is a difference between supportive enabling and premature untimely stimulation.

In England, there are so many government requirements to make each child a 'reader', a 'writer', a 'thinker', a 'counter' and a 'problem solver', that there is a failure to consider how imperative it is that such focus should only be addressed at the developmentally appropriate time, when a child is not only considered able, but ready too. These learning goals, and others, should never have been set in a Statutory Framework such as currently exists in the Early Years Foundation Stage (EYFS). In the early years, such compulsory targets have enormous potential for diverting practitioners and parents away from quality time with children into an increasingly time-consuming and unproductive bureaucracy. The outcome is more and more 'schoolifying' of young children before they have fully incarnated. Five years old is hardly enough time for such a marathon task, and six or seven years old could ensure a more healthy integration.

It may seem progressive to assess individuals on how much they can do, how fast they can do it, how early we can demand results and what degree of precision can be reached. However, such individuals may then be more aptly likened to those described in Iain McGilchrist's book *The Master and His Emissary* (2009), where he describes such requirements as those we expect from machines. It is also noteworthy that a former children's Minister of Education routinely referred to early years education as an 'industry'!

When too many untimely requirements and judgements are made, whether by parents or educators, the child experiencing failure retreats back into its shell, and the emerging personality becomes modified, taking on false images of itself before it reaches out again. The trouble is that these images are never again in line with the child's pure nature. The child seeks other, less natural ways of meeting those true needs with which to enhance self-esteem and well-being. Hence the negative parts of what Carl Jung called 'the shadow' are formed as the light retreats, creating even more problems and fragmenting the psyche. This shadow lies in the unconscious for the time when the individual feels it is safe, if ever, to re-present those aspects of their lost wholeness, in order to attempt healthy psychological integration.

The Birth of Identity

In early infancy, children are incredibly pure beings and are full of unconditional love, which literally shines out of them. They are at one with their parents and the other people in their lives. The awareness of being a separate self is not a sense which appears to be consciously felt during the first two years, but manifests like a dynamic energy directing the will towards those activities for which there is the greatest natural hunger. This hunger, in the first place, is for a sense of belonging and of trust so that the will can follow a natural path, rather than a deviating one.

Around the age of two years we do see a fascinating transition, however, from the child saying 'Sasha do it', 'Sasha have biscuit' to 'I do it', or 'Me do it', 'I have biscuit'. Often the incredible significance of this goes unnoticed, but it is the first step in real individuation, when for the first time spirit unites with matter; rather like the potter when the wobbly clay centres on the wheel for the first time. The 'I', the 'self' of the child, has incarnated at last! Now, with an emerging though clumsy sense of individuality, the child attempts to take hold of his 'I', his centre, and thereby to further integrate the previously fragmented parts of himself round that core. 'The ego has landed!' – albeit rather shakily. This is what is manifesting in the so-called 'terrible twos'. What degradation is made by calling attempts at incarnation by such a term! It is during this transition that 'great compassion' is needed for the child when he or she is undertaking this immense task. The child is attempting with this new sense of self to harness his own will, an unwieldy beast at the best of times, and attempt to make choices which provide the greatest sense of inner satisfaction and autonomy. The child needs to know its own value, mind, body and spirit, and there is a need to provide healthy boundaries to grant each child that freedom to be the person they were meant to be, despite all the initial chaos! 'The river would never reach the sea, if it weren't first hemmed in by the banks' (Rabindranath Tagore).

I often think this time in a young child's life could be likened to 'the fall of man'. The young infant at first so adored, and almost worshipped, can suddenly slip from grace, as the emerging ego provides parents with new unforeseen challenges and awareness that their child's purity and innocence have now taken on a different phase. The child, once so dependent, now has a will of its own, where the thrust for independence takes centre stage. The ego still has a long journey to travel before it is really independent, and it is still very much influenced by both parents and teachers. With this new-found state of being it becomes ever more imperative that each child receives a reflection back from those around it that it is still loved, still valued and that, despite any manifestations of negative and uncooperative behaviour, it needs to be protected from crystallizing a negative image of itself. Consistency with boundaries, so essential for a child's security and trust, as well as loving authority are now more important than ever.

Disadvantage

There seems to be something of a misconception about natural development being the unique property of privileged or middle-class children. All children are spiritual in essence and it is to this that all pedagogies need to be addressed. There is already a prevailing mind-set which sees the disadvantaged child as being limited, because they are viewed materialistically rather than spiritually. The word 'disadvantage' is bandied about without any clear definitions being given, or the realization that there are many kinds of disadvantage, other than economic. If we view all children as full of potential we are more likely to ignore their economic or social status and have the highest expectations for their future, providing healthy soil for their potential, and offering that extra encouragement and respect so essential for positive attitudes towards learning. If we believe in them, then they will believe in themselves. There needs to be a letting go of any mind-sets that disadvantage will inevitably lead to failure and lack of success. It can, of course, but it often does not, and, with the nurturing of a sense of value, much can be done to eliminate a loss of hope. This is the more healthy way of improving social mobility.

Pre-school is a time when, whatever form disadvantage takes, positive learning environments can be provided where there is an atmosphere of emotional warmth. This can have a dramatic impact on the self-esteem of all children. Disadvantaged children have the same inner core as other children and, given opportunities for realizing their own worth with positive encouragement to take risks, they will move forward with their self-esteem enhanced. Being a reflection back to a child that their light is seen and valued, has true healing potential. It must be self-evident that the prevention of low self-esteem in the first place is far easier than trying to establish it later, once the damage has been done. This is the real 'Sure Start'!

Without a good-enough foundation of a healthy integrated personality, the need for it will not go away, but will continue to reside in the lower unconscious, making its presence felt perhaps throughout life ... for example, the 'bully' or the 'victim' that we hear so much about; where did they come from? – as they certainly weren't there at birth!

Friedrich Froebel, the renowned German educator, felt that the duty of parents and teachers was to 'crystallize the good' inherent in every child. This done, when the child becomes an adolescent with all the confusions and insecurities that bombard this time, they will take care of any issues by virtue of the inherent sense of 'goodness' consolidated within. It's like having psychological money in the bank. Children who, in their teen years, degenerate into adolescent chaos are likely to be those who never had this inner goodness crystallized, and so are unable to find the necessary resources within with which to change. Their self-image has been formed on all the negative feedback they have experienced in their early years. They have donned false masks to protect their core self, hiding their natural beauty from the world. Their self-esteem is rock bottom. In a sense, it is like not having any psychological money in the bank; nothing with which to heal the fractured ego. From this point forward, children begin to see themselves in the negative ways often reflected back by others. Adults may be able to address such a state of affairs through counselling, therapy or psycho-analysis, or just plain commonsense and personal awareness, but such conscious choices elude the child.

Thus begins the individual's frantic search in the outside world for anything that puts that feeling to rest. Regrettably, that search, devoid of a sense that all is well, has now become modified by the attempt to satisfy, by deviated and unnatural means, that which was once their birthright. Once that essential selfhood gets obscured by masks, it is a painful journey to learn to risk taking the masks off again. Masks come initially from denial by others and ultimately by self-denial. However, for the evolving child there is a constant need to know that he is loved as he is, and not for what he can do or has achieved. Humanistic psychologist and founder of person-centred therapy, Carl Rogers, coined the term 'unconditional positive regard', which arguably should be the right of every child; and where this cannot happen in the family, then it should be addressed as a priority in early years education. A good foundation in early learning can, of course, enhance self-esteem, and for that foundation, unconditional positive regard is not instead of, but as well as. However, children who already have low self-esteem are likely to have negative dispositions and attitudes already well established; hence the need to address this as a priority.

It is an irrational assumption to conclude that failure to reach learning targets at 10 or 11 will be improved by targeting children as young as 4, 5 or 6, from some misguided idea that this will lead to economic well-being, even though there is no convincing research evidence to support such an assumption. Is this not what is happening with some of our teenagers? Did they experience failure before their essential foundation of self-esteem and autonomy was fully established? Do we really believe that setting earlier and earlier learning requirements is going to address that problem? The only thing that will halt the loss of self-esteem in children, the true disadvantage, is to ensure that they are given appropriate time and truly nurturing experiences. This will enable them to feel good about themselves … good about who they are … and good about their potential for the future by being aided in the first place in developing a healthy functioning personality in line with their own developmental agendas and their own unique souls.

Children should not be required to ripen early. They should not be required to be what we think they should be, whether at home or at school. Parents and teachers can, and usually will, be the sowers of healthy developmental seeds in the early years; but the harvest must be left to the children, and not quantified and managed with bureaucracy designed to inform the State, with little if any benefit to the child. The 'being' of the child is in process, for in the first place all children are learning 'to be', and that is the natural role of childhood.

Parents and teachers can become totally overwhelmed at the enormity of their task, whether in parenting or teaching. For teachers in the early years, it is all too easy to lose the original spark that brought them there in the first place. Routines, policies, structures and more and more external demands are capable of, and are, destroying their enthusiasm. It is not the setting of goals in the early years which will guarantee successful outcomes, but the enabling of the child's own developmental goals which can do that. The child's will is best developed through an emerging self-discipline through self-initiated and self-directed activities, which inform him about his value and sense of identity. For such choices to be made, there needs to be freedom and independence and sufficient time to just enjoy being a child.

Unfolding

In summing up, it is important to emphasize that only adults of the highest moral development and intuitive understanding of the natural stages of childhood should, ideally, work with our youngest children. High-flying graduates, currently thought to be necessary for education in the early years, cannot guarantee that they also have the necessary intuition, emotional warmth and real ability to see the uniqueness of each child (cf. Chapter 20). Teachers who are sufficiently developed to have an awareness of their own spiritual nature can know the real 'soul' of the child, enabling the child to know it for himself. Contact with this 'golden thread' enables each child to emerge with confidence, but this contact can so easily be broken if there is ignorance of its existence in the first place.

Self-confidence, self-respect, self-will, self-actualization, self-acceptance and self-discipline are not given this prefix without reason. This intrinsic 'self', the unique being, is in process, and starts unfolding its potentialities from birth; but so much more could be done to make this process as free from negative constraints as possible, by focusing on 'who a child is' rather than 'what a child can do':

> This fashioning of the human personality is a secret work of 'incarnation'. The child is an enigma. All that we know is that he has the highest potentialities, but we do not know what he will be. He must 'become incarnate' with the help of his own will.
>
> Maria Montessori

I have just finished watching a programme on television depicting a variety of behaviours by triplets under three years of age. It showed the stresses and anxieties, as well as the joys, of parenting so many emerging little personalities from birth. I immediately found myself thinking about the idealistic picture I have painted in this chapter, and wondered how parents and teachers can ever be expected to honour the light of the child more often with so many complexes and challenges in these early years. This is a tall order, but surely it is the whole crux of the matter? This idealism is the approach which is missing in our relationships, parenting and teaching. We all care passionately, and want so much to do the best we can for our children, but we get side-tracked through our fears, frustrations, ambitions and feelings that we, in some way, are failing. This frustration and desire to get it right has produced far too much control; far too much concern about early learning, emotional security and, above all, what I consider to be too much misguided intervention from central government in their endless and ever-changing endeavours to improve the education of all of our children. There seems to be a systematic reluctance by government and policy-makers to heed the message that we should stop looking towards the end-result for answers, and go back again and re-vision the beginning.

So let us consider taking a step back and re-examining our convictions that we have to make children into the people we think they should be. Let us consider trusting more that children can show us the way, by being willing to observe and provide those things which bring them the most satisfaction and joy. Let us also consider that, without a spiritual view of life, we are missing the bigger picture, and therefore denying to children their own spiritual birthright – the right to a fully functioning well-rounded personality with the soul intact and the inherent goodness unquestioned.

Let me end with a short quotation, taken from an ancient Egyptian Creation Myth:

> Out of the waters of chaos emerged the lotus. When its petals opened, within was the Golden Child. The Light from the child pushed back all the darkness, and this is where creation came from – the light of the Child!

References

Layard, R. and Dunn, J. (2009) *A Good Childhood: Searching for Values in a Competitive Age*; Report for the Children's Society, Harmondsworth: Penguin

McGilchrist, I. (2009) *The Master and His Emissary: The Divided Brain and the Making of the Western World*, New Haven, Conn: Yale University Press

Maslow, A. (1962) *Toward a Psychology of Being*, New York: Van Nostrand

Montessori, M. (1995) *The Absorbent Mind*, Carlsbad, Calif.: Holt, Rinehart and Winston

Steiner, R. (1999) *The Philosophy of Freedom: The Basis for a Modern World Conception*, Herndon, VA: Steiner Books Inc.

Chapter 11

The Democratization of Learning

Wendy Ellyatt

It is surely the case that schooling is only one small part of how a culture inducts the young into its canonical ways. Indeed, schooling may even be at odds with a culture's other ways of inducting the young into the requirements of communal living … What has become increasingly clear … is that education is not just about conventional school matters like curriculum or standards or testing. What we resolve to do in school only makes sense when considered in the broader context of what the society intends to accomplish through its educational investment in the young. How one conceives of education, we have finally come to recognize, is a function of how one conceives of culture and its aims, professed and otherwise.

JEROME S. BRUNER, *THE CULTURE OF EDUCATION*, 1996: IX–X

Finding Ourselves through Others

Human beings are extraordinary natural learners and undoubtedly the most successful and dominant species ever to walk the earth. Predictability and expectation have always played a fundamental role in our development as we need the solidity of a predictable world, particularly when we are very young, in order to feel secure. However, we also have an innate need and curiosity to seek out the unpredictable and unknown, and it is our desire for ongoing experience that allows for diversification, exploration, expansion and growth. It is this that has enabled man to evolve faster than any other species, and to become a consummate master of his environment. What is clear, however, is that man is not only immensely creative but is also an innately social animal, and this quest for learning is constantly constrained by the human need to 'do what is expected' within the confines of the surrounding culture.

Every society is organized in such a way that codes, rules, habits, expectations and customs fundamentally influence the way that its members behave. Human societies are unique in that we cannot survive without such interaction. Peter Farb talks of this in his book *Humankind*:

> Humans survive as a result of the things that they are able to learn, not the things they are born with … Culture is what is learned from the cumulative experience of past generations, shared among contemporaries, and preserved beyond the individual life-span of a society's members. (Farb, 1978: 76)

Man is therefore subject to a dialectical play between his developmental needs as a dynamic living spiritual being, and his needs to adapt to, and conform with, the needs and expectations of the dominant human culture. We are 'beings in process', with that process fundamentally reliant upon and informed by the relationship with others. The psychologist Colwyn Trevarthen talks of human children having an innate expectation of 'finding themselves through others' (Trevarthen, 1980). The social behaviour of a child depends upon the influences and examples set for him by his society; in fact the well-being, and often the very survival of each member of a human society, depends largely upon the reaction and behaviour of others.

The Role of Culture

What is it that a child draws from his culture? It is the mirror through which he creates the emotional attachments that accompany each and every sense impression. It is the means by which he sees his own reflection. A newly born baby cannot qualify the impressions that he receives in any complex way – he only knows that things either feel 'right' or 'not right'. The whole rhythm of his growth is directed towards a world in which he is open to the minds and feelings of others. This interplay between the immature learner and the more mature other creates a field of play that is culturally shaped and stretched. The inherited basic biological programmes of the human child continue, but are subject to the continuous pressures of the cultural environment, much of it based on the accepted development of social 'competence', which we know as education.

> In pre-literate societies, education was achieved orally and through observation and imitation. The young learned informally from their parents, extended family and grandparents. At later stages of their lives, they received instruction of a more structured and formal nature, imparted by people not necessarily related, in the context of initiation, religion or ritual.
>
> Wikipedia, retrieved 12 October 2010

Children are, therefore, actively involved in the social construction of their own lives. The lives of those around them and the societies in which they live are fundamental influences in their ongoing development. As the Russian psychologist Vygotsky said, 'Human learning presupposes a specific social nature and a process by which children grow into the intellectual life of those around them' (Vygotsky, 1978: 86). And Howard Gardner (1983: 239) includes 'interpersonal' and 'intrapersonal' intelligences in his theory of multiple intelligences:

> Interpersonal intelligence is the ability to understand other people: what motivates them, how they work, how to work co-operatively with them. Intrapersonal intelligence ... is a correlative ability, turned inward. It is a capacity to form an accurate, veridical model of oneself and to be able to use that model to operate effectively in life.

The Importance of Relationship

If we look at the social world of the child, it becomes immediately apparent that there are certain primary relational influences, i.e. the mother, father and other key caregivers. Numerous studies have demonstrated the levels of extreme deprivation experienced by children denied care, stimulation and love from these sources (Bowlby, 1969; Bronfenbrenner, 1968; Rutter, 1991). As Bronfenbrenner says, however, it is not sufficient to look at these influences in isolation. The larger world must pay a significant part in the overall attitudes of all concerned:

> Whether parents can perform effectively in their child-rearing roles within the family depends on the role demands, stresses

and supports emanating from other settings … The availability of supportive settings is, in turn, a function of their existence and frequency in a given culture or subculture.

(Bronfenbrenner, 1968: 7)

He emphasizes the principle of interconnectedness between settings and the enormous effect that public policies and practices can have on societal values and roles conducive to balanced family life. There are, for example, profound differences between the government-funded childcare provision within different EU countries. For example, parents and children living in Nordic countries, with their long-standing focus on more broad-based family and child well-being rather than the measurement of early developmental outcomes, can expect a very different experience to those living here in the UK.

When looking at the life of the modern child in the United Kingdom and the social environment in which it lives, it becomes clear that there have been enormous changes in the last 50 years – perhaps more than at any other period of time. 'Traditional' family life, where the mother devotes her time to caring for home and children, the father brings home the wage and everyone sits down together for meals, has now long gone. In 1996 a report revealed that out of 1,000 children interviewed, one in three had not sat down to a meal with his or her family in the preceding week. Nor are most children now allowed to go out to play after school. Gone are the hours of hopscotch and marbles, the games of cowboys and Indians, the intimate social network of children in the street. A 2009 'Family Trends' report showed that 71 per cent of adults reported playing in the street or near their home every day when they were children, compared to only 21 per cent of children in 2007 (Child and Parenting Institute, 2007). With the economic and social stresses of modern life, people are now having fewer children. Only 25 per cent of households have the classic 2.4 children, a decline of 13 per cent since 1971. In 2009 the provisional Total Fertility Rate (TFR) for the UK was 1.94 children per woman (Office for National Statistics, 2009). And approximately one in four children are being brought up by single parents, compared with one in fourteen in 1972 (Child and Parenting Institute, 2007). Those children live in areas where they are no longer surrounded by close-knit families with grandparents, uncles, aunts and cousins all living close by. Instead, they are living increasingly isolated lives where adults make all the major decisions about the way that they spend their time. Schools are therefore playing an increasingly dominant role in the social understanding of children.

The Need for Wholeness

What is it that a child needs in order to develop socially? All human beings need warmth, respect and acceptance from others, particularly 'significant others' such as parents. They need to reinforce their identities through the recognition of others, they need to know that they can relate and communicate with others, they need to be allowed to construct and co-construct meaning with others, and they need to feel that they, and their thoughts and opinions, matter to others. Children acquire identity in the context of their social group. As the Italian educator Malaguzzi says, 'A child can't develop a good sense of self isolated from other people' (Edwards et al., 1998: 219). The child has an inborn expectation of finding an atmosphere of reciprocal help and socialization. Implicit in this expectation is his desire to feel whole, and feeling whole is a vital biological and spiritual need for achieving a true sense of self.

The danger of cultures is that their influence is so profound that they can easily offer the child a vastly impoverished world in which to develop. As Bruner writes,

> A culture equips its members with such structured models of the world so that they may predict, interpolate and extrapolate. That much for knowledge. Without such models man would not be the species that he is. Nor would culture be so controlling.
> (Bruner, 1972: 11)

The extraordinary potentials and intelligences that young children possess can be stifled and bound down by the demands of society. Modern Western cultures have consistently been criticized for continuing to develop educational systems that emphasize the intellect, to the detriment of the social, emotional and spiritual development of children. Bruner goes on, 'Man's intellect … is not simply his own, but is communal in the sense that its unlocking or empowering depends upon the success of the culture in developing means to that end' (ibid.: 21).

The complexity of modern cultures has resulted in knowledge and skills far beyond the capacity of a single group. Increasingly, therefore, we have developed means of children being 'instructed out of context', rather than 'experiencing in context'. The danger of this way of learning for the child is that he cannot make the connections and relationships with an experience of meaningful reality in his mind. 'A piece of unreal learning has no hooks on it; it can't be attached to anything, it is of no use to the learner' (Holt, 1990: 169). In such environments, children sense the anxious expectations of the adults around them and begin to experience the fear of failure, of disappointing others. Malaguzzi talks of spoken language being increasingly imposed upon children: 'Through imitative mechanisms which are lacking or completely devoid of exchange, rather than strong imaginative processes linked to experience' (Malaguzzi, 1996: 35).

Language is the accumulated wisdom of a group of people. As Aldous Huxley says in his book *The Doors of Perception*, 'When you learn a language – you are the inheritor of the wisdom of the people who have gone before you' (Huxley, 1954: 118). You are, however, also the victim, in the sense that, of the infinite number of sensorial experiences that you could have had, certain ones are repetitive in the experience of your people and are therefore given more emphasis and more labels. Take, for example, the extraordinarily high number of words available in Eskimo culture to describe snow. Eskimo children have clearly defined labels for each recognizable difference in their sensory impression of this part of their environment. With only one label, European children only relate to that one over-riding impression, and their attention is therefore not drawn to the differences. Experiences on the sensory level that are given few or even no labels at all are hardly able to intrude into consciousness. Daniel Stern discusses how this can affect the development of the young child. Language, he says, provides a new way of being related to others. By sharing personal world knowledge in a common symbol system, there is a forging of shared meaning: 'They discover that their personal experiential knowledge is part of a larger experience of knowledge, that they are unified with others in a common culture base.' He describes the advent of language, however, as a very mixed blessing for the child: 'What begins to be lost (or made latent) is enormous … The infant gains entrance into a wider cultural membership, *but at the risk of losing the force and wholeness of original experience*' (Stern, 1998, emphasis added).

Dynamic Creativity

Educational systems have, therefore, a double responsibility: one is to ensure that the child has a real understanding of those elements that are important to his establishing a secure place in the particular society in which he lives; the second, however, is even more important, and that is to ensure that he or she as an individual is allowed to move beyond those values in order to express his or herself as a dynamic, creative individual sharing an entire world with others. Creativity is the dynamic force that enables us to transcend the confines of cultures and to delve into the immensely important properties and possibilities of the unknown. It is this that underpins all scientific, artistic and technological advances.

The world is rapidly becoming a smaller place. Information technology is creating an extraordinary environment where children no longer have to accept the barriers between countries, where they can communicate freely in a way that transcends cultural defences. Such freedom has never been known before and the impact has far-reaching consequences. We need no longer be bound quite so rigidly to the limitations of our own social and cultural experiences. We can open our minds to new ways of thinking. Educational policy-making needs to both acknowledge and adapt to the extraordinary diversity of social experience that is now available.

The language of education must not therefore continue to offer what Jerome Bruner terms 'the so-called language of fact and objectivity'. It must help to make the connections and associations necessary to extend the child's cultural 'library of labels'.

> It must express stance and must invite counter-stance, and in the process leave place for reflection, for meta-cognition. It is this that permits one to reach higher ground, this process of objectifying in language or image what one has thought and then turning around and re-considering it.
>
> (Bruner, 1986: 129)

For the children in our modern world, it is the rich tapestry of these connections and associations that is all too often being denied them. This is clearly demonstrated by studies such as that carried out by Fowler et al. (1997) who, having seen the dramatic results of providing a cognitive and language enriched environment for a controlled group of children, concluded that, 'It would appear that common forms of socialisation seriously underestimate and fail to stimulate the biological potentials for the development of competence of which most children are capable' (Fowler et al., 1997: 142). As Jones and Reynolds discuss in their own research into the interaction of teachers in children's play, 'Teachers do not really "trust" children as learners and most environments and lesson plans are therefore dependent on teaching, not on children's spontaneous learning activities' (Jones and Reynolds, 1992: xiii).

The 2010 television programme 'Gareth Malone's Extraordinary School for Boys' (BBC Radio 2, 2010) was a clear demonstration of how fundamentally learning can be compromised by the formality of current systems. In 12 weeks, this young choir teacher took a profoundly disengaged group of primary school boys and, by breaking all the stipulated curriculum rules, improved their developmental reading profiles by as much as 20 months. Not only that, but he started to reintroduce them to reading as the fascinating, highly meaningful and powerful tool that it can be, rather than something to be avoided and that led them to feel bad about themselves. Despite enormous investment over the past few years, England's performance in reading attainment has been steadily declining. The 2007 PIRLS Study, *Progress in International Reading Literacy*, showed us dropping from 3rd to 19th, and reported that children in England read *for pleasure much less frequently than their peers in other countries.* There had been significant increases in the proportion of English 10-year-olds with the 'least positive' attitudes to reading, and who said that they very seldom read stories or novels outside school:

> On average, children in England reported less frequent reading for pleasure outside school than children in many other countries: just a third of children reported reading for fun on a daily basis ... Of particular concern is the 15 per cent of children in the sample for England who had the least positive attitudes, a significant increase from 2001. This is one of the highest proportions in all the 2006 participating countries.

Surely it is levels of enjoyment and deep engagement that we should be seeking to achieve when children read, rather than the very arid measurement of their decoding abilities; and examples such as this reinforce the urgent need to re-examine the efficacy of current approaches. After all, what is it that we are trying to achieve?

Hundreds of thousands of students who have great paper results, but have lost a sense of who they are and their place in the world, or young adults who are deeply connected to their communities, have a true sense of self and whose worth comes from being able to develop their unique skills and capacities in ways that have real meaning for them.

Goleman lists the core emotional and social skills needed for life (Goleman, 1983). These include: self-awareness; identifying, expressing and managing feelings; impulse control and delaying gratification; handling stress and anxiety; reading social and emotional cues; listening; being able to resist negative influences; taking others' perspectives and understanding what behaviour is acceptable in a given situation. Such qualities can only be developed through rich interpersonal relationships. Teaching children with a bank of regurgitated, inert, unexciting words deprives them of the joy of learning through relationships and connectivity. 'Children expect living words, words that are rooted in reason and in ideas, in plans and actions, in situations of real human exchange' (Malaguzzi, 1996: 35).

Teaching children with isolated, inert and regurgitated subject material, particularly that has no connection to their own everyday lives and that serves primarily to answer examination questions, is an insult to their innate intelligences and deserves the lack of respect that it is so often given. Because our children aren't stupid. It's just that we have created a system that leaves a significant number of them feeling that way, and that even affirms it for them as they grow older.

The Task Ahead

AQA (The Assessment and Qualifications Alliance)

> So, on the one hand you have the AQA of the old world – we'll measure how clever you are by seeing how much information you can cram into your head and regurgitate in an hour or so in an exam hall with millions of other children on the same day and then forget it all on the following day – and on the other the twenty-first century AQA – the knowledge will cost you just £1 and then we'll see how clever you are by what you do with it.
>
> (Gilbert, 2010)

Our task, therefore, seems to be that we should help children to communicate using all their potential, intelligences and languages. We should protect them from the demands of cultures that in any way limit their possibilities. We should do everything we can to support their innate expectations of living and learning in vibrant social worlds. Roger Hart, in his work with UNICEF, recognized the dichotomy between the children in the poorest countries who, although denied high standards of schooling, can see and feel the enormous contribution that their work provides for their families. They were therefore valued and important members of their social communities (Hart, 1992). Research from 50 non-industrial societies revealed that the most common age for the assignment of responsibility of the following tasks was 5 to 7 years of age: the care of younger children, tending animals, household chores, gathering food and materials, and running errands. He argued that these activities have innate social meaning for the children, whereas in industrial nations we are now seeing the effects of young people who have had no opportunities to discover the pleasures of meaningful work (ibid.).

Sociality involves the development of competence, which is relevant to the expectations demanded by the culture, and through these experiences every child should find a route to his or her meaningful role in the community. What any schooling system should do is to maximize the child's opportunities to demonstrate competence. Self-esteem is the most critical variable affecting a child's successful collaboration with others, and self-esteem is a value judgement that is made based upon competence. Children who feel valued and important know where they stand, and will not be afraid to contribute to the work of others. Colin Rogers, in his article 'Early Admission: early labelling' (Rogers, 1989), recognized the enormous influence that teachers' expectations can have on the performance of children, and that a young child experiencing negative feedback can be profoundly affected. Low expectations from a teacher all too often result in a reality of low achievement from the child. As Bandura was quoted in one of Daniel Goleman's *New York Times* articles:

> People's beliefs about their abilities have a profound effect on those abilities. Ability is not a fixed property; there is a huge variability in how you perform. People who have a sense of self-efficacy bounce back from failures; they approach things in terms

of how to handle them rather than worrying about what can go wrong.

(Goleman, 1988)

Children are enormously perceptive. Teachers must understand that it is not only their words that children react to, *but also their emotional attitudes*. Back in 1990 Martin Woodhead argued that early years schooling should be seen as only one element in the transition that the child must make within a much wider social setting. Children's lives, he said, involve infinitely more than the schooling system, and what we should be concentrating on is the 'educational' process of enjoyable meaning-making, whatever the context (Woodhead, 1997). Perhaps we should, in fact, examine the very nature of schooling itself, and question the reasons that it developed in the way that it has. Perhaps we would then better appreciate the drastic transformation that has occurred in the last hundred years when work has been removed from its intrinsic connection with meaningful family life to become, instead, a means of producing an effective and controllable workforce. The new construction of childhood that began at that time significantly reduced the children's sense of their own value and meaningful contribution. Children were comprehensively removed from socially significant activity and given new imposed characteristics of dependence, vulnerability and immaturity. Thus the overall aim of Margaret Thatcher's education policies in the 1980s was to convert the nation's schools system from a public service into a market (Gillard, 2007).

Children have an expectation of taking part in vibrant social worlds in which they can feel secure and valued. They have an expectation of being empowered, and need their work to be meaningful to them so that they can make the connections and associations unique to their needs as individuals. Whatever learning environments we provide for children should, therefore, be fulfilling these expectations.

Empathy and Interconnectivity

The National Curriculum was written by a government 'quango' (quasi-autonomous non-government organisation). Teachers had virtually no say in its design or construction. It was almost entirely content-based. Dennis Lawton, of the University of London's Institute of Education, described it as 'the reincarnation of the 1904 Secondary Regulations'. It was huge and therefore unmanageable, especially at the primary level, leading to a significant drop in reading standards. It divided the curriculum up into discrete subjects, making integrated 'topic' and 'project' work difficult if not impossible. But perhaps the most damaging outcome of it was that it prevented teachers and schools from being curriculum innovators and demoted them to 'curriculum deliverers'.

(Gillard, 2007)

The problem, therefore, is to create learning environments that allow children this rich interplay between home, school and the community. Loris Malaguzzi clearly recognized this in his work at Reggio Emilia. The teachers in Reggio 'listen intently to the way children perceive and understand the world and respond with both appreciation and expertise to help them build on and expand what they understand' (Boyd Caldwell, 1987: 32); and 'The teacher's role is to ask good open-ended questions that stimulate children's thinking and provoke discussion – to facilitate, orchestrate and gently guide … In these conversations the teacher does not fish for right answers or impart information' (ibid.: 62).

Carlo Rinaldi says, 'We do not hurry to give them answers; instead we invite them to think about where the answers might lie … *It is not the answers that are important, it is the process that you and I search together*' (ibid.: 63, emphasis added). And that seems to be the fundamental difference to the approach taken by traditional educational settings in Britain. We do not have an educational culture built on recognition of children's extraordinary abilities and interests. All too often we rely on pre-planned curricula that assume that adults know best what children need to learn, that adults know the limits of children's abilities and that adults know best how to teach them.

An emergent curriculum requires teachers to listen to children's ideas and interests, and to adapt their learning goals to those of the children in responsive and creative ways. It is a co-constructivist view of education where child and adult participate in a mutual voyage of discovery. In Reggio the child is an important person in his own right. His thoughts, opinions, ideas and interests are all invited to be shared with the community. The adult's behaviour conveys to the children that all aspects of their work are taken seriously. As Lillian Katz comments, 'This message is not communicated directly by pronouncement or announcement; *it permeates the environment indirectly through a variety of actions, provisions and strategies*' (Edwards et al., 1998: 58, emphasis added). What Reggio has done, therefore, is to reproduce for the child the same sense of being an important contributor to the life of the community as children had before the advent of the schooling system. They are helped to feel that they matter, that people care about what they think and that they can make changes to the world around them. It is education based on relationships, shared understanding and participation, rather than education based on knowledge alone. As Jones and Nimmo say in their book *Emergent Curriculum*, 'You're not teaching children – you're living with them' (Jones and Nimmo, 1984: 1).

Children have an expectation of a co-operative, dynamic system of communication with others. If they experience emotionally unreactive or negative responses, they cannot effectively communicate their feelings. This is the same for a young baby left with an unresponsive mother or a young child left with a disengaged nursery teacher who is focusing more on filling in observation sheets than the quality of interaction. Mutual engagement and flow only happen when the process becomes a co-operative exchange. Daniel Stern talks of the adult 'attuning' to the child, and Trevarthen's work clearly demonstrates the importance of the child being with someone who is meaningful to him.

The ability to talk and think communicatively relies on there being a dynamic link:

> It appears that the development of communication is indissolubly linked to the formation and use of relationships and to a co-operation that depends on mutual liking and trust ... the evolution of language has been shaped by the needs of emotional minds that try to be conscious, interested and purposeful together.
>
> (ibid.: 28)

In Trevarthen's view, the child is born with an intersubjective mind that seeks an affectionate partner. These processes, he says, retain priority in control of cognitive and linguistic developments as well as in the formation of social attachments, as the child grows towards adulthood and a responsible life in society. In the period of time when the child has not yet developed his linguistic abilities and has limited experience of the world, it is therefore of critical importance that he spends his time with adults with whom he shares empathy.

What are we doing to a child when we leave him in the care of someone who does not interact with him, who perhaps does not even share the same language as him? What happens when a child is left for hours on end with only a television set or computer screen to interact with? How can that child express himself in ways that are meaningful, and which will be effectively reflected back to him? Speech and language therapists throughout the country are being flooded by referrals for children with some sort of language delay, and research shows that this is the commonest development problem in pre-school children. In some inner city areas the incidence was found to be over 30 per cent in 1996 (Faulkus, 1999), and a 2009 study by the *Archive of Pediatrics and Adolescent Medicine* reported that parents and children virtually stop talking to each other when the TV is on, even if they're in the same room. For every hour in front of the TV, parents spoke 770 fewer words to children, according to a study of 329 children, ages 2 months to 4 years of age (Park, 2009). The Family Policy Studies Centre produced a report in 1996 that stated 'The current focus throughout the educational system on academic and vocational achievement is in no way matched by a voiced concern for the development of social communication and relationship skills' (Family Policy Studies, 1996).

The Definition of Quality

> 'Quality', therefore, is neither neutral nor self-evident, but saturated with values and assumptions. It is not essential, but a constructed concept. Originally developed as a part of management theory, it has been incorporated into early childhood care and other services as part of the revolution of new public management and the growth of the audit society.
>
> (Power, 1997, quoted in Moss and Dahlberg, 2008: 5)

The most drastic change in our approach to early childhood has come with what Moss and Dahlberg (2008) call 'the paradigm of regulatory modernity' which has been significantly influenced by the twin disciplines of organizational management and economics:

> The concept of quality assumes the possibility of deriving universal and objective norms, based on expert knowledge. 'Quality' is an evaluation of the conformity of a product or service to these norms.

It values universality, objectivity, certainty, stability, closure; and presumes an autonomous observer able to make a decontextual-ised and objective statement of fact. It deploys certain methods, based on applying templates to particular settings (e.g. rating scales, check lists, standardised inspection procedures).

(Moss and Dahlberg, 2008: 4)

They go on to say:

It is a technology of normalisation, establishing norms against which performance should be assessed, thereby shaping policy and practice. It is a technology of distance, claiming to compare performance anywhere in the world, irrespective of context, and a technology of regulation, providing a powerful tool for management to govern at a distance through the setting and measurement of norms of performance.

(ibid.: 5)

The danger of such a normalizing and regulatory paradigm in a twenty-first century world is that it relies on the criteria of the past, and stifles the possibility of more expansive meaning-making and creativity. It uses the technical language and structures of the workplace which, in order to ensure the organizationally defined criteria and quality, then confine, limit and oppress the possibility of more risky and challenging new thinking and experimentation. The achievement of safe, externally acceptable and measurable outcomes is the core goal of the system. In his book *Why do I Need a Teacher When I've Got Google?*, Ian Gilbert refers to it as 'the world of right answers' (Gilbert, 2010: 45), and provides Mark Steel's simple example from one of his BBC Open University lectures typifying the current system (ibid.: 42):

TEACHER: What did the Vikings come in, children?

CLASS: Longboats, Miss!

TEACHER: No, no, now come on … – we did this last time, remember …

CLASS: Er, ships, narrowboats, er, don't know, Miss!

TEACHER: Oh, come on, we did this! They came in 'hordes', class. What did they come in?

CLASS: 'Hordes', Miss …

The actress Imogen Stubbs and her husband Sir Trevor Nunn recently challenged the obsession with results over the need for genuine engagement with the material when their children were going through their A-Level English exams. Whenever they tried to provide interesting anecdotes and related materials to the children over the dinner table they were told that it would just confuse them and wouldn't be relevant to the questions that they were going to be asked (Stubbs, 2010).

Sir Ken Robinson likens it to the fast-food model of quality assurance based upon standardization and conformity: 'Standardization tends to emphasize the lowest common denominator. Human aspirations reach much higher and if the conditions are right they succeed. Understanding those conditions is the real key to transforming education for all our children' (Robinson, 2010).

In 2010 IBM's survey of 1,500 global CEOs identified creativity as the number one 'leadership competency' of the future. And yet in July 2010, *Newsweek* published a new research report showing that American creativity appears to be drastically declining, especially in the youngest students. The increased focus on standardization was identified as a possible culprit:

> It's too early to determine conclusively why U.S. creativity scores are declining. One likely culprit is the number of hours kids now spend in front of the TV and playing videogames rather than engaging in creative activities. Another is the lack of creativity development in our schools. In effect, it's left to the luck of the draw who becomes creative: there's no concerted effort to nurture the creativity of all children.
>
> (Bronson and Merryman, 2010)

Most European countries place particular emphasis on the importance of social development and communicative skills, together with the importance of family and community. The Danish Government in particular has demonstrated its belief that the nurturing of self-confidence, independence and social competence is *of more importance* than the acquisition of knowledge and specific abilities. Britain has consistently been criticized for its stance in this area, and communicative and social skills even now remain secondary to the attainment of specific learning goals. The recent UK investment in the early years has come at the cost of an increasing need to justify this investment and the potential danger of doing so through flawed and old-paradigm definitions of what constitutes quality.

It is not as if we are leading the field in successful outcomes – in fact the latest findings of the PISA survey – the Programme for International Student Assessment – show the UK tumbling down the rankings, according to tests recently taken by an international sample of 15-year-olds. In 2000, when 32 countries took part in the survey, the UK came 7th in reading skills – but the figures for 2009 show that out of 65 countries and regions, the UK has fallen to 25th place. In maths, between 2000 and 2009 the UK has fallen from 8th to 28th, and in science from 4th to 16th (Coughlan, 2010). Almost one in five seven-year-olds in England did not reach government targets for literacy in 2010, and one in eleven boys in England – one in seven in some areas – starts secondary school with, at best, the reading skills of an average seven-year-old (BBC News, 2010). The danger of the political reaction to such statistics is that there is then a panicked call to increase the focus on isolated elements of the curricula, rather than the recognition that it may be developmentally inappropriate pressures that are actually causing the problem! Nor do we do well in assessments of child well-being. A 2009 European league table of young people's well-being placed the UK 24th out of 29 countries (Child Poverty Action Group, 2009), and this backs-up the 2007 table by UNICEF which placed the UK at the bottom of a list of 21 industrialized nations (UNICEF, 2007). A 2008 study by the World Health Organization showed that underage binge-drinking in Britain was amongst the worst in the world (Devlin and Porter, 2008).

About 10 per cent of children have a mental health problem at any one time, and the UK has one of the highest rates of self-harm in Europe, at 400 per 100,000 population (Mental Health Foundation, January 2011). The 2009 OECD report found only 36 per cent of children 'liked' school, and that British children were twice as likely to be drunk before the age of 15 than children in any other OECD country (OECD, 2009). Surely these statistics confirm that something is very wrong with how we are currently approaching learning and education. Government Ministers are quoted as being very concerned and determined to ensure that future investment reaps the acceptable results, but there remains damningly little investigation into the possibility that it may be the value systems themselves that may be at fault and, as Moss and Dahlberg have highlighted, virtually no investment in the possible value of alternative views and perspectives.

> Although today there is a sort of standard policy document, produced by governments and international organisations, which offers a predictable rationale and prescription for early child-hood education and care and draws on the same much-quoted research, it does not provide so much as one critical question or recognition that there may be different perspectives and views ... Not only do these documents make dull and repetitive reading. They stifle democracy.
>
> (Moss and Dahlberg, 2008: 9)

Conclusions

We are entering a new age of interpersonal social awareness unlike anything that we have known before. The skills and competencies needed in tomorrow's work-place are going to be significantly different from those that we have traditionally cultivated in schooling systems, and across the world key thinkers are starting to call for a re-definition of the role of education. The old models that measured value through the regurgitation of banks of memorized information simply aren't going to cut it any more. The obsession with the criteria of 'performance' has created a generation of children who are profoundly disengaged from the joy of learning, and who struggle to find any real meaning in their lives.

For it is personal meaning-making, deep engagement, adaptability and creativity that we need to nurture as we move into a drastically changing world. A curriculum that employs instructional strategies encompassing the needs of the whole child is the only one that is going to meet with the true needs of the twenty-first century. It should encompass the physical, emotional, intellectual and spiritual growth of the child with environments that stimulate and nurture the intuitive as well as the rational, the imaginative as well as the practical, and the creative as well as the receptive functions of each individual. As Mihalyi Csikszentmihalyi so succinctly stated 'the chief impediments to learning are not cognitive in nature. It is not that students cannot learn, it is that they do not wish to' (Czikzentmihalyi, 1991: 1).

We need to move from educational systems based upon conformity and standardization (thinking and moving only within the box) to ones that embrace complexity, diversity, subjectivity and multiple perspectives (thinking and moving in, over and beyond the box). And we need to actively seek out and encourage new thinkers and researchers who are exploring the importance and value of differing approaches, views and perspectives, and who are developing new frameworks for education, such as lifelong learning, learning on demand, self-directed learning, information contextualized to the needs of the learner, collaborative learning and community learning. We live in a complex and rapidly changing world that demands new, exciting and innovative responses, rather than more of the same old deeply flawed model that is serving neither the welfare of the child, nor society as a whole.

We know that children's learning dispositions are highly environ-mentally sensitive – meaning that they are nurtured or weakened by their experiences, especially those in relation to the significant adults in their lives. And yet we invest extraordinarily little in research studies that measure child well-being and flow, or that investigate whether what we are currently doing is enhancing or eroding those disposi-tions. After all, what good are acceptable outcomes or great test results if your whole sense of self-worth has been moved from an internal to an external focus, and you are no longer able to recognize or follow your innate developmental needs? Just as we are currently seeing the call for democracy in all corners of the world, so should we be calling for the democratization of learning for all children, and the protection of the extraordinary potential that is so clearly evident in the early learner.

References

BBC News (2010) 'One in 11 boys leaves primary school "unable to read"', accessible at: http://www.bbc.co.uk/news/education-12000886 (retrieved 30 June 2011)

BBC Radio 2 (nd) See: http://www.bbc.co.uk/programmes/b00tqrj1

Bowlby, J. (1969) *Attachment and Loss, Vol. 1*, 2nd edn, New York: Basic Books

Boyd Caldwell, L. (1987) *Bringing Reggio Emilia Home*, New York: Teachers College Press

Bronfenbrenner, U. (1968) *The Ecology of Human Development*, New York: Hawthorne Books

Bronson, P. and Merryman, A. (2010) 'The creativity crisis', *Newsweek*, 10 July 2010; http://www.newsweek.com/2010/07/10/the-creativity-crisis.html (accessed 29 June 2011)

Bruner, J. (1972) *Going Beyond the Information Given*, New York: Norton

Bruner, J. (1986) *Actual Minds, Possible Worlds*, Cambridge, Mass.: Harvard University Press

Bruner, J.S. (1996) *The Culture of Education*, Cambridge, Mass.: Harvard University Press

Child and Parenting Institute (2007) *Family Trends*, London

Child Poverty Action Group (2009) *Child Wellbeing and Child Poverty: Where the UK Stands in the European Table*, London; downloadable at: http://www.cpag.org.uk/info/ChildWellbeingandChildPoverty.pdf (30 June 2011)

Coughlan, S. (2010) 'UK schools fall in global ranking', BBC News, 7 December; http://www.bbc.co.uk/news/education-11929277 (accessed 29 June 2011)

Csikszentmihalyi, M. (1991) *Thoughts about Education, New Horizons for Learning*; see: http://www-bcf.usc.edu/~genzuk/Thoughts_About_Education_Mihaly_Csikszentmihalyi.pdf (accessed 1 July 2011)

Devlin, K. and Porter, A. (2011) 'Underage drinking in Britain "among worst in the world"' (report in World Health Organization study), *Daily Telegraph*, 16 June; http://www.telegraph.co.uk/news/uknews/law-and-order/2140278/Underage-drinking-in-Britain-among-worst-in-the-world.html (accessed 29 June 2099)

Edwards, C., Gandini, L. and Foxman, G. (eds) (1998) *The Hundred Languages of Children – Advanced Reflections*, London: Ablex

Family Policy Studies (1996) Proceedings of a conference on Families and Parenting held in September 1995, May

Farb, P. (1978) *Humankind,* Orlanda, Fla: Houghton Mifflin

Faulkus, G. (1999) Talk given at a meeting in the House of Lords for Children, May

Fowler, W., Ogston, K., Roberts-Fiati, G. and Swenson, A. (1997) 'The effects of enriching language in infancy on early and later development of competence', *Early Childhood Development and Care,* 125: 41–77

Gardner, H. (1983) *Frames of Mind*. New York: Basic Books

Gilbert, I. (2010) *Why Do I Need a Teacher when I've got Google?*, London: Routledge

Gillard D. (2007) 'Education in England: a brief history'; see http://www.educationengland.org.uk/history (accessed 1 July 2011)

Goleman, D. (1983) *Emotional Intelligence*, New York: Bantam Books

Goleman D. (1988) 'New scales of intelligence rank talent for living', *New York Times*, 5 April

Hart, R. (1992) *Children's Participation: From Tokenism to Citizenship*, Innocenti Essay No. 4, United Nations Environment Programme, UNICEF

Holt, J. (1990) *How Children Fail*, 2nd edn, Harmondsworth: Penguin Books

Huxley, A, (1954) *The Doors of Perception*, London: Chatto and Windus

Jones, E. and Nimmo, J. (1984) *Emergent Curriculum*, Washington, D.C.: National Association for the Education of Young Children

Jones, E. and Reynolds, G. (1992) *The Play's the Thing: Teachers' Roles in Children's Play*, New York: Teachers College Press

Malaguzzi, L. (1996) *The Hundred Languages of Children*, New York: Ablex Publishing Corporation

Mental Health Foundation (2011) London: MHF, January; see: http://www.mentalhealth.org.uk/help-information/mental-health-statistics (accessed 1 July 2011)

Moss, P. and Dahlberg, G. (2008) 'Beyond quality in early childhood education and care – languages of evaluation', *New Zealand Journal of Teachers' Work*, 5 (1): 3–12

OECD (2009) *Doing Better for Children*

Office for National Statistics (2009) *Fertility Rates 2009*, London

Park, A. (2009) 'TV may inhibit babies' language development', *Time* Magazine, 1 June

PIRLS (2007) *Study Progress in International Reading Literacy*, Chestnut Hill, Mass.: International Association for the Evaluation of Educational Achievement (IEA)

Power, M. (1997) *The Audit Society: Rituals of Verification*, Oxford: Oxford University Press

Robinson, Sir K. (2010) 'Bring on the learning revolution', http://sirken-robinson.com/skr/bring-on-the-learning-revolution (accessed 29 June 2011)

Rogers, C.R. (1989) 'Early admission: early labelling', *Journal of Humanistic Psychology*, 32

Rutter, M. (1991) *Maternal Deprivation Reassessed*, 2nd edn, Harmondsworth: Penguin Books

Stern, D. (1998) 'The process of therapeutic change involving implicit knowledge: some implications of developmental observations for adult psychotherapy', *Infant Mental Health Journal*, 19: 300–8

Stubbs, I. (2010) 'How to Get an A-Star', BBC Radio 4, Monday 16 August

Trevarthen, C. (1980) 'The foundations of intersubjectivity: development of interpersonal and co-operative understanding in infants', in D. Olsen (ed.), *The Social Foundations of Language and Thought*, Toronto: George J. McLeod, pp. 316–42

UNICEF (2007) *An Overview of Child Wellbeing in Rich Countries*, Innocenti Research Centre

Vygotsky, L.S. (1978) *Mind in Society: The Development of Higher Psychological Processes*, Cambridge, Mass.: Harvard University Press

Woodhead, M. (1997) 'Psychology and the cultural construction of children's needs', in A. Prout and A. James (eds), *Construction and Reconstruction of Childhood*, 2nd edn, London: Falmer, pp. 61–82

CHAPTER 12

The Steiner Waldorf Foundation Stage – 'To Everything There is a Season'

LYNNE OLDFIELD

'As the human lifespan becomes longer, why is childhood becoming ever shortened?'

This question appeared in the foreword of a book by Elizabeth von Grunelius, the teacher in the first Waldorf kindergarten, based on the philosophy of Rudolf Steiner, which opened in Stuttgart in 1926. It is still a question we should be asking. Grunelius encouraged Waldorf kindergarten teachers to resist premature intellectuality and over stimulation of the nerve–sense system in early childhood, and to make all decisions as to practice from out of a deep understanding of the phases of child development, rather than to meet centralized policy- and economy-driven targets. This is a genuinely developmentally attuned approach to care and education in the sensitive early years of human development (Oldfield, 2011).

The Unhurried Pathway

In relation to current trends, the Waldorf approach is notably unhurried. This unhurried mood embraces everything that the child experiences – the presentation of activities, the structure of the day, the attention to detail, the patient nurturing of the individual child and care for the environment, the assessment of school readiness. Most significantly the Waldorf foundation stage extends to the sixth birthday, with children entering school Class 1 in the year they turn seven.

The children are in mixed age groups, from three to six years of age, and remain, ideally, with the same teacher throughout the three years before entering school. There are seldom more than 16 children in a group.

In a Waldorf kindergarten we have the gift of time, and the young, developing child senses this at the deepest level. This gift of time together allows a valuable connection to be made between child and teacher, which finds resonance in attachment theory, and acknowledges the value of continuity in the early years of childhood. This is not an approach lacking in aspiration, but an active patience, with its roots in the wisdom of the natural laws of child development. The progressive stages of human development require educators to have not only a sense of '*what*' the curriculum should deliver, but also *why, when and how*, so that we develop a pedagogy which will acknowledge and enhance each stage of development, recognizing its specific characteristics and needs – a sense of what is truly appropriate at each age.

This approach to building a foundation does not directly, or narrowly, concern itself with 'school readiness', but a general readiness for life, and a meeting of the specific challenges inherent in the first seven years of human development.

A Hand-First, not Head-Start, Approach

The Waldorf kindergarten is essentially an activity-rich, and authentically play-based experience. It arises from what we term a Will-first pedagogy, which recognizes, respects and welcomes the active nature of the young child in the first seven years of life. The children will find many outlets for initiative; rather than waiting for instruction and direction, children in a Waldorf kindergarten develop the habit of taking initiative. They become initiators of their own learning, and as a result discover repeatedly 'I can do it!', with self-confidence and self-esteem developing as a consequence. They become empowered, exploratory learners rather than being 'set up' to meet imposed targets which, however well intended, require children to stretch into the next stage of development.

A significant number of primary school children have been identified as having poor balance and motor skills (see Chapter 9), which has implications for the hand and eye co-ordination necessary for reading and writing. We now know, through neuroscience, that movement establishes neural pathways and makes sense of sensory experience. The Waldorf kindergarten teacher is familiar with the sense of balance, touch and movement, and develops practice to support their development, understanding this as a significant part of a foundation for formal learning.

The Waldorf day is a healthy balance between indoor and outdoor play, child-initiated and teacher-led activities. Domestic skills – baking, bread-making, gardening, care of the environment – and artistic expression – painting, drawing, music, woodwork, sewing – combine with free, imaginative, child-led play. Waldorf kindergartens are communities of 'do-ers' where a 'be active' rather than 'sit still' culture prevails, with the much-desired qualities of attentiveness and self-management emerging from the active experience.

Guiding the naturally active nature of young children has implications for socialization – a further prerequisite for a foundation stage. Children need to move beyond instinctive and impulsive behaviour, and towards self-management, before they are ready for the more sedentary activities of reading and writing. Attentiveness and perseverance, the ability to sit still for the lengths of time required for the acquisition of literacy and numeracy – these abilities need to be developed first.

A Calming, Emotion-regulating and Nurturing Experience

In a Waldorf kindergarten the children certainly experience a sense of freedom of movement but importantly they are not limit-deprived. Boundaries are established by a rhythmical, repetitive, habit-forming experience, and the conscious use of example by informed, reflective, responsible yet relatively non-intrusive practitioners.

The children quickly learn what is required of them, as a result of the carefully structured experience in which rhythm and repetition have an innate authority for the child, removing the need for constant direction and instruction. They experience freedom within form and feel liberated, whilst recognizing boundaries. The young child is enabled, in this ordered environment, to develop a sense of purpose and to acquire self-management. This early experience of order and consistency is the foundation for future self-discipline. These elements are supportive in steadying emotional responses, leading children to act rather than react.

The repetition of activities, stories, songs, circle times and experiences allows children to make sense of their world – not only 'to know', but also to understand, and to imprint experience into memory. It is also an antidote to the speeded-up reality of our contemporary lifestyles. The child has time to grasp, and understand, a logical sequence in these repeated experiences. In-born trust is frequently shaken by the inconsistent, accelerated conditions prevailing in the lifestyles of many children, and the steady, returning, rhythmical quality of a Waldorf kindergarten allows the child to feel safe and trust what will be experienced there. The competence and self-esteem which are developed will accompany them into the next phase of a more formal approach to learning.

A Language-Rich Environment

The Waldorf early childhood educator is engaged in a linguistic mothering. She creates a language-rich, rather than print-filled, environment. Orality is acknowledged as the foundation for literacy.

The child's experience of language in the kindergartens is essentially that of human speech, as opposed to technological substitutes. Story tapes, white boards, television and computer software have no place in the Waldorf early childhood curriculum. Our foundation stage for literacy embraces phonological awareness, fine and gross motor skills, the development of speech and communication, the ability to listen and be attentive, opportunities for mark-making in painting and drawing, and a love of stories; in an unhurried way, these opportunities prepare the children for a later introduction to phonics, reading and writing. The children are noticeably articulate and communicative.

The curriculum is rich with songs, nursery rhymes, verses, finger games, puppet shows, circle and story time – all repeated over several days so that children can memorize and enrich their vocabulary, without anxiety. Speech is constantly practised and extended in the free social interaction of creative play. (Neuroscience has identified the connection between speech and motor skills, particularly hand-based motor skills, and the significance of the senses of balance and movement for language and speech development and the making of neurological connections [cf. Chapter 9]. The Waldorf approach works intensively with fine and gross motor skills.)

Literacy, in the narrow sense of reading and writing, is both a gain and a loss. We need also to be aware of what the child loses when introduced ever earlier to phonics. Literacy changes everything. It represents a significant shift in consciousness for the child – away from the unselfconscious state-of-being that is normal to the child below five, and which is necessary for authentic play to flourish. Literacy in its current narrow definition takes the child away from an earlier naturally concrete reality; the abstraction of the alphabet has only a very tenuous link to the reality of young children, and they can become anxious when pulled away, too soon, from this experience.

The Early Years Foundation Stage (England) goals for literacy belong to the next phases of development, according to the Waldorf understanding of child development. The ambition to have children reading and writing before they enter school represents an acceleration of intellectuality, self-consciousness and awakefulness, and does not allow sufficient time to establish a physiological foundation for reading and writing.

This analytical consciousness, and the physiological demands required for phonics, reading and writing, together with the emerging practice in early years care and education of constant instruction, direction and questioning, will eventually inhibit the genius of imitation and creative play, and result in the loss of their attendant rewards. What are the long-term implications of these early precocious achievements?

Authentically Play Based

The human ability 'to imagine' deserves our utmost respect. In the future work-place, in social interaction and in our homes, the prospect of adults who were play-deprived in childhood deserves our concerned attention.

The Waldorf early childhood educator creates an environment which acknowledges wonder as the foundation for the development of a natural seeker of knowledge. Wonder is cherished and nurtured as the very seed of enquiry. From our earliest beginnings, we have stated our intention to offer a play-based experience for children up to the age of seven. We have refined our definition of play, and developed our ability to create an enabling environment in which true, authentic, imaginative, creative, self-initiated exploratory play can flourish.

Our definition would exclude descriptions such as 'directed play', 'structured play' and 'purposeful play', but would embrace descriptions such as 'freely chosen' and 'child initiated'. The concept of play instigated by a practitioner for the purpose of acquiring a particular concept is considered a contradiction in terms. In our view, this is actually 'playful teaching' rather than authentic play, with the latter always requiring the child to be both instigator and navigator of the experience. The rights of the child should include the right to be a dreamer.

An even less well understood fact is that the 'enabling environment' which would need to be created for phonic, reading, writing and the ICT skills currently invading the preschool domain will, in time, actually disable true play. One requires a new self-conscious, separating, analysing, awakened viewpoint, whilst play requires the child to act out of an unselfconscious, unseparated, non-analytic state-of-being. They are incompatible environments.

The peak time for authentic play is between four and five years of age, when the demands of early introduction to formal literacy are now beginning to be felt. Once the window of opportunity for play is lost it cannot be re-opened. This will only make sense for teachers and politicians if play is understood, defined and valued.

We now know that interactive play is essential for optimal brain development in the frontal lobes, with a subsequent relationship to reasoning, reflecting, empathy and creativity. Play releases well-being chemicals which are also anti anxiety and anti aggression, and recent research suggests a correlation between play deprivation and 'ADHD', and that play may be as effective as low doses of Ritalin in addressing hyperactivity.

Article 31 of the United Nations Convention on the Rights of the Child acknowledges the importance of play for the young child. Waldorf kindergartens defend the child's right to time and space for play, confident that society will ultimately benefit from its qualities of enthusiasm, empathy, perseverance, inspiration, confidence, socialization, integrated learning and divergent thinking.

Dedicated Care of the Nerve–Sense System

The young child is open, utterly, to the environment. We now know the extent to which the brain is experience-dependent, formed by experiences which leave their neuron footprint. A policy report from the Centre for Social Justice (2008), 'The Next Generation', identified the nerve–sense system in early childhood as 'both a critical window of vulnerability and also a critical window of opportunity'.

The report also noted the stress which can arise when children are over stimulated through society's anxiety for the child 'to achieve'.

The Waldorf kindergarten aims to provide a calm, stress-free environment which is nevertheless demanding in a healthy way. Recognizing the vulnerability, there is a protective approach to the nerve–sense system, shielding children from early screen viewing, precocious intellectuality, and over abundant and negative sense impressions. Recognizing the opportunity, there is also a seizing of possibilities for sensory nourishment – carefully chosen stories, natural materials, direct experience of nature, organic food, colour, touch, smell, sounds – all are chosen for their integrity, beauty and truthfulness. Young children need a real rather than a virtual reality. They deserve no less. The vulnerability of young children to screen viewing is now well documented (see Chapter 19). Visual electronic media halts development of the frontal lobe and its ability to control anti-social behaviour. Once introduced, screen viewing quickly becomes addictive, and makes real-world experience uninteresting. Impulsive behaviour is stimulated and attentiveness weakened.

The Human Image

Rudolf Steiner, the founder of Waldorf education, gave imitation a central place in the child's transition from being a creature of instinct and impulse to one capable of self-direction and healthy social interaction, and in 1921 Sigmund Freud (1922) remarked that 'A path leads from identification by way of imitation to empathy'. In recent years neurological research has confirmed a link between mirror neurons which are activated by the act of imitation, and the quality of empathy which is enabled by the same neurons (Meltzoff and Prinz, 2002).

The child's overcoming of impulsive behaviour is a major problem in early years settings. This is considered to be a prime task for the Waldorf kindergarten teacher, and a key principle in laying a foundation for school entry. Consciously providing an example to imitate is a valued Waldorf early childhood principle, and a key element in our teacher training programmes. Children have a natural biological predisposition to imitate. They unconsciously look for the human example to emulate. They seek the human image, and Waldorf teacher training emphasizes the self-development of the teacher as an absolute necessity.

Our teachers are trained to be examples worthy of imitation, and view themselves as a significant part of the environment. Students study speech, movement and artistic activities as preparation for this responsibility. They recognize that the act of imitation, when used intensively, can strengthen attachment, affect behaviour, develop empathy and teach new skills, but essentially provide children with the human image they need to find the way forward.

'To Everything There is a Season'

Why is it assumed that 'quality' early childhood care and education necessitates an ever-earlier introduction to ICT, phonics, reading and writing? In the same week that a national newspaper reported that children born in 2011 can expect to live to the age of 100, an early years magazine quoted research which regarded preschool children as 'trailing behind' if they did not have access to digital technology as aids to early reading and writing! (see Chapter 19).

Is it accurate to assume that the disadvantaged child will benefit from this hurried approach? Surely they are the children who will most benefit from the unhurried pathway – with socialization, speech and communication, attentiveness, self-management, physiological readiness, and the healing power of play as central to their preparation for school entry.

Perhaps we need to define more clearly what we mean by 'a foundation stage', and its purpose, and to reinvigorate our instinct as educators for appropriate timing and appropriate intentions. Let us prepare, and empower, our trainee teachers with a deep understanding of child development so that they can confidently, and freed from centralized, one-size-fits-all legislation, make meaningful decisions as to what is right at each phase of the child's journey towards full humanity.

References

Centre for Social Justice (2008) 'The Next Generation', London: September; see: http://www.centreforsocialjustice.org.uk/default.asp?pageRef=267

Freud, S. (1922) *Group Psychology and the Analysis of the Ego*, New York: Boni and Liveright; Chapter 6: 'Identification'; accessible at: http://www.bartleby.com/290/7.html (accessed 1 July 2011)

Meltzoff, A.N. and Prinz, W. (2002) *The Imitative Mind: Development, Evolution and Brain Bases*, Cambridge: Cambridge University Press

Oldfield, L. (2011) *Free to Learn: Introducing Steiner Waldorf Early Childhood Education*, 2nd edn, Stroud: Hawthorn Press (in press)

CHAPTER 13

Can We Play?[*]

DAVID ELKIND

Play is essential to positive human development, but children are playing less and less. In this chapter, I explore what we can do to build a new culture of play.

Play is rapidly disappearing from our homes, our schools, and our neighbourhoods. Over the last two decades alone, children have lost eight hours of free, unstructured and spontaneous play a week. More than 30,000 schools in the United States have eliminated recess to make more time for academics. From 1997 to 2003, children's time spent outdoors fell by 50 per cent, according to a study by Sandra Hofferth (2009) at the University of Maryland. Hofferth has also found that the amount of time children spend in organized sports has doubled, and the number of minutes children devote each week to passive leisure, not including watching television, has increased from 30 minutes to more than three hours. It is no surprise, then, that childhood obesity is now considered an epidemic.

But the problem goes well beyond obesity. Decades of research has shown that play is crucial to physical, intellectual and social-emotional development at all ages (Elkind, 2007). This is especially true of the purest form of play: the unstructured, self-motivated, imaginative, independent kind, where children initiate their own games and even invent their own rules.

In infancy and early childhood, play is the activity through which children learn to recognize colours and shapes, tastes and sounds

---

[*] This chapter was originally published in the spring 2008 issue of *Greater Good* (www.greatergoodscience.org), the magazine of UC Berkeley's Greater Good Science Center; reproduced here with updating by kind permission of the editor.

– the very building blocks of reality. Play also provides pathways to love and social connection. Elementary school children use play to learn mutual respect, friendship, co-operation and competition. For adolescents, play is a means of exploring possible identities, as well as a way to blow off steam and stay fit. Even adults have the potential to unite play, love and work, attaining the dynamic, joyful state that psychologist Mihaly Csikszentmihalyi (1991) calls 'flow'.

With play on the decline, we risk losing these and many other benefits. For too long, we have treated play as a luxury that children, as well as adults, could do without. But the time has come for us to recognize why play is worth defending: it is essential to leading a happy and healthy life.

Play and Development

Years of research has confirmed the value of play. In early childhood, play helps children develop skills they can not get in any other way. Babbling, for example, is a self-initiated form of play through which infants create the sounds they need to learn the language of their parents. Likewise, children teach themselves to crawl, stand and walk through repetitious practice play. At the preschool level, children engage in dramatic play and learn who is a leader, who is a follower, who is outgoing, who is shy. They also learn to negotiate their own conflicts.

A 2007 report from the American Academy of Pediatrics (Ginsburg and others, 2007) documents that play promotes not only behavioural development but brain growth as well. The University of North Carolina's Abecedarian Early Child Intervention programme (Anon, n.d.; Campbell and Ramey, 2007) found that children who received an enriched, play-oriented parenting and early childhood programme had significantly higher IQ's at age five than did a comparable group of children who were not in the programme (105 vs 85 points).

A large body of research evidence also supports the value and importance of particular types of play. For example, Israeli psychologist Sara Smilansky's classic studies of sociodramatic play, where two or more children participate in shared make-believe, demonstrate the value of this play for academic, social and emotional learning. 'Sociodramatic play activates resources that stimulate social and intellectual growth in the child, which in turn affects the child's success in school', concluded Smilansky in a 1990 study (Smilansky, 1990; see also Smilansky and Shefatya, 1990) that compared American and Israeli children. 'For example, problem solving in most school subjects requires a great deal of make believe, visualizing how the Eskimos live, reading stories, imagining a story and writing it down, solving arithmetic problems, and determining what will come next.'

Other research illustrates the importance of physical play for children's learning and development. Some of these studies have highlighted the importance of recess. Psychologist Anthony Pellegrini and his colleagues (Pellegrini and Bohn, 2005) have found that elementary school children become increasingly inattentive in class when recess is delayed. Similarly, studies conducted in French and Canadian elementary schools over a period of four years found that regular physical activity had positive effects on academic performance. Spending one third of the school day in physical education, art and music improved not only physical fitness, but attitudes toward learning and test scores. These findings echo those from one analysis of 200 studies on the effects of exercise on cognitive functioning (Tomporowski and Ellis, 1986), which also suggests that physical activity promotes learning.

In recent years, and most especially since the 2002 passage of the No Child Left Behind Act, we have seen educators, policy-makers and many parents embrace the idea that early academics leads to greater success in life. Yet several studies by Kathy Hirsch-Pasek and colleagues (e.g. Hirsh-Pasek, 1991) have compared the performance of children attending academic preschools with those attending play-oriented preschools. The results showed no advantage in reading and math achievement for children attending the academic preschools. But there was evidence that those children had higher levels of test anxiety, were less creative and had more negative attitudes towards school than did the children attending the play preschools.

So if play is that important, why is it disappearing?

The Perfect Storm

The decline of children's free, self-initiated play is the result of a perfect storm of technological innovation, rapid social change and economic globalization.

Technological innovations have led to the all-pervasiveness of television and computer screens in our society in general (cf. Chapter

19), and in our homes in particular. An unintended consequence of this invasion is that childhood has moved indoors. Children who might once have enjoyed a pick-up game of baseball in an empty lot now watch the game on TV, sitting on their couch.

Meanwhile, single and working parents now outnumber the once-predominant nuclear family, in which a stay-at-home mother could provide the kind of loose oversight that facilitates free play. Instead, busy working parents outsource at least some of their former responsibilities to coaches, tutors, trainers, martial arts teachers and other professionals. As a result, middle-income children spend more of their free time in adult-led and -organized activities than any earlier generation. (Low-income youth sometimes have the opposite problem: their parents may not have the means to put them in high-quality programmes that provide alternatives to playing in unsafe neighbourhoods.)

Finally, a global economy has increased parental fears about their children's prospects in an increasingly high-tech marketplace.

For too long, we have treated play as a luxury that kids, as well as adults, could do without. Many middle-class parents have bought into the idea that education is a race, and that the earlier you start your child in academics, the better. Preschool tutoring in math and programmes such as the Kumon System, which emphasizes daily drills in math and reading, are becoming increasingly popular. And all too many kindergartens, once dedicated to learning through play, have become full-day academic institutions that require testing and homework. In such a world, play has come to be seen as a waste of precious time. A 1999 survey found that nearly a third of kindergarten classes did not have a recess period (e.g. Jambor, 1999).

As adults have increasingly thwarted self-initiated play and games, we have lost important markers of the stages in a child's development. In the absence of such markers, it is difficult to determine what is appropriate and not appropriate for children. We run the risk of pushing them into certain activities before they are ready, or stunting the development of important intellectual, social or emotional skills. For example, it is only after the age of six or seven that children will spontaneously participate in games with rules, because it is only at that age that they are fully able to understand and follow rules.

Those kinds of developmental markers fall by the wayside when we slot very young children into activities such as Little League. When Little League was founded in 1939, the adult organizers looked to children themselves in setting the starting age, which ended up being about age nine or older. But the success of Little League was not lost on parents eager to find supervized activities for young children. Before long, team soccer was promoted for younger children because it was an easier and less complex game for the six- to nine-year-old age group. The rapid growth of soccer leagues challenged the popularity of Little League. This led to the introduction of Tee Ball, a simplified version of baseball for children as young as four.

By pushing young children into team sports for which they are not developmentally ready, we rule out forms of play that once encouraged them to learn skills of independence and creativity. Instead of learning on their own in backyards, fields and on sidewalks, children are only learning to do what adults tell them to do. Moreover, one study found that many children who start playing soccer at age four are burned out on that sport by the time they reach adolescence, just the age when they might truly enjoy and excel at it (see Reilly, 1996).

Bring Back Play

Play is motivated by pleasure. It is instinctive and part of the maturational process. We cannot prevent children from self-initiated play; they will engage in it whenever they can. The problem is that we have curtailed the time and opportunities for such play. Obviously we cannot turn the clock back and reverse the technological, social and economic changes that have helped silence children's play. Television, computers, new family models and globalization are here to stay.

What is important is balance. If a child spends an hour on the computer or watching TV, equal time should be given to playing with peers or engaging in individual activities like reading or crafts. It is important to involve the child in making these decisions and setting the parameters for how they spend their time. If we give children some ownership of the rules, they are usually more willing to follow them than when they are simply imposed from above. It is also important to appreciate individual differences. You will not be able to keep some children from playing sports, while others prefer more sedentary activities.

Another way we can help bring play back into children's lives is to have schools restore recess for at least half an hour. As research demonstrates, academics are unlikely to suffer from this change; if anything, they will benefit. Schools also argue that they cannot afford

recess because of high insurance costs and parents' greater appetite
for litigation. But when I speak with insurance officers about this
issue, they claim that that argument is overblown. Either way, children could still be taken outside, or to the gym, for calisthenics to
exercise their bodies.

We must also address the more general problem of test-driven
curricula in today's schools. When teachers are forced to teach to the
test, they become less innovative in their teaching methods, with less
room for games and imagination. More creative teaching methods
build upon children's interests and attitudes – their playful disposition – and this encourages them to enjoy their teachers, which in
turn enhances their interest in the subject matter. Though computers
are one of the forces limiting play, they can be creatively used in the
service of playful learning. As more young teachers who are profi-
cient in technology enter the schools, we will have the first true
educational reform in decades, if not centuries.

But you don't have to be a teacher to help bring back play. Many
neighbourhoods badly need more playgrounds. This was also the case
in the 1930s; in response, we saw the 'playground movement', when
local communities set up their own playgrounds. A new playground
movement is long overdue, especially for our inner city neighbourhoods, where safe play spaces are often in short supply. A playground
should be required of any new large-scale housing development.

We could go further. In Scandinavian countries, there are play
areas in even the best restaurants, as well as in airports and train
stations. These countries appreciate the importance of play for
healthy development, and we could well follow their example.

Finally, children do as we do, not as we say. That gives us incen-
tive to bring play back into our adult lives. We can shut off the TVs
and take our children with us on outdoor adventures. We should
get less exercise in the gym and more on hiking trails and basketball
courts. We can also make work more playful: businesses that do this
are among the most successful.

Seattle's Pike Fish Market is a case in point. Workers throw fish
to one another, engage the customers in repartee, and appear to have
a grand time. Some companies, such as Google, have made play
an important part of their corporate culture. Study after study has
shown that when workers enjoy what they do and are well-rewarded
and recognized for their contributions, they like and respect their
employers and produce higher-quality work. For example, when the

Rohm and Hass Chemical Company in Kentucky reorganized its workplace into self-regulating and self-rewarding teams, one study found that worker grievances and turnover declined, while plant safety and productivity improved.

When we adults unite play, love and work in our lives, we set an example that our children can follow. That just might be the best way to bring play back into the lives of our children – and build a more playful culture.

References

Anon (n.d.) The Carolina Abecedarian Project, see: http://www.fpg.unc. edu/~abc/ (visited 1 July 2011)

Campbell, F.A. and Ramey, C.T. (2007) 'Carolina Abecedarian Project', paper presented at National Invitational Conference of the Early Childhood Research Collaborative, University of Minnesota Center for Early Education and Development, 7–8 December; accessible at: http://www.earlychildhoodrc.org/events/presentations/campbell-ramey. pdf (retrieved 1 July 2011)

Csikszentmihalyi, M. (1991) *Flow: The Psychology of Optimal Experience*, New York: HarperPerennial

Elkind, D. (2007) *The Power of Play: How Spontaneous, Imaginative Activities Lead to Happier, Healthier Children: Learning What Comes Naturally*, Cambridge, Mass.: Da Capo Press

Ginsburg, K.R. and others (2007) 'The Importance of Play in Promoting Healthy Child Development and Maintaining Strong Parent–Child Bonds, Pediatrics,' 119 (1): 182–91, accessible at: http://www.aap.org/ pressroom/playfinal.pdf (retrieved 1 July 2011)

Hirsh-Pasek, K. (1991) 'Pressure or challenge in preschool? How academic environments affect children', *New Directions for Child and Adolescent Development*, 53 (Fall): 39–46

Hofferth, S.L. (2009) 'Changes in American children's time – 1997 to 2003', *International Journal of Time Use Research*, 6(1): 26–47; accessible at: http://www.ncbi.nlm.nih.gov/pmc/articles/PMC2939468/ (retrieved 1 July 2011)

Jambor, T. (1999) 'Recess and social development', *Earlychildhoodnews*, available at: http://www.earlychildhoodnews.com/earlychildhood/ article_view.aspx?ArticleID=39 (retrieved 1 July 2011)

Pellegrini, A.D. and Bohn, C.M. (2005) 'The role of recess in children's cognitive performance and school adjustment', *Educational Researcher*, 34 (1): 13–19

Reilly, T. (1996) 'Special populations', in T. Reilly, *Science and Soccer*, London: Spon Press/Taylor & Francis, pp. 109–19

Smilansky, S. (1990) 'Sociodramatic play: its relevance to behavior and achievement in school', in E. Klugman and S. Smilansky (eds), *Children's Play and Learning: Perspectives and Policy Implications*, New York: Teachers College Press, pp. 18–42

Smilansky, S. and Shefatya, L. (1990) *Facilitating Play: A Medium for Promoting Cognitive, Socio-emotional, and Academic Development in Young Children*, Gaithersburg, MD: Psychological & Educational Publications

Tomporowski, P.D. and Ellis, N.R. (1986) 'Effects of exercise on cognitive process: a review', *Psychological Bulletin*, 99: 338–46

CHAPTER 14

Play – Transforming Thinking

TRICIA DAVID

The review of the Early Years Foundation Stage (EYFS) by Dame Clare Tickell (2011: 27) has given a powerful endorsement for 'effective teaching' as promoted through 'playing and exploring, active learning, and creating and thinking critically'. This chapter examines some of the reasons why play is favoured as the most appropriate approach in provision for babies and children in their earliest years, as well as some of the challenges involved.

What Are Children to Do with Their Time in Their Earliest Years?

The Jesuits' maxim 'Give me a child until he is seven and I will give you the man' has perhaps been debated even more fiercely since neuroscientists' evidence began to be widely circulated, indicating the ferocious activity of a baby's brain cells, and that learning has been taking place even in the womb. There were fears that brain 'wiring' during this first phase of life might predestine lives of ignorance, indolence and incapacity in children who had not been sufficiently or appropriately stimulated. Some young children's experiences began to be planned, timed and checked almost to exhaustion by aspiring parents, whose emotional (and financial) investment seemed crucial to their own feelings of success. Others were left, as their parents termed it, to 'enjoy their childhoods'.

In many ways, the issue of what young children should be doing during their time in nurseries and childcare settings rests on the same basic issue – to what extent should babies and young children be allowed to do what seems to come naturally – to explore and play, to engage in self-selected activities? Or, to what extent should adults direct children's foci, time and space? This leads on to the questions: what is happening during play? Does play contribute to learning? What should young children be learning anyway, and how do they learn best? What are the implications in relation to the role of adults?

Play: What's Going on when Children Play?

Thankfully, babies come into the world full of enthusiasm to explore the place where they find themselves – both its inhabitants (with whom they seem programmed to seek contact and communication) and everything else they can smell, hear, see, touch and taste. They are overwhelmed by desire to investigate what attracts them in that world, and will single-mindedly pursue their goal if at all possible, becoming broken-hearted (and perhaps ultimately broken-willed) if too often thwarted in that quest. They are scientists desperately seeking answers to questions they pose themselves, even before they have the language to explain this. Most are passionately fascinated by what goes on around them, wanting to become accomplished and recognized members of their communities. So above all, they are going to observe, mimic, construct and seek their places or roles in that community.

In Western/Northern societies, play has long been promoted as the most appropriate occupation for young children. Play – real play – is freely chosen by the player. It is often serious in the initial epistemic stages, when the player is posing the question 'What is this, and what does it do?' (Hutt et al., 1989). During this phase of play, a baby or young child will show great concentration, their earnest faces bearing witness to intense brain activity. The fun/ludic stage of play, which is said to follow on after the epistemic phase, uses the information gained so that, in effect, the player is asking 'What can I do with this?', often laughing and using a sing-song voice. Either phase may last a long time, negating the idea that young children cannot concentrate for sustained periods. Equally, the activity may be abandoned and regenerated. However, defining play is problematic (Nutbrown, 2006). Some researchers argue that it is easier to say what play is not.

Almost 20 years ago, I related my six-month mental struggle (David, 1993) following observations and discussions in Denmark, concerning the place of print literacy in early childhood. Similarly, when working with a group of classroom assistants in Coventry as part of my role at Warwick University many years ago, I was struck by the clear division in views within the group about what children might be expected to be capable of and know on entering the reception year of primary school. The views of participants from Asian British families were clearly focused on certain aspects that the White British group members regarded as too formal, their own views being strongly rooted in play as the 'correct approach' to learning. Recently, research by Liz Brooker (2005) has exposed important questions challenging the universal advocacy of play. Similarly, contact with countries like China (Powell and David, 2010) demonstrate that different expectations of parents and ECEC (Early Childhood Education and Care) professionals in other countries with strongly held cultural traditions and beliefs about the need for young children to be able to participate in those valued practices mean that Western play approaches will be adapted rather than adopted wholesale.

Other issues involve exclusion, where some children control play bouts in ways that prevent others from taking part, or even involve threatening, negative behaviours (Wood, 2007). Meanwhile, Singer and de Haan (2009) argue that adults often intervene too early in conflict, rather than giving children time to resolve their differences. However, practitioners need to be aware of the issues, and thoughtfully consider interventions enabling excluded children to participate meaningfully, as well as working with families, explaining and listening to parents' views, so that adults and children explore together how to ensure that no-one's rights are being infringed (Wall, 2006).

So emphasis on play is not without its critics. For example, the Western/Northern assumption that playing in a nursery is preferable to working is justified for extreme, hazardous, exploitative situations, but in some societies the interactions afforded by employment may be viewed as contributing to a child's socialization (Woodhead, 2005). Bjorklund (2007), while recognizing that the urge to play is universal and that children learn during play experiences, adds that it is not the sole mode of learning, nor are all children able to recognize what they have learnt from play; some will need adults to make their implicit learning explicit for them.

Widening cultural understanding of childhood has caused reflection about the deep belief in play as pedagogy held in the West, so it is at this point that we must ask ourselves if we are justified in doing this. We cannot simply dig our heels in and refuse to examine our own faith in play approaches. As Rogoff (2003: 368–9) has argued:

Understanding different cultural practices does not require determining which one way is 'right' (which does not mean that all ways are fine). We can be open to possibilities that do not necessarily exclude each other. Learning from other communities does not require giving up one's own ways, but it does require suspending one's assumptions temporarily to consider others carefully ... There is *always* more to learn. (author's emphasis)

The Benefits of Play Approaches in Early Childhood Education and Care

Play was recognized as a valuable element in the education of young children by influential thinkers such as Rousseau and Owen over two hundred years ago. Perhaps the main benefit of adopting a play approach is that throughout the world, children generally enjoy playing and choosing how they spend their time (Konner, 1991).

Might the tradition of play as *the* modus operandi of early years education and care be immaterial? Child labour notwithstanding, perhaps children prefer 'real' activities shared with a loving adult and/ or other children who make the explorations and executions of the tasks stimulating and enjoyable, because it is the interaction with other people and with objects or materials which proves attractive? However, because children enjoy sharing activities with an adult, this does not mean it is wise to resort to dominance of children's time by teacher-led activities aimed at covering specific, set goals. In their searching analysis of the Reggio Emilia experience, Hall et al. (2010: 163) suggest that 'In a world that is increasingly preoccupied with measurement, targets, international comparisons, competition, outcomes and productivity, the ideas inherent in the Reggio Emilia experience represent a refreshing and attractive counter-discourse of process, diversity and attention to relationships and self-expression' (cf. Chapter 11).

Vygotsky (1978), emphasizing the social nature of children's development and learning, argued that development is a dialectical process in which transitions are revolutionary, not evolutionary. Thus, development does not simply lie dormant within the child but takes place when that child participates in cultural activities in their families and communities, building up an understanding of 'this is what we do ... '.

Further, McLachlan et al. (2010) demonstrate how cultural-historical approaches based on Vygotsky's ideas are respectful of the cultural backgrounds of children and their families. Similarly, relational pedagogy (Papatheodorou and Moyles, 2009) is informed by the cues of the children themselves, who are respected as people. Here the community of learners – children, professionals and parents – are said to actively engage in relationships and pursue knowledge together. Play acts as a mechanism for promoting and cementing relationships. Children are developing socially and emotionally as well as physically and intellectually when engaging in shared activities which afford the forging of relationships and opportunities to interact with others. Such interactions – with either adults or children – are important, because they are likely to involve social, emotional, cognitive and physical aspects, and development is holistic.

Building on her earlier insightful research on role play, Rogers (2010: 14) argues that play is being used to ensure 'future competencies, rather than the transformative, mimetic and life-enhancing qualities of play', and she urges practitioners to try to view play from the children's perspective, in a 'reciprocal and relational way'.

As Brooks (2011) and Baron-Cohen (2011) argue, positive, sensitive early relationships with parents, family members and others are embedded in meaningful, supportive cultural communities and these promote the development of empathy and resilience.

Some of the advantages of play over sedentary instruction include:

- opportunities for movement, which enable the embodiment of learning and the strengthening of the central nervous system
- humans are big-brained animals with plastic minds and play: promotes adaptive human behaviour; involves imagining alternatives ('what if … ?' type of thinking); eliminates the idea that there is one correct answer and the pressure to come up with that; and fosters negotiation of meanings (Rogoff, 1990; Strandell, 2000)
- interactions with adults, but especially with other children, promote the development of a theory of mind in each child (Gopnik et al., 1999), as well as engagement in everyday life, which may form the basis for democratic understanding
- human development is holistic, and psychologists now agree that the historical approach of separating physical, cognitive, social and emotional development has led to a lack of recognition for the ways in which all areas of development and learning intertwine (David et al., 2003). Children's emotional development, resilience and self-esteem are promoted by play, as it contributes to their holistic development (Howard, 2010)

- play for adults is often referred to as recreation, but for young children, new to many of the experiences they encounter during play, their experiences are allowing them to create themselves and their worlds (David, 1996).

Bruce (2005, 2010) details 'free-flow play', suggesting that its characteristics include: being active; controlled by the player; intrinsically motivated; lacking external pressure; sensitive paired, grouped or solitary activity; an integrating mechanism in a child's learning. Similarly, Broadhead (2004) argues that young children need time, space and, sometimes, specific meaningful objects but, above all, agency to build momentum in play narratives. What seems to be important during the early years is the provision of environments in which young children can interact and negotiate, make choices about what they will do, with whom, where and for how long, exercising agency safely.

Has Play Been Highjacked?

Advised about the centrality of play, the Department for Education and Skills (2007: 37) stated:

> Providers must plan and organise their systems to ensure that every child receives an enjoyable and challenging learning and development experience that is tailored to meet their individual needs ... that there is a balance of adult-led and freely chosen or child-initiated activities, delivered through indoor and outdoor play.

A year later, metamorphosed into the Department for Children, Schools and Families (2008: 11), play was officially endorsed – children and young people should be provided with opportunities to follow 'their own ideas and interests, in their own way and for their own reasons, having fun while respecting themselves and others'.

However, after systematically studying the statements from various government sources, Powell (2008) concluded that the policy discourse revealed an emphasis on containment and control of where, how and when children might have opportunities to play and, therefore, with what and with whom. In England in particular, it was argued that the prescribed curricula and outcomes, and the legal requirement for providers of Early Childhood Education and Care (ECEC), to comply with the demands of the government's Early Years Foundation Stage (EYFS) (Department for Education and Skills, 2007) and the National Curriculum in primary schools (which includes children from five to seven) (Department for Education and Employment/Qualifications and Curriculum Authority, 1999) were creating a restrictive context (British Educational Research Association, 2003) and 'potentially overpower[ing] the intentions of the child' (Goouch, 2009: 142). This was found to be particularly marked in Year R (reception) classes of primary school (British Educational Research Association, 2003; Broadhead, 2004).

While it seems there may have been a lack of consensus amongst different government departments about play, there has certainly been very strong support for play as pedagogy, as well as recognition for issues such as how to plan *for* play, rather than imagining one can actually plan play (DCSF/QCDA, 2009).

If there is an emphasis on adult direction and a curriculum which is inappropriately 'pre-primary' rather than 'socio-cultural' (Bennett, 2005; OECD, 2001, 2006), play will be both highjacked and sidelined. While many ECEC professionals are comfortable with the governmental advocacy of play, some still find it difficult to ensure children are enabled to attain the learning goals. They therefore resort to instruction, especially if they believe the inspectorate require them to adopt more formal approaches (BERA, 2003; David et al., 2000). In other words, there is a demand that children have time and space for play, but predetermined goals are imposed which mean true play is difficult for many ECEC professionals to encourage because they lack either the confidence or the competence to achieve this. Play is highjacked by being stressed in documentation which will often be interpreted to mean the adult must set up playful but adult-directed activities.

Play and learning

Even in the field of ECEC in England there is a range of opinions about how to implement play approaches in ECEC settings. At one end of the spectrum are those who argue that children should be free to play without adult involvement or interference – but is the provision of materials and particular types of spaces or routines a kind of adult intervention? Others claim that it is important for adults to observe children's play and to intervene in appropriate ways, extending the play through the provision of props or language, ideas and reflection (cf. Chapter 12) – but can all adults manage to skilfully ensure that the children are still in control? Some educators plan playful activities which they lead and direct, considering that making an activity fun justifies their actions because they have intended to teach through the experiences offered – but by definition this is not child-selected, child-directed or child-controlled – so it is not play.

These examples are gross categorizations, but they are intended to highlight the fact that such varied views are unsurprising because they stem from underlying knowledge, theories and philosophies about child development, the early childhood curriculum and learning. Perhaps the focal point of this debate should be the differences between play *as* pedagogy and play *for* pedagogy. For example, Bernstein (1997) argued that teachers adopt play approaches for surveillance purposes. He added that teachers' interpretation, evaluation and diagnosis, ultimately, subtly shape each child's learning.

The role of adults in children's play

The extent to which formal instruction is considered necessary will relate to adult understandings about the complexity of the curriculum, the processes through which young children learn and are able to comprehend, and educators' knowledge of each child's earlier experience and achievements.

ECEC professionals have been very aware that they were being judged by their ability to perform in particular ways, that the children with whom they work were expected to achieve particular outcomes. The danger of such a regime is that most young children are compliant and eager to collaborate with adults, seeking partnerships and dialogic opportunities. Many educators identified what central and local government agencies required, and they worked hard to meet these demands, becoming what Hall (2004: 48) called 'restricted professionals'. Some have attempted to overcome policy contradictions through creative compliance, particularly when they believed they had divined what inspectors expected. Meanwhile other colleagues have adopted a relational pedagogy which enables young children to play and learn as participants in a community of learners (David et al., 2011). Dame Clare Tickell (2011) has, thankfully, recommended that the inspectorate ensure they communicate effectively with local authority staff and educators, so that their judgements are transparent, and it is also further recommended that all inspectors be well informed.

During the last 20 years, early childhood educators have been advised that there should be a balance of adult-led and child-led activities (Sylva et al., 2004; Siraj-Blatchford et al., 2002) and, as discussed earlier, this was enshrined in the Statutory Framework (Department for Education and Skills, 2007). Thus, child-initiated play has been promoted and it has again been emphasized by the report (Tickell, 2011), but some anxious practitioners have asked what 'balance' means in this context, and what their role should be if play is to be at the heart of young children's experiences.

In a democracy where individual citizens are expected to think for themselves and to express their views in civilized, informed discussion, what young children require of the adults who share their spaces and offer a 'play as pedagogy' approach means educators need to know each child well, informed by parents and colleagues, as well as by their own professional judgement in order to achieve that balance. Such educators' expertise would include:

- their ability to observe and listen;
- their ability to recognize achievements and concerns as exposed by children's play and talk (or other forms of communication, such as body language, dance, music, painting …);
- their ability to intervene to offer materials, experiences and words, or to suggest ideas, which the children may choose to incorporate in continuing play narratives;
- their sensitivity;
- their ability to take the lead from the children and to join play as a member of a pair or group without dominating;
- their ability to model behaviour, actions, language – especially meta-cognition through 'thinking aloud';
- their ability to create a welcoming, inspiring and exciting place where everyone learns together;
- their ability to be reflexive about their own influence, and to articulate their practices in relation to policies, theories, beliefs, knowledge and professional responsibilities;
- their ability to cherish each of the children, to recognize the knowledge they bring with them and to form loving relationships.

Play: Transforming Thinking

Young children are probably the most gifted observers bar none of life around them. They avidly watch the behaviour and rituals of those in their families and communities (including portrayals in books, television, films, computer games and so on). Above all, human infants come into the world seeking love, acceptance and interaction. They are aware – and wary – of dissonance, while at the same time learning to 'mind read' (Dunn, 1999), a facility which not only gives them power over older siblings but also the power to understand how to please parents and other familiar adults. During imaginative play, they will be 'trying on' roles, just as in other types of play, such as play with paint or clay, they will be investigating the properties of the materials as well as experimenting with their own ideas and concepts.

When three-year-old twin brothers Sam and Noel were playing at running a café with their grandparents, Sam was ever amenable but Noel constantly (and noticeably enjoyably) denied that they had any of the goodies requested. After ordering several apparently unobtainable items, Grandad stated, leaving the room, that this was a 'rubbish café' and that he would have to report the matter to a café inspector. Despite never having come into contact with anyone in such a role, when Grandad returned as the supposed inspector, Sam was again highly polite and amenable. He was then questioned as to his partnership in the café ownership with his brother, the 'inspector' adding that he now wished to speak to 'Mr Noel', who had actually disappeared beneath the table, from where a voice called 'Tell him I'm in Spain'. This play episode demonstrated, among other knowledge and skills, both boys' understanding of cafés, their tremendous repertoire of social skills, imagination, sense of humour and ingenuity.

When sufficient time and space allow, young children will, in Piaget's (1959) words, 'assimilate' their discoveries and 'accommodate' their thinking, adjusting their knowledge, skills and attitudes accordingly.

Because play has 'what if … ?' qualities and there are numerous possible solutions to situations raised during play, it will have afforded children experiences which propel them to make creative transformations of earlier understandings, learning and achievement. Janet Moyles (2010) lists 21 examples of the ways in which children's cognitive, physical, social and emotional abilities were evident as observed during one episode of role play in a reception class. A teacher-directed activity would have been unlikely to engender such an observable range of achievements.

Whilst an adult might offer new ideas and reflection on earlier learning, it is during play episodes that young children are challenged and contradicted in non-threatening ways which cause them to transform their thinking. Similarly, if adults truly listen and observe during interactions with children (Goouch, 2010), their own thinking is constantly transformed – about that particular child, children, families, development and learning in general, about the world – and most importantly, about themselves as educators.

The Tickell Report (2011) stresses the essential nature of a professional, appropriately skilled ECEC workforce, and that the value of that work needs to be more widely understood. Clearly, such an effort to achieve wider understanding should include debate about the complexity of early learning and the important role of play.

References

Baron-Cohen, S. (2011) *Zero Degrees of Empathy*, London: Allen Lane

Bennett, J. (2005) 'Curriculum issues in national policy-making', *European Early Childhood Research Journal*, 13: 5–23

Bernstein, B. (1997) 'Class and pedagogies: visible and invisible', in A.H. Halsley, H. Lauder, P. Brown and A.S. Wells (eds), *Education, Culture, Economy, Society*, Oxford: Oxford University Press

Bjorklund, D.F. (2007) *Why Youth Is Not Wasted on the Young*, Oxford: Blackwell

British Educational Research Association Early Years SIG (2003) *Early Years Research: Pedagogy, Curriculum and Adult Roles, Training and Professionalism*, Southwell, Nottinghamshire: BERA

Broadhead, P. (2004) *Early Years Play and Learning*, London: Routledge Falmer

Brooker, L. (2005) 'Learning to be a child: cultural diversity and early years ideology', in N. Yelland (ed.), *Critical Issues in Early Childhood Education*, Maidenhead: Open University Press

Brooks, D. (2011) *The Social Animal*, New York: Random House

Bruce, T. (2005) 'Play, the universe and everything', in J. Moyles (ed.), *The Excellence of Play*, Maidenhead: Open University Press

Bruce, T. (2010) Play, the universe and everything', in J. Moyles (ed.), *The Excellence of Play*, 3rd edn, Maidenhead: Open University Press

David, T. (ed.) (1993) *Educating our Youngest Children: European Perspectives*, London: Paul Chapman

David, T. (1996) 'Their right to play', in C. Nutbrown (ed.), *Respectful Educators – Capable Learners*, London: Paul Chapman

David, T., Goouch, K. and Powell, S. (2011) 'Play and prescription: the impact of national developments in England', in M. and E. Singer (eds), *Peer Relationships in Early Childhood Education and Care*, London:

Routledge

David, T., Goouch, K., Powell, S. and Abbott, L. (2003) *Birth to Three Matters: Review of the Literature,* Research Report 444, London: DfES

David, T., Raban, B., Ure, C., Goouch, K., Jago, M., Barrière, I. and Lambirth, A. (2000) *Making Sense of Early Literacy,* Stoke-on-Trent: Trentham Books

Department for Children, Schools and Families (2008) *The Play Strategy,* Nottingham: Department for Children, Schools and Families Publications

Department for Children, Schools and Families/Qualifications and Curriculum Development Agency (2009) *Learning, Playing and Interacting: Good Practice in the Early Years Foundation Stage,* London: DCFS/QCDA

Department for Education and Employment/Qualifications and Curriculum Authority (1999) *The National Curriculum,* London: DfEE/QCA

Department for Education and Skills (2007) *Early Years Foundation Stage,* Nottingham: DfES Publications

Dunn, J. (1999) 'Mindreading and social relationships', In M. Bennett (ed.), *Developmental Psychology,* London: Taylor and Francis, pp. 55–71

Goouch, K. (2009) 'Forging and fostering relationships in play: whose zone is it anyway?', in T. Papatheodorou and J. Moyles (eds), *Learning Together in the Early Years,* London: Routledge, pp. 139–52

Goouch, K. (2010) *Towards Excellence in Early Years Education,* London: Routledge

Gopnik, A., Melzoff, A. and Kuhl, P. (1999) *How Babies Think,* London: Weidenfeld and Nicolson

Hall, K. (2004) *Literacy and Schooling, Towards Renewal in Primary Education Policy,* Hampshire: Ashgate

Hall, K., Horgan, M., Ridgway, A., Murphy, R., Cunneen, M. and Cunningham, D. (2010) *Loris Malaguzzi and the Reggio Emilia Experience,* London: Continuum Books

Howard, J. (2010) 'The developmental and therapeutic potential of play: re-establishing teachers as play professionals', in J. Moyles (ed.), *The Excellence of Play,* 3rd edn, Maidenhead: Open University Press/McGraw-Hill, pp. 201–15

Hutt, S.J., Tyler, S., Hutt, C. and Christopherson, H. (1989) *Play, Exploration and Learning,* London: Routledge

Konner, M. (1991) *Childhood,* Boston, Mass.: Little Brown

McLachlan, C., Fleer, M. and Edwards, S. (2010) *Early Childhood Curriculum: Planning, Assessment and Implementation,* Cambridge: Cambridge University Press

Moyles, J. (2010) 'Introduction', in J. Moyles (ed.), *The Excellence of Play,* 3rd edn, Maidenhead: Open University Press/McGraw-Hill, pp. 1–16

Nutbrown, C. (2006) *Key Concepts in Early Childhood Education and Care*, London: Sage

OECD (2001) *Starting Strong I*, Paris: Organization for Economic Cooperation and Development

OECD (2006) *Starting Strong II*, Paris: Organization for Economic Cooperation and Development

Papatheodorou, T. and Moyles, J. (eds) (2009) *Learning Together in the Early Years*, London: Routledge

Piaget, J. (1959) *The Language and Thought of the Child*, London: Routledge & Kegan Paul Ltd

Powell, S. (2008) 'The value of play: constructions of play in England's national policies', *Children and Society*, 23: 29–42

Powell, S. and David, T. (2010) 'Play in the early years: the influence of cultural difference', in J. Moyles (ed.), *The Excellence of Play*, 3rd edn, Maidenhead: Open University Press/McGraw-Hill, pp. 244–58

Rogers, S. (2010) 'Play and pedagogy: a conflict of interests?', in S. Rogers (ed.), *Rethinking Play and Pedagogy: Contexts, Concepts and Cultures*, London: Routledge, pp. 5–18

Rogoff, B. (1990) *Apprenticeship in Thinking: Cognitive Development in Social Context*, Oxford: Oxford University Press

Rogoff, B. (2003) *The Cultural Nature of Human Development*, Oxford: Oxford University Press

Singer, E. and de Haan, D. (2009) 'Conflicts and togetherness in childcare centers', Barcelona, June: European Seminar on Respect for Diversity, Equity and Social Exclusion; see: www.decet.org/barcelona06/09

Siraj-Blatchford, I., Sylva, K., Muttock, S., Gilden, R. and Bell, D. (2002) *Researching Effective Pedagogy in the Early Years*, London: Department for Education and Skills, Research Report 356

Strandell, H. (2000) 'What is the use of children's play: preparation or social participation?', in H. Penn (ed.), *Early Childhood Services: Theory, Policy and Practice*, Buckingham: Open University Press

Sylva, K., Melhuish, E., Sammons, P., Siraj-Blatchford, I. and Taggart, B. (2004) *The Effective Provision of Pre-school Education Project*, London: University of London, Institute of Education

Tickell, C. (2011) *The Early Years: Foundations for Life, Health and Learning*, London: DfE

Vygotsky, L.S. (1978) *Mind in Society: The Development of Higher Psychological Processes*, Cambridge, Mass.: Harvard University Press

Wall, K. (2006) *Special Needs and Early Years*, London: PCP/Sage

Wood, E. (2007) 'New directions in play: consensus or collision?', *Education 3-13*, 35: 309–22.

Woodhead, M. (2005) 'Early childhood development: a question of rights', *International Journal of Early Childhood*, 37(3): 79–98

CHAPTER 15

Challenging the Reggio Emilia Approach with Relational Materialist Thinking and an Ethics of Potentialities[*]

Hillevi Lenz Taguchi

Introduction

The focus of this chapter relates to the problem that the majority of pedagogical practices deployed in schools are still based on instrumental strategies, which do not take into account the provision of contexts for creative and experimental learning that incorporate the body and material artefacts as a part of learning environments. It seems as if the more we know about the complexities and new possibilities of learning, the more we are inclined to find yet another 'one-size-fits-all' strategy for teaching (Lenz Taguchi, 2010b; Osberg and Biesta, 2009). Although the benevolent political aim is usually equated with the desire to achieve a fair and inclusive system for all students, what actually happens in the educational or schooling process might be the opposite of what we intend, and thus exclude students who are positioned on the margins of gender, race, sexuality and (dis)ability.

---

* This chapter is an abridged version of the paper 'Investigating learning, participation and becoming in early childhood practices with a relational materialist approach', *Global Studies of Childhood*, 1 (1), 2011: 36–50

During the past decade, new teaching strategies have been introduced to challenge the instrumental teaching and learning strategies that have dominated the schooling experience for a majority of students. These include the Reggio Emilia-inspired approach, which was in fact first developed in the 1950s in northern Italy in the city of the same name. Over the last ten years Reggio Emilia has enjoyed increasing celebrity and emulation, not just in Scandinavia and Sweden, where it has been taken up by a large number of municipalities as the main approach mainly in preschools, but there are also numerous networks and experimental preschools and schools in Latin and North America, Australia, New Zealand and various European countries (Ceppi and Zini, 1998; Dahlberg et al., 2008; Dahlberg and Moss, 2005; Edwards et al., 1998; Gardner, 1994; Katz, 1998; Rinaldi, 2006). The Reggio approach to teaching and learning is often referred to as being constructivist or social constructionist. It is embodied in the notion of 'the hundred languages'; that is, teaching and learning contexts that engage and use multiple forms of expression and modalities beyond the traditional spoken and written words. These include drawing, painting, sculpture and construction work, but also sounds and music (Reggio Children, 2001, 2008).

In spite of the Reggio Emilia approach incorporating opportunities for both creativity and participation in learning, the approach still basically focuses on conceptual creativity and development. Moreover, in relation to the learner's construction of identity in learning, the Reggio approach constitutes a one-sided social class position, neglecting issues of gender, sexuality and race. In this chapter, I will argue that the approach can be understood as being both logocentric (language-based) and anthropocentric (human-centred), and that it basically ignores students' constructions of identity/subjectivity in relation to some crucial social aspects. Thus, I will argue, what is otherwise a very engaging approach, when it comes to children as co-constructors of knowledge, is missing an opportunity to widen the scope of contexts to promote creativity, experimentation and collaborative participation in relation to the *material* world as well as in relation to each student's continuously transforming learning subjectivity – with creativity and participation being so strongly needed in an era of the vast global problems of overpopulation, climate changes and refugee emigration.

Thus, the aim of this chapter is to investigate and further challenge this growing and otherwise very successful learning strategy, with a *relational materialist* theoretical approach (Hultman and Lenz Taguchi, 2010). In this relational materialist analysis offered as an example from a Reggio Emilia-inspired preschool in Sweden, I will focus on what kinds of *learning* are being encouraged and also what kinds of *creativity and participation in learning* are achievable as a result of their implementation. The chapter also considers what kind of *child and subjectivity as learner* is enacted and *made real* by this specific practice.

The Problem of Anthropocentrism and Logocentrism in Teaching and Learning

Although there are new strategies for teaching and learning that try to challenge instrumental pedagogies, all of our contemporary teaching and learning practices tend to regard, as a taken-for-granted, that learning takes place inside the individual student. This means that the student is understood as a separate organism from the concepts to be learnt and the things involved, such as books and learning environments. What counts, and is valued and evaluated, as knowing, is what an individual child is able to conceptualize linguistically, emerging from within the child. Thus, the problem that I will address, with inspiration from my colleague Hultman (forthcoming), is what she has spelled out as the problem in teaching and learning of *anthropocentrism and logocentrism*. The problematic anthropocentric and humanocentric notion takes human beings as the taken-for-granted starting-point and centre, and thus gives humans a self-evident higher position above matter in the process of learning. This makes our understanding of learning events neglectful of the indispensable force and importance of the material in learning, and it leads us to over-emphasize human *language* as the superior way to understand learning. In a recent study, Sorensen (2009) shows how we can understand learning in primary education, if we change our anthropocentric view, and take into account the interplay between discursive concepts and the materiality of learning.

Contemporary educational thinking is deeply enmeshed in the ideological realm of liberal humanism, and is thus concerned with an idea of the learner as a unique and self-actualizing agent (Lee, 2001). Developmental and constructivist learning theories outline increasingly refined stages of cognitive and conceptual development. They identify a growing range of cognitive knowledge constructs and abilities that are seemingly neutral and applicable to everyone, irrespective of the social factors and subjectivities involved in learning. It is not the case that these cognitive and constructivist theories entirely dismiss the learning environment and the material (Gestwicki, 2006). On the contrary, they have made good efforts to understand their impact on learning, as for example in the learning-study approach (Marton and Tsui 2004; Runesson 2005). However, when analysing learning-study practices, what is produced through those practices is actually strategies to *get around* or *eliminate* what is considered to be a distorting impact of the material, as well as students' social positionings and experiences (Lenz Taguchi, 2011, 2010a). As we delve deeper into understanding human cognition, theories and methods of conceptual development, it seems as if some of us think that we can produce a scientifically grounded context-free, neutral and truly individualized pedagogy that works, irrespective of gender, race, ethnicity, class, sexuality and other cultural and social factors. The fact that the proponents of scientifically based constructivist and cognitive learning theories think that neutral, value-free and culturally independent theories can actually exist is one of the major problems that I can see today (Biesta, 2007).

As I have already hinted at, what is so deeply problematic with this dominant thinking is that it is so firmly based on a set of binary divisions, and thus constitutes a thinking of *separatedness* (Barad, 2007; Lee, 2001; Prout, 2005). *Cognition and the mind* are understood as basically separated from *the body*; *thinking and talking* are separated from *embodied doing and handling* the world and things around us; *scientific concepts* are separated from *everyday words and expressions*; *human subjects* are separated from *non-human organisms and matter*; and to summarize: *human learning* is separated from identity construction in relation to *materialized positionings and expressions of gender, race, ethnicity, sexuality, class and other cultural dispositions* within the learning process. This way of thinking, from the starting point of the mind, has dominated in the Western world since Plato, and was firmly established with the Cartesian notion of 'I think therefore I am' (Descartes, adapted by Bennett, 2007). It is the view that what human beings are able to think, say and conceptualize determines what is real. 'If I – the human being – cannot identify or be conscious about it, it might as well not exist!'

The childhood sociologists Nick Lee (2001) and Alan Prout (2005) both separately write about how Western philosophy has developed around the project of giving humanity itself value, grounded on the separation of culture from nature, and thinking ourselves as more and other than animals. The child is seen as closer to the animal than the adult, and Lee (2001) argues that the more the child is able to foreground its separatedness and independence from nature, but also from other people, parents and caretakers, the more developed and closer to adulthood and maturity the child gets. The more independent as an intellectual and rational mind you become, i.e. the more you can *detach* yourself from the influence of others and other things, the freer as an autonomous human subject you become. Contrary to such thinking, Hultman (forthcoming) argues very differently, in line with a *relational materialist* way of thinking. She states that the *more* connections the learner is able to make, and the *more* s/he acknowledges *dependence* on other human beings, things, artefacts, milieux and environments with which to form connections, the 'freer' s/he becomes to make new and increasingly more complex inter-connections. In other words, inter-connections multiply and overlap, so that *dependence* in these relations with others and things opens up new possibilities; that is, increases your relative 'independence' through multiple dependencies.

A Relational Materialist Approach on Learning and Becoming

A relational materialist theoretical approach on learning and becoming complements contemporary increased voicing and visibility of *the material* in research and education, which has been conceptualized as a 'material turn', 'material feminism', a 'post-humanist turn' and a 'new empiricism' (Alaimo and Hekman, 2008; Barad, 2007; Bennett, 2010; Hekman, 2010; Mol, 2002). This turn, however, is not about doing a 'switch' or 'swap' to the other extreme – from mind to body, or from discourse to matter. Rather, this approach reads reality in ways that, so to speak, *flatten out* the hierarchies between humans and matter: we read from our embodiedness and *being a part of the world*, and being in an equal state *among* other organisms and matter (Barad, 2007).

The physicist and feminist science theorist Karen Barad writes in her ground-breaking book titled *Meeting the Universe Halfway* (2007) about an *onto-epistemology*, defining it as 'the study of practices of knowing *in* being' (p. 185, my italics). She writes that it is impossible to isolate knowing from being, since they are mutually implicated. Thus, Barad's onto-epistemology constitutes a theory of immanence, and what can be called a *posthumanist* understanding of the 'human' where the ontological and epistemological cannot be separated but merge (Barad 1998, 2007). We are nothing until we connect to something else (Hultman, 2010; Hultman and Lenz Taguchi, 2010; Latour, 2005), even if it is simply the intra-activity with the molecules of oxygen in our breathing. Every organism connects with at least one other organism or matter in order to live, as a condition of its existence. 'To be is to be related', writes Annemarie Mol, and she concludes: 'nothing ever "is" alone' (Mol, 2002: 54).

In*tra*-activity relates to physicist terminology and to a relationship between any organism and matter (human or non-human) which are understood *not* to have clear and inherent boundaries, but are always in a state of intra-activity taking place on a horizontal level (Barad, 2007). For this chapter it is important to note that Barad's concept of in*tra*-activity is different from the more familiar concept of in*ter*activity, which refers to inter-personal relationships between at least two persons or entities that are understood to be clearly and inherently separated from each other. The concept of intra-activity makes it clear to us why we cannot consider ourselves as a separate entity *in* the world, but rather as a consequence *of* the world in a state of mutual inter-dependence with everything else. We are in processes of *'becoming-with'*, as Haraway contends (2008: 4).

The Reggio Emilia-inspired Approach

The so-called 'Reggio Emilia-inspired approach' is based on multiple constructivist learning theories, cybernetics and complexity theories such as those by Maturana and Varela (Steier, 1991), as well as relying on aesthetic work, and what Loris Malaguzzi, the founder of the schools, has called 'the hundred languages of children' (Reggio Children, 2001; Rinaldi, 2006). The approach has been developed since the Second World War in the city of Reggio Emilia in Italy, but the practice that I will refer to here is from a Reggio Emilia-*inspired* practice in Sweden. In Sweden and Norway and elsewhere, this approach is still growing, with new energy, as something of a resistance movement to traditional approaches in education.

In the Reggio Emilia approach *pedagogical documentation* constitutes an inevitable tool to document the learning processes of children in order to *challenge* their learning. Pedagogical documentation is also performed with the aim of making visible *different ways of understanding and doing* things among the children. Ann Åberg, the preschool teacher who has published the example below, writes that when you start a project in the Reggio approach, you aim to start it with what the children *already know*. This constitutes an ethical move which is about respecting what children bring with them into the learning event, and to make active *use* of what they bring with them *throughout* the learning process.

In the Reggio Emilia approach, the learning project does not have a preset goal, as is the case in most other pedagogical approaches, whether traditional or alternative. Goals are conceptualized only on a general level, and are of the kind that the teachers decide with regard to performing collaborative investigative mathematics during the upcoming semester. Instead of starting at the end with a specific learning content, these teachers claim to start *in the middle of things* – in the middle of what children already think and know (Lenz Taguchi, 2010a). The idea of doing a learning project in the Reggio approach is to upgrade and value children's thinking to the same level as adults' thinking about the world, and from this positioning collaboratively investigate children's questions *as they emerge* in the process.

In relation to the above-presented relational materialist thinking, I will make an analysis of an example from a book involving children in mixed-age groups with children of 3–5 years of age (Åberg and Lenz Taguchi, 2004). This book is called *A Pedagogy of Listening* (2004). I wish to analyse this example in order to understand what kind of child, what kind of learning and what kind of participation in learning that this practice, as it is enacted in this example, makes real. I will argue that although this practice is very interested in the material environment of learning, and although it engages in close documentation of the pedagogical space to understand children's learning, it *still* doesn't manage to transgress the dominant binary divides that haunt modern liberal humanist education; that is, human/non-human; discourse/matter; culture/nature; mind/body. Thus, in a very specific sense this practice remains both humanocentric (anthropocentric) and logocentric in its enactment as a practice. I will also argue that this practice produces learning activities that, in spite of its strong engagement in issues of equality between social groups, are still neglectful of students' constructions of identity/ subjectivity in learning and in relation to the learning contents, and especially in relation to gendered constructions of identity.

The example

The children had been involved with investigating birds in various ways – from detailed studies of claws, to birds' behaviour, the technique of flying and identifying different kinds of birds and how they live. The blue-tits were intimately studied, alongside the crow, since both of these birds stay in Sweden during the winter. The children had been amazed with differences connected to the size of them. Several months after the project on birds was formally finished, the children still discussed birds and the size of birds. Jonathan insisted that he must know the size of the biggest bird in Sweden, the sea-eagle.

One morning he told a group of children that he had experimented with his parents and brothers to find the answer. He said:

> I now know how big a sea-eagle is. It is just as big as four kids standing in a row with their arms stretched out. There are four children on the wingspan of an eagle. It is possible to say that four kids equal an eagle.
>
> (Åberg and Lenz Taguchi, 2004: 126)

He asked four children to stand in a row stretching their arms out. The children were fascinated by how big the sea-eagle was. Its huge size was accentuated as a crow scampered about the row of children who were dramatizing the eagle. Victor said: 'A crow is a tiny tot compared to the eagle'. The children took photographs, and Jonathan made a drawing. Pontus then wanted to know how many blue-tits equalled a sea-eagle. Since all of these children knew the blue-tit very well, this seemed to be a good way to measure the sea-eagle. Pontus asked four children to stand in a row again and then he made a blue-tit-measurement using his hand – the thumb and index-finger showing the size of a regular-sized blue-tit. He measured along the arms of the children: 'one, two, three ... ' until reaching 81. He concluded: '81 blue-tits equals a sea-eagle'. Sitting down in the group for a discussion, Pontus explained: 'When I wanted to know how many blue-tits there are on a sea-eagle, I fantasized with my fingers, and then the eagle ended up being 81 blue-tits.' Elsa wrote in the children's documentation-book: '81 blue-tits = 1 sea-eagle. 4 kids = 1 sea-eagle.'

Now Jonathan and Kevin wanted to know how many blue-tits equals the height of Elsa. Jonathan told Elsa to lie down to be able to measure her with his blue-tit hand-measure: 'One, two, three … there are eleven blue-tits on Elsa!' Then Kevin measured Josephine the same way and said: 'There are 27 blue-tits on Josephine. 'What?' There was great confusion among the children now. 'How can Josephine be 27 blue-tits and Elsa only eleven, when both of these girls are almost the same height?' Jonathan asked Elsa and Josephine to lie down alongside each other, and the children made them lay very still.

ALVA: 'This is strange. In fact, Elsa is somewhat taller than Josephine!'

JOHANNA: 'Actually, it should have been eleven on Elsa and ten on Josephine.'

JONATHAN: 'I think Kevin did shorter steps with his fingers so he ended up measuring 27 blue-tits. Perhaps Kevin used blue-tits babies? If you fantasize bigger with your fingers it will be less blue-tits, not as many. And if you do smaller steps with your fingers you will have more blue-tits!'

He talked this out very slowly, thinking at the same time, and then he eagerly concluded: 'When you measure with a smaller measure it becomes more!' The children looked bewildered, and Kevin said: 'I want to try again and using a larger measurement with my fingers this time' (Åberg and Lenz Taguchi, 2004: 128).

The children then worked together to experiment, and were thrilled to find out that the result of measuring depends on the kind of measurement tool they used. The project now exploded into various kinds of measuring. The children also decided to produce a common and standardized blue-tit measurement tool. They chose among the blue-tits which they had previously drawn, and picked one they all liked, and copied it in hundreds to use as a measure.

Then yet *another* discovery was made. If you put the blue-tits or buttons somewhat apart from each other or closely attached to each other, the result will differ, even though you are using a standardized measurement. They came to realize that measuring has to be accurate. But although they realized that the ruler and folding rule can measure more accurately than using buttons or blue-tits, the children preferred making up many different ways of measuring to compare the differences in their results, so that they could discuss the reasons for such differences.

A Relational Materialist Analysis of the Reggio Emilia Approach Example

In a relational materialist analysis of this example we see that what the children *say* is foregrounded in the writing. Although a lot of emphasis is put on what children *do*, what they *say* is understood as a reflection and representation of their doing (Olsson, 2009). The materials are *still* put in the background and understood as passive and *handled by active children*, and given meaning only in what the children say about them (ibid.).

However, when we look a bit closer at the example carrying out a relational materialist analysis, the ambitions and attempts to bridge, or move beyond, the liberal humanist binaries become visible. Consider how the maths project started. With a relational materialist approach we can understand that questions of size and measurement emerge from multiple encounters, where previous intra-actions with birds and questions about size are still active. These multiple encounters assemble themselves into a strong desire to know the size of the sea-eagle. When the children use their bodies to enact a sea-eagle, we can understand this in terms of them installing their *bodyminds* (Merrell, 2003) in the event of enacting a sea-eagle together. This constitutes a strong embodied experience, working as an 'interference' with their everyday thinking about both birds and size. The previously big crow now becomes a tiny tot. This sets in motion new and strong waves of diffraction through the space of the preschool, carrying with it all of the previous experiences of birds, graphical work, constructions and conceptualizations that have been made, as well as the *bodymind* affects, imaginations and other experiences of children and adults: from all of these encounters, something new emerges.

When the children reassemble around the documentation, new problems that warrant investigation, and new solutions emerge. They fetch other materials to measure with, or measure using their own bodies. They decide to solve the problem of inaccurate results caused by arbitrary measures, by making a standardized blue-tit measure. The children in this event *collaboratively negotiate* to determine that there is a need for a standardized measure from their own unique experiences of measuring with various materials. Instead of having the *teacher* structure the space of learning in terms of what to do, what materials, words and phrases to use, both the children and the documentation can be understood to be *performative agents in an immanent flow of learning* in the Reggio approach. In other words, the children's learning is constructed by their active participation in the learning event, where all varieties of contributions are valued in the collaborative negotiations that emerge between all matters involved.

This constitutes a relationship which is definitely more flattened and un-hierarchical, and which can enable a process of multiple relations and encounters with multiple performative agents, not just other children, but also things, materials and concepts.

In these events, the teacher actually becomes only *one of many* other performative agents. Her central position as teacher is significantly displaced. Her first-most job is to see to it that the children as *bodyminds* are assembled around the documentation.

So, what child is enacted and becomes real as an effect of this practice? This child can indeed be understood as part of an assemblage where non-human matter is also understood as active in learning. Moreover, this is a child who is an active participator; active in suggesting meaning, conceptual understanding, solutions to problems and posing new questions, and formulating new problems to investigate. However, it is clear in the writing of this example that it is what individual children *say* that is the absolute focus of this example. The child and the spoken words used can *still* be regarded as being hierarchically 'above' all other matters involved in the process (Hultman, forthcoming). The child, and conceptual meaning-making, are foregrounded.

Concluding Discussion on a Relational Materialist Analysis and Approach to Learning, Participation and Becoming

When doing a relational materialist analysis of this example we can make visible how different kinds of children, learning and participation in learning are made real as an effect of the practices performed (Mol, 2002). Although there are significant differences between these practices in relation to children's *participation in learning*, as well as in the attempts to bridge the binaries between mind and body, rational thinking and aesthetic doing, for example, it is clear that it is the superior status of the child and what the child says, and is able to conceptualize, that is foregrounded. Thus, both of these practices can be understood to be both anthropocentric and logocentric in a relational materialist analysis (Hultman, forthcoming).

A relational materialist approach to learning is critical to the idea of learning in terms of inner mental activities inside a separated human being. We can never reflect upon something on our own: to reflect means to inter-connect with something. Thus, thinking and learning are always *an encounter*; something that 'hits us' as we engage with the world (Bennett, 2001). Thinking and learning take place *in-between* heterogeneous actors, rather than being something localized inside a human superior mind, separated and located above the material world and other organisms. 'Something in the world forces us to think. This something is an object not of recognition but of a funda- mental encounter' (Deleuze, 1994: 139). This corresponds to what historians of evolution say about how human language, communica- tion and culture have emerged as an effect of humans intra-acting with the non-human world (Bell et al., 2010). Learning can, in a relational materialist approach, be understood as emerging from what happens in distributed networks and assemblages consisting of both human and non-human matter and organisms, which are in intra-action with each other (Deleuze and Guattari, 1987).

Despite the fact that the practices of the Reggio example are inclusive of what children bring into the learning process, we can observe that the strategies focused and encouraged by the teachers follow a quite conventional understanding of mathematical learning. Moreover, in this example, as in numerous other examples from the Reggio approach, it is apparent that the ideas and commentary made by verbally clever boys are put to the front in the collaborative learning process. The strategies of the children that are not verbally clever and do not verbalize well what they do are not acknowledged in a way that make their strategies central to where the collaborative learning process will go next. Contrary to this, a relational mate- rialist focus on what emerges as an effect of the intra-activity that takes place *in-between* children and material artefacts, and which is not necessarily put into words by the children, would actually allow for a less hierarchical relationship between the 'hundred languages' that the Reggio advocates put forward as their learning strategy. As for now, the spoken language still prevails as the 'language' given the highest value, and as a tool for representing the learning taking place when using other 'languages'.

Learning can take many directions. Its flows are always rhizomatic (Deleuze and Guattari, 1987). It is my conviction that if we are to *seriously* engage in questions of learning, participation and becoming with an ethical and participatory stance, *then* we need to make yet another effort to flatten and spread ourselves out in the world around us, and pay far greater attention to the multiple encounters in which children and we ourselves are engaged (see also Hultman, forthcoming). We need to make ourselves aware and inclusive of the diversities in thinking and doing amongst children that emerge in their intra-actions with non-human matter in the events of learning. Diversity here should not be understood in terms of the social categories that tend to fix the child in specific positions in its encounters with others, as Todd (2009) asserts. Rather diversity should be thought upon in terms of the uniqueness that emerges in what Todd calls the *reciprocal narrative character of any encounter* in which the child is engaged.

In a relational materialist approach, we understand that gender, race and culture are part of a multiplicity in the process of becoming continuously *anew* in each new encounter (Hultman, forthcoming; Hultman and Lenz Taguchi, 2010; Lenz Taguchi, 2010a). This does not mean that gender and race, for example, are not important in the process of learning and becoming. Quite the contrary, it means that we cannot continue to understand diversities in terms of what an individual *represents* in terms of a group category of, for example, gender or race (Todd, 2009). Rather, we need to look to the singularity in each becoming, and how gender or race, or both, matter *differently* in different events for different children (Lenz Taguchi, 2010a; Olsson, 2009).

Performing events of learning and becoming with what I have called an *ethics of immanence and potentiality* is about opening yourself up to the endless possibilities of what children do, are capable of, and can become (Lenz Taguchi, 2010a). This frame of mind is ethically and politically different from the outcome-based one-size-fits-all curriculum of our dominant educational learning practices. We need to challenge ourselves to go beyond that which we already think we know as a truth about children's development and learning, and instead engage in an ethics of potentialities, where it becomes impossible to judge, value or diagnose children in relation to pre-set ideas or truths. The teacher cannot understand the student, the content or the methodology in terms of being a fixed entity apart and separated from everything else. An ethics of immanence and potentialities is concerned with the inter-connections and intra-actions *in-between* human and non-human organisms, matter and things, in processes of *constant* movement and transformation, where all of us continuously become different in ourselves (Deleuze, 1994).

The consequences of this thinking are that the teacher needs to become aware of how the room, space, time and things are organized and structured, and what kinds of intra-action between different organisms and matter *might* be possible. S/he needs to be ready for what kinds of learning emerge in the rhizomatic movement that can take multiple directions, and as an effect of multiple intra-activities, expressions and modalities beyond the traditional spoken and written words. S/he needs to welcome the transformative singularities of children, and what they continuously become.

To Conclude

If we think about the learning event above with a relational materialist approach, we involve our whole *bodymind* to activate an ethics of potentiality: we see a child involved in an encounter of mutual engagement and transformation with different kinds of materials. These different bodies are in a *mutual state of responsibility* for what happens in the multiple intra-actions emerging in the events unfolding. We acknowledge that we *affect and are being affected* by everything else in the event (Deleuze, 1988). The flow of events thus becomes a collective and collaborative responsibility on behalf of *all* organisms present, whether they are human or non-human. Responsibility is thus built *into* the immanent relationship *in-between* everything in the encounters. Thus, responsibility is nothing we can choose to have or take on; rather it *comes* with living, which is about affecting, and being affected (Deleuze, 1988). This is because we are, as Barad (2007) concludes, in a mutual state of co-existence with everything else. Being involved in an ethics of immanence and potentialities pays serious attention to interdependencies and responsibilities, but moreover, it means looking for future possibilities and potentialities in what *might become*, rather than getting stuck in determining what *is*, what *was* and what *should* be, in ways that will only fixate positionings, differences and knowledges (Smith, 2003).

References

Åberg, A. and Lenz Taguchi, H. (2004) *Lyssnandets pedagogik* [Pedagogy of Listening], Stockholm: Liber

Alaimo, S. and Hekman, S. (2008) 'Introduction: Emerging models of materiality in feminist theory', in S. Alaimo and S. Hekman (eds), *Material Feminisms*, Bloomington and Indianapolis: Indiana University Press, pp. 1–19

Barad, K. (1998) 'Getting real: technoscientific practices and the materialization of reality', *Difference: A Journal of Feminist Cultural Studies*, 10 (2): 87–126

Barad, K. (2007) *Meeting the Universe Halfway: Quantum Physics and the Entanglement of Matter and Meaning*, Durham: Duke University Press

Bennett, J. (2001) *The Enchantment of Modern Life: Attachments, Crossings and Ethics*, Princeton: Princeton University Press

Bennett, J. (2007) *Meditations of First Philosophy in which are demonstrated the existence of God and the distinction between the human soul and body. René Descartes*; see http://www.earlymoderntexts.com/pdf/descmed.pdf

Bennett, J. (2010) *Vibrant Matter: A Political Ecology of Things*, Durham: Duke University Press

Biesta, G. (2007) 'Don't count me in: democracy, education and the question of inclusion', *Nordisk Pedagogik*, 27(1): 18–31

Ceppi, G. and Zini, M. (1998) *Children, Spaces, Relations: Metaproject for an Environment for Young Children*, Reggio Children and Domus Academy: Italy, Reggio Children

Dahlberg, G. and Moss, P. (2005) *Ethics and Politics in Early Childhood Education*, London/New York: Routledge/Falmer

Dahlberg, G., Moss, P. and Pence, A. (2008/1999) *Beyond Quality in Early Childhood Education and Care: A Postmodern Perspective*, London: Routledge/Falmer Press

Deleuze, G. (1988) *Spinoza: Practical Philosophy*, San Francisco: City Lights Books

Deleuze, G. (1994) *Difference and Repetition*, trans. Paul Patton, New York: Colombia University Press

Deleuze, G. and Guattari, F. (1987) *A Thousand Plateaus. Capitalism and Schizophrenia*, trans. B. Massumi, Minneapolis: University of Minnesota Press

Edwards, C., Gandini, L. and Forman, G. (1998) *The Hundred Languages of Children*, Greenwich, Conn.: Ablex Publishing

Gardner, H. (1994) 'Foreword: Complementary perspectives on Reggio Emilia', in C. Edwards, L. Gandinin and G. Forman (eds), *The Hundred Languages of Children: The Reggio Approach to Early Childhood Education*, Norwood, New York: Ablex

Gestwicki, C.L. (2006) *Developmentally Appropriate Practice: Curriculum and Development in Early Education*, 3rd edn, Clifton Park, New York: Delmar Learning

Haraway, D. (2008) *When Species Meet*, Minneapolis and London: University of Minnesota Press

Hekman, S. (2010) *The Material of Knowledge: Feminist Disclosures*, Bloomington and Indianapolis: Indiana University Press

Hultman, K. (forthcoming) 'Making matter *matter* as a constitutive force in children's subjectivities', *Contemporary Issues in Early Childhood* (accepted).

Hultman, K. and Lenz Taguchi, H. (2010) 'Challenging anthropocentric analysis of visual data: a relational materialist methodological approach to educational research', *International Journal of Qualitative Studies in Education*, 23 (5): 525–42

Katz, L.G. (1998) 'What can we learn from Reggio Emilia?', in C. Edwards, L. Gandini and G. Forman (eds), *The Hundred Languages of Children: The Reggio Emilia Approach: Advanced Reflections*, Norwood, NJ: Ablex, pp. 27–45

Latour, B. (2005) *Reassembling the Social: An Introduction to Actor-Network-Theory*, Oxford: Oxford University Press

Lee, N. (2001) *Childhood and Society: Growing up in an Age of Uncertainty*, Maidenhead: Open University Press

Lenz Taguchi, H. (2010a) *Going Beyond the Theory/Practice Divide in Early Childhood Education: Introducing an Intra-active Pedagogy*, London/New York: Routledge

Lenz Taguchi, H. (2010b) 'Rethinking pedagogical practices in early childhood education: a multidimensional approach to learning and inclusion', in N. Yelland (ed.), *Contemporary Perspectives in Early Childhood Education*, Maidenhead: Open University Press, pp. 14–32

Lenz Taguchi, H. (2011) 'Investigating learning, participation and becoming in early childhood practices with a relational materialist approach', *Global Studies of Childhood*, 1 (1): 36–50

Marton, F. and Tsui, A.B.M. (eds) (2004) *Classroom Discourse and the Space of Learning*, Mahwah, NJ and London: Lawrence Erlbaum

Merrell, F. (2003) *Sensing Corporeally: Toward a Posthuman Understanding*, Toronto: University of Toronto Press

Mol, A. (2002) *The Body Multiple: Ontology in Medical Practice*, Durham, NC: Duke University Press

Olsson, L. (2009) *Movement and Experimentation in Young Children's Learning*, London and New York: Routledge

Osberg, D.C. and Biesta, G.J.J. (2009) 'The end/s of school: complexity and the conundrum of the inclusive educational curriculum', *International Journal of Inclusive Education*, 14(6): 593–607; see: http://dx.doi.org/10.1080/13603110802530684

Prout, A. (2005) *The Future of Childhood*, London and New York: RoutledgeFalmer

Reggio Children (2001) *Making Learning Visible: Children as Individual and Group Learners*, Italy: Municipality of Reggio Emilia, Reggio Children

Reggio Children (2008) *Dialogues with Places*, Italy: Municipality of Reggio Emilia, Reggio Children

Rinaldi, C. (2006) *In Dialogue with Reggio Emilia: Listening, Researching and Learning*, London and New York: Routledge

Runesson, U. (2005) 'Beyond discourse and interaction: variation, a critical aspect for teaching and learning mathematics', *Cambridge Journal of Education*, 35(1): 69–87; http://dx.doi.org/10.1080/0305764042000332506

Smith, D.W. (2003) 'Deleuze and Derrida, immanence and transcendence: two directions in recent French thought', in P. Patton and J. Protevi (eds), *Between Deleuze and Derrida*, London and New York: Continuum

Sorensen, E. (2009) *The Materiality of Learning: Technology and Knowledge in Educational Practice*, Cambridge: Cambridge University Press

Steier, F. (1991) *Research and Reflexivity*, London and Thousand Oaks, Calif.: Sage

Todd, S. (2009) 'Educating beyond cultural diversity: redrawing the boundaries of a democratic plurality'. paper for presentation at SCAPE Symposium, Vancouver, BC, 16–18 October

Part III

Advocacy, Research and Policy-Making for Children's Early Years' Learning

Part III consists of five substantial chapters which look in close detail at various aspects of early development and learning from a policy-relevant vantage point. A strong policy-making theme runs through the chapters, especially around the highly controversial area of literacy learning in chapters by Sue Palmer (of 'toxic childhood' fame) and Dr Sebastian Suggate; and also in editor Richard House's chapter, which subjects early years research, and the politicized uses to which it is routinely put, to a searchingly critical analysis.

A very notable chapter is also contributed by Dr Aric Sigman (of *Remotely Controlled* fame), who presents a relentless litany of highly disturbing research evidence on the harm done to young children by exposure to televisual and ICTs (extraordinarily, currently compulsory in the EYFS curriculum). Finally in this part, there is an interview with Open EYE's own Margaret Edgington, whose campaigning zeal, and deep wisdom and insight on a wide range of early years themes, shine through in this very informative and thought-provoking interview. Again, anyone wishing to acquaint themselves with leading-edge thinking on key issues that really matter in current early years practice – early literacy, ICT, research – could do little better than read the provocative chapters in Part III.

CHAPTER 16

'If I Wanted My Child to Learn to Read and Write, I Wouldn't Start from Here'

SUE PALMER

I bet I'm the only contributor to this book whose background is in the teaching of phonics, spelling and grammar at Key Stage 2 – but it does give me another perspective on the current debate. A decade ago, I was working for the government's National Literacy Strategy (NLS), and so was able to watch from the sidelines as my NLS colleagues got together with early years specialists to devise the literacy goals that became part of the Early Years Foundation Stage (EYFS).

Starting on the Roof

At the time, the NLS gurus were under pressure – they'd been charged with raising standards in the tests at age 11, and had tough targets to hit. But they also had enormous power, because the government was prepared to back them to the hilt to ensure success. So when they noticed that, to hit the prescribed target at 11, children needed to master certain skills by age seven, NLS experts made nice neat lists of the skills, and worked out a schedule (starting at five) that could help them all get there.

The schedules started at five, because that was the school starting age in England – not for any educational reason, but because the Victorian politicians who set up the state system wanted to get poor children off the streets as early as possible. (There's also an apocryphal story that Prussia had just instituted a state system starting at six, and the English wanted to trump them. From what I learned during my years working for politicians, it seems highly possible.)

But it was very handy for NLS that, with the creation of a new 'Foundation Stage', there were now going to be an extra two years before primary education officially began to get children up and running towards their five-year-old competencies. And since 'aspiration' was the word of the moment, it seemed reasonable to expect foundation practitioners to help the drive to raise standards by bringing children up to that elementary level of competency by five.

This is how the literacy goals of the Curriculum Guidance for the Foundation Stage, introduced in 2000, and later lifted wholesale into the EYFS, came about. A top-down process of politically motivated thinking, based on educational targets and a deep belief in the power of 'aspiration'.

The whole intellectual process was rather like trying to build a house by starting with the roof and working downwards.

Goals and Aspiration

I remember how hard the early years experts fought against my colleagues. But it didn't matter how much developmental theory they sited, the literacy targets were the guiding light of the process, and the Literacy Strategy could just about do what it liked. So the notorious literacy goals for five-year-olds found their way into the document, including

- use their phonic knowledge to write simple regular words and make phonetically plausible attempts at more complex words;
- write their names and other things such as labels and captions, and begin to form simple sentences, sometimes using punctuation.

In 2008, these goals were actually enshrined in law, because the EYFS requirements were made a statutory duty for anyone looking after children outside the home – *anyone*, even a childminder, who has never had any training in early literacy.

But back at the dawn of the new millennium, I fear I didn't take much notice. As well as my Strategy work, I was busy researching a book about the possible effects of too much early TV-watching on children's spoken language development, and its long-term implications for literacy. But the Foundation Stage goals did leave me feeling slightly edgy. Before specializing in literacy, I was a primary teacher and head-teacher for many years, and I reckoned that most of the five-year-olds in my schools couldn't achieve those targets. Quite a few of the seven-year-olds would have found it a struggle. Still, perhaps we'd just not been aspirational enough …

My book on television and language never happened. The more I worked on it, the more I realized that language was only one aspect of development affected by children's changing life-styles, and it turned into a much more comprehensive book, eventually published in 2006 as *Toxic Childhood.* One of the areas I had to cover was the question of whether Britain's children were starting formal education too soon.

Tuning Minds and Ears

During my research into early years education in Britain, lots of the people I consulted mentioned that in other European countries, children didn't start formal education till age seven. With my literacy background, I couldn't but be interested in their claims that many of these countries still achieved high standards in literacy. When, in 2003, the PISA survey (Programme for International Student Assessment) found that Finland was top of the international charts for literacy, I decided to go there and see what they did in their kindergarten stage.

It was an enlightening experience. The Finnish kindergarten schools I visited did all the play-based activities you'd see in good UK settings, but with a gentle emphasis on song, story and language development that clearly had a significant effect on children's language development, attention skills and social behaviour.

Through telling and retelling of folk stories, the teacher introduced children to the rhythms and patterns of narrative language. The children turned the stories into plays (making props, costumes and scenery) and acted them for their parents. They had story-telling sessions themselves, and demonstrated remarkable control over language. All this repetition developed their auditory memory, something which today's children often struggle with, since they've lived since birth in a highly visual world.

Songs were used for the same purpose. They were threaded throughout the kindergarten day – number songs, phonic songs,

songs for the register and to signal change-over times, songs covering information children were learning or needed to remember, and, of course, lots of folk songs and other songs just for fun. Adults sometimes provided accompaniment using simple musical instruments, and children had many opportunities for music-making, and listening and moving to music.

'Why do you do so much music?', I asked one teacher. 'Music trains the mind to pattern and the ears to sound', she replied. It also, clearly, had a wonderful socializing effect on the children, who joined in lustily, sometimes marching around to the rhythm, sometimes doing the actions, sometimes trilling away as they got on with some other task. (They carried their repertoire through to the primary classroom, where the teacher added to it with songs that helped embed their more formal learning.)

This emphasis on using, remembering and internalizing narrative and rhythmic patterns of language – along with all the other play-based learning (including a great deal of outdoor play) – clearly built on learning methods that come naturally to children. If you think about it, human beings have always passed on their culture to their young through stories and song. In a more sophisticated society, they also seem to set them up for formal learning of literacy skills.

When I visited the first-year class of a Finnish primary school (where the children were the equivalent age to our Year 2), I asked the teacher how long he expected before they were all literate. It was August at the time. 'Oh … ,' he said casually, 'by Christmas'.

Shades of the Prison House …

Once back home on the research trail, I found plenty of evidence to support Finnish methods of language and literacy acquisition. If you want a good summary of the evolutionary and developmental basis of literacy, try Maryann Wolf's *Proust and the Squid* (Icon Books, 2008). What the Finns were doing was building their educational house from the bottom up, starting by laying down sound foundations.

This didn't 'hold children back' (the traditional anxiety of UK early-start enthusiasts). The kindergartens had writing areas and library corners where children could choose to go during their free playtime, and plenty of them did. The role-play areas had lots of environmental print, and children added to it with their own signs and symbols, which they also used in devising their plays. And kindergarten workers supported and encouraged them in much the way a parent would in a loving, literate home. So many children arrived at primary school with good levels of 'emergent literacy'. However, no one pushed a child to read and write before he or she was ready. Formal teaching of literacy skills waited until the vast majority of children were physically, socially, emotionally and cognitively equipped to succeed.

The contrast with English practice is stark. The NLS – urged on by politicians – has turned literacy into a sort of educational hurdle race, where all children are expected to achieve certain standards at adult-prescribed ages, and practitioners are charged with the responsibility of getting them there.

Literacy and Humanity

I'm now convinced that in doing this, we seriously damage the chances of many children, particularly those from disadvantaged backgrounds. At three or four years of age, they don't have the conscious control – of their bodies and their thought processes – that are needed to move their eyes along a line of print or to manoeuvre a pencil across a page (cf. Chapter 9).

Some can be trained, like dogs, to perform these tasks, but it's not proper learning, and may be physically or psychologically painful. Others can't do it at all. So they end up demotivated and disengaged. When children fall at the first fence at such a tender age, they're not very inclined to rejoin the race (see Chapters 10 and 11).

Some children, from better-off homes, *are* interested in reading and writing. So they adapt to the system, do as they're told to please the grown-ups, and manage to tick all the boxes. But it gives them a rather strange idea of what reading and writing are all about. They aren't really capable of rational thought at this tender age, so their achievement is just a matter of submitting to adult control and mastering a range of decontextualized skills. It sets them up for a future of box-ticking themselves (which, thanks to the tests and targets that now litter primary education, it often is), rather than reading for pleasure and writing to communicate meaning.

A couple of months ago, a secondary teacher gave me the following chilling poem, written by a holocaust survivor:

Dear Teacher,
I am the victim of a concentration camp.
My eyes saw what no one should witness:
gas chambers built by learned engineers;
children poisoned by educated physicians;
infants killed by trained nurses;
women and babies shot and burned
by high school and college graduates.
So, I am suspicious of education.
My request is:
help your students become human.
Your efforts must never produce
learned monsters, skilled psychopaths, educated Eichmans.
Reading and writing are important
only if they serve to make our children more human.

There are chapters in this book from much more authoritative pens than mine on the huge importance of emphasizing children's social and emotional development in the early years. So I'll just emphasize the significance of these developmental strands on long-term literacy development – true literacy is about a lot more than pursuing top-down targets.

Starting Afresh ...

After 15 years of an NLS-type approach to primary literacy, it's clear that it hasn't worked – our children might be better at passing tests and ticking boxes, but they're not doing well by any non-governmental educational measures, either national or international. And after ten years of literacy targets for five-year-olds, there's no evidence that achieving these targets makes any difference to children's reading and writing at the age of seven, or eleven or beyond. We have to rethink our approach to early years education, basing it on developmental psychology (see Chapter 17), not political requirements.

The EYFS is soon to be revised, but as long as it treats 'developmental milestones' as though they're 'goals' or 'targets' (cf. Chapters 2 and 20), childcare workers and early years practitioners will be locked into a system that confuses children's natural learning drive with formal education. Politicians will always be at their backs, looking for results. And parents will continue to worry that, unless early years settings crack on with formal work, their children are somehow being 'held back'.

But tinkering with the EYFS isn't enough. To help promote the significance of child development to a wider public – so that early years practitioners can respect and build on children's natural capacity to learn – we need root and branch reform. I now believe the only way to change the culture is to raise the school starting age to six (or preferably seven), and institute a separate Foundation Phase with a totally different ethos, similar to the Finnish kindergartens. The Welsh have already started to make this change, so it's certainly not impossible.

Changing the culture is about much more than literacy, but – to go back to where I came in on this whole discussion – it's the only way we'll ever raise standards. If asked how to ensure that all children in England learn to read and write, my response would be the same as the Irishman in the old joke. When a motorist asked him for directions to a distant destination, he replied: 'Well, if that's where you want to go, I wouldn't start from here.'

CHAPTER 17

Viewing the Long-Term Effects of Early Reading with an Open Eye

SEBASTIAN P. SUGGATE

My theme for this chapter is reading and the role of reading in child-hood. Reading is, of course, a central activity in modern childhood, and the precedence placed on this ahead of other more traditional childhood activities is insidious, such that it infiltrates and domi-nates many parent–child interactions, toys and games.

To take concrete examples, there are early reading packages such as 'Phonics for Babies' and then, of course, flash cards. Incredibly, I have seen a children's book that makes the promise 'this book will increase your child's vocabulary by associating it [*sic*] with beautiful pictures', which, to all intents and purposes, sounds lovely. However, it takes only a cursory glance to see the lack of substance behind this bold claim; the book consists almost entirely of pictures of cats and the only words – one per page, that is, one per cat, and remember that each word is to be associated with each picture to improve my child's vocabulary – are 'Taffy' and 'Toffee'!

This perhaps reflects the obsession in ensuring that children learn reading skills early: just observe, for example, the way many adults pick up a book to show a child, pointing out the letters first *before* the pictures. I do not believe that this obsession with text arises from having considered thoroughly the benefits for children; it is instead a form of easiness – or perhaps even laziness – to point out letters to children, to teach them the letters of the alphabet, to plaster these all over the fridge, to make this a priority, as opposed to directing them to the rich language and imaginative world around them. Certainly, in my view the latter is far more challenging and stimulating for both parent and child. But for now I would like to lay aside these more provocative, introductory arguments and turn specifically to the question: are there grounds to believe that early reading brings long-term advantage to children?

Certainly, when I began reading the literature – that is, the scientific literature, policy documents and advice to parents – these nearly always mentioned the importance of early reading. At the beginning of my PhD studies, therefore, I had been reading the persuasive arguments of my contemporaries for quite some time, which run something like this:

> We know that children who are behind when they are young are more likely to be behind when they are older. There are some reading programmes, like synthetic phonics programmes, that improve pre-reading skills. Then, there are Matthew effects (Stanovich, 1986), which show that children who fall behind, will fall ever further and further behind. Thereby, the poor become poorer, the rich become richer; thus we need to start early and intervene early.

This line of reasoning is everywhere: it is implicit in our culture and it is explicitly stated in many publications. It is a very compelling line of reasoning. I have much respect and admiration for this line of reasoning. But when I began to look for what hard evidence there was, I found that direct evidence was lacking.

It is indeed an interesting line of research to study the association between early reading and later reading, so let me delineate this more clearly. If you take children who are behind at time A and you see whether they are behind at time B, all that this really tells you is that children who are relatively behind at one point are relatively behind at another point later on. Would it not be more worrying if our schools had the effect of taking the best readers and turning them into the worst, and the worst into the best? That would be more worrying. This research can draw our attention to what skills and what factors are important in later reading, but in of itself it does not actually tell us a lot – not least, it cannot say whether children should have learnt the reading skills early in the first place.

Again, when we look at the data around early reading interventions to help those struggling readers (e.g. National Reading Panel, 2000) often we just do not see the follow-ups (Suggate, 2010) that would be necessary in order for us to conclude that this is having a long-term effect on later reading. Often the data are just not there.[1]

I would like to point out, first, that there are some very good, very famous studies that have taken disadvantaged children from Head Start, or from other disadvantaged backgrounds, and placed them in what are considered to be better environments for children (e.g. Lazar and Darlington, 1982) than regular head start programs or under-stimulating, even neglectful, home environments.[2] These studies have generally shown better outcomes for children later on in life. But an important distinction about these programmes is that children are not just getting extra reading, but they also get language, they get better play environments and all sorts of other factors. So we cannot say that it is the early reading that has made these children into better readers because we cannot isolate which component was effective.[3]

When I began to look at what specific evidence there is that directly relates to later reading,[4] I could really find nothing! I found one paper at the beginning of my PhD studies, and this was published in 1974–5, by Dolores Durkin. She recruited families from the newspapers who would be willing to enrol their children in her two-year pre-kindergarten programme that emphasized reading and language. It was an academic kindergarten programme. Durkin then looked at these children two years down the line, comparing them to children who stayed at home with their mothers, finding in the beginning that the children who were in the academic programme had better reading skills. But they were also more intelligent (as measured through IQ), which probably is a feature, on average, of parents who volunteer their children for such a programme. Two further years down the line, however, after two years of school, and once IQ had been accounted for, there was no benefit of the early-reading programme on later reading skill (Durkin, 1974–5).

This is a crucial finding. I do not wish to criticize other people's research unnecessarily, but the recent report from the Office for National Statistics claiming benefits for the early years curriculum (Early Years Foundation Stage) in England (Hopkin et al., 2010) did not have a good comparison group and did not have good controls of important background factors. In this report, there was a strong tendency for the poorer children to not receive the early years curriculum. So when the researchers found that on the early years criteria there seemed to be a minor effect of the curriculum, they could not rule out that this was just because these were the more disadvantaged children. There was also no control for intelligence, just for ethnicity and gender. Despite stacking the measures in their favour by selecting those directly related to their curriculum, and by not having a good control group, they still only found small effects!

Unfortunately, a lot of evidence comes out like this. It is really important to have a good understanding of what actually comprises 'evidence' (cf. Chapter 19). Saying 'Evidence says … !' has so much power nowadays, but we need to stop and say, 'OK, what evidence? How is it done, and what are you telling me?' For often, when we dig a little deeper, the evidence does not actually match the statement.

Subsequent to starting my PhD, I discovered another study on the effects of early reading, conducted in Germany around 1970 (Schmerkotte, 1978). The government in North Rhineland–Westphalia decided that they wanted to lower the school entry age to improve achievement, from six or seven to five or six years. But unlike governments in the English-speaking world, they said: 'Before we do this, let's test it!' And they did duly test it, and being German, they tested it very well! They took 50 kindergartens, assigning 25 to an early academic programme emphasizing maths and reading, and they took 25 kindergartens with a very play-centred, very child-centred approach.

Lo and behold, after the first year of school, the children who had the academic instruction did better at reading, they did better at maths, and there was interestingly some evidence for slightly lower social skills. By grade 2, the reading and maths advantage had disappeared, and in grade 3, there was nothing left. So on the basis of these research findings, the German Government decided not to lower the school entrance age (Schmerkotte, 1978).

There are also international studies of reading, usually conducted every 4 or 5 years. We know that children in many parts of the world begin reading and schooling later, when they are seven years old, and most countries begin at six. The English-speaking countries tend to begin at five. When I began my PhD, as far as I could tell there was only one quantitative analysis of this rich data. The reason why I say 'quantitative analysis' is because it is all very well taking children from Finland – the world champions in reading – and comparing them with children from Scotland or New Zealand, but this approach has its problems. Comparing New Zealand with

Finland is difficult because New Zealand has a lot more immigration than Finland, perhaps more socio-economic diversity, and the language is English, which is not an easy language in which to learn to read, as it is irregular in terms of its spelling and its spelling-to-sound correspondences (Seymour et al., 2003).

However, in quantitative analyses there are ways of indexing the immigration, the wealth of the countries, and the provision of education, in order to obtain a fairer control of factors, such as when children begin school. One analysis was carried out in 1992 by Elley, a New Zealander. He took the top ten and the bottom ten performing countries and compared them with respect to the age when they began school. Elley found that children in countries where they began school a little bit later did a little bit better. Then he brought in his controls for economic factors, the social development of the countries and the health of the citizens, comparing the top and the bottom ten countries again. He found that now, the best countries were the countries where school began a little bit earlier (Elley, 1992).

However, the devil is always in the detail! There were two populations in Elley's study: children aged 9 and children aged 14. Reading through the reports, one could see that Elley only looked at the reading achievement of the younger children, with respect to this question. So what does this leave us with? We have a situation where children enter school at age seven and go to school for two years, versus children who enter school at five and go to school for four years. Then at age nine, after two years in the one group and four years in the other, he compared them and found a very small difference. It is a sure bet that if you looked at the data for the 14-year-old children there would have been no difference!

I therefore decided to replicate this study using data from the 2006 PISA study, doing much the same as Elley had done, except that I had 54 countries (Suggate, 2009b). I looked to see whether there was any effect (benefit) in reading for these countries where schooling begins earlier, but I found nothing. There was not even a difference that would have become significant with a larger sample. There was a tendency, though, for countries that began school later to have a larger variance in reading.

In trying to find a way to test this question, I realized that in the New Zealand education system, children enter school at the age of five. In New Zealand, fairness is everything, so it does not really matter which background you are from, everybody is entitled to an education. It is supposed to be free, and in fact, the schools from the richer areas receive less funding, so the more disadvantaged you are, the better the funding. Children get a good class size, and they come into school when they turn five. So in New Zealand, the joke runs: 'Happy birthday son, now get to school. I am going to the pub!'

Between ages five and six, children's reading development is regularly screened and monitored. If they are behind at age six, which is approximately 15 to 20 per cent of children, they often get referred for extra tuition. By age six, the vast majority of children can read fairly fluently. Conversely, in Rudolf Steiner schools in New Zealand, children enter school when they are six or seven, and they are certainly not encouraged to learn to read before then. This gives rise to two groups of children; one of fluent readers shortly after age five, and another who learn to read around age seven. To reiterate, both systems receive government funding, such that there is no socially biased selection. This was confirmed by our parent questionnaires investigating education and profession. There was probably a bit more ethnic diversity in the Steiner schools, but the samples were otherwise very similar.

I looked at their reading three times a year across the first six years of school, also measuring aspects of language and the home-reading environment. There were really marked differences in reading skill at the beginning of school; however, by around age 10, the differences were no longer present – a finding confirmed by our computer modelling accounting for the host of background variables.

I also made an observation while doing this testing, which is also borne out by the data. I would go along to these different schools and observe that in the state schools, the children could read fluently. Then I would visit the Steiner schools and the children in the beginning were hopeless! But what would happen is that I would go back, and go back again a few months later, and they would still be down at the bottom in terms of reading. And then suddenly, a child's reading would take off. It might happen a little bit earlier for some children, a little bit later for other children, but there was a burst in the development of the skills; it was really fascinating. This development actually followed a typical learning curve, whereas with the earlier readers, I noticed that they made progress each time, but it was more incremental and linear. I do not yet know what the significance of this is, but I suspect that what it means is probably that once the language foundation is there, the reading fluency skills can develop quite quickly. Whilst you certainly can exert improvements in reading in young children, it is harder work.

About half-way through the longitudinal study, I began to worry about how attrition might affect sample size, so we conducted an additional, cross-sectional study involving children who were about 12 years old, using similar measures and schools. After we had controlled for the necessary background factors, the later and earlier starters had similar reading fluency scores, but the later starters were slightly ahead in reading comprehension (Suggate, 2009a).

Importantly, we now have data from international studies, from the English-speaking world – which is very important because of the irregularity of the English language (Seymour, et al., 2003) – and from pre-school studies. It is a good evidence base, converging from many different angles, but for the absence of elusive randomized-controlled trials, believed to be the gold standard in positive empirical research.

Therefore, given the imperfect state of the evidence, these findings need an explanation; and this presents a good riddle, given the compelling arguments to begin reading early that I mentioned earlier. Why is it not the case that reading is like a snowball rolling down a mountain, becoming ever larger? That is, if begun earlier, reading can become more automatic, allowing one to read more, encountering more words – but this does not appear to happen, and thus needs explaining. If our findings are to be accepted, they need to be explained. Thus, I will now point to six aspects of reading that I think explain why earlier readers lose their advantage.

The first point is that reading comprises mastering the code of the language (i.e. in English, the alphabet) and the language itself. This is well known and obvious.

Second, it is really important to recognize that reading is therefore constrained by language, and language is constrained by reading. If you can read text brilliantly, but the requisite language is not there, then it is a little like being able to decode Russian texts without knowing the words or grammar. Thus, part of what might be going on here is that the early readers develop reading skills, yet do not have sufficient development in language and other skills to derive profit. Language comprehension comprises many factors, such as thinking, memory, attention, concentration and the ability to learn, and it therefore depends on much more than mere alphabetic and decoding skills. Thus, one idea behind the so-called 4th-grade slump in reading,[5] sometimes observed in English-speaking countries (where reading begins early), is that these reading skills develop but then have to wait for the language to catch up before developing further (Reese et al., 2010). A similar phenomenon may occur for early readers, which also fits with the findings from our longitudinal study discussed above.

Third, children learn and develop without being readers. Play contains much that is important to development and learning that is not reading-based (Golinkoff et al., 2006). Again, this is quite obvious, but is often forgotten.

Fourth, an important and controversial point: many people seem to believe that early reading improves language. I hold this to be unlikely: certainly, reading might improve language if a child is not getting language in the first place, although this is also paradoxical because you need to have language to read and to learn new words in the first place. But the key question is, what does reading give to language that a play-rich environment cannot give to language? Certainly, there is a point in which reading does improve language; there are certain words that one reads that are not used in spoken language. But when is this point? There is one estimate of this point being around grade 3 to 4 (Nagy and Anderson, 1984), based on the complexity of vocabulary in text. It might be earlier for some children, and it might be improved in some ways through reading before then, but it is important not to forget that language improves without reading, through story-telling, talking about events, conversing with adults and peers and even through having an imaginary friend (Trionfi and Reese, 2009).

One exception to this is phonemic awareness, which improves through rudimentary reading and language activities. According to what is called the lexical restructuring hypothesis (Walley et al., 2003), vocabulary improves phonemic awareness. For example, as one learns the words 'dig', 'dug' and 'dog', one is forced to make fine phonemic distinctions, to understand and convey the differences between these words. So just through language, an important skill for reading develops to some extent.

The fifth aspect is that reading skills are comparatively more difficult to acquire when children are younger. In all probability, comparatively older children's greater language, learning and thinking skills allow them to more easily learn to read (Suggate, 2011b).

Sixth and finally, it is really important to consider what course the development of skills follows. The English language has, depending on how you calculate it, from between 50,000 and 1,000,000 words. Depending on whether you count different participles and stem variations, the estimate can vary widely. In contrast, there are only 26 letters in the English language! Likewise, there is a very finite number of letter-to-sound correspondences in English, far fewer than 50,000. Clearly, language – when one considers grammar, nuances and vocabulary – takes much longer to learn than reading skills. I am always discovering new understandings of words I have known since I was four, including new nuances and new meanings.

So what are we doing when we start teaching explicit reading skills when children are young, say when they are five years old? We are teaching them skills that are easier to acquire when they are older; that is, they could have learned these in a shorter amount of time, because of having better attention, language, thinking skills, better memory, and abstract reasoning, for example. Instead of taking the more cost-effective approach, we drive these skills into children when they are young, and do not look to see whether we may be depriving them of opportunities for language development. Moreover, this will not even improve the reading! To depict this, I have coined the term the Luke Effect (Suggate, 2011b), derived from the Bible:

> A farmer went out to sow his seed. As he was scattering the seed, some fell along the path; it was trampled on, and the birds of the air ate it up. Some fell on rock, and when it came up, the plants withered because they had no moisture. Other seed fell among thorns, which grew up with it and choked the plants. Still other seed fell on good soil. It came up and yielded a crop, a hundred times more than was sown. (Luke, 8: 5–8)

From this analogy, I wish to emphasize the importance of capital- izing on developmental experiences and the development of children so as to introduce reading when it is going to provide meaningful and unique benefit to them, when they have less likelihood of failing at acquiring that skill and being put off reading. It is important to plant the seed in the right season where it is most likely to grow, yielding a good crop.

This brings me to my final point: *ableness is not readiness*. Being able to learn to read is not the same as readiness – if we view readiness in terms of what is the long-term benefit from learning to read early. Certainly, many children can learn to read when they are young, many children will acquire reading skills through all kinds of experiences; but the question is, if we are going to make this part of policy, if we are going to tell teachers that this is really important to teach, and children that it is really important to learn, then both personally as a father and as a developmental scientist, I would want to know that learning reading early has a long-term benefit on the future development of children. And if it does not, I would rather children did something else.

Acknowledgements

This chapter was written when I was an Alexander-von-Humboldt post-doctoral research fellow at the University of Würzburg and was edited from a talk given at the Open EYE conference in London on 12 June 2010. I am grateful to Natascha Gerstner for transcribing the original presentation.

Notes

1   Around 20 per cent of published reading intervention studies report follow-up data, but few of these go beyond one year. A serious concern arises as to whether there is bias in what is published, in that authors do not publish studies showing no effect of their intervention long term (Suggate, 2011a).
2   For example, the Abecedarian Project and the Preschool Perry project.
3   A recent review of these programmes (Suggate, 2011b) that reports results for reading measures suggests that even these programmes do not lead to better reading skills; the long-term improvement is usually in other domains.
4   Evidence that Matthew Effects are caused by reading skill has not been found (Suggate, 2011a).
5   This refers to the observation that children in the fourth grade seem to make little progress.

References

Durkin, D. (1974–5) 'A six year study of children who learned to read in school at the age of four', *Reading Research Quarterly*, 10: 9–61
Elley, W.B. (1992) *How in the World do Students Read? IEA Study of Reading Literacy*, The Hague: International Association for the Evaluation of Educational Achievement
Golinkoff, R.M., Hirsh-Pasek, K. and Singer, D.G. (2006) 'Why play = learning: a challenge for parents and educators', in D.G. Singer, R.M. Golinkoff and K. Hirsh-Pasek (eds), *Play = Learning: How Play Motivates and Enhances Children's Cognitive and Social-emotional Growth*, Oxford and New York: Oxford University Press, pp. 3–12

Hopkin, R., Stokes, L. and Wilkinson, D. (2010). 'Quality, outcomes and costs in early years education', London: National Institute of Economic and Social Research, June

Lazar, I. and Darlington, R. (1982) 'Lasting effects of early education: a report from the consortium for longitudinal studies', *Monographs of the Society of Research in Child Development*, 47(2–3): 1–151

Nagy, W.E. and Anderson, R.C. (1984) 'How many words are there in printed school English?', *Reading Research Quarterly*, 19: 304–30

National Reading Panel (ed.) (2000) *Teaching Children to Read: An Evidence-based Assessment of the Scientific Research Literature on Reading and Its Implications for Reading Instruction*, Bethesda, MD: National Institute of Child Health and Development

Reese, E., Suggate, S., Long, J. and Schaughency, E. (2010) 'Children's oral narrative and reading skills in the first three years of reading instruction', *Reading and Writing*, 23: 627–44

Schmerkotte, H. (1978) 'Ergebnisse eines Vergleichs von Modellkindergärten und Vorklassen in Nordrhein-Westfalen' [Results from a comparison of typical kindergartens and preschools in Northrhein-Westphalia], *Bildung und Erziehung*, 31: 401–11

Seymour, P.H.K., Aro, M., Erskine, J.M. and COST Action Network (2003) 'Foundation literacy acquisition in European orthographies', *British Journal of Psychology*, 94: 143–74

Stanovich, K.E. (1986) 'Matthew effects in reading: some consequences of individual differences in the acquisition of literacy', *Reading Research Quarterly*, 21: 360–407

Suggate, S.P. (2009a) 'Response to reading instruction and age-related development: Do later starters catch up?', University of Otago, Dunedin, NZ : unpublished D.Phil. thesis

Suggate, S.P. (2009b) 'School entry age and reading achievement in the 2006 Programme for International Student Assessment (PISA)', *International Journal of Educational Research*, 48: 151–61

Suggate, S.P. (2010) 'Why "what" we teach depends on "when": grade and reading intervention modality moderate effect size', *Developmental Psychology*, 46, 1556–79

Suggate, S.P. (2011a) 'Are Matthew Effects caused by initial differences in reading skill?', manuscript submitted for publication

Suggate, S.P. (2011b) 'Matthew, Luke, and the Gospel of Early Literacy: a model of what becomes of early reading', manuscript submitted for publication

Trionfi, G. and Reese, E. (2009) 'A good story: children with imaginary companions create richer narratives', *Child Development*, 80: 1301–13

Walley, A.C., Metsala, J.L. and Garlock, V.M. (2003) 'Spoken vocabulary growth: its role in the development of phoneme awareness and early reading ability', *Reading and Writing*, 16: 5–20

Chapter 18

Early Childhood Research and its Political Usage: Some Cautionary Remarks*

Richard House

In this chapter I urge a cautionary approach with regard to accepting at face value the simplistic 'headline' reports of research into early childhood development and learning – favouring, instead, a sceptical view which teases out the 'politicized' interests involved in such research, and the taken-for-granted assumptions about reality that inevitably underpin any and every research methodology.

Features on research methodology in early-childhood professional magazines are highly unusual if not entirely absent, with the vast majority of early years practitioners (excepting those involved in university-level research) probably having little if any exposure to arguments about what constitutes legitimate and appropriate research methodology in the field. Research results presented in the media and in the professional journals – and even in the academic literature – are often far from what they seem, as there is commonly a much more complex and 'messy' story underlying the research process and product than ever comes across in the simplistic, often tabloid-esque way in which 'findings' are routinely presented. In short, research findings can often be misleading, and even grossly distorted – and especially when either the researchers' paymasters

---

* This chapter is based in part on the article 'Research – you can prove anything', *Early Years Educator*, 10 (6) (October), 2008, pp. 17–21.

(e.g. the government) or the researchers themselves have some vested (material) interest in their reported findings.

Conventional quantitative empirical research also tends to encourage uncritical acceptance of the myth of detached 'objectivity', whereas in reality, all research necessarily entails material or vested *interests*, along with what are often *unconscious, unarticulated assumptions* about reality – and which it is then the task of critical thinking to unmask and problematize (e.g. House, 2010; Lather, 1991; Slife and Williams, 1995). Thus, there exist taken-for-granted metaphysical assumptions that unavoidably underpin *any and every* research methodology in the social sciences. One of my core arguments in this chapter, then, is that *the making explicit of research assumptions is essential if we are to be in any position to make an informed and rational assessment of reported research findings.*

It is certainly easy for academic research, and writing about research, to come across as mystifying or patronizing (at times I am guilty of this myself, especially when writing for a narrow academic audience) – yet my goal here is to help empower early childhood practitioners to gain a critical sensibility towards the often daunting output of research 'experts' who claim a monopoly on assessing the subtle and complex work that you yourselves do with young children. Contrary to current preoccupations with so-called 'evidence-based practice' and 'objective' empirical research, I believe that *every individual practitioner* is, in a very real sense, a researcher whenever they work with children – and that the *actual experience* of practitoners yields 'research findings' that are potentially just as valid, if not sometimes more so, as are the results of sophisticated empirical research projects.

A recent example of this concerned new research on introducing ICT (in the form of I-pads) into early-childhood settings (Learner, 2011). In the reported research, Dr Rosie Flewitt of the Open University and Dr Sylvia Wolfe of Cambridge University found that many early years practitioners lacked confidence in how to use technology, were uncertain about its value, or feared the potential harm to 'childhood'. These researchers' finding, that 'most practitioners feared [new technologies'] potential harm to "childhood"', might actually be those practitioners' *accurate* perception of what counts in early childhood environments, made by experienced practitioners with an intuitive feel for what is developmentally appropriate, rather than being the fear-driven, reactionary viewpoint that the researchers uncritically seemed to be assuming.

One key metaphysical assumption that informs my own thinking in this chapter is the *assumption of uniqueness*, which holds that every relational experience between adult and child(ren) is a unique one which can never be repeated, nor 'measured', in all its subtlety and complexity. This kind of view, championed by qualitative or so-called 'phenomenological' research theorists like Max van Manen (1990) and Clark Moustakas (1994), contrasts markedly with more conventional, so-called 'positivistic' research, that claims to discover generalizable, universal cause-and-effect relationships between 'variables' which are, *from the outset*, assumed to be distinct and mutually excluding, and accurately quantifiable and measurable.

'Positivism' is a broad term in the philosophy and methodology of science which refers to a particular approach to empirical research which seeks to quantify key 'variables', and then to specify 'cause and effect' relationships between them, based on (often sophisticated) statistical analysis. Positivistic research has many well-documented problems – not least, that the kinds of research themes that many would deem of critical relevance and interest are often simply not quantifiable; that positivistic research can only 'discover' what the *initial specification* of quantified variables self-fulfillingly assumes to exist in the first place (with what is excluded from analysis being at least as important as what is chosen to be included); that positivistic research is intrinsically atomistic rather than holistic, in that it starts by splitting reality up into analysable parts or 'variables', rather than beginning with the (at least equally plausible) assumption that it is *the whole functioning system* that is determining of the constituent parts (the latter sometimes being termed 'structural causality'; see Balibar, 1996); and it assumes, finally, that it is somehow both possible and valid to reach *standardizing, generalizing* (so-called 'nomothetic') statements about reality, rather than assuming that uniqueness and diversity are the norm, with every situation requiring its own separate analysis and understanding that honours its uniqueness.

At its worst, then, positivistic research can easily end up self-fulfillingly 'proving' what was assumed to be the case at the outset! – and I maintain that a great deal of 'empirical' research, though seeming on the surface to be sophisticated and impressive, is of this essentially circular nature (House, 2010).

Most early-childhood practitioners are probably (and appropriately) so involved in their work with children that they understandably have little or no time to engage with the complexities of research methodology – making it all the more important that practitioners can develop tools for taking a robustly critical view of research findings – and especially when it can so easily be *politicized* (that is, used, and even distorted, for political purposes). More of the latter later.

The Early Years Foundation Stage (EYFS): A Revealing Tale of Two Pieces of Research

To help illustrate my argument, I will critically examine several pieces of EYFS research that have been reported in the professional press over the past few years. I will argue that far from proving what the headline findings claim, the research quoted was methodologically flawed, and by no means proved what was being claimed by the researchers and/or its reporters. This clearly has major implications for the political use to which research findings are put – to which crucial issue I return below. In following the occasionally technical argument through to the end, readers will hopefully then be equipped to take a more critical, appropriately sceptical viewpoint when they encounter the reported results of empirical early years research.

I will refer to two pieces of research on the EYFS conducted or sponsored by (the then) Department for Children, Schools and Families (DCSF), termed the 'Super Scale Points Project' – research which met with very different fates. In summary, one piece of research led to findings which embarrassingly contradicted core aspects of the EYFS framework, and these findings were quietly 'shelved' by the Department – and were only released to the public via a Freedom of Information request by the then Shadow Minister Annette Brooke MP (who has written the Foreword to this book) (Curtis, 2008). In stark contrast, another piece of DCSF research was widely reported in the media and professional press (Gaunt, 2008a) – and unsurprisingly, it was claimed that this particular research vindicated the EYSF framework. When looked at more closely and critically, I show below that this latter research did not begin to make the case for the EYFS that the then government's DCSF was claiming it to make.

Early in 2008, the Open EYE campaign in which I was (and am) involved was anonymously contacted about some DCSF independently commissioned research which contradicted aspects of the EYFS framework. Once released under the Freedom of Information Act, the *Guardian* then reported on this apparently suppressed research (Curtis, 2008) which, they reported, 'runs counter to ministers' curriculum plan'.

One has to question, first, the motivation driving the decision not to make this research report public. If the research had yielded results which had *supported* the government's policy framework, the DCSF would have almost certainly very actively trumpeted its results. This episode, then, merely confirmed the suspicions of those who believe that research of this kind is inevitably and unavoidably 'politicized' in nature.

A close perusal of the released research report indicated that the research was conducted in an impeccably rigorous way, according to the standards and procedures of this kind of research. We are told that (quoting from the released report) 'Schools were chosen that were distributed throughout England and which represented a range of demographic situations from urban to rural settings.' Furthermore, 'FSP practitioners were themselves chosen by recommendation from Early Years specialists in various authorities'; and

> internal data checks were made within the data sets looking for obvious inconsistencies that would cast doubt on the validity of the rest of the data. ... [This] rigour severely reduced the total number of data. [Some] 202 matched records were suitable for the statistical analysis.

An independent statistician then assessed the data's validity and suitability. This is clearly serious research, therefore, whose findings certainly deserved to be taken seriously. Nor should the comparatively small size of the sample necessarily be seen as significantly detracting from any research findings, as (for example) case-study and qualitative research are not necessarily inferior to more statistically representative, large-scale empirical research (e.g. Hatch, 2002; Lichtman, 2009). Indeed, the Scottish study so often cited by 'synthetic phonics' supporters was also very small-scale (Johnston and Watson, 2005), yet the policy influence it has had has been enormous – perhaps because its findings just happened to coincide with what politicians were wanting to do anyway.

More damning still is the fact that the results obtained *directly contradicted* key aspects of the EYFS framework – thus comprehensively undermining the Department's reported claim, made at the time, that it was 'inconclusive'. Thus, the suppressed research discovered that (again quoting from the unpublished report):

- In every aspect of attainment at Key Stage 1 (KS1), DA 8, 'Maintains attention and concentrates' was a distinguishing factor in final attainment;
- Overall the data suggests use of spoken language is important to becoming an accomplished writer;
- Two scale points did ***not*** seem crucial ... to high performance at KS1. These were LSL8, 'Attempts to read more complex words, using phonic knowledge' and W8, 'Begins to form captions and simple sentences, sometimes using punctuation';
- The following scale points ***did*** show an association with performance at KS1:

  - ✓ **DA8** 'Maintains attention and concentrates';
  - ✓ **SD6** 'Understands that there need to be agreed values and codes of behaviour for groups. ... ';
  - ✓ **ED8** 'Understands what is right and wrong and why';
  - ✓ **CD4** 'Sings simple songs from memory';
  - ✓ **CD7** 'Uses imagination in art and design, music, dance, imaginative role-play and stories' (emphases added).

These extraordinary findings strongly support the Open EYE campaign's advocacy of an informal, story and play-based early learning milieu, with strong emphasis on naturalistic and artistic learning experiences; whilst the government's emphasis on preschool *cognitively biased* learning (e.g. in literacy) is, at the very least, thrown into considerable doubt. Indeed, these findings could easily be used to make a strong case for shifting the start of formal schooling to 6 or 7 years of age (as occurs in much of continental Europe) (see Chapter 16).

Then, in July 2008, the Department *did* choose to release research findings which, they alleged, supported its EYFS framework. The latter DCSF analysis compared the results of a 10 per cent sample of Foundation Stage Profile assessments in 2005 and Key Stage 1 in 2007, and found 'a direct link' between the two sets of results. Thus, those children who achieved well in reading, writing and spoken language in the Foundation Stage Profile were *statistically* very likely to continue to do well in primary school. The prestigious early years magazine *Nursery World* reported that 'Clear evidence has emerged that shows that children who do well in assessments at the age of five are more likely to go on to continue to achieve in primary school'; and that there was 'a strong connection between the CLL assessments "linking sounds and letters", reading, and writing and KS1, reading, writing, maths and APS scores' (Gaunt, 2008a).

The assumption seems to be being made that it is the EYFS 'learning goals' *per se* that are somehow *causing* higher performance at KS1 several years later; and so by extension, if you simply make sure that the goals are somehow reached at age 5, then *ipso facto*, you will increase (or, should I say, *drive up*) educational standards by age 7. Thus, the then children's minister Beverley Hughes was quoted as saying, 'Of those children who achieve at least six points in all the personal, social and emotional development and CLL scales, a very high proportion go on to achieve the expected level and above in KS1 maths (99 per cent), reading (98 per cent) and writing (97 per cent)' – as if this says anything meaningful or useful whatsoever about the efficacy or otherwise of the EYFS!

So-called 'positivistic' research of this kind, by its very nature, has severe methodological shortcomings (cf. Masters, 2008) – to such an extent that one really has to ask what the point is of such research, in light of the essentially meaningless statements derived from it, as quoted above. Richard Masters (2008) wrote the following withering critique to *Nursery World*:

> The research with which the Government tries to justify ever-earlier learning and assessment is woefully inadequate. It just compares FS performance with KS1 performance. ... It fails to ask or answer a single interesting question. All it 'discovers' is that those who can answer FS questions well at five years old are, surprise, surprise, also more able to answer KS1 questions at seven years old. This is laughable. The research doesn't even compare performance at age seven of one group who have done FS assessments against a group who have not. But even if it did, and demonstrated that those assessed at five were better exam fodder at seven, it would remain a desperately narrow piece of research. Something has gone badly wrong when a Government has to use non-evidence to justify trying to force reading, writing and other types of abstract thinking on children before their make-up is suited to such focused thinking.

Don't sit on the fence, Richard! ...

Presumably, then, the only conceivable rationale for this research is the assumption that data on children's achievements at age 5 can somehow be used to ensure what their achievements will be at age 7, at Key Stage 1 – or why else do this kind of research at all? Yet to maintain such a view would entail entirely fallacious assumptions. Most notably, what is being assumed is precisely what remains to be discovered! – that is, *how it is* that children reach their measured achievements at age 5. If the government is wanting to claim or imply that it was the 'delivery' of the Foundation Stage curriculum that led to the measured achievements at 5, then this simplistic empirical research doesn't even begin to show that.

Secondly, there is the crucial issue of *causality*. It is very well known that the existence of a statistical *correlation* between certain achievements at ages 5 and at 7 tells us absolutely nothing about the learning dynamics and the trajectory of how children's learning actually progresses between those ages. As already argued, it certainly cannot be assumed that simply making sure that the age-5 children can attain the narrowly measured profile competencies will necessarily then lead to healthily integrated and well founded competencies at a later age. Yet the very fact that this kind of research is being done suggests that this is, *indeed*, the kind of crassly mechanistic assumption that the DCSF is making; for again, if not, then why do such expensive and resource-consuming research at all? – if not for politicized propaganda purposes...

Finally, to place any faith in research of this kind, one has to assume that what is being measured is what the researchers *believe* is being measured (which it might well not be); and even more importantly, that it is possible to capture and then measure those factors which are most important in early learning. Yet many prominent authorities believe early learning to be a largely *unconscious,* sub-cortical process (e.g. Claxton, 1997; Hooper Hansen, 2008; Salzberger-Wittenberg et al., 1983; cf. Chapters 10 and 21) – in which case it follows that research that only gives credence to what is measurable and quantifiable may well be grossly distorting, to the point of caricature, what it is claiming to measure.

That the results of such research are so sensitive to the way the research is set up and operationalized also means that if you repeat the research enough times in enough different ways, using varying specifications and populations, you are eventually *bound* to find at least one analysis that yields results that 'support' the assumptions you're seeking to justify. Yet such an 'EU Referendum'-type approach to research is dishonestly expedient and brazenly opportunistic, in that you cynically keep repeating the research using different specifications until you get the results you want, and disregard all the uncomfortable disconfirming findings in the interim. This is essentially what appears to have happened in this particular DCSF research exercise.

The Millennium Cohort Study: More Questionable Research

A second example of questionable early-childhood research is that of the so-called Millennium Cohort Study (MCS).[1] As background, the Millennium Cohort Study is a multi-disciplinary research project following the lives of around 19,000 children born in the UK in 2000–1, being the most recent of Britain's national longitudinal birth cohort studies. The study has tracked the Millennium children through their early childhood years, and intends to follow them into adulthood. The MCS's field of enquiry covers such diverse topics as parenting; childcare; school choice; child behaviour and cognitive development; child and parental health; parents' employment and education; income and poverty; housing, neighbourhood and residential mobility; and social capital and ethnicity.

Again, considerable caution is required before substantive policy implications are drawn from the MCS data – and more specifically for current purposes, the alleged causal relationship that is claimed to exist between childcare and children's developmental progress. Researchers into early childhood are perhaps understandably preoccupied with finding scientific evidence which will somehow provide the 'magic bullet' that will enable policy-makers to guarantee healthy development and learning for all young children, irrespective of background and the many and varied vicissitudes of children's home environments. Research findings from the MCS reported in February 2010 (Gaunt, 2010), examining the alleged impact of formal childcare on child development, cannot pass without some detailed reservations being expressed about the way in which the MCS data is being interpreted. The concerns fall into four broad categories:

- first, the problem of assuming causation from aggregate data and mere statistical association (cf. earlier discussion);

- secondly, the uncritical and unwarranted assumption that measurable attainments in young children's capabilities are necessarily positively beneficent and developmentally appropriate;
- thirdly, the possible ignoring of subtle and intangible 'imponderables' that might well be beyond quantitative specification and measurement, and yet might well be more important than those variables that *are* measurable; and finally,
- the possible impact of subtle and longer-term unintended (negative) side-effects that might well outweigh any benefits that early formal childcare interventions confer.

First, it is well known within the research methodology literature that the discovery of a statistical assocation between alleged independent and dependent variables can never be assumed to represent a linear *cause-and-effect* relationship.[2] Even if we accept linear-causal thinking as a legitimate framework of explanation, with the MCS research as in all such empirical research, it is, at the very least, plausible that there exists a variable (or variables) to which both the 'independent' and 'dependent' variables are causally related, and that it is this third variable which generates the observed association between the 'independent' and 'dependent' variables – a methodological problem referred to as 'multi-colinearity' in the research jargon. In such a situation, then, it would very possibly be entirely spurious to assume that by somehow intervening in and manipulating the allegedly 'independent' variable (in the current case, formal childcare) that the so-called 'dependent' variable will then change in a predictable and necessarily beneficent way. Thus, in the aforementioned *Nursery World* report (Gaunt, 2010), we read that 'If you're a parent with low educational qualifications, you can offset that disadvantage by sending your child to formal childcare'. Yet this viewpoint assumes a mechanistically causal relationship between formal childcare per se and child development which may mislead, rather than elucidating matters.

Thus, for example, it seems highly plausible that it is not formal childcare *per se* that is the crucial variable here, but rather, that in whatever environment the child finds herself, if she is receiving more language-rich contact and high-quality relating than she would experience in the environment where she would otherwise be (e.g. in a deprived family home), then all other things being equal, she will make more progress according to measurable criteria. In other words, then, these research findings are not at all necessarily an argument in favour of formal childcare *per se*, but rather, for children being in language-rich, loving relational environments, *wherever* they may be. Note my invoking of the crucial term 'loving relational environments' here; for my strong hunch is that this latter 'variable' is an essential and necessary accompaniment of a language-rich environment, if the child is to derive the maximum developmental benefit from such an experience.

Sadly, it *will* sometimes be the case, of course, that a formal childcare environment will provide a relatively more enabling and 'growthful' environment according to these criteria, compared to a child's home life; but policy-makers should surely be looking at *every conceivable way* in which young children can have such healthily formative experiences – and they should certainly not be assuming that only institutional formal childcare can provide them. On this kind of view, then, *to claim that it is formal childcare per se that is the decisive variable is at best misleading, for it is to misrepresent and claim far too much from the research findings*. Indeed, if policy-making decisions are based on data like this, the result could easily be a huge waste of public resources, and even policy interventions that in some cases bring about the very opposite of their original intention.

Interestingly, the principal researcher in this latest Millennium Cohort research study, Dr Kirstine Hansen, is quoted as acknowledging that 'daily reading to children could be an indicator of more general parenting behaviour that benefits child development', and that 'the finding should be examined further'. So given her recognition of this issue, one can only wonder why the research ended up being quoted in a way that significantly, and potentially misleadingly, oversimplified the alleged findings, and relegated the kinds of methodological reservations I am highlighting here firmly to the background.

Secondly, there is the highly problematic assumption that measurable attainments in young children's capabilities are necessarily positively beneficent and developmentally appropriate. By way of illustrating the point, we presumably wouldn't be celebrating the fact if a child of 5 or 6 were performing highly complex algebra calculations, or a child of 6 or 7 were highly knowledgeable about the procedural detail of adult human sexual relationships. Yet on the kind of argument implicitly adopted in this research, it is assumed quite uncritically that for young children to be able to 'achieve' the kinds of learning requirements set out in the EYFS statutory guidance is *necessarily* a good thing. Yet from the standpoint of educational and childhood theorists like Donald Winnicott or Rudolf Steiner (House, 2009), quite the opposite might well be the case, with children possibly having been 'awakened' into kinds of quasi-adult consciousness which is actually harmful to their all-round, long-term healthy development. This in turn touches on the fault-line that lies at the heart of the flawed EYFS – namely, its conflation of guidance and requirements, and the way in which its normalizing discourse about 'requirements', 'expectations' and 'goals' is continually contradicting what it says elsewhere in the framework about 'The Unique Child'.

The use of the tell-tale word 'ahead' gives a graphic example of such ideological positions camouflaged in the spuriously 'objective' language of science. Thus, we read that 'Overall, girls were two months *ahead* of boys in their mathematical scores and four months *ahead* of boys in their CLL scores. In creative development, girls were nine months *ahead* of boys' (emphases added). Yet the very use of the term 'ahead' necessarily assumes that this is somehow preferable and beneficent; whereas from the kind of viewpoint held by authorities like Carl Honoré and David Elkind in their books, respectively, *In Praise of Slow* (2004; see also Honoré, 2008) and *The Hurried Child* (2007), it could be convincingly argued that 'more is often less' in early learning, and that terms like 'ahead' entail all manner of adult-centric normalizing assumptions about child development that are, at the very least, open to major challenge.

Thirdly, there is the possible neglect, or even outright ignoring, of subtle and intangible variables, sometimes referred to as 'imponderables', that might well be beyond quantitative specification and measurement. It was educationalist Rudolf Steiner who paid especial attention to these subtle qualities in education (House, 2009), and who argued that a deep understanding of the child is far more important and helpful than is a focus upon (for example) measurable literacy 'outcomes'.

Finally, and related to the latter point, the possible impact on child development of subtle and longer-term unintended (negative) side-effects is routinely ignored in 'positivistic' research such as that under discussion here, yet the latter might well outweigh any benefits that early formal childcare is claimed to confer. Thus, how can we be sure, for example, that in those circumstances in which children are exposed to more language-rich experience via formal childcare, there are not other, more subtle effects of (for example) children being separated from their parent(s) at an early age, that more than counterbalance any early-learning advantages conferred by formal childcare? For example, there is the interference with a strong early attachment relationship in which parent and child learn about each other very deeply, and which could well have major implications for the parent–child relationship throughout the rest of their childhood. By focusing merely upon mechanistic measurable quantitative 'outcomes', these kinds of possible long-term effects are simply ignored.

Another poignant example is afforded by disturbing research on long-term learning competencies. Research from 2006 by Philip Adey and Michael Shayer at Kings College, London discovered that far from getting cleverer, 11-year-olds are less 'intelligent' than their counterparts of 30 years earlier. And more recently, we hear of new research by Professor James Flynn of the University of Otago showing that there has been a very unexpected decline in British teenagers' IQ scores between 1980 and the present day (Gray, 2009; Shayer, 2006).

There is a distinct possibility that this observed decline in children's cognitive abilities may be, at least in part, a direct result of those same children having been subjected to unbalanced, overly cognitive learning at earlier ages, leading to ephemeral short-term gains (e.g. higher attainment or test scores), but at the expense of a longer-term cognitive malaise. One notable culprit may well be the imposition of cognitively unbalanced learning in the early years, through the introduction of the Curriculum Guidance for the Foundation Stage in 2000 (DfEE and the QCA, 2000), and the associated intrusion of an increasingly ubiquitous ICT screen culture into early childhood, both in the home and now in early-years settings through the EYFS (see Chapter 19).

Evidence from a rich variety of sources strongly suggests that a stable and lovingly consistent early attachment relationship is crucial in early children's development. Such a relationship is also vital for parents, in terms of learning about being a parent to their child(ren), and developing a deep, intimate relationship that will inform, support and 'hold' both child and parent(s) throughout the rest of childhood. Some even believe that the compromising of early attachment relationships through early institutional childcare, and the associated drive to get young mothers back into the (often low-paid) workforce, may well be significantly responsible for the growing malaise in children's behaviour and mental health.

It therefore needs to be emphasized that there is a major problem with the way in which research like this is reported in the media and in the professional literature. Research methodology is widely known to be a procedural minefield with very considerable associated complexities, and unless the full reservations and shortcomings of research data and their accompanying methodologies are spelt out in detail, alleged headline 'findings' which are in reality not supported by the data and the methodology can be grossly misleading. This is of particular concern when such reported findings are often seized upon in a highly uncritical way to support culturally fashionable but ultimately ephemeral policy-making fads, which may well not be in the best developmental interests of at least some of our young children.

Similar kinds of objections can be made to the much-vaunted Effective Provision of Pre-School Education (EPPE) Research Project's findings, and the way they are routinely reported and interpreted. Thus, in late 2008 (Gaunt, 2008b; Ward, 2008), it was reported that there seems to be some association between 'quality' early experience and later 'outcomes'; but this 'finding' merely begs the crucial questions about what such 'quality' actually consists in. Without doing the very complex and subtle research necessary to ascertain the latter information, it may well be that what EPPE (and the government) are uncritically assuming to be the 'active ingredients' in 'quality' provision may actually be a wild goose chase that misses the crucial factors at work. Certainly, the dramatically impressive results of the developmentally appropriate and comparatively cheap Reading Recovery Programme for six-year-olds strongly suggests that the almost £2 billion spent in 2007 on early years programmes (including most prominently, the EYFS) might well have been far better spent in well-targeted interventions for deprived and educationally challenged children (Ward, 2010), instead of the kind of expensive and non-discriminating policy interventions, like EYFS, that are arguably unnecessary for the majority of young pre-school children, and possibly harmful and constraining for at least some children.

Empirical, 'positivistic' research which seeks to make generalizations raises enormously complex issues, and is routinely open not only to withering methodological critique but also to a range of often very diverse interpretations. The notion of 'equifinality', for example, refers to the phenomenon that an infinite range of processes can generate a given measured outcome. Given the latter case, one always has to be extremely cautious before assuming what might have caused an observed outcome in one's measured data. Indeed, it is at the very least sometimes the case that researchers' empirical findings can be accounted for by factors (often unmeasurable ones) *other than* the ones they claim to be the causal or 'active' variables – and this may well be the case with the EPPE research.

Conclusions

In sum, then, I have argued that headline research findings are very rarely what they seem, and commonly mask all manner of unarticulated assumptions about reality. *Every* early years practitioner is a researcher whenever they work reflectively with children; and I believe that we should empower practitioners by recognizing this phenomenon, rather than condescendingly adhering to a false hierarchy of 'knowledge' in which personal experience is seen as being inferior to so-called 'objective', generalizable (academic) knowledge.

Officially commissioned government research on the EYFS was shown to have yielded highly variable results, some of which were reported, and some not – simply confirming suspicions that research of this kind is more 'politicized' than it is 'objective'. Research inevitably entails material interests and (often taken-for-granted) metaphysical assumptions about what constitutes 'reality' (e.g. Cary, 2006; Stronach and MacLure, 1997), with issues of *power* always being present (e.g. Peters and Besley, 2006; Popkewitz and Brennan, 1998); and until both are questioned and sufficiently articulated, our ability to make mature and discerning assessments of reported research findings will be severely limited.

My strong wish from this chapter is *not* that readers will necessarily agree with my own sceptical 'take' on the DCSF's EYFS research reported here – for as I made clear earlier, we all have our own particular interests in research and in how it is reported – and I am by no means immune from that unavoidable partiality. However, if readers come away from reading and reflecting on these questions with a wish and a capacity to think more critically about what is routinely presented as 'objective' and 'factual' research findings – especially when there is a political agenda involved – then it will have more than served its purpose.

Notes

1 See http://www.cls.ioe.ac.uk/text.asp?section=000100020001
2 And within certain cosmologies, the very notion of linear-causal thinking itself is squarely rejected as a legitimate way of understanding reality.

References

Balibar, E. (1996) 'Structural causality, overdetermination, and antagonism', in A. Callari and D. Ruccio (eds), *Postmodern Materialism and the future of Marxist theory*, Hanover: Wesleyan University Press, pp. 109–20

Cary, L.J. (2006) *Curriculum Spaces: Discourse, Postmodern Theory and Educational Research*, New York: Peter Lang

Claxton, G. (1997) *Hare Brain, Tortoise Mind: Why Intelligence Increases When You Think Less*, London: Fourth Estate

Curtis, P. (2008) 'Early-years writing lessons "do no good"', The *Guardian*, 14 July; retrievable at: http://www.guardian.co.uk/education/2008/jul/14/schools.uk (retrieved 20 June 2011)

Department for Education and Science (DfEE) and the Qualifications and Curriculum Authority (QCA) (2000) *Curriculum Guidance for the Foundation Stage* (London)

Elkind, D. (2007) *The Hurried Child: Growing Up Too Fast Too Soon*, New York: Perseus Books (orig. 1982)

Gaunt, C. (2008a) 'FS Profile assessments point to future success', *Nursery World*, 24 June; retrievable at http://www.nursery-world.co.uk/news/822599/FS-Profile-assessments-point-future-success/?DCMP=ILC-SEARCH; (retrieved 20 June 2011)

Gaunt, C. (2008b) 'EPPE study affirms pre-school benefits to end of KS2', *Nursery World*, 4 December; downloadable at http://www.nurseryworld.co.uk/news/866659/EPPE-study-affirms-pre-school-benefits-end-KS2/?DCMP=ILC-SEARCH (retrieved 23 June 2011)

Gaunt, C. (2010) 'Formal childcare boosts Foundation Stage Profile scores', *Nursery World*, 24 February; downloadable at: http://www.nurseryworld.co.uk/news/985743/Formal-childcare-boosts-Foundation-Stage-Profile-scores/?DCMP=ILC-SEARCH; (retrieved 23 June 2011)

Gray, R. (2009) 'British teenagers have lower IQs than their counterparts did 30 years ago', *Sunday Telegraph*, 7 February; downloadable at: http://www.telegraph.co.uk/education/educationnews/4548943/British-teenagers-have-lower-IQs-than-their-counterparts-did-30-years-ago.html (retrieved 23 June 2011)

Hatch, J. A. (2002) *Doing Qualitative Research in Education Settings*, Albany, NY: State University of New York Press

Honoré, C. (2004) *In Praise of Slow: How a Worldwide Movement is Challenging the Cult of Speed*, London: Orion

Honoré, C. (2008) *Under Pressure: Rescuing Our Children from the Culture of Hyper-parenting*, London: Orion

Hooper Hansen, G. (2008) Letter of the week: 'Play is vital as brains develop', *Times Educational Supplement*, 8 August; http://www.tes.co.uk/article.aspx?storycode=6000712 (retrieved at 20 June 2011)

House, R. (2009) 'The mind object and "dream consciousness": a Winnicottian and a Steinerean rationale for challenging the premature "adultisation" of children', in R. House and D. Loewenthal (eds), *Childhood, Well-being and a Therapeutic Ethos*, London: Karnac Books, 2009, pp. 155–69

House, R. (2010) 'Psy research beyond late-modernity: towards praxis-congruent research, *Psychotherapy and Politics International*, 8 (1): 13–20; extended version as Chapter 20 in R. House, *In, Against and Beyond Therapy: Critical Essays Towards a Post-professional Era*, PCCS Books: Ross-on-Wye, 2010 pp. 269–90

Johnston, R.S. and Watson, J.E. (2005) *A Seven Year Study of the Effects of Synthetic Phonics Teaching on Reading and Spelling Attainment*, Insight 17; Edinburgh: Scottish Executive Education Dept; downloadable at: http://www.scotland.gov.uk/Resource/Doc/933/0044071.pdf

Lather, P. (1991) *Getting Smart: Feminist Research and Pedagogy within/in the Postmodern*, London: Routledge

Learner, S. (2011) 'Middle-class angst over technology in the early years', *The Guardian*, Education Supplement, 7 June; retrievable at http://www.guardian.co.uk/education/2011/jun/07/early-years-anxiety-digital-technology (retrieved 20 June 2011)

Lichtman, M. (2009) *Qualitative Research in Education: A User's Guide*, 2nd edn, Thousand Oaks, Calif.: Sage

Masters, R. (2008) Letter of the week: 'The questions to ask', *Nursery World*, 10 July; retrievable at: http://www.nurseryworld.co.uk/news/830453/Opinion-Letters/?DCMP=ILC-SEARCH (retrieved 20 June 2011)

Moustakas, C. (1994) *Phenomenological Research Methods*, London: Sage

Peters, M.A. and Besley, A.C. (eds) (2006) *Why Foucault?: New Directions in Educational Research*, New York: Peter Lang

Popkewitz, T.S. and Brennan, M.(eds) (1998) *Foucault's Challenge: Discourse, Knowledge and Power in Education*, New York: Teachers College Press, Columbia University

Salzberger-Wittenberg, I., Williams, G. and Osborne, E. (1983) *The Emotional Experience of Learning and Teaching*, London: Routledge

Shayer, M. (2006) 'Thirty years on – a large anti-Flynn effect? The Piagetian test volume and heaviness norms, 1975–2003', reported in *Science*, 311 (5763)

Slife, B.D. and Williams, R.N. (1995) *What's Behind the Research?: Discovering Hidden Assumptions in the Behavioral Sciences*, Thousand Oaks, Calif.: Sage

Stronach, I. and MacLure, M. (1997) *Educational Research Undone: The Postmodern Embrace*, Buckingham: Open University Press

van Manen, M. (1990) *Researching Lived Experience: Human Science for an Action Sensitive Pedagogy*, Albany: SUNY Press

Ward, H. (2008) 'Quality nurseries pay long-term dividends', *Times Educational Supplement*, 28 November; downloadable at: http://www.tes.co.uk/article.aspx?storycode=6005702 (retrieved 23 June 2011)

Ward, H. (2010) 'Effect of Reading Recovery is long term, study finds', *Times Educational Supplement*, 8 January; downloadable at: http://www.tes.co.uk/article.aspx?storycode=6032777 (retrieved 2 July 2011)

CHAPTER 19

Does Not Compute, Revisited: Screen Technology in Early Years Education[*]

ARIC SIGMAN

Central Government and local education authorities are placing increasing emphasis on the use of screen technology (e.g. computers, 'educational' DVDs) in the classroom, and promoting 'visual literacy' and 'media literacy' as part of the educational curriculum. This trend has been accompanied by assertions that information presented by computers and DVDs – especially moving images – is more engaging, and thereby engenders greater learning in children (Marsh et al., 2005). There has been increasing use of the term 'interactive', which by default gives the impression that existing methods of teaching and learning are not, or are less so.

The growing acceptance of screens in education is further reflected in statements by the former Department for Children, Schools and Families (DCSF), which expressed the view that ' … mainstream policymakers have – perhaps erroneously – seen curriculum subject areas revolving around literacy … ', and which posited ' … a curriculum where noun, verb and adjective sit alongside other types of "grammatical" vocabulary such as pan, zoom and edit' (DCSF, 2008). To give one example, the London Education

---

* This chapter is an edited and updated version of 'Does Not Compute', a Research Paper originally commissioned by the Ruskin Mill Educational Trust, Nailsworth, Stroud, 2008, Copyright © Aric Sigman and Ruskin Mill Educational Trust 2008; and reproduced here by kind permission of the Ruskin Mill Educational Trust.

Authority of Hackney states: 'Visual images are fast becoming the most predominant form of communication, with the ratio of image to text increasing' (London Grid for Learning, 2007). More generally, schools are increasingly showing animated Hollywood films as part of the school day, and referring to this activity with descriptions such as 'Golden Time'.

The trend towards screen technology in education is now being directed at children from the age of 22 months. The former DCSF referred to children using Information and Communications Technology (ICT) as being 'legal requirements' for 'learning and development' (DCSF, 2007). As part of the Early Years Foundation Stage (EYFS) introduced in 2008, from the early age of 22 months, ICT became formally considered by the Department as a 'development matter'. Children should 'show an interest in ICT. Seek to acquire basic skills in turning on and operating some ICT equipment.' From 30 months, schools should 'Draw young children's attention to pieces of ICT apparatus they see or they use with adult supervision'.

From 40 months, children should 'Complete a simple program on a computer. Use ICT to perform simple functions such as selecting a channel on the TV remote control. Use a mouse and keyboard to interact with age-appropriate computer software.' Teachers should 'Teach and encourage children to click on different icons to cause things to happen in a computer program. Provide a range of programmable toys, as well as equipment involving ICT, such as computers.' (ibid.)

'Educational' vs 'Non-educational' Screen Time

There has been a concerted effort to distance and differentiate so-called 'educational television' and 'educational DVDs' from entertainment television and DVDs. A similar distinction is being made between 'educational computer games' and those that are merely entertaining, whilst the Internet is increasingly seen as offering phenomenal educational benefits to children. The previous British Government established the 'Home Access Task Force' to provide every child with home internet access, and encouraged companies such as BT, Sky, Virgin, Microsoft and RM to provide cheaper internet access and computer technology (BETT, 2008). Children are certainly enthusiastic about this 'home access', but not in the way envisaged by the

Government. A British report describes an enormous increase in 'social networking' sites amongst younger children, which 'has overtaken fun (online games) as the main reason to use the Internet, and study is now far behind' (Childwise Monitor, 2008).

'Quality Time'

The advocates of introducing young children to screen technology contend that it is the 'quality' of what the children see on the screen – the content – that is critical. It is suggested that provided what the young child sees on the screen is 'educational' and 'age-appropriate', there are cognitive and intellectual advantages and educational benefits forthcoming. Moreover, there is an implicit message that *not* to expose young children to this screen material puts them at a developmental and educational disadvantage. Presumably this is why it is currently a legal requirement, as stated in the EYFS.

It is also implied that if children do not 'get used to' screen technology early on, they will in some way be intimidated by it, or be less competent at using it later. However, new research has found that even Rhesus monkeys are comfortable with, and capable of using, the same screen technology that children are exposed to (Deadwyler et al., 2008; Tulane University, 2006). Monkeys are even willing to forego their food and drink in exchange for the opportunity to look at screen images of the dominant, 'celebrity' monkeys of their pack. The Dallas Zoo reports that their gorillas each have their favourite television shows. They all like Disney cartoons; The Little Mermaid, The Lion King and Beauty and the Beast are their favourites (Dallas Morning News, 2004).

While this trend in introducing screen technology in early years education is gathering strength, a growing body of empirical evidence – most of it from beyond the domains of media studies, education and psychology – is providing a very different account of how exposure to screen technology affects children now and in the long-term future (Sigman, 2007, a, b, 2009, 2010). There seems to be a direct conflict between the advocates of ICT in early years education, on the one hand, and the warnings arising from studies in paediatric medicine and biology, on the other.

There are now sound medical reasons for delaying the introduction of technology to children. In August 1999, the American Academy of Pediatrics (AAP) issued guidelines recommending that children under the age of two watch no screen entertainment at all because television 'can negatively affect early brain development'. They have more recently issued another statement on 'TV and Toddlers':

> It may be tempting to put your infant or toddler in front of the television, especially to watch shows created just for children under age two. But the American Academy of Pediatrics says: Don't do it! These early years are crucial in a child's development. The Academy is concerned about the impact of television programming intended for children younger than age two and how it could affect your child's development.

The US Department of Health and Human Services (2010) has announced a 'national 10-year health promotion and disease prevention objective', a main aim of which is to

> increase the proportion of children aged 0 to 2 years who view no television or videos on an average weekday. Increase the proportion of children and adolescents aged 2 years through 12th grade [18yrs] who view television, videos, or play video games for no more than 2 hours a day.

The Australian Government is now considering a similar national policy guideline. And it is highly significant that France's Government has recently banned French channels from airing all TV shows – 'educational' and otherwise – aimed at children under three years of age. It has declared:

> Television viewing hurts the development of children under three years old and poses a certain number of risks, encouraging passivity, slow language acquisition, over-excitedness, troubles with sleep and concentration as well as dependence on screens … even when it involves channels aimed specifically at them.

Preschool institutions in Belgium now have similar warnings posted on walls.

The Video Deficit

State and private ICT production interests have cultivated a belief that almost from birth, so-called 'age-appropriate, educational' television and DVDs will provide children with cognitive/intellectual advantages, including improved language acquisition. Yet studies have found that 'When learning from videos is assessed in comparison to equivalent live presentations, there is usually substantially less learning from videos' (Anderson and Pempek, 2005). A phenomenon called the 'video deficit' is being used to describe the observation that toddlers who have no trouble understanding a task demonstrated in real life often stumble when the same task is shown onscreen. They need repeated viewings to learn it. Yet the young children's 'educational' television and DVD market has perpetrated the view that learning and experiencing via a screen rivals, and often exceeds, the process of learning via real-life interactions.

A study of 1–3-year-olds found that even

> background TV significantly reduced toy play episode length, as well as focused attention during play. Thus, background television disrupts very young children's play behavior even when they pay little overt attention to it. These findings have implications for subsequent cognitive development. (Schmidt et al., 2008)

Language Acquisition

Screen-based education is found to be less effective, and in some cases deleterious. For example, despite claims that educational DVDs and videos are beneficial to young children, a study published in the medical *Journal of Pediatrics* found that the use of such productions might actually retard their language development (Zimmerman et al., 2007a). Furthermore, even 'educational' television programmes, DVDs and videos showed no positive effects on children age 2 and under; and there were no benefits, whether the children watched 'educational' or 'non-educational' media or adult television programmes such as 'The Simpsons', 'Oprah' and sports programming. Whether parents sat and watched the screen with the children also made no difference to the outcome. In particular, the researchers found that for every hour per day spent watching specially developed baby DVDs and videos such as 'Baby Einstein' and 'Brainy Baby', children under 16 months understood an average of six to eight fewer words than children who did not watch them. One of the authors stated,

> The evidence is mounting that they are of no value and may in fact be harmful. Given what we now know, I believe the onus is on the manufacturers to prove their claims that watching these programs can positively impact children's cognitive development. The bottom line is the more a child watches baby DVDs and videos the bigger the effect. The amount of viewing does matter.
>
> (ibid.)

Disney has now offered refunds to parents who bought Baby Einstein DVDs (Evans, 2009).

'Educational' Computers

Enthusiasm for the advantages offered by screen technology is more pronounced when considering computer use in schools. Yet few people working in education are aware of large, well-controlled studies that fail to support this presumption of benefit. For example, a study of 15-year-old students in 31 countries concluded that those using computers at school several times a week performed 'sizeably and statistically significantly worse' in both maths and reading than those who used them less often (Fuchs and Woessmann, 2004).

Another study from Duke University involving 150,000 pupils aged 10 to 14 compared the same children's reading and maths scores before and after they acquired a home computer. Researchers could also compare their scores to those of peers who had always had a home computer and to those who never had access to one. They found that providing children with regular access to a computer could actually hinder their reading and maths skills: 'the introduction of home computer technology is associated with statistically significant and persistent negative impacts on student math and reading test scores' (Vigdor and Ladd, 2010). Researcher Jacob Vigdor concluded that for schools hoping to maximize attainment or reduce the impact of socio-economic disparities, 'a programme of broadening home computer access would be counter-productive'.

Malamud and Pop-Eleches (2010) compared the educational effects of government-provided home computers on Romanian school children, and concluded that children given these home computers 'had significantly lower school grades in Math, English and Romanian but significantly higher scores in a test of computer skills'.

In a randomized controlled study of 6–9-year-old boys who did not have their own computer games, the boys were offered a computer-game system and 'child-appropriate' games in exchange for participating in an 'ongoing study of child development'. The results were unequivocal:

> Boys who received the system immediately spent more time playing video games and less time engaged in after-school academic activities than comparison children. Boys who received the system immediately also had lower reading and writing scores and greater teacher-reported academic problems at follow up than comparison children. ... Altogether, our findings suggest that video-game ownership may impair academic achievement for some boys in a manner that has real-world significance.
>
> (Weis and Cerankosky, 2010)

Adults too have been encouraged to believe that computerized mental workouts and 'brain training devices' advertized widely will improve their general cognitive functioning. With this in mind, a study examining this assumption, published in *Nature* involving 11,430 subjects, concluded: 'Computerized mental workouts don't boost mental skills. ... There were absolutely no transfer effects from the training tasks ... [the claims are] completely unsupported.' As is the case with educational software for children, the authors noted that for adults, 'brain training', or the goal of improved cognitive function through the regular use of computerized tests, is a multimillion-pound industry' (Owen et al., 2010).

The idea that children leaving primary school are becoming more and more intelligent and competent is also called into question by uncomfortable findings. After examining certain measures of cognitive development, the researchers concluded that, 'An 11-year-old today is performing at the level an 8- or 9-year-old was performing at 30 years ago ... '. The decline was attributed in part to the growing use of computer games. Children, especially boys, are playing more in virtual worlds instead of 'outdoors, with tools and things ... ' (Shayer, 2006).

Redefining 'Interactive'

A major study, which few in the education field have heard of, by London University's Institute of Education has also raised doubts about the growing use of 'interactive whiteboards'. Moss et al. (2007) reported that, 'Although the newness of the technology was initially welcomed by pupils, any boost in motivation seems short-lived. ... Statistical analysis showed no impact on pupil performance in the first year in which departments were fully equipped.'

Many pupils were relegated to that of 'spectators' as teachers used this ICT to create faster and more complicated lessons. It was reported that some children became distracted by the technology, and the pace of some classes slowed as teachers sought to give each child 'turns' at using the board: 'For instance, the focus on interactivity as a technical process can lead to some relatively mundane activities being over-valued. ... '; and 'In lower ability groups it could actually slow the pace of whole-class learning as individual pupils took turns at the board'.

Larry Cuban, education professor emeritus at Stanford University, summarizes the situation:

> There is hardly any research that will show clearly that any of these machines will improve academic achievement. But the value of novelty, that's highly prized in American society, period. And one way schools can say they are 'innovative' is to pick up the latest device.
>
> (Cuban, 2010)

Brain Function and Computer Use

While playing computer games is thought to be more stimulating than watching television or DVDs, evidence indicates that even this so-called 'interactive media' is associated with limited neurological activity. For example, a study looking at differences in cerebral blood flow between children playing computer games and children doing very simple repetitive arithmetic adding single digit numbers found that computer games only stimulated activity in those parts of the brain associated with vision and movement, as compared to arithmetic-stimulated brain activity (Kawashima et al., 2001). Adding single-digit numbers activated areas throughout the left and right frontal lobes; playing computer games did not. The findings were described by the World Federation of Neurology as 'alarming ... computer games stunted the developing mind. ... '

The frontal lobe is the brain's executive control system, responsible for planning, organizing and sequencing behaviour for self-control, moral judgement and attention. The frontal lobe continues to develop until the age of about 20. It is imperative that children and young adults pursue activities which thicken the fibres connecting neurons in this part of the brain, and the more the person is stimulated, the more the fibres will thicken. The study reported by the World Federation of Neurology expressed great concern over the way in which visual electronic media are affecting children by

> ... halting the process of frontal lobe development and affecting their ability to control potentially antisocial elements of their behaviour ... the implications are very serious ... children should also be encouraged to play outside with other children, interact and communicate with others as much as possible.

It is suggested that the more work done to thicken the fibres connecting the neurons in this part of the brain, the better the child's ability will be to control their behaviour (Kawashima et al., 2001).

As a point of comparison, real-world cognitive demands – especially early ones – physically improve and enlarge children's brains. For example, a study published in the journal *Nature* has found that learning a second language literally increases the density of a child's grey matter in the left inferior parietal cortex of the brain (Mechelli et al., 2004). This part of the child's brain is active during both procedural and declarative learning.

Brain Function and Reading

Reading has been observed to increase brain activity in the left hemisphere and to build the neural mechanisms for better reading, and the nature of the words that are read appears to influence brain structure and function. Moreover, reading figurative language – sentences containing irony or metaphor – produces more brain activity than reading factual, literal sentences (Turkeltaub et al., 2003; Eviatar and Just, 2006). It is thought that in reading the printed word, the medium is secondary: the child is required to analyse and interpret.

In contrast, watching a televized account of the same material does not place the same cognitive demands upon the child.

Stimulating young children through the early use of screen technology may therefore have an inhibitory effect on their later ability to be engaged by traditional written information as presented in books, or by propositional learning through lessons given by a teacher in a classroom (Sigman, 2007a). Early introduction to screen technology may, in effect, render the real world less arresting and compelling.

Screen Viewing Leads to Less Reading

Early exposure to, and increasing time spent watching, screen technology is strongly linked to a significant continuing decline in time spent reading books as a regular pass-time (Childwise Monitor, 2008). Pre-school children spend three times longer in front of a television or computer than they spend reading; and those with a screen in their bedroom are less likely to be able to read by age 6 (Rideout et al., 2003). A comparative study of children in 41 countries found that England has dropped from 3rd to 19th in the international reading literacy league table since 2001 (PIRLS, 2007; cf. Chapters 16 and 17, this volume). More than a third (37 per cent) of 10-year-olds in England play computer games for more than three hours a day, the study found – one of the highest proportions internationally; and researchers found a link between this use of computer games and lower attainment in reading and literacy. Interestingly it was the lower achievement of better readers that has had the most influence on the overall decline. A survey by Britain's National Literacy Trust (2010) found that a third of children did not now enjoy reading and found it 'boring'. And less than half of children aged 9–14 read fiction more than once a month; websites were far more popular.

The effects are also found in adults. A quarter of US adults say they read no books at all (Associated Press – Ipsos, 2007), while a quarter of Britons say they have not read a book in the past year, including almost half of males aged between 16 and 24 (Office of National Statistics, 2008). The rapid decline in reading has lead to the recent 'million book giveaway' launched in Britain on 'World Book Night', intended to entice people to read again.

Educational Achievement

Television viewing amongst children under 3 is found to have 'deleterious effects' on mathematics ability, reading recognition and comprehension in later childhood. Along with television viewing displacing educational and play activities, this harm may be due to the visual and auditory output from the television actually affecting the child's rapidly developing brain (Zimmerman and Christakis, 2005). A 26-year longitudinal study, tracking children from birth, has recently concluded that 'television viewing in childhood and adolescence is associated with poor educational achievement by 26 years of age. Early exposure to television may have long-lasting adverse consequences for educational achievement and later socioeconomic status and well-being.' The authors describe a dose–response relationship between the amount of television watched and declining educational performance, which has 'biological plausibility'. Significant long-term effects occurred even at so-called modest levels of television viewing: between one and two hours per day. They also concluded that 'the overall educational value of television viewing was low. … These findings offer little support for the hypothesis that a small amount of television is beneficial' (Hancox et al., 2005).

Canadian researchers conducted a prospective study examining weekly hours of television exposure at 29 and 53 months of age and later academic, psychosocial and physical well-being at age 10. Among the many negative associations identified, they reported that adjusting for pre-existing individual and family factors,

> every additional hour of television exposure at 29 months corresponded [years later] to 7% and 6% unit decreases in classroom engagement and math achievement. … Higher levels of early childhood television exposure predicted less task-oriented, persistent, and autonomous learning behavior in the classroom … early childhood television exposure undermines attention … early television exposure could eventually foster risk toward a more passive rather than active disposition when attending to learning situations.

The authors stated, 'we might have expected the prospective associations to disappear after 5 years. Remarkably, the results suggested adverse effects despite having a low-risk sample, making the "potential for harm" public health argument stronger.' (Pagani et al., 2010)

Autism

Research from Cornell University strongly suggests that for children under 3, screen-viewing may be 'an important trigger for autism', the incidence of which appears to be increasing. Researchers estimated that just under 40 per cent of autism diagnoses studied were linked to watching screens below the age of 3 (Waldman et al., 2006). While it is not clear how watching screens could trigger autism, it is possible that the lack of social interaction could render children who are prone to autism more withdrawn. If screen technology is involved, the damage must be done early in life, as most cases of autism are diagnosed by age three. In discussing the findings, the lead researcher commented, 'we have evidence that is awfully suggestive of a link between watching TV and autism'.

Mechanisms Affecting Learning

If early exposure to screen technology compromises learning, the mechanism may be alterations in the child's developing attentional system. A study of 2,500 children (Christakis et al., 2004), published in the journal *Pediatrics*, looked at whether early exposure to television during critical periods of synaptic development would be associated with subsequent attentional problems.

About 5 per cent of children now exhibit the symptoms of 'attention deficit hyperactivity disorder' (ADHD), and the incidence of this disorder (Castellanos et al., 2002) appears to be increasing (Schonwald, 2005). Although genetic inheritance may account for some of the prevalence of ADHD, and despite decades of research, little thought has gone into the potentially crucial role that early childhood experiences may have on the development of attentional problems. Christakis and his colleagues wondered whether there was an omnipresent environmental agent that is putting some children at risk of developing ADHD. They found that early television exposure was associated with attentional problems at age 7, which was consistent with a diagnosis of ADHD. Children who watched television at ages 1 and 3 had a significantly increased risk of developing such attentional problems by the time they were 7. For every hour of television a child watched per day, there was a 9 per cent increase in attentional problems. The authors also suggest that their findings may actually be an understatement of the effects on children (Christakis et al., 2004).

A more recent study has found later attention damage in children who watched average amounts of screen time when they were over 5. The study was the first to investigate a possible long-term link between television viewing in childhood between the ages of 5 and 11, and attention problems in adolescence. Symptoms included short attention span, poor concentration and being easily distracted. The study concluded:

> Childhood television viewing was associated with attention problems in adolescence, independent of early attention problems and other confounders. These results support the hypothesis that childhood television viewing may contribute to the development of attention problems and suggest that the effects may be long-lasting.
>
> (Landhuis et al., 2007)

These findings could not be explained by early-life attention difficulties, socio-economic factors or intelligence. The authors stated that even after all of these factors were taken into account, watching more television was associated with teenage attention problems.

Another controlled study on children of 14 to 22 years also concluded that:

> Frequent television viewing during adolescence may be associated with risk for development of attention problems, learning difficulties, and adverse long-term educational outcomes. Youths who watched 1 or more hours of television per day at mean age 14 years were at elevated risk for poor homework completion, negative attitudes toward school, poor grades, and longterm academic failure. Youths who watched 3 or more hours of television per day were the most likely to experience these outcomes. In addition, youths who watched 3 or more hours of television per day were at elevated risk for subsequent attention problems and were the least likely to receive postsecondary education.
>
> (Johnson et al., 2007)

A recent longitudinal study in *Pediatrics* included computer game exposure in its assessments of attention, and widened the age-range to include subjects who were 8–24 years old. Yet the effects seemed ageless:

Viewing television and playing video games each are associated
with increased subsequent attention problems in childhood …
late adolescence and early adulthood. … The association of
television and video games to attention problems in the middle
childhood sample remained significant when earlier attention
problems and gender were statistically controlled. The associations of screen media and attention problems were similar across
media type (television or video games) and age (middle childhood or late adolescent/early adult).

(Swing et al., 2010)

Yet attention is not merely confined to everyday descriptions such
as concentration or attention span (Sigman et al., 1985), and new
brain-imaging studies are finding that different parts of the brain
deal with different types of attention, and so there can be types of
attentional damage different from ADHD (Stuss et al., 2002). If
early exposure to television does affect aspects of attention later on,
what mechanisms may be involved?

Screen technology elicits what Pavlov first described as the
orienting response, our instinctive sensitivity to movement
and sudden changes in vision or sound. The orienting response
to screen stimulation is apparent almost from birth (Kubey and
Csikszentmihalyi, 2004). Computers or educational DVDs/TV
offer additional stimulation to children in early years education
compared to the world around them, or they would not sit and look
at a screen. And the stimulation has intensified over the past decades:
for example, in television programmes, there are more zooms, pans
and edits. Children's television programmes increasingly 'demand
constant attentional shifts by their viewers but do not require them
to pay prolonged attentional shifts to given events'. Researchers
are now asking whether it 'is possible that television's conditioning
of short attentional span may be related to some school children's
attentional deficits in later classroom settings', and whether ' … the
recent increase of attention deficit disorders in school age children
might be a natural reaction to our modern speeded-up culture …
we live in an attention deficit culture' (Hooper and Chang, 1998;
Healy, 2004, respectively).

Screen technology is the perfect medium for producing strong
rewards for paying attention to something. Compared to the pace
with which real life unfolds and is experienced by young children,

television, DVDs and computer games portray life with the fast-forward button fully pressed. Rapidly changing images, scenery and events, colours and high-fidelity sounds are highly stimulating and extremely interesting. Screen technology provides unnatural levels of sensory stimulation, but little in real life is comparable to this. Screen technology may overpay the child to pay attention to it, and in so doing may physically corrupt the reward system underpinning his ability to pay attention when the screen is off (Christakis et al., 2004; Healy, 2004).

The currency used to pay off and corrupt the reward system may be the neurotransmitter, dopamine. Dopamine release is associated with reward and dopamine rewards paying attention – especially to what is novel and stimulating (Nieoullon, 2002). Computer screen entertainment causes our brain to release dopamine (Koepp et al., 1998). More research is needed that looks at the extent to which this reward system involving dopamine (and other neurotransmitters) is set in childhood by exposure to screen technology.

Brain Development

What humans do better than any other species is to learn, and whatever happens in the environment will leave its mark on the child's brain. Every moment counts in building brain circuits, and the story of an individual's life is based on their brain connections. The young brain is a physically sensitive organ, and repeated exposure to any experience will have a powerful impact on the child's mental and emotional development by either building specific brain circuitry in relation to that experience, or by simply depriving their brain of other experiences. The types and degrees of stimulation the child receives from his environment affect the actual number and the density of his brain-cell connections, and width of blood vessels, which supply the brain. This process of moulding, referred to as 'structural neuro-plasticity', affects both the brain structure and function, and appears to influence brain cell development and the regulation of the brain's chemical messengers (neurotransmitters). Even difficult-to-quantify concepts such as a child raised without nurturing or love can affect the size and function of that child's brain. The frontal-temporal part of the brains of Romanian orphans have been found to be underdeveloped and showing little or no activity. The author later commented, 'these children appear to have altered brain growth'. Brain scans showed that neglected three-year-olds actually had smaller heads than children raised in loving families (Perry, 2000).

Contrary to the cultural notion that the child's brain needs constant external stimulation to develop properly, new research finds that the opposite can be true (cf. Chapter 7). Restricting stimulation by meditating actually increases the thickness of the brain's cortex in areas involved in attention and sensory processing. The scientist remarked, 'You are exercising it while you meditate, and it gets bigger', adding that yogis 'aren't just sitting there doing nothing' (Lazar et al., 2005).

A child's brain cells are literally 'up for grabs'. Plasticity is political, in that there is a constant battle for the child's neurons to quite literally develop in a certain way. Therefore, we need to have a far better understanding of the overwhelming lobbying power of media screen interests. Irrespective of the content, the medium alone may cause powerful irreversible changes to a child's brain, either directly or by displacing other critical experiences, which have sell-by dates on their consumption. The newest and greatest environmental factor in the child's daily life is the screen. England's legally compulsory Early Years Foundation Stage is likely to add to both the early age of exposure and the number of hours per day that children look at a screen.

Hours of Screen Time

There is growing concern over the sheer number of hours children now spend looking at a screen (Sigman, 2007a, 2009). In the United States, by 3 months of age 40 per cent of infants are regular viewers of television, DVDs or videos, and by the age of 2, this number increases dramatically to 90 per cent (Zimmerman et al., 2007b). Nearly two-thirds of children under 2 spend a couple of hours a day in front of the screen (Rideout et al., 2003). The average seven-year-old will have already watched for more than one full year of their lives; and when other screen time is included, the figure is growing far higher. British children aged 11–15 now spend 55 per cent of their waking lives – 53 hours a week, seven and a half hours a day – watching TV and computers – an increase of 40 per cent in just a decade (BMRB, 2004). More than half of three-year-olds now have a TV set in their bedrooms (Winston, 2004). At least two-thirds of young British children watch television before they go to school, and even more watch when they return home (Childwise Monitor, 2008). A quarter of British five-year-olds own a computer or laptop (Childwise Monitor, 2008). These already-escalating levels of screen exposure occur in the context of screen viewing in early life, leading to higher levels of screen viewing later on (Vandewater et al., 2005). The most modest calculation shows that even at below average levels of television viewing alone, by the age of 80 the average child will have spent at least 13 full years of 24-hour days awake in front of a television screen; and adding computer time will raise this figure substantially.

Biological Changes

There are an increasing number of empirical studies finding significant links between hours of screen viewing in childhood and physiological changes, along with the development of health risks (Sigman, 2007b). These biological changes range from reduction in child resting metabolic rate, increase in body fat, elevated blood cholesterol levels, clinically increased risk of abnormal glucose metabolism and new Type 2 diabetes in adults (Hu et al., 2003), through substantial increases in myopia (Morgan and Rose, 2005). Watching screen technology, irrespective of the content, is increasingly associated with unfavourable biological and cognitive changes. These alterations occur at viewing levels far below the population norm. When considering the content, there is now strong evidence of neurological alterations and body dissatisfaction among healthy females in response to screen images of female body shapes, and a link with the development of eating disorders (Sigman, 2010).

Social Disengagement

Childhood is increasingly about 'private space' and sedentary activities, which are directly displacing social interaction or self-generated imagination. Many people now talk of the benefits of 'interactive' media and the Internet because it is used for communication, but even that has damaged family relationships. Studies at Stanford University have led to a 'displacement' theory of Internet use:

> In short, no matter how time online is measured and no matter which type of social activity is considered, time spent on the

Internet reduces time spent in face-to-face relationships ... an hour on the Internet reduces face-to-face time with family by close to twenty-four minutes.

(Nie et al., 2005)

An ongoing study of families by University of California–Los Angeles has found that social disengagement is now rapidly increasing, as side-by-side and eye-to-eye human interactions are being displaced by the eye-to-screen relationship (Campos et al., 2009). The impact of multi-tasking gadgets is one of the most dramatic areas of change, described by the scientists as 'pretty consequential for the structure of the family relationship' (Ochs, 2006). With increasing screen time, any consequent reduction in social interaction and connection is linked to physiological alterations, along with increased morbidity and mortality (Sigman, 2009).

Yet young children can now join the website 'MyCBBC', which the BBC describes as being 'about trying to develop their Internet skills and social networking ... '. And there is now a pre-school version – 'MyCBeebies' – where preschoolers are encouraged to 'create your own CBeebies Me: a personal avatar that represents you'. The Controller of BBC Children's TV says that this will 'help a child understand itself and its place in the world'.

Multi-Tasking

Scientists are now witnessing compound effects. Children and teen-agers are spending an increasing amount of time using 'new media' like computers, the Internet, ipod videos and video games, without cutting back on the time they spend with 'old' media like televi-sion. Instead, because of the amount of time they spend using more than one medium at a time, they're managing to pack increasing amounts of media content into the same amount of time each day, and at younger and younger ages (Kaiser Family Foundation, 2005; Childwise Monitor, 2008). Brain imaging reveals that multi-tasking activates a different brain region (the striatum) to the one used when you learn one thing at a time (medial temporal lobe), and this is a significant hindrance to learning (Foerde et al., 2006).

Studying with a television on makes learning less efficient, and renders what you manage to learn less useful. Homework can take 50 per cent longer to complete. Neuroscientists behind this research are describing the benefits of modern multi-tasking as 'a myth. ... The toll in terms of slowdown is extremely large – amazingly so ... you will never, ever be able to overcome the inherent limitations in the brain for processing information during multitasking' (Myers, 2006). A study of multi-tasking performance conducted at Stanford University, published in the *Proceedings of the National Academy of Sciences*, compared groups of young people assessed as being either 'heavy' or 'light media multitaskers'. Ironically, they reported 'the surprising result that heavy media multitaskers performed worse'. One of the researchers commented, 'The shocking discovery of this research is that [high multitaskers] are lousy at everything that's necessary for multitasking' (Ophir et al., 2009).

Discussion

The introduction of screen technology in the early years of child development increasingly conflicts with empirical evidence that it may have deleterious effects on learning and development. Paradoxically, the premature introduction of these technologies – which could later be used as tools – may ultimately undermine the cognitive and academic skills they are intended to cultivate in the first place. It appears that the timing of screen exposure is crucial. The claim that these findings do not apply to 'supervised', educational use of 'age-appropriate' DVDs and computer software is unjustified, as it appears that it is the time spent during a child's early years looking at and relating to *the medium* of the screen that is the central factor. Moreover, in addition to the American Academy of Pediatrics, a growing number of well-conducted studies have concluded that children under 2 should be kept away from computer and TV screens, and other researchers, clinicians and governments are now recommending drastic reductions in, or abstinence from, screen exposure for children over the age of 2.

The use of screens in early years education must be viewed in the context of a society of children spending increasing amounts of daily time relating to screens, and in the context of financial and political interests encouraging society to see screens in the early years as an allegedly beneficial component of modern-day child development. For example, recent years have seen a substantial increase in screen-based 'toys' for British children aged 0–3 (Sunday Times, 2007). Above all, there is a systemic problem in the relationship between the

ICT industry and academics – who receive research funding directly or indirectly from suppliers of screen technology, software, internet, advertising and television production. Government departments involved in education, as well as the educational establishment, increasingly liaise with suppliers of ICT, which again constitutes a conflict of interest when considering policy-making on introducing screen technology in early years education.

In terms of school preferences, when affluent British private schools have the resources and latitude to use screen technology in teaching, they do not appear to subscribe to it. The public schools examined did not refer to television or 'visual literacy' when presenting their approach to education. Nor did private schools show images of pupils watching a television screen. Pupils were typically shown reading books, writing by hand and taking part in tutorial discussions (Sigman, 2007c).

An Educational Buffer Zone

Until it is demonstrated otherwise, we should assume that young children are predisposed – 'hard-wired' – to learn through real-world experiences and interaction with real human beings. If they do not experience this throughout the critical first 3–6 years of their life, their learning, and possibly their personality, will be impeded. In particular, until their brains are fully formed, children's attentional development appears to need protection. Attention is the prerequisite to what we consider being alive; one has to be able to pay attention to things in order to experience them. Attending to something is the first stage in processing and analysing it, and learning and remembering it. Once a child's attention is damaged, then everything that comes from it is compromised. Learning language, reading, school work, exams, job performance, relationships, and even one's sense of identity – all can suffer. It is akin to damaging the focus control on the child's lens that looks out on life. In damaging a developing child's attentional system, one has damaged the prerequisite to experience. It appears that exposing children to screen technology at increasingly earlier ages, along with the sheer amount of exposure, may well be placing unhealthy demands on our children's developing attention, which is undergoing a fragile period of key development.

Legally requiring the introduction of screen technology to 20–60 month-old children is likely to lead to even higher levels of daily screen viewing. Early introduction to ICT is likely to lead to a greater lifetime dependency on screens. I therefore propose that parents and the educational establishment should, in effect, 'cordon off' the early years of education, providing a buffer zone where a child's cognitive and social skills can develop without the distortion that may occur through premature use of ICT. We must all be reminded of the ancient medical imperative: 'First, do no harm'.

Conclusion

There is ever-mounting evidence, then, that:

a   Exposure to screen technology during key stages of child development may have counterproductive effects on cognitive processes and learning.
b   Learning through watching screens neither rivals nor exceeds early years learning through more traditional 'non-virtual' means.
c   These salient issues occur in the context of screen viewing in early life, leading to higher levels of screen viewing later on.
d   Even moderate levels of screen viewing are increasingly associated with a wide range of health risks.

In light of this accumulating evidence, there is an increasingly overwhelming case for education authorities explicitly reconsidering the role of screen technologies in schools.

References

Anderson, D.R. and Pempek, T.A. (2005) 'Television and very young children', *American Behavioral Scientist*, 48 (5): 505–22

Associated Press – Ipsos poll (2007) 'One in four Americans read no books last year', reported by AP, Wednesday 22 August and *Guardian Unlimited*

BETT educational technology conference (2008) Statement by Schools minister Jim Knight, 'Home access: Internet for all children', *The Guardian* (Education), Tuesday 8 January; see http://www.guardian.co.uk/education/2008/jan/08/link?INTCMP=SRCH (accessed 1 July 2011)

BMRB International (British Market Research Bureaux) (2004) 'Increasing screen time is leading to inactivity of 11–15s', Youth TGI Study

Campos, B., Graesch, A.P., Repetti, R., Bradbury, T. and Ochs, E. (2009) 'Opportunity for interaction? A naturalistic observation study of dual-earner families after work and school', *Journal of Family Psychology*, 23 (6): 798–807

Castellanos, F.X. and others (2002) 'Developmental trajectories of brain volume abnormalities in children and adolescents with attention-deficit/ hyperactivity disorder', *Journal of the American Medical Association*, 288: 1740–8

Childwise Monitor, UK, 2007/2008

Christakis, D.A. and others (2004) 'Early television exposure and subsequent attentional problems in children', *Pediatrics*, 113 (4): 708–13

Cuban, L. (2010) Quoted in 'Some educators question if whiteboards, other high-tech tools raise achievement', *Washington Post*, Friday 11 June

Dallas Morning News, June 2004

Deadwyler, SA. (2008) 'Systemic and nasal delivery of Orexin-A (Hypocretin-1) reduces the effects of sleep deprivation on cognitive performance in nonhuman primates', *Journal of Neuroscience*, 27 (52): 14239–47

Department for Children, Schools and Families (DCSF) (2007) *Early Years Foundation Stage from Birth to Five*, London: Section 4.4, Learning and Development: ICT

Department for Children, Schools and Families (DCSF) (2008) Primary National Strategy Story Shorts: Using films to teach literacy; accessible at: http://www.standards.dfes.gov.uk/primary/features/literacy/659883/918015

Evans, C. (2009) 'Disney offers refund after furore over Baby Einstein DVDs', *The Times*, 27 October

Eviatar, Z. and Just, M.A. (2006) 'Brain correlates of discourse processing: an fMRI investigation of irony and conventional metaphor comprehension', *Neuropsychologia*, 44 (12): 2348–59

Foerde, K. and others (2006) 'Modulation of competing memory systems by distraction', *Proceedings of the National Academy of Sciences*, 1, 103 (31): 11778–83

Fuchs, T. and Woessmann, L. (2004) 'Computers and student learning: bivariate and multivariate evidence on the availability and use of computers at home and at school', CESifo Working Paper no. 1321; Analysis of OECD's Programme for International Student Assessment (PISA), 24 November

Hancox, R.J. and others (2005) 'Association of television viewing during childhood with poor educational achievement', *Archives of Pediatric Medicine*, 159: 614–18

Healy, J.M. (2004) Commentary: 'Early television exposure and subsequent attentional problems in children', *Pediatrics*, 113 (4): 917–18

Hooper, M.L. and Chang, P. (1998) 'Comparison of demands of sustained attentional events between public and private children's television programs', *Perceptual and Motor Skills*, 86: 431–4

Hu, F.B. and others (2003) 'Television watching and other sedentary behaviors in relation to risk of obesity and type 2 diabetes mellitus in women', *Journal of the American Medical Association*, 289: 1785–91

Johnson, J.G. and others (2007) 'Extensive television viewing and the development of attention and learning difficulties during adolescence', *Archives of Pediatrics and Adolescent Medicine*, 161: 480–6

Kaiser Family Foundation (2005) 'Generation M: media in the lives of 8–18 year-olds', Kaiser Family Foundation, 9 March

Kawashima, R. and others (2001) Reported in *World Neurology*, 16 (3) (September): 3

Koepp, M.J. and others (1998) 'Evidence for striatal dopamine release during a video game', *Nature*, 393: 266–8

Kraut, R. and others (1998) 'Paradox: a social technology that reduces social involvement and psychological well-being?', *American Psychologist*, 53 (9): 1017–31

Kubey, R. and Csikszentmihalyi, M. (2004) 'Television addiction is no mere metaphor', *Scientific American*, Special Edition, 14 (1): 48–55

Landhuis C.E. and others (2007) 'Does childhood television viewing lead to attention problems in adolescence? Results from a prospective longitudinal study', *Pediatrics*, 120 (3): 532–7

Lazar, S.W. and others (2005) 'Meditation experience is associated with increased cortical thickness', *NeuroReport*, 16 (17) (28 November): 1893–7

London Grid for Learning (2007) 'Literacy live: Teaching and Learning', Hackney, London: The Learning Trust, The Future for Education in Hackney: Visual Literacy; see: http://www.lgfl.net/lgfl/leas/hackney/accounts/staff/literacylt/web/visual/index/

Marsh, J. and others (2005) 'The 'Digital Beginnings' project: young children's use of popular culture, media and new technologies in the home', funded by BBC Worldwide and the Esmée Fairbairn Foundation

Mechelli, A. and others (2004) 'Neurolinguistics: structural plasticity in the bilingual brain', *Nature*, 431: 757

Morgan, I.G. and Rose, K.A. (2005) 'How genetic is school myopia? Progress in retinal and eye research', *Progress in Retinal and Eye Research*, 24 (1): 1–38

Moss, G. and others (2007) 'The interactive whiteboards, pedagogy and pupil performance evaluation: an evaluation of the Schools Whiteboard Expansion (SWE) Project', London: London Challenge, Research Report No. 816, Department for Education and Skills

Myers, D. and others (2006) 'Multitasking and task switching', University of Michigan: Brain, Cognition and Action Laboratory

National Literacy Trust (2010) As reported in S. Adams, 'Half of children don't read fiction', *Daily Telegraph*, 17 February 2010; accessible at: http://www.telegraph.co.uk/education/educationnews/7250303/Half-of-children-dont-read-fiction.html (retrieved 5 July 2011)

Nie, N.H. and others (2005) 'Ten years after the birth of the internet: how do Americans use the Internet in their daily lives?', Stanford University: special report

Nieoullon, A. (2002) 'Dopamine and the regulation of cognition and attention', *Progress in Neurobiology*, 67(1): 53–83

Ochs, E. (2006) UCLA Center on Everyday Lives of Families

Ofer Malamud, O. and Pop-Eleches, C. (2010) 'Home computer use and the development of human capital', Cambridge, Mass.: National Bureau of Economic Research, NBER Working Papers, No. 15814, March

Office of National Statistics (2008) National Year of Reading campaign

Ophir, E. and others (2009) 'Cognitive control in media multitaskers', *Proceedings of the National Academy of Sciences*, 106 (37): 15583–7

Owen, A.M. and others (2010) 'Putting brain training to the test', *Nature*, 10; 465 (7299) (June): 775–8

Pagani, L.S. and others (2010) 'Prospective associations between early childhood television exposure and academic, psychosocial, and physical well-being by middle childhood', *Archives of Pediatrics and Adolescent Medicine*, 164 (5): 425–31

Perry, B.D. (2000) 'The neuroarcheology of childhood maltreatment: the neurodevelopmental costs of adverse childhood events', in B. Geffner (ed.), *The Cost of Child Maltreatment: Who Pays? We All Do*, Haworth Press

PIRLS (Progress in International Reading Literacy Study) (2007) Reported 28 November

Rideout, V.J., Vandewater, E.A. and Wartella, E A (2003) 'Zero to six: electronic media in the lives of infants, toddlers and preschoolers', Kaiser Family Foundation Report, 28 October

Schmidt, M.E., Pempek, T.A., Kirkorian, H.L. and others (2008) 'The effects of background television on the toy play behavior of very young children', *Child Development*, 79: 1137–51

Schonwald, A. (2005) 'Update: attention deficit/hyperactivity disorder in the primary care office', *Current Opinion in Pediatrics*, 17(2): 265–74

Shayer, M. (2006) 'Thirty years on – a large anti-Flynn effect? The Piagetian test volume and heaviness norms, 1975–2003', reported in *Science*, 311 (5763)

Sigman, A. (2007a) *Remotely Controlled: How Television Is Damaging Our Lives*, London: Vermilion

Sigman, A. (2007b) 'Visual voodoo: the biological impact of watching television', *The Biologist*, 54 (1): 14–19

Sigman, A. (2007c) 'Television in education: salience in affluent British private schools', Houses of Parliament, Westminster: Preliminary findings reported at Children and the Media conference, 23 April

Sigman, A. (2009) 'Well connected?: the biological implications of social networking', *The Biologist*, 56 (1): 14–20

Sigman, A. (2010) 'A source of thinspiration?: the biological landscape of media, body image and dieting', *The Biologist*, 57 (3): 116–21

Sigman, A., Phillips, K.C. and Clifford, B. (1985) 'Attentional concomitants of hypnotic susceptibility', *British Journal of Experimental and Clinical Hypnosis*, 2 (2): 69–75

Stuss, D.T. and others (2002) 'Dissociations within the anterior attentional system: effects of task complexity and irrelevant information on reaction time speed and accuracy', *Neuropsychology*, 16 (4): 500–13

Sunday Times (2007) Jim Silver, as quoted in S. Griffiths, 'The rise of the techy toddlers', 16 December

Swing, E.L. and others (2010) 'Television and video game exposure and the development of attention problems', *Pediatrics*, 126 (2): 213–21

Tulane National Primate Research Center (2006) How Smart are Monkeys?. Tulane University; see: http://www.tnprc.tulane.edu/public_faq.html#20

Turkeltaub, P.E. and others (2003) 'Development of neural mechanisms for reading', *Nature Neuroscience*, 6 (7): 767–73

United States Department of Health and Human Services (USDHHS) (2010) Proposed Healthy People 2020 Objectives, Washington, D.C.

Vandewater, E.A. and others (2005) 'When the television is always on', *American Behavioral Scientist*, 48 (5): 562–77

Vigdor, J.L. and Ladd, H.F. (2010) 'Scaling the digital divide: home computer technology and student achievement', National Bureau of Economic Research, Working Paper no. 16078, June

Waldman, M. and others (2006) 'Does television cause autism?', study presented to the National Bureau of Economic Research health conference, Working Paper no. 12632, October; revised December 2006

Weis, R. and Cerankosky, B.C. (2010) 'Effects of video-game ownership on young boys' academic and behavioral functioning: a randomized, Controlled Study', *Psychological Science*, 21(4): 463–70

Winston, R. (2004) 'The damning proof that TV DOES corrupt our young', editorial accompanying the BBC documentary series 'Child of Our Time', written for *Daily Mail*, 9 January: 12

Zimmerman, F.J. and Christakis D.A. (2005) 'Children's television viewing and cognitive outcomes: a longitudinal analysis', *Archives of Pediatric and Adolescent Medicine*, 159: 619–25

Zimmerman, F.J. and others (2007a) 'Associations between media viewing and language development in children under age 2 years', *Journal of Pediatrics*, 151 (4): 364–8; and press release, Baby DVDs, videos may hinder, not help, infants' language development, University of Washington, 7 August

Zimmerman, F.J. and others (2007b) 'Television and DVD/video viewing in children younger than 2 years', *Archives of Pediatrics and Adolescent Medicine*, 161 (5): 473–9

CHAPTER 20

Margaret Edgington: Inveterate Campaigner for Early Childhood

MARGARET EDGINGTON IS INTERVIEWED
BY RICHARD HOUSE

RICHARD: Margaret, we first made contact many years ago now, when I spotted a letter of yours in *Nursery World*, regarding a petition you were organizing. Can you say a bit about how you first started working with early years, and perhaps something about the first campaigning stance or activity you were engaged in?

MARGARET: I started my teacher training the year after the influential Plowden Report *Children and Their Primary Schools* (1967), with its emphasis on child-centred individualized learning, was published. I opted for the nursery/infant specialist B.Ed. course because I had a real interest in how the very youngest children learn, and also because I knew from extensive baby-sitting experience that I had a real rapport with young children. Amongst the lecturers at Edge Hill College I was fortunate to have a number of really passionate advocates who instilled in us a desire to focus on the needs of each child, and to set ourselves the highest standards for learning and teaching. In those days, we studied child development and the thinking of a range of influential theorists, and we were also (particularly in sessions on the philosophy and sociology of education) taught to question and reflect. A characteristic of many of the teachers I know who trained at this time is that they are passionate about their work, they put children's needs first (deploying great creativity to do so) and they deplore simplistic, mechanistic approaches.

I emerged into the profession in 1972 with a strong passion and with a real sense of wanting to ensure my practice was appropriate to the developmental needs of each child. From my own experience at school, I always tried to focus on those children who struggled to cope with the expectations within a community outside their home, and I mostly worked in what would now be termed 'disadvantaged' areas.

As a nursery teacher, I became acutely aware of the need to act as an advocate for maintained nursery classes and schools, and the wonderful practice they have developed over many years. These settings have always been subject to political will, and their future has always been vulnerable to cuts. When I moved to London, I became aware of the National Campaign for Nursery Education, which had been campaigning since the mid-1960s to insure that every three- and four-year-old child had the right to a state-funded, high-quality nursery education place. I joined this campaign and voluntarily worked in a number of roles such as publications officer, Vice Chair and Chair. This experience taught me a great deal about how national and local government works, and about dealing with politicians and the press. I am still involved as a Vice President, and our work is even more necessary now, as the cuts being made by the current British coalition government begin to impact on local areas, and everything we believe in is under threat.

I have been a long-standing, active campaigner for high-quality early childhood education, including trying to prevent the destruction of the Inner London Education Authority (ILEA) (where I was working at the time). Since I've worked as an independent consultant, I've seen it as my responsibility to speak out on early years issues, when others feel constrained. I have written many challenging letters to the education and national press and, in 2001, I single-handedly launched a petition to protect the Foundation Stage from the top-down pressure from SATS, achieving over 2,500 signatures in just a few months. This petition was presented to the House of Commons by my Member of Parliament. My involvement with the Open EYE campaign was therefore pretty inevitable. We share a deep concern for early childhood, and are committed to challenging any policy initiatives that work against the developmental needs of very young learners.

RICHARD: That gives us a graphic picture of a rich, varied and
committed career, Margaret – thank you. Britain has a proud
tradition in the nursery education field, going back to the seminal
work of great pioneers like Margaret McMillan and Susan Isaacs.
Could you summarize for us what you see as the broad features
of this tradition and its benefits for young children; and what it
is about the current policy-making *Zeitgeist* that puts these values
and practices at risk?

MARGARET: It is hard to encapsulate in a few words the distinctive
characteristics of specialist nursery schools, but I believe that the
best have built on the strong traditions of the pioneers, taking
their basic principles and beliefs into the twenty-first century.
The best-maintained nursery schools have passionate, inspirational head-teachers who act as powerful advocates for the children and families they cater for. They instil in their staff team
(which includes other specialist qualified early years teachers and
nursery practitioners) a passion for children, and for a child-
centred approach to early learning. The best nursery heads I
know remind me of the people who trained me (both at college
and on teaching practice), and I know how powerful a model
that is for a young practitioner.

Observation is central to their work – not in a mechanistic
way, but as a means of enjoying, and learning more about, children. The environment is highly organized to promote informed
choice, creativity and independence, and the outdoor environment is seen as being equally important as the rooms. The aim
is first and foremost for children to develop important life skills
such as persistence, resilience, curiosity, creativity, imagination,
resourcefulness etc. Teaching focuses on encouraging, and sensitively supporting, child-initiated activity and modelling skills
(including language and social skills) that children may need.

In addition, never content to stand still, nursery schools have
taken a strong lead on innovative practice, such as the development of forest schools and creative projects with artists. Partnership with parents is given high priority, and the parents often
see the senior nursery staff as being sources of information on
a range of issues. For example, I recently witnessed a nursery
school head-teacher offering to speak to a utility provider on
behalf of a parent, who was in danger of having a vital service
cut off through no fault of her own. It is because of this that a

majority of nursery schools were well placed to become the core of the first Sure Start Children's Centres. In a nutshell, the best nursery schools are joyful places which put the needs of children and their families first.

The problem for nursery schools and classes has always been their cost. Because all the staff are qualified to teacher or NVQ 3 level, staffing costs are fixed by national pay scales. Premises also have set costs. Maintained nursery education, being a non-statutory service, has always been vulnerable to cutbacks. However, in the last 15 years, the policy of extending the label of 'nursery education' to all types of provider, including those operating in poor premises with minimally trained staff, has meant that to the less-than-well informed national or local politician, nursery schools and classes seem too expensive. This is in spite of the fact that both OFSTED and the Audit Commission have said they offer value for money.

The Single Funding Formula is proving to be particularly devastating. Many local authorities are not valuing their nursery schools enough to protect them from devastating cuts, and I am hearing about huge budget losses which will take place over the next year or so. The recently elected coalition government claims that it has made enough money available to protect Sure Start Children's Centres, but because this money was not ring-fenced, it is relatively easy for local authorities to spend it elsewhere.

Essentially, this indicates to me that our politicians, in spite of their rhetoric, do not value young children, and are not prepared to pay for the best services.

RICHARD: Can I pick up on your final point here, Margaret, as I think there are very complex questions wrapped up in the question of politicians' attitudes to children and education. I'm tempted to introduce some psychoanalytic thinking here about what some theorists claim to be adults' unconscious envy and considerable ambivalence towards children, and how the latter then plays out in all kinds of ways – not least in the policy-making process. There's also the more familiar argument that the 'short-termist' party-political system, with ambitious ministers often using the Education portfolio as a way of advancing their careers as they climb up the 'slippery pole', is a singularly inappropriate way of making far-reaching decisions about children's educational experience and provision. In this context, do you think it might help if early-years policy-making were taken out of the hands of party politicians altogether – as long as there was a way of ensuring that resourcing levels were statutorily protected, and the sector was administered by an appropriately diverse body of 'the great, the good and the informed'.

MARGARET: I do think that the short-term approach taken by politicians is very unhelpful when considering important policy matters such as education and health. I have had contact with many different government ministers over the years, and it is very frustrating that many of them have little or no awareness of the issues that concern us on the ground when they first take up office. Inevitably, these politicians need to be seen to be having an impact, and this is almost certainly why they have become so devoted to easily measurable short-term outcomes. Unfortunately, the truly beneficial outcomes of quality early childhood education are unlikely to be seen in the short term, and may take many years to become apparent. Government departments have always sought advice from academics and other interested parties, but it seems that this advice is only heeded if it fits with a narrow agenda. It would certainly be interesting to explore how all public services could be administered differently, but I'm not sure I have the answers to this one.

I do wonder, though, whether the cross-party House of Commons Select Committee would bring more balance and stability to policy-making. Their reports, which have focused on early years, have been well-researched, very thoughtful, and have been highly regarded throughout the sector. If successive governments had acted on the recommendations contained within these reports, we might be in a much stronger position.

Recently, I found myself agreeing with Peter Moss, who, in his article 'Supermarket childcare' (*Early Years Educator*, Vol. 13, No. 2, June 2011), points out that there has never been a proper public debate about the kind of early years services we want in the UK. He comments:

> There was no moment when government explicitly determined a market approach in childcare, no policy document where different options were considered and the market approach preferred, no parliamentary debate on the future policy direction to be taken. Yet by 2008, a senior civil servant could state in a public presentation that a 'diverse market (is) the only game in town'.

Moss urges us to recognize that 'there are alternatives, that these should be vigorously debated and that we can collectively decide as a democratic society to take another direction. In short we can and should resist the dictatorship of no alternative'. He proposes an early years sector 'imbued with democracy, co-operation and entitlement.'

RICHARD: I think your comment about the Parliamentary Select Committee's work is a very important one, Margaret. The much-respected ex-chair of the Education Select Committee, Barry Sheerman, has a chapter in this book (Chapter 22) in which he considers some of these issues. It certainly seems that when Education *is* taken out of partisan party-political hands and is placed with independently minded politicians who are not unduly driven by party-political ideology and orthodoxy, some very beneficent and enlightened thinking does indeed start to occur; and perhaps there are lessons here for any future government with the courage to think outside of the policy-making box, and which is prepared to put children's long-term well-being ahead of narrowly circumscribed partisan power-politics.

Coming out of your previous answer, a related question that comes to mind is: what, for you, would constitute an appropriate balance between statutory intervention and professional autonomy in the early childhood sphere; and what changes, if any, would be needed to the current situation to achieve such a virtuous balance?

MARGARET: I have always been clear that there is a need for a statutory framework to protect the welfare of young vulnerable children. I have therefore always supported the welfare requirements within the Early Years Foundation Stage (although not the excessive amounts of paperwork which some of these seem to have generated). I also think it is helpful to have some agreed clear values or principles to underpin and guide early childhood practice. The themes and principles of the EYFS are by no means new – they have been around for many years in one form or another; but I believe that their central role in the statutory framework has been helpful, particularly when used by effective leaders and training providers to deepen the understanding of less experienced practitioners.

I'm certainly not averse to having some national guidance on the areas of experience that young children should be entitled to.

However, I will never believe it is desirable, or necessary, to have statutory learning and development *requirements* for such young children – particularly when these are used to judge children and their settings. The idea that a child can be below an arbitrary 'expected' level of development is abhorrent to me, and I regularly challenge the use of phrases such as 'less able' and 'below expectations' when applied to young children (who may be nearly a year younger than those they're being compared with).

I have some sympathy with the view, and one that is regularly argued, that we need statutory frameworks to support less effective settings and practitioners. However, I do not believe a framework or document can single-handedly change poor practice, and I would rather see poor settings closed down. If all that remained were good and outstanding settings, it should be possible for them to be encouraged to interpret nationally agreed principles to develop their own innovative approaches (whilst also taking account of the welfare requirements). However, this option would require a more sophisticated inspection/evaluation framework, and a more diverse group of inspectors/evaluators who are able to appreciate different approaches. When statutory frameworks are too prescriptive, innovation and creativity are stifled, and practitioners and those who evaluate their practice become afraid to take risks, and lose sight of what can be possible.

RICHARD: Again, all very interesting – I wish we had a book for this dialogue, rather than a mere chapter! Moving on to your training experience as described earlier, Margaret, this sounds like a really empowering one which encouraged critical reflective thinking, and was led by teachers who were left relatively free to bring their passion to their teaching – and which in turn rubbed off on their students. Drawing on your extensive experience as a training consultant, would I be right in saying that current early years training is a long way from this ideal? – and if so, where does the responsibility for this lie, and what do you think needs to be done to rectify the shortcomings in early years training today?

MARGARET: I'm not sure that my training was ideal, but I do believe it was vastly superior to the initial training that teachers and other early years practitioners have been receiving in recent times. Changes started to happen with the arrival of the National Curriculum in the 1980s and the more generic model of primary teacher training, where specialism was not necessarily seen as an asset. Instead of fostering passion and a knowledge of children and how they learn, courses tended to focus on curriculum content. From my experience I would say that, at worst, this has meant that many teachers working with young children in nurseries and reception classes do not have the passion or specialist knowledge which they need in order to be strong advocates for young children. More specifically, instead of reflecting on whether they are meeting each child's unique needs, they tend to worry more about whether they have got the planning and paperwork right. On the other hand, the recent expansion of early childhood studies degree courses has meant that some teachers are joining the profession with both passion and in-depth understanding. So perhaps we are seeing a virtuous change here.

In terms of other early years practitioners, the replacement of the NNEB (National Nursery Nursing Board) qualification with National Vocational Qualifications (NVQs) has caused considerable concern. NNEB-trained nursery nurses spent two years partly in college, learning about children and studying at their own level, and partly in a variety of carefully chosen placements, which gave them experience of working with children from birth to 7. An employer of an NNEB knew exactly what had been covered on their course, and could therefore have clear expectations of what their role was. This is not true, through no fault of their own, of NVQ candidates. Different assessment centres seem to have different standards, and many employers feel that candidates move through NVQ 2 and NVQ 3 qualifications too quickly. Additionally, because this is a vocational qualification, assessed in the work-place, the quality of the qualification is very much dependent on the setting in which the student happens to be working at the time.

All of these changes have been the result of government initiatives, and frankly it seems disingenuous of any government to say that it wants a highly qualified early years work-force. It seems to me that successive governments have been more concerned about increasing the number of places for children (regardless of quality), and have in practice 'dumbed down' the qualifications to make it look as if they are fulfilling their stated ambition.

Interestingly, in her recent review of the EYFS, Dame Clare Tickell (see Chapter 6) seems to agree that something needs to be done about the quality of training. She recommends that 'the

Government review the content of early years training courses to test the strength and quality of these qualifications', and that 'the Government ensures that new entry qualifications are of a high standard and, once introduced, reviews whether they succeed in conferring the equivalent status of the NNEB qualification'.

Overall, I would like to see all early years practitioners recognize that it is a privilege and a joy to work with young children and their families, and that in order to do their job well, they need specialist knowledge and understanding of child development, and the context in which children develop and learn most effectively.

RICHARD: Again, all very interesting and thought-provoking, Margaret. As a counsellor and psychotherapist, I'm particularly interested in the place of *experiential learning* in practitioner development. One way into this issue is to consider your welcoming, above, of recent developments in Early Childhood Studies university degree courses. I got into trouble with some much-respected colleagues several years ago by challenging in print the strong move towards the 'academicization' (awful word!) of early years training – my argument being that an over-intellectual or overly academic way of thinking about, and being with, very young children can actually get in the way of a *developmentally appropriate* way of relating with young children. In contrast, the Steiner Kindergarten training which I did over a decade ago was very experiential and artistic in focus, and I felt that this really prepared practitioners very well for working with young children. But perhaps my concerns are misplaced; I suppose this is really another training question, and as a highly experienced trainer yourself, it would be interesting to hear whether you think my concerns have any substance.

MARGARET: I don't think your concerns are misplaced, and I agree that experiential learning should be given high priority in early years training, as much of the day-to-day work is practical in nature. It has concerned me for some time that many newly qualified practitioners do not seem to be able to prepare an inviting environment for the children. Many also appear to lack the creativity and ingenuity to think outside the box (or beyond the catalogue!) when collecting and developing resources. The art of story-telling (as opposed to story *reading*) also seems to be undervalued. All of these were a strong part of my initial training, *alongside* more academic study. I strongly believe that practitioners need both theory *and* practical experience, as practice has to sit within a context of values. Practitioners who don't understand the reasons why something is important for young children find it difficult to make, implement and justify appropriate practice decisions. However, I don't think that every practitioner needs to be a graduate, or that every graduate will necessarily make an effective early years practitioner.

Alongside theory and practical experience, I also believe that practitioners need to be supported to develop, and go on developing, emotional maturity and self-awareness in order to enable them to support each unique child and family with empathy and without negative judgement. They also need a degree of emotional maturity to work effectively as part of a team.

We need to remember, though, that initial training is not enough by itself, and that regular professional development opportunities are vital to keep practitioners reflecting and reviewing. The courses which I have found most useful when it comes to balancing theory and experience are those where participants have time between sessions to carry out small-scale action research projects in their settings. I have been very moved to hear course members sharing their questions, their actions and their findings, and have recognized that this approach enables even the least experienced practitioners to question and challenge themselves and their own practice in a safe and supportive way.

RICHARD: As something of an inveterate campaigner yourself, could you say something about the Open EYE campaign, and how it compares with your other various campaigning activities? If it *has* been successful in any sense, to what do you attribute that success, and what might be the implications for campaigning in this or other public-policy fields?

MARGARET: I think the Open EYE campaign has been phenomenally successful – way beyond anything I have ever experienced before. We have had more top-level media coverage than many more established groups, and we have been very difficult to ignore. In fact we have generated very strong emotions, with people either loving or hating us! This doesn't worry me; I simply think it is a measure of our effectiveness in either speaking for those who feel they have no voice, or rattling the cages of those who may have vested interests.

This campaign brought together a group of people who, although very different in personality and professional background, shared some core values and beliefs. We have certainly not agreed with each other all the time, but we have been able to debate our differences in a professional and respectful manner (albeit with a great deal of passion) and find common ground for the campaign. Once we had a core message (and, I acknowledge, that took time to refine), we have stuck to that doggedly, and have not allowed ourselves to become distracted.

Open EYE Steering Group members have consistently worked as a democratic team, and have given a huge amount of energy to the cause. Because of this, we have been able to mobilize each other very quickly when needed to write a letter or make a comment. I have to mention your role, Richard, because, right from the beginning, you have never missed or failed to circulate a relevant press article or public comment, never failed to come up with an innovative idea (not all acceptable to the rest of the group), and your editing skills are legendary. However, all of the steering group have put a huge amount of time and commitment into the campaign, and none of us has been afraid to speak out, or write strongly about what we believe in. We have all been proactive in our different ways, seeing opportunities and using all our connections and contacts. This is what is needed for a campaign to be successful in the longer term.

We have also been risk-takers. Our conferences were huge gambles for an unfunded organization, but, in both cases, they were a great success and gained us much support and respect. This support is evident in this book, with its fantastic list of contributors. We have always used available research evidence to back up our arguments, and have been able to showcase the work of some less well known academics alongside more established names. The Open EYE newsletter, so ably edited by Wendy Ellyatt, is another great achievement, and keeps our supporters up to date with the campaign and other early years issues.

But, I guess, campaigns should be measured by their concrete successes, and we know there is a huge amount still to be done. We have undoubtedly influenced Dame Clare Tickell's review of the EYFS. If her recommendations are accepted by the government, Steiner Kindergartens and groups of independent schools will be able to apply *en masse* for exemption from the EYFS learning and development requirements. She has recognized the central importance of Personal, Social and Emotional Development, Communication and Language, and Physical Development by naming them as 'Prime Areas', and appears to have accepted that paperwork has increased to unreasonable levels, either because of the EYFS or its interpretation.

However, we have not achieved the central goal of our campaign, which is to remove the statutory learning and development requirements, changing them to 'guidance' instead. Reducing the early learning goals is not enough – in fact, it is debatable whether there has actually been a reduction in Tickell, since each of the 17 goals that the Review proposes contains several goals within each goal. The three-point scales, setting out whether children's achievement of a goal is emerging, as expected, or exceeding expectations, play into the hands of those who wish to measure children and make predictions of, or set targets for, their future achievement. Open EYE members have consistently spoken out about this appalling lack of respect for young children's unique developmental pathways, and will continue to do so.

Implications for other campaigns that we can draw from our experience might be the need to:

- ensure there is a clear message and goal, and stick to that without deviation;
- adopt a democratic team approach to getting things done, drawing on diverse skills and experience – the team needs to include people who are not afraid to take a risk or stick their head above the parapet; and there is no place for egos;
- be proactive with the media – offering stories and letters, and building up relationships with key journalists;
- have a core group of people who are willing to give time and energy to the campaign, and to be available to contribute at short notice;
- use research evidence to back up the message, and boost support for the message through conferences and newsletters;
- never give up on the core message or the belief that you can make a difference.

As Margaret Mead famously said: 'Never doubt that a small group of thoughtful, committed citizens can change the world. Indeed it's the only thing that ever has.'

RICHARD: I think your summarizing of the Open EYE campaign could hardly be bettered, Margaret; and it feels good to have such a clear and resounding summary of our work going out into the public sphere through the medium of this book.

One final question for you: what are your hopes and fears for the future of the early years in Britain? Is there anything to be optimistic about?

MARGARET: I'm going to start with my fears, as they are prevalent at the moment.

Maintained nursery schools and the role of the specialist nursery teacher

I fear that with the current and future cut-backs to public services, maintained nursery schools will cease to exist, or be so starved of resources that they will wither and be unable to offer anything close to the quality for which they are currently renowned. If we lose these fantastic role models, I believe that *all* provision will suffer, as there will be little in the public domain to provide a vision for practitioners to aspire to – this applies especially to practitioners working in areas of disadvantage, which is where the majority of maintained nursery schools are situated. It will also damage career prospects for those who wish to train to teach the youngest children (and receive a salary based on national pay scales), as specialist teacher training courses will diminish, and job opportunities will dry up.

Early years services in the wider context

I fear the separation of early years services from the rest of the education system. Children in reception classes and Key Stage 1 are still very young, and need an approach which builds on the best nursery education approaches. I have witnessed excellent nursery teachers moving through reception into Key Stage 1 and taking their child-centred practice with them. This will be significantly more difficult if specialist nursery teachers are few and far between.

I also think it will do nothing for the status of early years practitioners if they are seen to be quite separate from all other parts of the education system. Although there is the danger of top-down pressure, I believe the danger of being marginalized and seen as second rate is worse.

The early years curriculum

As far as the curriculum is concerned, I fear the revised learning and development requirements in the EYFS, in as much as I think they will make it easier for children to be measured, counted and deemed to be failures at a very young age (cf. Chapters 10–12, this volume). It will also be easier to measure early years practitioners and move towards payment by results! I worry that, instead of supporting children within the Prime areas (which I support), there will still be an over-emphasis on literacy and preparation for a phonics test in Year 1. If this happens, it is those children who need a playful, joyful experience the most who will lose out, as they are called away to do additional phonics sessions or other small group work. Overall, I fear that even though the EYFS is lauded as a play-based framework, the reality will be a move towards preparation for Year 1 and SATs, particularly in reception classes.

I struggle to find anything to be optimistic about in the current climate, but never being one to give up entirely, I think it's appropriate to list some hopes. I therefore hope that:

- **We can take up Peter Moss's call (op. cit.) for a debate on what kind of early years services we want in the UK;**
- **Nursery schools will once again be recognized for the fantastic work they do**. Governments would ring-fence their funding to enable then to continue to act as inspirational role models to others. Enabling them to become teaching schools, in the same way that primary and secondary schools can, would be an important first step;
- **Specialist training courses for all level of early years practitioner, including nursery teachers, will be re-established.** All of these courses would balance theoretical study with practical experience and personal development, and would be long enough for candidates to develop the attitudes, skills and understanding they need for their role;
- **Early childhood will be seen as the vital foundation on which everything else should be built.** Rather than early years being seen as a time to prepare for school, it would be

seen as unpressured time for children to develop as individuals, form relationships, make sense of their world in their own unique ways and develop their love of learning. Schools would prepare for a group of unique, creative individuals, and would not expect children to have achieved predetermined goals; and

- **The curriculum for young children will be left to those working with them who know their needs best.** It would be underpinned by nationally set welfare standards and some core values and entitlements, but would leave scope for each setting to develop in innovative, creative ways.

Overall, I would like to think that the early years work-force as a whole will become less passive and less willing to do things just because they have been told to. We all need to continue to stay informed, and to reflect, question and challenge. Above all, we need to keep in mind the young vulnerable children, who have no political voice, and ask ourselves, what would they vote for?

RICHARD: One never knows how an exercise like this interview chapter is going to work out beforehand, but I must say that it has far exceeded any expectations I might have had – so thank you, Margaret, for making it so. In having the last word, and not sparing your blushes, I would like to finish by thanking you for having been, and continuing to be, an inspiration to a generation of early years practitioners in your fearless advocacy of independent, child-sensitive critical thinking, and your refusal to allow your core values and beliefs to be compromised or distorted by political expediency. And it's for that very reason that, were I the Early Years minister, you would most definitely be my chief advisor; and if the current minister, Sarah Teather, or her successor(s) or advisors, happen to read this, there is still time! ...

Ways Ahead
to Achievable Futures

In the final part, Part IV, we consider what positive changes might be made to current early years policy and associated pedagogical practices, which would respond to the major concerns about the 'too much, too soon' ideology that have been detailed throughout this book. Grethe Hooper Hansen first offers us some incisive 'new paradigm' thinking, introducing us to ideas that rarely if ever get considered in the early years literature, and yet which might just be the ideas of the future, in a radically 'post-modern' world that dares to fundamentally challenge many of the tacit metaphysical assumptions underpinning mainstream praxis. Certainly, this chapter brings home very clearly how there is an urgent need to consider just how young children learn, and that the phenomenon of *unconscious* learning is a phenomenon that we must take very seriously indeed.

Very different in tone and content is the book's penultimate chapter, in which the distinguished ex chair of the parliamentary Education Select Committee, Barry Sheerman MP, offers us a unique first-hand policy-maker's perspective on early childhood. In a characteristically measured and thoughtful contribution, Barry urges campaigners to engage with policy-makers in a positive, constructive way; and in their final concluding chapter, Wendy Scott and Richard House attempt to respond to this *cri de coeur* by setting out what they argue to be eminently achievable changes to current policies, the embracing of which would go a considerable way towards responding to the concerns raised in this book. In any rational world, the proposed changes would surely be implemented without demur; and we still retain hope that informed rationality will ultimately prevail in the early years sphere – notwithstanding the many instances that regrettably point in the opposite direction.

CHAPTER 21

Education and Paradigm Shift

GRETHE HOOPER HANSEN

We live in a transforming world. The reason for the fierce disagreement over early years practice is the paradigm shift in progress now from belief in a purely material reality to acceptance of its multi-dimensionality. A 'paradigm' is a set of beliefs that affects us before we even begin to frame a thought, colouring every impulse. Paradigms are so deeply engrained in a culture that it takes immense time to flush them out: Galileo was imprisoned and tortured for repeating what Copernicus had proved no less than a century before, that the world is *not flat*. During the period of paradigm disintegration (which we are in now), we live in a limbo of contradiction as the old dies and is slowly replaced: hospitals stock up with MRI scanners without realising the quantum implication behind them of the accuracy of energetic transmission, by comparison with the fallibility of the chemical, on which modern pharmaceutical medicine is based.

So it is with education, firmly rooted in logical positivism. The real issue in early years is whether to work at the quantum level of 'very small' effects, or at the material and cognitive level. Government expectations are entirely materialist, and to meet them, practitioners are forced to impose that paradigm on the children. For those used to working at subtle levels, this is outrageous. As the only member of the Open EYE team who is not a specialist in early years work, I bring a perspective from a 'quantum' educator, Dr Georgi Lozanov from Bulgaria, who as a scientist created a systematic way of teaching directly to the unconscious mind, by shaping an environment to invoke a 'natural'/organic response. Rudolf Steiner's cosmology is probably the most profound and complex example of a quantum system, but because there was no conventional science to support his insights, it was ridiculed and excluded, which has left an imprint of traumatization, generating in turn a degree of rigidity. However, that rigidity served to protect his method from well-meaning but misguided alteration. I hope that this chapter will help to demystify his work.

Materialist science addresses the world that we perceive through the five physical senses; they are called 'physical' because they are biologically limited to respond to only a narrow range of experience, so that we can orientate ourselves in the world and manage normal life; in reality, there is infinitely more 'out there' (which is the stuff of quantum science). Conscious awareness is like the narrow beam of a torch, offering a glimpse into the complexity of the unconscious. In order to be conscious, it processes only one thing at a time, and can hold no more than nine items at once,[1] whereas unconsciously, we process 'in parallel', seeing, hearing, smelling, touching and moving simultaneously. This is vital because we also perceive holographically:[2] even the mind of a child is at every moment performing complex mathematics (fourier transforms) in fractions of a second too small to count – but this is neither visible nor knowable. Cell biologists report that 95 per cent of our mental process is unconscious; only about 5 per cent is conscious.[3]

This has enormous implications for education, indicating that in the natural state, learning is largely unconscious; we notice only a tiny segment. The rest is processed unconsciously, and surfaces in its own time. Educators such as Steiner, Montessori, Froebel and particularly Lozanov have approaches to facilitate this. Mainstream educational theory has only a vague notion of 'tacit' awareness, and no concept of how to use it. But this is vitally important because it involves presenting material and activating the mind in a very different way. In the old days, there were many brilliant school-teachers who followed their intuition (Sukhomlinsky, Sylvia Ashton Warner, et al.), but their skills could not be replicated because there was no theory to explain them. Unfortunately, now that the government presumes to prescribe how teachers should teach, all effort and intention is directed relentlessly at the conscious mind, the 5 per cent. Teacher training has also for many years been aimed at the 5 per cent. Successive governments made a point of offering early retirement to get rid of older teachers on high salaries, with the result that expertise has been drained from the profession.

Focus on the 5 per cent has vastly increased 'learning disorder'; one might more realistically call it 'preventing-from-learning' disorder.

Much worse is the imposition of cognitive focus on the early years sector, because this is the time when the basic sub-cortical structures are being created, on which the cortical will eventually depend. These are the result of *sensory* stimulation, giving rise to imagination, now drained from the early years classroom by premature cognitive focus. William Blake might serve as an example, sixth son of a simple hosier, who became one of the greatest geniuses of our literature. How? Having happily avoided school, he took an 8-year apprenticeship in copper engraving, which could provide the neural structure to be elaborated later by copious reading. As for genetics, cell biology now reveals that genes are only a potential waiting to be selected.

Georgi Lozanov

Lozanov was 18 when Communism rampaged into Bulgaria, imposing its suffocating blanket of control. He rebelled, was imprisoned and repeatedly tortured for not revealing the names of collaborators, but was eventually released on parole. By continually changing address over many years, he surfed the Communist blacklist and managed to attend University in Sofia, where he eventually gained doctorates in medicine, neurology and psychology, and earned a professorship. His major interest was what we refer to now as psychoneuroimmunology (PNI), advanced in the Eastern bloc when still unknown in the West. His life had been profoundly affected by the trauma of his mother's death when he was 2, and by the weeks of torture, which may have contributed to the extreme sensitivity that enabled him to pursue the work he did. Like Viktor Frankl, he emerged from the darkness with a vision: he saw humanity as *locked gods,* socio-hypnotically frozen into a belief of 'restricted humbleness', and set to work to find the key to their release, as professor, doctor and therapist by day, and in the evenings, researcher at the Institute of Experimental Sciences.

Dealing with an endless stream of people traumatized by the conditions of life within the grim interpretation of Communism in Bulgaria (worse than but not unlike the 'controlism' of our previous Labour government), he gradually learned how to release and resuscitate the life energy within by weaving around his patients a delicate cobweb of suggestion. To counter the implication of hierarchy in the doctor–patient relationship, and being skilled in the Eastern tradition of group therapy, he set about designing a method of language learning that could achieve the same effect simply through the suggestion inherent in its manner of presenting information, the way it caused students to think and act and to process that information. He developed it meticulously over many years, researching every intervention. The results were astounding: not only did his patients lose their symptoms, but their language learning was phenomenal.

The government heard about his work and saw its potential for general education, and to add to the greater glory of Communism. He was funded to set up an institute with a large staff of scientists, researchers and teachers, and allowed to run large-scale projects in schools, which soon gained a world-wide reputation for extraordinary results, attracting foreign delegations to study the method, and his first book was published.[4] But eventually, his past resurfaced, his institute was taken over, his research papers were destroyed in a mysterious fire, and he found himself once again under surveillance and harassment. When the Iron Curtain fell, he moved with his collaborator Dr Evalina Gateva to Austria, where they continued to develop the work, attracting enthusiasts from all over the world to study with them. But the problem was that the Western world was deeply immersed in materialism, and unaware of the kind of thinking that lay behind PNI.

To show the nature of his work, I give an example from one of the few records that escaped the fire, of a film of young children learning to read (at 7, not 4). It is astonishing to watch the dramatic differences that appeared almost immediately between the control and experimental groups. Both teachers were highly skilled – one trained in Lozanov's method, the other using a traditional teaching approach of incremental progress from letter to syllable to word. By contrast, the experimental group absorbed meaningful units (words or sentences) *unconsciously*: the teacher simply told a story, talked about it, told it again and asked questions. The same story was posted in writing and pictures on the walls, which she at first ignored. But the children did not, and soon found themselves recognizing words and, in response to questions, reproducing them, having learnt in the tacit, peripheral or semi-conscious way. They became more and more involved and excited, and within a very short period, had mastered reading (since at age 7, the mind is ready for it). By contrast, the control group, labouring to 'get it right' and please the teacher, passed from high expectation to disappointment, self-doubt, anxiety, competitiveness for teacher favour, and teacher dependence – a dramatic decline in a short time, although the teacher was excellent by conventional standards.

The most obvious immediate difference is enormous *volume*: a whole story as a first reading lesson! But the experimental teacher embedded it in a web of delicate suggestion and expectation: it was not a 'lesson', just a story-telling. Answers to questions were met with a smile of recognition, but there was no praise or reward because there was no demand for learning; the children did not know at first that they were learning. Nothing was made explicit because when learning is restricted to the 'tacit', the brain is activated differently, a 'bottom-up' process of absorption and assimilation, a difference that is recognized in the psychoanalytic world.[5] It was evident that no child experienced 'difficulty', linked to the absence of direct correction (which was instead very subtle and indirect) since there was no expectation. It was assumed that each child would learn only that which was appropriate for him or her. If this seems absurd and impossible, think of William Blake; he probably learned to read in much the same way. Reduction of information, objective standards, assessment and measurement collapse the vast quantum complexity of the (holographically processing) mind.

Brain Bias

Western escalation of the cognitive-material was illuminated by a recent study of brain hemispheric differences, *The Master and his Emissary*, by Dr Iain McGilchrist, psychiatrist and Oxford professor of poetry.[6] In it, he links the cultural shifts and pendulum swings in Western history with hemispheric dominance, reaching the conclusion that we are now in an endgame of pathologically extreme left hemisphericity. As a university teacher, he has great respect for the rational, organizational and linguistic skills of the left, its reason, logic and ability to give form to thought. But McGilchrist maintains that the brain is designed to hold a balance whereby the more complex possibility of the right, which can be expressed and realised only through the left, always remains supreme. The right is the *master*, who needs the emissary as a vehicle for expression, but must retain the position of power and control. (To apply this to education, we must allow children to learn as nature intended, primarily through the right, holographic process.)

If the left succeeds in dominating, which it naturally seeks to do, being limited in its perception and unaware of its own deficiency, which it imagines to be superiority, its myopic fixation on the material, factual and logical can lead us into separation, judgement and compartmentalization of mind, as well as conflict, war and ego obsession. There is an affinity between the left-hemispheric and materialist science, whereas the right hemisphere mediates multi-dimensional awareness. Lozanov does not speak of hemisphericity, focusing instead on fragmentation or integration of mind, but he has a similar understanding in terms of conscious and unconscious awareness, with his learning target of the 'para-conscious' holding the balance on the threshold between.

Our five physical senses cannot reveal to us that at the sub-atomic level, everything is in constant flux, changing or being changed by all that it engages with (which explains how the teacher's expectation of the student affects what s/he achieves).[7] As a therapist attuned to the more subtle levels, Lozanov could sense these mercurial realities and anticipate the influence that one thing would exert upon another. He realised that 'telling' creates an authority–receiver hierarchy that determines the way the brain will work (top-down reproduction), whereas 'suggesting' has the opposite effect since it leaves the student free to accept or refuse spontaneously, whether consciously or not, and this results in a bottom-up dynamic. The name *Suggestopedia*, dismissed derisively by the academic world,[8] simply indicates that when something is suggested or offered rather than demanded, the response becomes one of choice, not obedience, which involves a different brain reaction, causing a bottom-up rather than top-down manner of processing and further spin-off of a myriad subtle effects. While conventional language teaching (my speciality) rejects 'passive' learning as useless, since it cannot immediately be tested, Lozanov targets the passive, and has a plethora of ingenious means to bring it to awareness, including drama, role-play and games. Materialist approaches target the conscious-rational, whereas the quantum/multi-dimensional target the para-conscious and passive. In his method, one reason for play (and there are many) is to allow the brain freedom from constraint so as to absorb, in its natural holographic way, infinitely more than it possibly could if narrowly focused by traditional insistence on 'concentration'.

Early Years

Similar considerations lie behind the differences between materialist and multi-dimensional concepts of early years education. In the early years classroom, for example, the child's mind responds entirely differently if play is adult-directed, as in the Early Years Foundation

Stage (EYFS) model, which uses play as a format to disguise instruction. Children are hyper-sensitive to adult intent, and automatically respond to what the teacher *really* wants behind the pretence. In a child-led approach, ideas arise spontaneously from the child's own psyche. As Lozanov explains, learning is *state dependent*: what we learn, and the quality of our learning, depends on the mental state we are in when the learning takes place – and it is up to the facilitator/teacher/carer to create conditions that will orchestrate an appropriate state. For older children, the constant stress that prevails in the 'audited' classroom causes a narrowing of receptive faculties, reducing focus to that which is prioritized (what the teacher wants them to perceive), which is all they see and memorize; this is the traditional, left-brain-intensive classroom mode. By contrast, the 'safety' of a non-competitive[9] classroom allows the mind to relax, open and receive a wider picture. The greater the load of safety/pleasure/support signals, the more extensive the students' understanding will be. Lozanov offers a cornucopia of reassurance, relaxation and mental expansion effects, using music, aesthetics and the arts.

When he came to the West, this was misinterpreted as a 'play method' and led to the concept of Accelerated Learning – as mechanistic as the name implies, involving such activities as goal-setting and review of targets, which collapse Lozanov's complex wave forms into restrictive particles. His means to motivation is *inspiration*, the opposite of competition, which holds the mind open and aloft. But this is never made explicit, only implied – through characters and dialogue in the texts, music, poetry and delicate aesthetic effects. He avoids all suggestion that might bump the mind back into mundane realities: jokey cartoons, loud colours, dialogue involving accident, violence, gossip or complaint. Instead, beauty, arts and intimations of morality enhance attitude, motivation and expectancy, creating a 'suggestive set-up', priming the mind for high achievement.

He pays close attention to what he calls the 'dual plane', explaining that there are always two levels of response, conscious and unconscious, often paradoxical, and teachers must learn to cater for both. For example, if I say that 'Italian is easy', at the unconscious, implicational level, a) I am lying, and b) implying that the learner who finds it difficult must be stupid. Traditional pedagogy is full of such mixed messages, but since traditional pedagogy keeps the students' mind narrowed into concentration and self-defence, they are less sensitive. However, its customary barrage of negative suggestion does become apparent in behaviour: aggression is *triggered* in the classroom by such things as implications of criticism and control, and the weight of a relentlessly adversarial environment. Lozanov would regard the teacher as having the responsibility of holding the learners' mind in an appropriate space for learning, so that distress is avoided.

Since the richest and most voluminous learning is acquired *indirectly* (through unconscious parallel processing, as in the example of children learning to read), Lozanov also provides a myriad ingenious ways of distracting the conscious mind from the target material (the *polar opposite* of conventional education). This is easy to do in a language-learning situation: through games and activities, asking, explaining, and so on. Outside of language learning, the kind of method used would be such things as discussion, discovery, experimentation, films and stories. Lozanov was able to measure the conspicuous qualitative differences achieved through direct or indirect learning, with the indirect showing far more complexity, plasticity and durability. When a teacher complains that things 'aren't working', he typically advises her to treble the volume of her text, i.e. if it is not too much for the conscious mind to comprehend, the conscious mind will take over and quantum learning will grind to a halt. This is the most common mistake that teachers make, since it is very difficult to adjust pedagogical practice to absolute faith in the enormous capability of the unconscious.

When passive learning surfaces to awareness (in a language-learning situation, through role play, drama, games and particularly, story telling), the experience is very different from that of conventional classroom learning. Students find words and sentences emerging from their mouths 'of their own accord', without any conscious preparation (just as a small child learns to speak). This is an exhilarating experience, bringing a glorious feeling of autonomy and capability, the opposite of repetition-reproduction. To the same end, correction is extremely sensitive, always 'peripheral': the teacher embeds a correct version within a sentence of her own, which is presented *indirectly* (as if by chance) so that it will be picked up *unconsciously*, and therefore trigger the more complex bottom-up process of assimilation and analysis. This fine adjustment has immense effects; the negative impact of direct correction in conventional classrooms has more damaging consequences than the conscious mind can comprehend.

These are just a few examples and comments on an intricately conceived quantum methodology, which relies on the complexity that can be reached only by targeting the *unconscious* mind. Its practice is full of methods and techniques equally relevant to early education, such as framing questions so as to avoid the startle reflex (horribly emphasized by the EYFS accountability procedures) and keep the learners' minds in the relaxed, para-conscious state that will optimize their learning. It also requires a degree of psychological maturity and awareness in teachers, as opposed to academic qualifications which, in the early years sector, might only predispose the teacher to think from head rather than heart (cf. Chapter 20).

Lozanov does not demand therapeutic skills as such (it was his job to provide them in the design of the method!), but a warm heart, sufficient sensitivity and awareness, and the willingness to take full responsibility for every problem that arises in the classroom, seeing it as an opportunity to look more deeply into one's own psychological mirror, and to increase sensitivity and awareness. A good teacher is dedicated to lifelong learning.

Notes

1 See G. A. Miller, 'The magical number seven, plus or minus two: some limits on our capacity for processing information', *Psychological Review*, 63, 1956: 81–97.

2 See K. Pribram, 'Primary reality may be frequency realm', *Brain/Mind Bulletin*, 2, 1977: 1–3.

3 See B. Lipton, *The Biology of Belief*, Santa Rosa, Calif.: Mountain of Love/ Elite Books, 2005.

4 G. Lozanov, *Suggestology and Outlines of Suggestopedy*, New York: Gordon & Breach, 1978.

5 See J.D. Teasdale and P.J. Barnard, *Affect, Cognition and Change: Remodelling Depressive Thought*, Hove: Lawrence Erlbaum, 1996.

6 Iain McGilchrist, *The Master and His Emissary: The Divided Brain and the Making of the Western World*, New Haven, Conn: Yale University Press, 2009.

7 See R. Rosenthal and L. Jacobson, *Pygmalion in the Classroom*, New York: Holt, Rinehart & Winston, 1968.

8 One critic, a teacher of English as a Foreign Language from a prestigious East Coast American university, dismissed his book as 'pseudo-scientific gobbledy-gook', although he clearly had no understanding of science, and was evidently unaware of Lozanov's three doctorates. This ignorant and egotistical review effectively destroyed Lozanov's reputation in the academic world.

9 This is not to say that competition is necessarily harmful. If a safe and friendly classroom climate is established first, competition can be taken as a game that is useful and stimulating. But because it can so easily degenerate, Lozanov avoids it.

CHAPTER 22

Early Childhood:
A Policy-Making Perspective

BARRY SHEERMAN

The very first inquiry the Education Select Committee embarked upon under my chairmanship was on Early Years in 2000. It was originally suggested that we would cover 3–8-year-olds, but I thought this inadequate. It was therefore decided that it should be extended to span the period from birth to 8 years. In addition, we agreed to appoint a clinical psychologist as a special advisor to inform the Committee on the development of a child's brain and early learning processes. Ten years later my final inquiry as Chairman of the Children, Schools and Families Select Committee was an evaluation of the impact of Sure Start Children Centres and its influence on the preschool environment.

There are many highly qualified professionals in the educational sector, few of whom have a full understanding of the impact that an effectively organized Select Committee can have on the policy-making process. The prime responsibility of a Select Committee is to ensure that the Government and its Ministries are accountable to Parliament. This role involves interviewing Ministers, senior civil servants and key influentials such as Her Majesty's Chief Inspector of Schools (OFSTED). At the core of the Committee's work is the desire to assess value for money for the taxpayer. However, following a General Election there is also a responsibility to evaluate the degree to which Government policies are successfully delivering the promises made in the election manifesto.

Select Committees must not be constrained by a purely negative role and should seek to proactively examine areas that have been neglected, and should not be afraid to tackle subjects which Governments are reluctant to engage with. At its best, a Select Committee should not only improve the quality of policy-making but should also make a substantial contribution to the improvement of the broader educational environment.

At the very heart of the Select Committee process is a unique method of enquiry. The process begins with the choice of subject and the refinement of its terms of reference. Our Committee introduced an extremely useful tool, the navigational seminar, which enabled us to meet with many of the leading experts in a field like Early Years. The seminar, also attended by our small core staff consisting of clerks and committee specialists, was then able to refine the topic, discuss potential witnesses to be called and visits to be made. In addition, such seminars assisted us in identifying the team of Special Advisors who would assist us throughout the enquiry. These advisors were drawn from leading academic researchers and practitioners, and were crucial to the success of the work that followed. The significance of this link between the Select Committee, the Research Community and the policy context cannot be overestimated. Over time, an enduring relationship can develop, and the opportunity for academic research to directly influence policy is palpable. As a Committee we were always looking for talented advisers with a fresh perspective, as well as ensuring that we were aware of the depth and breadth of various current fields of research. The quality of those who offered their services to the Committee was remarkable, and had a significant impact on how an enquiry was shaped and focused, the oral evidence we invited, and the settings, schools and locations we visited.

The Committee's ability to call on these special advisors to share their expertise, knowledge and research findings was unique, and highlighted the fact that the policy context is not an entirely closed one, and that one way to open up policy formation to researchers, practitioners, parents and teachers is to use the system well.

The Early Year's sector has the benefit of a wealth of high-quality research, much of it conducted over significantly long periods of time. Due to the diversity of the expertise available from both academics and practitioners, we had the confidence to write a highly original report, the recommendations of which still resonate today.

The report, published in 2000, clearly stated that the first two years of a child's life were critical to later development and that the need for early stimulation was vital. We also emphasized the prime role of parents and called for a Parent's Charter; we urged parents and early year's professionals to work together to develop individual profiles on children; and we called for better training and remuneration for the work-force. These recommendations have not only stood the test of time, but have had a positive influence on policy development in Government and the delivery of a holistic service for children. On the remuneration of the Early Years work-force, it had shocked the Committee during visits to some settings to be told that the passing of the minimum wage legislation in 1999 would mean that preschools would be unable to cope with the increased wage burden. We discovered that payment of a rate of £1 per hour to childcare professionals was common in many settings.

The committee also recommended that 0–5 years should be seen as the first phase of education, and that informal teaching methods used in this phase, as well as structured learning practices, should be introduced slowly, as 'stepping stones'. Evidence provided to the committee convinced us that formal learning should not be thrust upon children too early. Whilst we were less concerned with age of entry into schools we worried that some schools would transform the reception class into the first part of Key Stage 1.

We were strong in emphasizing parental choice, and the need for practitioners to be both well trained in working with parents and families as well as possessing the requisite skills for assisting a child's personal and social development. We were somewhat ahead of our time in calling for one Ministry to provide a universal service covering care and education, and right in our enthusiasm for early years stimulation. Our belief in the benefit of smaller class sizes and the aspiration of having an adequately trained teacher in every setting was also progressive, and we were also slightly ahead of the curve in advocating the key role of learning outside the classroom.

This Early Years report was a wonderful induction for a new chair, and the lessons learned from that first inquiry stay with me. Over the subsequent ten years I never lost the belief in evidence-based policies, which always returns to the notion of prioritizing the quality of staff and their continued training and professional development, an idea which is true at every level; schools, colleges and universities, as well as early years.

After ten years of inquiries across a broad spectrum, I am still convinced that early years remains the most critical time for a young human being, that early stimulation of the brain should be developmentally appropriate, enlightened, informed and provided by highly trained and well remunerated professionals. However, the Select Committee in March 2009, which I also chaired, did recommend that the Early Learning Goals should apply to slightly older children, so that they are genuinely something that children at the end of the fifth year would be able to achieve rather than having unrealistic expectations for younger children. Since this original inquiry, we have witnessed a continued search by all parties for a diverse preschool sector that meets the needs of both children and parents. Politicians often make strong claims for policies that they introduce, and exaggerate the differences between themselves and those of other parties. Looked at logically and dispassionately, I suspect that when it comes to all stages of education policy, the differences between the three parties are not that great. Indeed, the policy retrospective inquiry which the Committee conducted at the end of 2010, entitled 'Baker to Balls', highlighted the similarities rather than the differences between the Labour and Conservative Governments in the post-1944 period.

Prime Minister Jim Callaghan opened the 'great education debate' at Ruskin College, Oxford in 1976, speaking of the need for a more effective inspectorate, and greater testing and assessment, as well as a national curriculum. However it was Kenneth Baker who introduced all of these changes in the educational landscape under Mrs Thatcher's premiership. During much of this time, there had been little dramatic difference in practice between the Conservative and Labour policies. However, in 1996 the new Labour leader, Tony Blair, once again at Ruskin College, launched the era of 'Education, Education, Education', and we began to see the strong emphasis on diversity and choice at all levels of our education system.

There is no doubt the 'triple E' commitment was accompanied by a vast expansion of resources devoted to the education sector. Early years in particular became a major beneficiary of the Blair years. The Callaghan and Baker enthusiasm for testing and assessment, inspection and a national curriculum were now embraced on all sides of the political spectrum. It was not surprising that early years would soon be influenced by policy thinking that was originally designed for school years evaluation and monitoring. If testing and assessment, a national curriculum and a more intrusive Inspectorate were sufficient for other educational phases, then why not for preschool settings? This seismic shift is still being debated as to its real benefits, and will need to be kept under constant review.

To give Ministers their due, it is understandable that a growing expenditure on early years would have to be defended to the taxpayer with evidence of value for money. Early years characterized by a rather patchy and uneven provision, and staffed by an under-paid and under-trained work-force, was not expected to put up much resistance to the changes. However, the challenge of increasing training and qualifications, as well as properly remunerating the profession, must have looked not only daunting, particularly in the short term, but also expensive. Ministers might have been persuaded that a prescriptive early year's curriculum that even the less well-trained could deliver, alongside more inspection and assessment, could be the quickest and cheapest way of transforming the system.

Over the period of my chairmanship, the pace of change in early years has been immense, with a rapid growth of preschool education and a landscape that has been littered with innovation in Birth to Three Guidance (DfES: 2003), the Foundation Stage Curriculum for three- and four-year-olds (DfEE and QCA, 2000), the National Standard for Day Care (e.g. Sure Start, 2004), the Early Years Foundation Stage Framework (DCSF, 2008), and more recently the review of the Early Years Foundation Stage (Tickell, 2011).

As I embarked upon my last inquiry into early years in 2009/2010 on Sure Start Children Centres, I could not resist thinking that although so much has happened in early years during my chairmanship, many of the challenges remain the same.

We *are* in a profoundly better position in early years; I believe that the Sure Start Children Centres model of breaking down silos between professions to provide seamless and universal support for families across health care and education is a wonderful innovation. This holistic approach is one that we should learn from, and should be used as an exemplar across all stages of the educational journey.

In the course of our inquiry into young people Not in Education, Employment or Training (or 'NEETs'), we visited the Netherlands, a country with consistently low rates of youth unemployment. We were struck by the number of features of the Dutch approach: the fact that support for young people was available to those up to the age of 27; that payment of benefits was dependent on participation in education, employment or training; and the provision of support and guidance in 'one-stop shops' that were remarkably similar to our holistic Children's Centre model.

In terms of curriculum, testing and assessment, and inspection, I believe that we have seen a healthy retreat from the more intensive policies of the past. The recent recommendations of the Tickell review (DfE, 2011) are an important stage in this process, and I hope that the Education Committee will play a part in the restoration of balance between trusting parents, families and professionals instead of allowing too much interference from central Government. With a larger, better-trained and better remunerated work-force, we can have an early years agenda that truly fits the twenty-first century, one with which we can hopefully respond to with a softer and more flexible policy stance.

I am struck and impressed by what Professor Lilian Katz has said in her chapter in this book, namely that

> those who make national policy decisions should resist the temptation to become opponents. Adversaries and enemies tend to become alike in many ways. Come together with your colleagues – those you disagree with, as well as those you agree with, and work out a position statement, then propose modification in the law that will address our best current understanding of how children best grow, develop and learn with the sincere intention of helping the decision-makers to achieve their well-meaning intentions.

It is beyond doubt that campaigns within organizations such as 'Open EYE' have played an important role in the changes that we are now seeing, resulting in a fundamental policy approach that extends beyond all parties. As a result of all of this I believe we are rethinking the balance between making children 'ready' for schooling and preparing them for happy and fulfilled lives. In this connection it might be worth mentioning that the Select Committee did also recommend that the Rose Review should not pursue its interim recommendation that entry into reception class in the September immediately following a child's fourth birthday should become the norm.

We are in a much better place in early year's settings than we were in 2000. This is something I wish could be said as emphatically about every stage of the educational journey. We have developed an education system from a constructive dialogue between academics, researchers, practitioners, policy-makers and politicians, and I am proud that the Select Committee has been able to play a constructive and influential part in this debate.

References

Department for Children, Schools and Families (DCSF) (2008) *Statutory Framework for the Early Years Foundation Stage*, Annesley, Nottingham: DCSF Publications, revised edn, May (orig. 2007); downloadable at: https://www.education.gov.uk/publications/eOrderingDownload/eyfs_res_stat_frmwrk.pdf (retrieved 6 July 2011)

Department for Education and Science (DfEE) and the Qualifications and Curriculum Authority (QCA) (2000) *Curriculum Guidance for the Foundation Stage*, London

Department for Education and Skills (DfES) (2003) *Birth to Three Guidance*

Sure Start (2004) 'What Works in Promoting Children's Mental Health: The Evidence and the Implications for Sure Start Settings', Department for Education, EOR-SBU-2003-174, July; accessible at: https://www.education.gov.uk/publications/RSG/Surestart/Page7?viewAs=full&sortBy=DateIssued_Descending (retrieved 6 July 2011)

Tickell, Dame C. (2011) *The Early Years: Foundations for Life, Health and Learning*, An Independent Report on the Early Years Foundation Stage to Her Majesty's Government, accessible at: http://www.education.gov.uk/tickellreview (retrieved 6 July 2011)

Conclusion and Ways Ahead: Recommendations for Educators and Policy-Makers

Wendy Scott and Richard House

Taken together, the many and diverse contributions to this book make a very strong case for the principle of developmentally appropriate support for children's development and learning in the early years. Contributors also argue for the corollary, the avoidance, where possible, of pedagogical and cultural practices that drag young children into premature, precocious development in an unbalanced way dominated by an adult agenda that compromises their medium- and long-term welfare as well as their current well-being. The evidence is now overwhelming that 'too much, too soon' is deeply damaging both to individual children and to our culture more generally. One key implication of this conclusion is that educators, parents and policy-makers have a grave responsibility (a big challenge?) to arrest and reverse the 'adultification' of children and childhood in whatever ways they can. Later in this concluding chapter, we will make some clear, deliverable recommendations that are eminently practicable. These can be adopted right now, as a contribution to a cultural movement which is against the ideology of 'too much too soon', and *for* developmentally appropriate childhood experience. This in turn would help to create the child-friendly conditions for young children in the Anglo-Saxon world that Dutch and Scandinavian children routinely enjoy.

The authors contributing to this book have major concerns about the developmental inappropriateness of some of the expectations we have of our young children, as seen in aspects of the Early Years Foundation Stage (EYFS), and which presents difficulties in several key areas:

- the disturbance of the subtle balance between physical, emotional, cognitive and spiritual development;
- the tension between each child's unique pattern of development and normalized standards;
- the disruption of dispositions to learn;
- the undue emphasis on conscious as opposed to unconscious learning;
- counter-productive premature pressures on early literacy development;
- the influence of arbitrary goals on early development and learning;
- the erosion of provision of opportunities for authentically free imaginative play;
- potentially damaging early exposure to information and communication technology and the screen culture; and
- the exceptionally early age for starting formal school.

The wide-ranging contributions in this book have engaged variously with all of these key issues, with the discussions framed by principle, observation and research, and grounded in critical thought, reflection and long experience. They therefore offer us a provocative stimulus to thinking and practice for all those wanting to deepen their understanding, and to develop their work with young children and families.

The book's contributors challenge much of the current early years orthodoxy, drawing on lessons from the past and raising questions about the evidence that is used to justify expected learning outcomes. Thoughtful consideration of the current complex situation in England inevitably generates pertinent questions about the process of policy development itself (see Chapters 3, 5, 20 and 22) – with policy too often being driven by ill-advised political priorities, in the face of convincing evidence of the prime importance of respecting individual children's unique needs and patterns of development. Despite the government's repeatedly stated intention to trust the judgement of professionals, the required learning goals in the EYFS, although now to be reduced in number, continue to distort the integrity of learner-centred early years pedagogy. It is difficult for practitioners to challenge this top-down shaping of their work, and it takes courage to counter expectations that have a strong influence on many parents' views, particularly as these continue to be reinforced through league tables and OFSTED inspections, and now also a simplistic test of phonics in Year 1 and an ill-defined concept of school readiness.

As well as foreclosing on the necessary breadth of open-ended experience that children need across all areas of learning, current statutory requirements are short-changing parents too. The UK government is a signatory to the European Convention on Human Rights, which includes protocols designed to ensure the collective enforcement of certain rights and freedoms. Article 2 of these protocols states that:

> No person shall be denied the right to education. In the exercise of any functions which it assumes in relation to education and to teaching, the State shall respect the right of parents to ensure such education and teaching in conformity with their own religious and philosophical convictions.

It is largely due to the persistent lobbying of the Open EYE campaign and its supporters that Dame Clare Tickell, in her review of the Early Years Foundation Stage, recommended that it should be more straightforward in future for organizations, settings and individual parents to gain exemptions from aspects of the statutory requirements (see Chapters 3–5, this volume). It remains to be seen whether the government will accept her proposal.

England's Current Policy-making Landscape

There are issues quite specific to policy-making in England that cannot be ignored. Staff training, particularly continuing professional development, is a casualty of the current financial pressures. The recently introduced single funding formula is another obstacle to improving practice. What is an ostensibly fair and sensible measure to equalize the amount of money paid per child is already causing grave difficulties. Funding was never enough to cover the real costs of high-quality provision, including professional development, and it does not take into account the salaries of the qualified teachers required in schools.

Levels of qualification have been shown to be the most important indicator of successful practice, yet pay scales are not sufficient to attract and retain staff of the calibre that is needed. The government appears to be content to settle for second best, which will result in an unavoidable levelling down of quality, at the key stage when investment in early learning and family support is most effective. It is beyond irony that, just when colleagues abroad are looking to enlightened British traditional nursery education, with its emphasis on direct experience and learning through play (see Chapters 13 and 14) as a model for the future development of their early years provision, our proud heritage is tragically disappearing (see Chapter 20). It is essential that the very specific knowledge and skills that are needed for effective early years work are recognized. There is also a need to develop initial training, for health and social services as well as for childcare, education and outreach staff, and to ensure that multi-agency professional development is available in addition to specialist courses. As this book makes clear, there really is no substitute for shared reflective practice and the capacity to engage in critical professional thinking, maturely grounded in fundamental principles.

The established and widely embraced themes of the unique child, learning and developing through positive relationships in an enabling environment, continue to underpin England's Early Years Foundation Stage, but they are being undermined in practice through prescribed outcomes, and counter-productive premature pressures, particularly in many reception classes. Statutory schooling starts very early in the UK compared with continental Europe, and new admissions arrangements make it imperative that developmentally appropriate provision is offered in the reception year and the transition through to Year 1. It is entirely logical to insist that any children who have not reached expected levels as measured by the EYFS profile should be entitled to teaching in Year 1 that continues the learner-centred approach advocated in the foundation years. Yet many pupils, especially summer-born children and boys, are misdiagnosed as having special educational needs at this stage, when the difficulty lies in the unsuitable learning environment within the school.

As has been repeatedly argued in this book, young children need time to explore and consolidate concepts through first-hand experience, before they are expected to learn through instruction. An emphasis on academic rather than intellectual development results in confusion, a dip in confidence and, crucially, a loss of motivation to learn. And this is at the cost of all the positive things children could be doing which would build up their capacity to learn more formally later (see Chapter 8). The reality of this experience of 'too much, too soon' is having a pernicious impact on too many of the current generation of young children in England.

The contributors to this book bring a wide range of knowledge and experience to their varied but complementary topics. Discussions in the earlier sections on the particular situation under both Labour and Coalition governments, and explanations of the implications of their fundamental commitment to protect childhood from damaging cultural and technological influences, create a platform for the third part of the book, which provides evidence and encouragement for a strong campaign to free our youngest children from statutory targets and top-down pressures. The phenomenal development that takes place in the early years, which is enabled most notably through creative play, is recognized, celebrated and respected. The crucial case for adults allowing and facilitating learning through self-directed play, rather than taking control of children's own initiatives, is powerfully made. In emphasizing the importance of investing in a strong start, the book's authors encourage thinking parents and professionals to speak out and influence future developments.

There are serious concerns about some aspects of the government's response in July 2011 to the recommendations made in the recent Tickell review of the Early Years Foundation Stage in England (cf. Chapter 6), which reveals a depressing lack of understanding of the role of play in learning, and an emphasis on readiness for formal schooling which runs directly counter to what we know through hard evidence from brain research as well as empirical knowledge and experience. There is very little to help parents and practitioners understand development and learning in the earliest months and years, and the importance of identifying and building upon children's existing knowledge and interests.

However, it is important to acknowledge that the vital importance of the early years is now widely recognized, and Ministers have generally endorsed the existing themes and principles of the EYFS. Given a well-qualified work-force, free of central diktat and able to interpret these underpinning tenets appropriately, little more is needed beyond the enlightened philosophy and framework they offer. However, this book has shown repeatedly that a number of other urgent imperatives exist that must be heeded by practitioners, policy-makers and parents, if early childhood experience is to be sufficiently protected from inappropriate and counter-productive intrusions.

Since its foundation in 2007, the Open EYE campaign has opposed the statutory imposition of government policy on early years practitioners. We have always been clear that the *principles* on which the statutory requirements are based are sound, but crucially, some of the content of the framework is both controversial and not supported by any research evidence, which makes its imposed statutory nature all the more problematic (e.g. see Chapter 6). The EYFS is not – and in principle never could be – the final word on the best way to care for young children and facilitate their learning. However, once these principles were enshrined in law the majority of practitioners felt obliged to comply with them. We believe this compliance has already resulted in many unhelpful and counterproductive unintended consequences, and unless the statutory nature of the requirements is withdrawn, will result in many more.

It is, of course, much easier to list objections to the current regime than to propose concrete, positive recommendations for the future. This book therefore marks Open EYE's development from advocacy and critique to a constructive engagement with policy-makers, educators, parents and academics for improving children's well-being and learning. Certainly, in Chapter 22, Barry Sheerman MP refers favourably to Lilian Katz's view that people in the field should...

> Come together with your colleagues – those you disagree with, as well as those you agree with – and work out a position statement, then propose modification in the law that will address our best current understanding of how children best grow, develop and learn with the sincere intention of helping the decision makers to achieve their well-meaning intentions.

This is precisely what we have striven to do in the following positive recommendations, which are derived directly from arguments presented in this book.

Recommendations

1 The Early Years Foundation Stage

a **Empowering guidelines**: with the exception of the welfare requirements and some broad agreed principles to underpin practice, the statutory nature of the Early Years Foundation Stage should be dropped, and replaced with a rich diversity of guidance, drawing on different pedagogical traditions, with the aim of encouraging mature, reflective practice by people from differing disciplines. Practitioners need to be able to think with respect and subtlety about individual children, unencumbered by adult agendas around school readiness, premature academic pressures, or any sense that children are failing to meet expectations. This change would mean that the vexed exemption procedures would be redundant, and would also recognize parents' fundamental human right to freedom of choice in educational provision for their children.

b **Privileging physical, emotional and social development and communication**: while acknowledging the interconnections between areas of learning, EYFS guidance needs to ensure the proposed prime areas of physical development, emotional and social development and communication are properly emphasized from birth.

c **Uniqueness versus state-defined normality**: there must be a clear, unequivocal message in the EYFS guidance that each child's unique developmental path should be given clear precedence over any normalizing definitions of child development.

d **Literacy**: the early learning goals in relation to literacy should be abolished and replaced by a wide-ranging diversity of guidance that emphasizes that children's capabilities develop at very different rates, and that the foundations for literacy, including a rich oral culture, the enjoyment of books and the disposition to learn to read, write and spell, should be securely in place before children are introduced to more formal literacy learning.

e **Play**: the central place of play in children's development and learning needs to be reaffirmed, with the sanctity of free imaginative play being protected from distortion by adult agendas. Practitioners need to find ways of engaging effectively with children which do not include intruding into their play with inappropriate goals or targets, but with a genuine interest in aiding each child's natural unfolding potential. It must be made clear that 'directed' and 'structured' play is different, as it involves adults building on each child's own interests and extending their understanding in playful ways.

f **Minimizing the impact of the 'audit culture' and unnecessary bureaucracy**: The Department for Education, OFSTED and Local Authorities should take a lead by acknowledging that values associated with the audit culture have the potential to do great harm in early childhood, and that the effects need to be reduced to a minimum in all settings. The less that educators have to carry out unnecessary audit, the more time they have for their children. Accountability should be primarily to children and families.

g **ICT and televisual technologies**: as some authorities have major philosophical concerns that are backed by research evidence, the EYFS guidance should include full and up to date information from research.

2 How Young Children Learn

There needs to be informed discussion across the early years field about the nature of young children's learning. As described at various points in the book, many notable authorities believe that young children naturally learn unconsciously, and are developmentally attuned to learn in an unconsciously competent way. The development of conscious competence in learning comes much later, and it is harmful to introduce self-conscious cognitive awareness at too young an age. At the very least, there needs to be research into this issue, and dissemination of the implications of findings from brain research for practice, so that practitioners can make informed professional judgements based on the most up-to-date evidence.

3 Training

A fundamental reappraisal of the content of initial training for work in the early years is needed. Academically oriented training risks reinforcing an overly cognitive bias in pedagogy, and should be balanced with plenty of mentored practical experience. Approaches such as Montessori, Reggio Emilia and Steiner Waldorf place great emphasis on the personal and artistic development of early years teachers, and on their subtle 'quality of being' with young children. Practitioners need a repertoire of skills and a capacity for sensitive observation and interpretation of children's behaviour, coupled with the ability to work with parents and adults from other disciplines involved in services for young children. This is acquired through reflective practice together with opportunities for rigorous continuing professional development. It is to be hoped that the planned review of early years qualifications in England will open up a wide-ranging dialogue across the field about the content of training, and for a diversity of approaches which should include the involvement of professionals from other disciplines.

4   School Starting Age

Statutory school starting age is very low in England, and children now enter school up to a year earlier than the term after they become five. In theory, the Early Years Foundation Stage continues until the start of Year 1, when around two-thirds of the children are still under statutory school age. Downward pressures have resulted in the concerns associated with 'too much, too soon' that have been expressed in this book. It is essential that the EYFS approach is sustained until the end of the reception year, and into Year 1 or beyond for all children who need it. As reported in this book (see Chapters 16 and 17), there is evidence that children who start formal literacy learning at the age of seven achieve as well at eleven as those who are taught phonic skills earlier, at the expense of other more worthwhile activities. Government should note this very important finding, and pay attention to the expressed concerns of literacy and child development specialists as well as early years experts, and ensure that provision for our youngest children in school is developmentally appropriate. Rather than focusing on an ill-defined notion of school readiness in children, it would be more effective to ensure that schools are ready to take forward the learning of all their pupils from the start. Rather than testing phonics in Year 1, teachers should be empowered to support all children, including those who can already read, to develop their capacity and disposition to make progress according to their particular needs and interests.

These recommendations are practical and achievable. Enlightened and open-minded parents, practitioners, educationalists, researchers and policy-makers will wish to consider them. The government's intention to involve a wide spectrum of people in the co-creation of policy for the development of services is a promising start. What is then required is the collective will to bring about change: the benefit that this would bring to young children's overall well-being is inestimable.

From Awareness to Action

The arguments in this book are just one aspect of a wider cultural movement that is centred around reversing the erosion of childhood that is endemic in modern Western culture. In September 2006, the *Daily Telegraph* published an Open Letter signed by over 100 experts in education, psychology and allied fields (to which we were both signatories), entitled 'Modern life leads to more depression among children'. The letter argued that children's well-being was being adversely affected in multiple ways by modern technological and commercial culture. This book, *Too Much, Too Soon*, seeks to renew and deepen the concerns raised both then and since, in calling for the development of a new grass-roots cultural movement whose central aim will be arresting and reversing the erosion of childhood (see www.savechildhood.net).

By the time you read this text, a new Open Letter will have been published and, hopefully, will have caught the imagination of the many citizens who are deeply concerned about the parlous state of too many of our young children's current experience at school and in the wider community. Children growing up too quickly has now become a ubiquitous cultural theme, repeatedly revisited by the media, politicians and a wide range of organizations. The Bailey Report, published in June 2011 with the backing of Prime Minister David Cameron, addresses the commercialization of childhood and children's premature sexualization, and has thrown this issue into the spotlight once again. Despite numerous government initiatives on children's well-being since 2006, commercial, technological and performance imperatives are still dominating children's lives, and some believe that childhood experience is in crisis as a result.

Those expressing these concerns are not nostalgic sentimentalists, nor technological Luddites, nor sufferers from moral panic, but concerned and informed professionals and citizens who believe that children are being dragged into premature adulthood by all kinds of cultural imperatives beyond their control and without their informed consent. Survey evidence shows parents to be deeply concerned about this issue, yet they often feel powerless to arrest these seemingly irresistible cultural trends. The contributors to this book, and many other supporters of what we hope will soon be a new cultural movement, urge professionals, parents, politicians and all concerned citizens to join this urgently needed conversation about what we can collectively do to protect our children from the pernicious 'too much, too soon' syndrome. In principle, all citizens can become the proactive *creators* of modern culture, rather than its hapless victims – and for the authors of this book, it is a matter of urgency that we take the actions necessary to reverse the erosion of childhood.

We can all take inspiration from the well-argued and thought-provoking propositions debated in this book, and apply them in our own lives and work. Moreover, we can and should raise the issues widely in order to counter the erosion of childhood, and to inform and influence future policy-making and practice for improving children's learning and well-being right across the globe. This might be a somewhat grandiose aspiration; but the considerable enthusiasm that greeted this book even before it was published suggests that this is one 'goal' and 'outcome' that might well be eminently achievable.

Afterword

Richard Brinton and Gabriel Millar

Considering all of the contributions in this book, the reader will appreciate that the subject of early years education and the Early Years Foundation Stage is not a simple legislative matter, but constitutes a highly complex suite of issues that are far from easy to disentangle. At a first, cursory analysis, these include:

- child development, from physical, emotional and cognitive perspectives, and how these influence what we do with children, and at what age;
- politics and policy-making, including the question of what level of involvement is appropriate for politicians in educational matters; and
- the historical and cultural context which may be influencing both our experiences and our thinking.

Each of these areas could, in itself, occupy several volumes when considering all the obvious as well as the more subtle attendant complexities.

The first years of a child's life are a time when it is very possible to get things fearfully wrong – not least, through compulsory legislation which downgrades perennial wisdom, and which enshrines in law 'old-paradigm' thinking and its associated practices (cf. Chapter 21). As Open EYE has emphasized from its inception, our education system treats children as though they were 'mini-adults'. This is a Victorian legacy: apparently, Queen Victoria was so impressed with the Prussian army's way of putting soldiers in rows, eyes front, to listen to a man standing at the front, that she decided the nation's children should do the same. It is under such influences that, since the Education Act of 1895, children have routinely been 'chained' to chairs, as though there were no other way of educating them.

In the summer 2007, Open EYE began as a burst of rage on a terrace in Stroud, Gloucestershire, with Lynne Oldfield (see Chapter 12) and Gabriel Millar alternately hooting and wincing over the inappropriateness of up to a third of the impending Early Years Foundation Stage 'learning goals'. With EYFS becoming statutory from September 2008, the law had surreptitiously brought compulsion into a pre-compulsory setting, as children are not legally obliged to be in school before age five years and three months.

Since late 2007, Open EYE has had an active nucleus (nearly all of whom are contributing to this book), and has been a consistent voice in countering the contradictions and inconsistencies of a preschool curriculum, a 'one-size-fits-all' that doesn't respect the unique sizing and timing of the young child's unfolding, whilst parroting fashionable, platitudinous phrases like 'the unique child' and 'developmental appropriateness'. For us, the EYFS is shot though like a stick of rock with the cultural contradictions and paradigmatic confusions of the modern technocratic world. Not least, Open EYE has pointedly blown the whistle on the harmful effects of screen viewing on the developing young brain and bodily co-ordination (see Chapters 9 and 19), and its re-wiring of the frontal lobe; and have linked up with research into 'ADHD' and the numbing of children's rich natural imaginative faculties.

In no other EU country is there such draconian and detailed government interference in the early years domain. The compulsory intrusion of the EYFS was the brain-child of the then 'New Labour' government, extolling the virtues of childcare provision to meet the needs of deprived children. With then Prime Minister Gordon Brown saying 'Education is for national economic survival', George Orwell's *1984* prophecy that the child will exist for the state suddenly seemed perilously real.

Open EYE has deplored the unholy, anxiety-driven hurry to impose intellectual pressure on a young unready mind, realising that the young child lives in his unconscious will (this being where Freud, Steiner, Isaacs and Winnicott most fruitfully meet), and needs to move and explore the world (see, for example, Chapters 9 and 12, this volume). Open EYE has shown how this is far from being an antiquated, outmoded view, but one borne out in many countries where formal education begins at six or seven years of age. Certainly, both anecdotal experience and research studies, including Robin Alexander's influential Cambridge Primary Review and many others cited in the chapters of this book, are increasingly demonstrating the harmful effects of the 'too much, too soon' mentality.

The Open EYE campaign has had its impact: our championing of the child's right to play has come into public awareness through scores of letters and articles in newspapers and professional literature, radio interviews and meetings with MPs, including an Early Day Motion tabled by Annette Brooke MP and signed by over 80 MPs. The campaign has made an acclaimed early years film (see http:// openeyecampaign.wordpress.com/video) and a conference dvd, it has hosted two highly successful conferences in London with keynote talks by acclaimed international speakers (see Chapters 1, 8, 17 and 19), and it has gained the support of a wide range of senior figures across the early years sector (though at least some are reluctant to show their support in public – itself surely symptomatic of a deep malaise in the field). Our campaigning also won a significant concession from the previous government on EYFS exemptions, with an exemption process that at least frees kindergartens from the compulsion of early literacy, numeracy and ICT; but to date, we have hoped in vain that the exemption procedure would be made genuinely open and negotiable.

Dame Clare Tickell's EYFS review has suggested that the EYFS be substantially simplified (see Chapter 6), with a substantial reduction in bureaucracy and at least some attenuation of the learning goals. This is some vindication, at least, for an exhausting campaign spearheaded by a volunteer team with laptops, facing a department of state backed by all its vast administrative resources; and it has warmed our child-loving hearts to discover that it is still possible *to speak truth to power*, and to have at least some favourable 'outcomes' as a result.

On 3 May this year the *Guardian* Education supplement published the results of a survey in which it asked primary school children what they would like to see in schools. In a new 'Children's Manifesto' they wrote, *inter alia*: a timetable that is not a one-size-fits-all but takes account of individual pupils' interests and needs. Fewer tests. Tree houses 'so we can learn more about nature'. Fortnightly trips to farms to see animals (without worksheets).

The children are telling us what they need. It sounds for all the world what Open EYE would suggest for them.

Acknowledgement

We would like to thank and acknowledge our colleague **Graham Kennish** for both his advice on this Afterword, and for his invaluable contribution to the Open EYE campaign in the 'early years' of its existence. We would like also to acknowledge here the major contribution that our colleague **Anna Firth** made to the campaign and its many successes in its early phase.

Contributors

Arthur Adams has been married to Pat Adams for 34 years. They have one daughter. In his day job, Arthur is a computer programmer and has also seen many changes in his working life.

Pat Adams lives in Cheshire and has been a registered childminder for over 23 years, in which time she has cared for more than 50 children, and is still in regular contact with many of the families she has worked with. She has seen a number of initiatives come and go, of which the EYFS is the latest.

Steve Biddulph has been a psychologist for 30 years. His books, including *Secrets of Happy Children*, *Raising Boys*, and *Manhood*, are in four million homes worldwide. He is a husband and father, and is Adjunct Professor in the School of Psychology, Cairnmillar Institute, in Melbourne, Australia.

Richard Brinton studied biology at St Lawrence University, USA, subsequently taking the Waldorf teacher training in Switzerland. He taught in Switzerland and in England before becoming Principal of Hawkwood College, an adult education centre in Gloucestershire, UK, where he has been for 15 years. With his wife a class teacher and his four children having gone through Steiner schools, he has always been keenly interested in issues of developmentally appropriate education, including when these move on to political agendas. Richard was part of the founding Open EYE group, in response to the EYFS legislation introduced by the previous Labour government.

Annette Brooke MP has been Liberal Democrat Member of Parliament for Mid Dorset and North Poole since 2001. She was previously a teacher and economics lecturer, has worked in schools, colleges and for the Open University, and has a BSC(Econ) from the LSE and a Cert Ed from Cambridge University. A Councillor for Poole Borough Council for 17 years, when Poole gained unitary status Annette became its first Chair of Education. She was the Liberal Democrat Spokesperson for Children, 2004–10, and was a member of the Children, Schools and Families Select Committee. Annette is a Parliamentary Ambassador for the NSPCC and a Champion for Save the Children. She believes strongly that our education system should be about developing a life-long joy in learning.

Tricia David, Emeritus Professor of Education at Canterbury Christ Church University (2003–9), and Honorary Emeritus Professor of Early Childhood Education at the University of Sheffield, has been involved in the field of Early Childhood Education and Care for 50 years. She has enjoyed all the areas in which she has worked, and counts herself blessed to have made many friends locally, nationally and internationally in the course of her career. Tricia continues her involvement in research and writing. Most of all, she appreciates the time she now has to observe, to think and to read widely.

John Dougherty is a former primary school teacher with extensive classroom experience who, after eleven years of tick-boxes, OFSTED and endless government initiatives, decided that enough was enough. He is now a full-time writer of fiction for children, published mostly but not exclusively by Random House. John is also the father of two children who spent most of their early years education in the kindergarten of a school which subscribes to a well-respected alternative educational philosophy. He believes that state education should offer access to a range of philosophies, and that government micro-management is bad for schools.

Margaret Edgington is an Independent Early Years Consultant and a specialist in work with young children and their families, having worked as an early years teacher, educational home visitor, NNEB tutor, advisory teacher, and nursery school head-teacher. She now offers a training, advice and consultancy service across the UK (and sometimes abroad), and writes on the subject of early childhood education (including her books *The Foundation Stage Teacher in Action*, 3rd edition, 2004 and *The Great Outdoors*, 2002). Margaret is also a Vice President of Early Education and of the National Campaign for Real Nursery Education, and a founder member of Open EYE.

David Elkind is currently Professor Emeritus of Child Development at Tufts University in Medford, Massachusetts. His research and theorizing have been in the areas of perceptual, social and cognitive development, where he has attempted to build on the work of Jean Piaget. Professor Elkind's bibliography now numbers more than 500 items, and includes 19 books as well many book chapters and articles. Perhaps David is best known for his books, *The Hurried Child, All Grown Up and No Place to Go, Miseducation*, and most recently, *The Power of Play*. His new book, *Giants in the Nursery: Grandmasters of Early Childhood Education*, is in press.

Wendy Ellyatt is a freelance writer and researcher who specializes in the early years and who has a particular interest in creativity and the optimization of natural learning potential. She has worked as a consultant, researcher and feature writer in Integral Education, and is the founder of The Unique Child Network. She was recently recognized by Demos as a leading thinker in the field of creativity and early learning.

Sally Goddard Blythe is the Director of the pioneering Institute for Neuro-Physiological Psychology (INPP) in Chester, UK. She has worked in the area of neuro-development for more than 20 years, and is the author of several books and published papers on child development and neurodevelopmental factors in specific learning difficulties including: *Reflexes, Learning and Behavior, What Babies and Children Really Need, Attention, Balance and Coordination – the A,B,C of Learning Success* and *The Genius of Natural Childhood.* Sally is the author of The INPP Screening Test and Developmental Programme for Use in Schools, which has been piloted with thousands of children across the world, and is due to be published by Wiley-Blackwell in 2012.

Sylvie Hétu has three grown-up children, has a BSc in Education (pre-school/primary) and is a qualified Steiner teacher. She has worked in both mainstream schools and a Steiner school, and with the International Association of Infant Massage (IAIM) since 1983, teaching families, and, since 1989, training instructors worldwide. A current member of the IAIM International Education Committee, Sylvie was the IAIM international president for 12 years (1992–2004). With her colleague Mia Elmsäter, she is also the co-founder of the Massage in Schools Programme (MISP) (2000) for children 4 to 12 years old. She is the author of the book *The Song of the Child* (2004) and co-author of *Touch in Schools: A Revolutionary Strategy for Replacing Bullying with Respect and for Reducing Violence* (2008).

Grethe Hooper Hansen, MA, RSA, Dip TEFL was formerly head of SEAL (the Society for Effective Affective Learning), an international organization founded to explore the pedagogy of Dr Georgi Lozanov and other innovative approaches to learning based on the concept of a multi-dimensional world. Originally, a school teacher, she moved into teaching English as a Foreign Language and worked in Italy and England. Grethe is currently writing a book on a new concept of education based on Lozanov's approach.

Richard House Ph.D. is Senior Lecturer in Psychotherapy and Counselling, Research Centre for Therapeutic Education, University of Roehampton. His nine other books include *Therapy Beyond Modernity* (Karnac, 2003), *Childhood, Well-being and a Therapeutic Ethos* (co-editor Del Loewenthal,

Karnac Books, 2009), and *In, Against and Beyond Therapy* (PCCS Books, 2010). The Theory Editor of the *European Journal of Psychotherapy and Counselling*, Richard helped found the Independent Practitioners Network and the Alliance for Counselling and Psychotherapy. A trained Steiner class and kindergarten teacher, with Sue Palmer he co-orchestrated the two *Daily Telegraph* Open Letters on 'toxic childhood' and 'play' in 2006 and 2007 respectively. Richard writes regularly on childcare and educational issues for the professional literature, and contributes regularly to peer-reviewed psychotherapeutic journals.

Lilian G. Katz, Ph.D. is Professor Emerita of Early Childhood Education at the University of Illinois (Urbana-Champaign) and is Co-Director of the Clearinghouse on Early Education and Parenting (CEEP) at the University of Illinois. Dr Katz served as Director of the ERIC Clearinghouse on Elementary and Early Childhood Education for 33 years and as Past President of the (US) National Association for the Education of Young Children, and is Editor of the first on-line peer reviewed trilingual early childhood journal, *Early Childhood Research and Practice.*

Frances Laing is a freelance writer, blogger (Parent's Guide to the Early Years Foundation Stage) and a campaigning journalist. She holds a BA Hons in German Studies, a PGCE in Adult Education and a Master of Science in Human Ecology. Frances has been a teacher, trainer, postperson and call centre employee. She maintains an organic allotment, and her parenting style is informed by the ethics and practice of martial arts. Both she and her daughter Ruth (aged five) attend the Black Belt Family Martial Arts Leadership Academy in Chester. Ruth's dad Richard (who has MS) has managed a council-run welfare and disability rights unit for several decades.

Penelope Leach is a research psychologist, specializing in child development. Best known as the author of *Your Baby and Child* (new edition, 2010) and as an advocate for children and parents (*Childcare Today: Getting It Right for Everyone*, A.A. Knopf, 2009, and *The Essential First Year,* (Dorling Kindersley, 2010), she is a Fellow of the British Psychological Society, and an Hon. Senior Research Fellow at the Tavistock Clinic and at the Centre for the Study of Children, Families and Social Issues, Birkbeck College, University of London.

Hillevi Lenz Taguchi is Associate Professor in Education at the Department of Education, Stockholm University, having majored in Sociology and Literature, with a Ph.D. in Education from Stockholm University in 2001. Her publications include books and articles in international journals on her research and experiences with collaborative and deconstructive learning processes with preschool teachers and teachers, using pedagogical documentation as a methodological tool. Her latest book is titled *Going Beyond the Theory–Practice Binary in Early Childhood Education: Introducing an Intra-active Pedagogy* (Routledge, 2010). Current research projects concern gender equality in academia, and teaching and learning of science theory and methodology courses in different social sciences disciplines.

Gabriel Millar was born in New York in 1944 and graduated *cum laude* from Columbia University, subsequently doing post-graduate work at Edinburgh University. Her social therapeutic work began with a pilot scheme for the children of alcoholics at the Drug Addiction Research Center in Toronto. She has lived in England for 40 years and has two daughters and two stepsons. For several years she taught part of the English A-level at Wynstones Steiner School. Then for 28 years she was a therapist in Camphill Communities and at Ruskin Mill, a college for challenged adolescents. One of the co-founders of Open EYE, she now teaches mothers to massage their babies.

Lynne Oldfield has been involved in early childhood education for 45 years, both in mainstream and Steiner Waldorf education. She is author of *Free to Learn* (2nd edn, Hawthorn Press, 2011) and a speaker on early childhood development and Waldorf Education, both in the UK and internationally. Lynne is currently the Director of the London Steiner Waldorf Early Childhood Studies training, and a member of the Steiner Waldorf early childhood steering group and of the Association of Steiner Waldorf teacher trainers. She was co-founder of the Open EYE Campaign.

Sue Palmer is the author of over two hundred books, software packages and TV programmes for the education market. She is a popular speaker on the subject of literacy and, more recently, child development in the modern world, about which she frequently writes and comments in the press and other media. Since publishing *Toxic Childhood* in 2006 (her first book for a more general audience), Sue has been involved in many campaigns around education, outdoor play, screen-based entertainment and the commercialization of childhood. Her latest book is *21st Century Boys*. www.suepalmer.co.uk

Wendy Scott is a Froebel-trained teacher and psychology graduate, with many years of early years experience, including headship of a demonstration nursery school, lecturing, advisory and inspection posts, and specialist work with the Department for Education and Skills. As chief executive of the British Association for Early Childhood Education, she chaired the national Early Childhood Forum, and has also worked abroad with the British Council and UNICEF. Wendy remains committed to the development of high-quality support for young children and their families worldwide.

Barry Sheerman MP was Chairman of the House of Commons Select Committee for Children, Schools and Families from 2007, and of the Education and Skills Committee from 2001 to 2007. He has extensive experience in educational issues and has played a key role in education policy and debates. His interests include economic affairs, environmental sustainability and transport safety. Barry is an energetic social and political entrepreneur, having initiated over 30 different social enterprises over the past 20 years. He is currently actively involved in Policy Connect, the Parliamentary Advisory Council on Transport Safety, Urban Mines and the John Clare Education and Environment Trust, all of which he helped establish.

Dr Aric Sigman is a Fellow of the Society of Biology, Associate Fellow of the British Psychological Society, a recipient of the Science Council's Chartered Scientist award and Fellow of the Royal Society of Medicine. He has worked on health education campaigns with the Department of Health, and gives health education lectures to schools and parents. He recently addressed the European Parliament Working Group on the Quality of Childhood in the European Union, in Brussels. He is the author of several biology papers and four books on child health and development.

Kim Simpson is married with three children and two grandchildren. She has been deeply involved in Montessori education, running nurseries for over 30 years, and was voted 'Montessorian of the Year' in 2006–7. Kim is a qualified psychotherapist, running a private practice in Kew and also providing Parent Coaching. She has acted as Chairperson on three Educational Boards, including the Psychosynthesis & Education Trust in London. A regular contributor to early years' magazines, she also gives talks on Montessori education, child behaviour and the spiritual development of both child and adult. Kim is also a core group member of the Open EYE campaign.

Sebastian Suggate, Ph.D. is a lecturer in education at the University of Regensburg in Germany, although he is originally from New Zealand. He is interested in researching developmentally appropriate practices in education and developmental psychology, currently with a focus on reading and language development. His personal career highlights are his Ph.D. thesis being placed on the University of Otago's 2009 list of distinguished theses, having this research reported and recognized internationally, being awarded an Alexander-von-Humboldt research fellowship to Würzburg (in Germany), and being invited to speak at conferences and meeting other like-minded people.

Index

Page numbers in **bold** indicate a particularly important mention.

HAWTHORN EARLY YEARS EDUCATION SERIES

The purpose of the series is to deepen our respect for the right to a whole childhood. This can mean slowing down and protecting children from 'too much, too soon' so they have time to grow. Hawthorn early years books address key aspects of child development such as creativity, holistic learning, health, wellbeing, play, stories, storytelling, literacy and child development. Respecting each child's right to a healthy childhood arises from some basic attitudes, including:

- Childhood is a significant phase of life which needs protecting so as to be a positive experience
- Each child needs support in developing their unique capacities and exploring ways of realising their potential in a social context
- The causes of poor child mental and physical health need addressing
- Children may be experiencing conflict and poor social and economic conditions, which need tackling

Hawthorn's authors and their books, then, help support creative family life ways, promote a developmentally appropriate early years curriculum, encourage better health, challenge the over exposure to the electronic media too early, counter commercialism directed at children and encourage the development of a child and family friendly society.

To order Hawthorn Press books please visit our website www.hawthornpress.com, or contact our distributor BookSource: Tel 0845 370 0063, email orders@booksource.net

What Babies and Children Really Need
How mothers and fathers can nurture children's growth for health and wellbeing
SALLY GODDARD BLYTHE

This book represents a milestone in our understanding of child development and what parents can do to give their children the best start in life. *What Babies Really Need* draws on the latest scientific research to show how a baby's relationship with its mother has a lasting and fundamental impact. Sally Goddard Blythe calls for a new Charter for Childhood in which nutrition, play, affection and discipline are valued as the basic building blocks for meeting children's needs.

368pp; 234 × 156mm; 978-1-903458-76-1; pb; **£16.99**

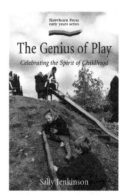

The Genius of Play
Celebrating the spirit of childhood
SALLY JENKINSON

Imagine a teaching aid which enhanced a child's self esteem and social skills, enriched their imagination, and encouraged creative thinking. That teaching aid is play. Sally Jenkinson argues that even as a growing body of research helps us to understand the genius of play we are eroding children's self-initiated play with inappropriate toys, TV and consumerism.

'... a book of genius, which celebrates childhood magically and enchantingly by capturing its spirit throughout ...'

Diane Rich, *Early Education*

224pp; 216 × 138mm; 978-1-903458-04-4; pb; **£12.99**

Storytelling with Children
NANCY MELLON

Telling stories is a peaceful, magical way of creating special occasions with children, whether it is at bedtime, around the fire or on rainy days. Nancy Mellon shows how you can become a confident storyteller with a wealth of ideas for using stories with dance, rhyme, puppets and creative play.

'Nancy Mellon's experience, advice and suggestions work wonders. They are potent seeds that give you the creative confidence to find your own style of storytelling.'
Ashley Ramsden, Director of the School of Storytelling, Emerson College

192pp; 216 × 138mm; 978-1-903458-08-2; pb; **£9.99**

Healing Stories for Challenging Behaviour
SUSAN PERROW

Susan Perrow writes, collects and documents stories that offer a therapeutic journey for the listener – a positive, imaginative way of healing difficult situations. Her collection of modern and traditional folk stories includes stories for challenging behaviours such as dishonesty, stealing, bullying and fighting; and stories for challenging situations such as moving house, a new baby, nightmares, illness or grieving. Each story is introduced with notes and suggestions for use. There is also a guide to help readers create their own healing stories.

'Explore the ancient art of storytelling with this inspiring book, strengthening your connection with your child along the way.'   *Kindred Magazine*

320pp; 234 × 156mm; 978-1-903458-78-5; pb; **£14.99**

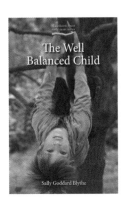

The Well Balanced Child
Movement and early learning
SALLY GODDARD BLYTHE

'Learning is not just about reading, writing and maths,' says Sally Goddard Blythe. 'A child's experience of movement will help play a pivotal role in shaping his personality, his feelings and achievements.' Her book makes the case for a 'whole body' approach to learning which integrates the brain, senses, movement, music and play. *The Well Balanced Child* examines why movement matters; how music helps brain development; the role of nutrition, the brain and child growth; and offers practical tips for parents and educators to help children with learning and behavioural problems.

'... compelling and enthusiastic. A strong book with important messages about early years learning.'   *The Teacher*

240pp; 216 × 138mm; 978-1-903458-63-1; pb; **£12.99**

HAWTHORN EARLY YEARS EDUCATION SERIES

You Are Your Child's First Teacher

What parents can do with and for their children from birth to age six

RAHIMA BALDWIN DANCY

This lucid, practical and common-sense guide will help you navigate safely through the early years of childhood and find solutions that work for your own family situation. Create your own family rituals to ease the daily routine, nourish your child's imagination with simple, home-made toys and materials from the garden and kitchen cupboard, and use imitation, repetition and setting limits to promote a harmonious family life.

'One of the most readable and accessible books on parenting... Rahima shows a way of understanding child development that encourages respect and love for the natural unfolding of emotional life, intelligence and creativity in the young child.'

Kindling

400pp; 234 × 156mm; 978-1-903458-65-5; pb; **£14.99**

Free to Learn

Introducing Steiner Waldorf early childhood education

LYNNE OLDFIELD

Free to Learn is a comprehensive introduction to Steiner Waldorf kindergartens for parents, educators and early years' students. It draws on the theory and practice of kindergarten education around the world with stories, helpful insights and lively observations. Author Lynne Oldfield is Director of the London Waldorf Early Childhood Teacher Training Course.

' ... a timely contribution to the debate about appropriate early education and a balanced approach to what, when and how children learn.'

Nursery World

256pp; 216 × 138mm; 978-1-903458-06-8; pb; **£11.99**

Other Books by Richard House

Implausible Professions: Arguments for Pluralism and Autonomy in Psychotherapy and Counselling (co-editor, Nick Totton), Ross-on-Wye: PCCS Books, 1997; 2nd edition, 2011.

Therapy Beyond Modernity: Deconstructing and Transcending Profession-Centred Therapy, London: Karnac Books, 2003.

Ethically Challenged Professions: Enabling Innovation and Diversity in Psychotherapy and Counselling (co-editor, Yvonne Bates), Ross-on-Wye: PCCS Books, 2004.

Against and For CBT: Towards a Constructive Dialogue? (co-editor, Del Loewenthal), Ross-on-Wye: PCCS Books, 2008.

Compliance? Ambivalence? Rejection? – Nine Papers Challenging the Health Professions Council July 2009 Proposals for the State Regulation of the Psychological Therapies (co-editor, Denis Postle), Wentworth Publishing, London, 2009.

Childhood, Well-being and a Therapeutic Ethos (co-editor, Del Loewenthal), London: Karnac Books, 2009.

Critically Engaging CBT (co-editor, Del Loewenthal) Maidenhead: Open University Press, 2010.

In, Against and Beyond Therapy: Critical Essays Towards a 'Post-professional' Era, Ross-on-Wye: PCCS Books.

Child Education and Learning for Reflective Parents: Cutting-edge Thinking for a New Zeitgeist [with Sebastian Suggate, forthcoming, 2012].